Django 3 Web Development Cookbook
Fourth Edition

Actionable solutions to common problems in Python web development

Aidas Bendoraitis
Jake Kronika

BIRMINGHAM - MUMBAI

Django 3 Web Development Cookbook
Fourth Edition

Commissioning Editor: Ravit Jain
Acquisition Editor: Joshua Nadar
Content Development Editor: Keagan Carneiro
Senior Editor: Hayden Edwards
Technical Editor: Suwarna Patil
Copy Editor: Safis Editing
Project Coordinator: Kinjal Bari
Proofreader: Safis Editing
Indexer: Tejal Daruwale Soni
Production Designer: Nilesh Mohite

First published: October 2014
Second edition: January 2016
Third Edition: October 2018
Fourth Edition: March 2020

Production reference: 1230320

Published by Packt Publishing Ltd.
Livery Place
35 Livery Street
Birmingham
B3 2PB, UK.

ISBN 978-1-83898-742-8

www.packt.com

Packt>

Contributors

About the authors

Aidas Bendoraitis has been professionally building websites for the past 18 years. For the last 14 years, he has been working at a design company, studio 38 pure communication, in Berlin. Together with a small dedicated team, he has mostly used Django in the backend and jQuery in the frontend to create cultural and touristic web platforms.

Among different side projects, he is bootstrapping a SaaS business with strategic prioritizer 1st things 1st.

Aidas Bendoraitis is active on Twitter and other social media under the username DjangoTricks.

I want to thank my wife, Sofja, and son, Joris, and also other family members and friends for their support while writing this book. I am grateful to my colleagues for sharing knowledge and creating exciting projects together. Also, I want to thank the Django community for great, friendly conferences, and meetups. Last but not least, I appreciate Vilnius University, for planting the initial seeds of my career.

Jake Kronika, a software engineer with 25 years of experience. He has been working with Python since 2005 and Django since 2007. Evolving in lockstep with the web development industry, his skill set encompasses HTML, CSS, full-stack JavaScript, Python, Django, React, Node.js, Ruby on Rails, and several other technologies.

Currently a software architect and development team lead, Jake collaborates with designers, business stakeholders, and engineers around the globe to build robust applications. In his spare time, he provides full-spectrum web services as a freelancer.

In addition to authoring this book, Jake has reviewed several other Packt titles – most recently, *Django 3 By Example, Third Edition* by Antonio Melé.

I would not have accomplished nearly all that I have if it were not for the support and encouragement of my family, friends, and professional connections. In particular, I would like to thank my wife, Veronica, and my children, Mykaela and Kaden, whose love and devotion continue to be an inspiration daily. Also, I want to recognize my childhood friend, Andrew, without whom I may not have built my first website, thus discovering software.

About the reviewers

Darian Schramm has over 14 years of experience working on the web with Python. Starting as a systems administrator in the university CS department and continuing his work at agencies in New York City, San Diego, CA, and beyond. Darian has used Python and other technologies as a tool for web development, system administration tasks, statistics gathering, and everything in between. His career path began with Zope, then on to Plone, and then eventually, Flask, Django, and Pyramid.

Scott Sharkey is President of LANshark Consulting Group, LLC. in Troy, Ohio. He has a master's degree in computer science from Ohio State University and has been working in the industry since 1984, having founded LANshark in 1990. He specializes in remote work using Django/Python for web application development. During his long career, he has worked on projects as diverse as an in-car data collection system for IndyCar, TurboTax Pro for Intuit, two dating sites, an Internet of Things data collection application, several medical applications, and many other systems, along with publishing over 30 software packages through LANshark.

Packt is searching for authors like you

If you're interested in becoming an author for Packt, please visit `authors.packtpub.com` and apply today. We have worked with thousands of developers and tech professionals, just like you, to help them share their insight with the global tech community. You can make a general application, apply for a specific hot topic that we are recruiting an author for, or submit your own idea.

Table of Contents

Preface

The Django framework was specifically engineered to help developers construct robust, powerful web applications quickly and efficiently. It takes much of the tedious work and repetition out of the process, solving questions such as project structure, database object-relational mapping, templating, form validation, sessions, authentication, security, cookie management, internationalization, basic administration, and an interface to access data from scripts. Django is built upon the Python programming language, which itself enforces clear and easy-to-read code. Besides the core framework, Django has been designed to enable developers to create third-party modules that can be used in conjunction with your own apps. Django has an established and vibrant community where you can find source code, get help, and contribute.

Django 3 Web Development Cookbook, Fourth Edition, will guide you through every stage of the web development process with the Django 3.0 framework. We start with the configuration and structuring of the project. Then, you will learn how to define the database structure with reusable components, and how to manage it throughout the lifetime of your project. The book will move on to the forms and views used to enter and list the data. We'll proceed with responsive templates and JavaScript to augment the user experience. Then we will enhance Django's template system with custom filters and tags to be more flexible for frontend development. After this, you will tailor the administration interface in order to simplify the workflow of content editors. From there, we shift focus to the stability and robustness of your project, helping to secure and optimize your apps. Next, we examine how to efficiently store and manipulate hierarchical structures. Then we will demonstrate that collecting data from different sources and providing your own data to others in a range of formats is simpler than you might think. We will then introduce you to some tricks for programming and debugging your Django project code. We will move on with a few of the available options for testing your code. Just before the end of the book, we will show you how to deploy your project to production. Lastly, we will complete the development cycle by setting common maintenance practices.

In contrast to many other Django books, which are concerned only with the framework itself, this book covers several important third-party modules that will equip you with the tools necessary for complete web development. Additionally, we provide examples using the Bootstrap frontend framework and the jQuery JavaScript library, both of which simplify the creation of advanced and complex user interfaces.

Who this book is for

If you have experience with Django and are looking to enhance your skills, this book is for you. We have designed the content for intermediate and professional Django developers who are aiming to build robust projects that are multilingual, secure, responsive, and can scale over time.

What this book covers

Chapter 1, *Getting Started with Django 3.0*, illustrates the fundamental setup and configuration steps necessary for any Django project. We cover virtual environments, Docker, and project settings across environments and databases.

Chapter 2, *Models and Database Structure*, explains how you can write reusable code for use in the construction of your models. The first things to define with new apps are the data models, which form the backbone of any project. You will learn how to save multilingual data in the database. Also, you will learn how to manage database schema changes and data manipulations using Django migrations.

Chapter 3, *Forms and Views*, shows ways to construct views and forms for data display and editing. You will learn how to use microformats and other protocols to make your pages more readable by machines for representations in search results and social networks. You will also learn how to generate PDF documents and implement multilingual search.

Chapter 4, *Templates and JavaScript*, covers practical examples of using templates and JavaScript together. We combine these facets like so: rendered templates present information to the user, and JavaScript provides crucial enhancements in modern websites for a rich user experience.

Chapter 5, *Custom Template Filters and Tags*, reviews how to create and use your own template filters and tags. As you will see, the default Django template system can be extended to meet template developers' needs.

Chapter 6, *Model Administration*, explores the default Django administration interface and guides you through extending it with your own functionality.

Chapter 7, *Security and Performance*, delves into several ways, both inherent to and external from Django, to secure and optimize your projects.

Chapter 8, *Hierarchical Structures*, examines tree-like structure creation and manipulation in Django, and the benefits of incorporating the django-mptt or treebeard libraries into such workflows. This chapter shows you how to use both for the display and administration of hierarchies.

Chapter 9, *Importing and Exporting Data*, demonstrates the transfer of data to and from different formats, as well as its provision between various sources. Within this chapter, custom management commands are used for data imports, and we utilize sitemaps, RSS, and REST APIs for data exports.

Chapter 10, *Bells and Whistles*, shows some additional snippets and tricks that are useful in everyday web development and debugging.

Chapter 11, *Testing*, introduces different types of testing and provides a few characteristic examples of how to test your project code.

Chapter 12, *Deployment*, deals with third-party app deployment to the Python Package Index and Django project deployment to a dedicated server.

Chapter 13, *Maintenance*, explains how to create database backups, set cron jobs for regular tasks, and log events for further inspection.

To get the most out of this book

To develop with Django 3.0 using the examples in these pages, you will need the following:

- Python 3.6 or higher
- The **Pillow** library for image manipulation
- Either the MySQL database and the mysqlclient binding library, or the PostgreSQL database with the psycopg2-binary binding library
- Docker Desktop or Docker Toolbox for complete system virtualization, or a built-in virtual environment to keep each project's Python modules separated
- Git for version control

Software/hardware covered in the book	OS recommendations
Python 3.6 or higher Django 3.0.X PostgreSQL 11.4 or higher/MySQL 5.6 or higher	Any recent Unix-based operating system, such as macOS or Linux (although it is possible to develop on Windows too)

All other specific requirements are mentioned separately in each recipe.

If you are using the digital version of this book, we advise you to type the code yourself or access the code via the GitHub repository (link available in the next section). Doing so will help you avoid any potential errors related to the copy/pasting of code or incorrect indentation.

For editing project files you can use any code editor, but we recommend **PyCharm** (https://www.jetbrains.com/pycharm/) or **Visual Studio Code** (https://code.visualstudio.com/).

I would be thrilled if, after successfully publishing your Django project, you would share your results, learnings, and outcomes with me by email at aidas@bendoraitis.lt.

 All code examples have been tested using Django 3. However, they should work with future version releases as well.

Download the example code files

You can download the example code files for this book from your account at www.packt.com. If you purchased this book elsewhere, you can visit www.packtpub.com/support and register to have the files emailed directly to you.

You can download the code files by following these steps:

1. Log in or register at www.packt.com.
2. Select the **Support** tab.
3. Click on **Code Downloads**.
4. Enter the name of the book in the **Search** box and follow the onscreen instructions.

Once the file is downloaded, please make sure that you unzip or extract the folder using the latest version of:

- WinRAR/7-Zip for Windows
- Zipeg/iZip/UnRarX for Mac
- 7-Zip/PeaZip for Linux

The code bundle for the book is also hosted on GitHub at `https://github.com/PacktPublishing/Django-3-Web-Development-Cookbook-Fourth-Edition`. In case there's an update to the code, it will be updated on the existing GitHub repository.

We also have other code bundles from our rich catalog of books and videos available at `https://github.com/PacktPublishing/`. Check them out!

Conventions used

There are a number of text conventions used throughout this book.

`CodeInText`: Indicates code words in text, database table names, folder names, filenames, file extensions, pathnames, dummy URLs, user input, and Twitter handles. Here is an example: "For this recipe to work, you will need to have the `contenttypes` app installed."

A block of code is set as follows:

```
# requirements/dev.txt
-r _base.txt
coverage
django-debug-toolbar
selenium
```

When we wish to draw your attention to a particular part of a code block, the relevant lines or items are set in bold:

```
class Idea(CreationModificationDateBase, MetaTagsBase, UrlBase):
    title = models.CharField(
        _("Title"),
        max_length=200,
    )
    content = models.TextField(
        _("Content"),
    )
```

Any command-line input or output is written as follows:

```
(env)$ pip install -r requirements/dev.txt
```

Bold: Indicates a new term, an important word, or words that you see on screen. For example, words in menus or dialog boxes appear in the text like this. Here is an example: "We can see here that the upload-related action buttons are also replaced with a **Remove** button."

Warnings or important notes appear like this.

 Tips and tricks appear like this.

Sections

In this book, you will find several headings that appear frequently (*Getting ready, How to do it..., How it works..., There's more...,* and *See also*).

To give clear instructions on how to complete a recipe, use these sections as follows:

Getting ready

This section tells you what to expect in the recipe and describes how to set up any software or any preliminary settings required for the recipe.

How to do it...

This section contains the steps required to follow the recipe.

How it works...

This section usually consists of a detailed explanation of what happened in the previous section.

There's more...

This section consists of additional information about the recipe in order to increase your knowledge of it.

See also

This section provides helpful links to other useful information for the recipe.

Get in touch

Feedback from our readers is always welcome.

General feedback: If you have questions about any aspect of this book, mention the book title in the subject of your message and email us at customercare@packtpub.com.

Errata: Although we have taken every care to ensure the accuracy of our content, mistakes do happen. If you have found a mistake in this book, we would be grateful if you would report this to us. Please visit www.packtpub.com/support/errata selecting your book, clicking on the Errata Submission Form link, and entering the details.

Piracy: If you come across any illegal copies of our works in any form on the internet, we would be grateful if you would provide us with the location address or website name. Please contact us at copyright@packt.com with a link to the material.

If you are interested in becoming an author: If there is a topic that you have expertise in and you are interested in either writing or contributing to a book, please visit authors.packtpub.com.

Reviews

Please leave a review. Once you have read and used this book, why not leave a review on the site that you purchased it from? Potential readers can then see and use your unbiased opinion to make purchase decisions, we at Packt can understand what you think about our products, and our authors can see your feedback on their book. Thank you!

For more information about Packt, please visit packt.com.

Getting Started with Django 3.0

1

In this chapter, we will cover the following topics:

- Working with a virtual environment
- Creating a project file structure
- Handling project dependencies with pip
- Configuring settings for development, testing, staging, and production environments
- Defining relative paths in the settings
- Handling sensitive settings
- Including external dependencies in your project
- Setting up STATIC_URL dynamically
- Setting UTF-8 as the default encoding for the MySQL configuration
- Creating the Git ignore file
- Deleting Python-compiled files
- Respecting the import order in Python files
- Creating an app configuration
- Defining overwritable app settings
- Working with Docker containers for Django, Gunicorn, Nginx, and PostgreSQL

Introduction

In this chapter, we will see a few valuable practices to follow when starting a new project with Django 3.0 using Python 3. We have picked the most useful ways to deal with scalable project layout, settings, and configurations, whether using virtualenv or Docker to manage your project.

We are assuming that you are already familiar with the basics of Django, Git version control, MySQL as well as PostgreSQL databases, and command-line usage. We also assume that you are using a Unix-based operating system, such as macOS or Linux. It makes more sense to develop with Django on Unix-based platforms as the Django websites will most likely be published on a Linux server, meaning that you can establish routines that work in the same way, whether you're developing or deploying. If you are locally working with Django on Windows, the routines are similar; however, they are not *always* the same.

Using Docker for your development environment, regardless of your local platform, can improve the portability of your applications through deployment since the environment within the Docker container can be matched precisely to that of your deployment server. We should also mention that for the recipes in this chapter, we are assuming that you have the appropriate version control system and database server already installed on your local machine, whether you are developing with Docker or not.

Technical requirements

To work with the code of this book, you will need the latest stable version of Python, which can be downloaded from `https://www.python.org/downloads/`. At the time of writing, the latest version is 3.8.X. You will also need a MySQL or PostgreSQL database. You can download the MySQL database server from `https://dev.mysql.com/downloads/`. The PostgreSQL database server can be downloaded from `https://www.postgresql.org/download/`. Other requirements will be requested in specific recipes.

You can find all the code for this chapter at the `ch01` directory of the GitHub repository at `https://github.com/PacktPublishing/Django-3-Web-Development-Cookbook-Fourth-Edition`.

Working with a virtual environment

It is very likely that you will develop multiple Django projects on your computer. Some modules, such as virtualenv, setuptools, wheel, or Ansible, can be installed once and then shared for all projects. Other modules, such as Django, third-party Python libraries, and Django apps, will need to be kept isolated from each other. The virtualenv tool is a utility that separates all of the Python projects and keeps them in their own realms. In this recipe, we will see how to use it.

Getting ready

To manage Python packages, you will need pip. If you are using Python 3.4+, then it will be included in your Python installation. If you are using another version of Python, you can install pip by executing the installation instructions at `http://pip.readthedocs.org/en/ stable/installing/`. Let's upgrade the shared Python modules, pip, setuptools, and wheel:

```
$ sudo pip3 install --upgrade pip setuptools wheel
```

The virtual environment has been built into Python since version 3.3.

How to do it...

Once you have your prerequisites installed, create a directory where all your Django projects will be stored—for example, `projects` under your home directory. Go through the following steps after creating the directory:

1. Go to the newly created directory and create a virtual environment that uses the shared system site packages:

   ```
   $ cd ~/projects
   $ mkdir myproject_website
   $ cd myproject_website
   $ python3 -m venv env
   ```

2. To use your newly created virtual environment, you need to execute the activation script in your current shell. This can be done with the following command:

   ```
   $ source env/bin/activate
   ```

3. Depending on the shell you are using, the `source` command may not be available. Another way to source a file is with the following command, which has the same result (note the space between the dot and `env`):

   ```
   $ . env/bin/activate
   ```

4. You will see that the prompt of the command-line tool gets a prefix of the project name, as follows:

   ```
   (env) $
   ```

5. To get out of the virtual environment, type the following command:

```
(env)$ deactivate
```

How it works...

When you create a virtual environment, a few specific directories (`bin`, `include`, and `lib`) are created in order to store a copy of the Python installation, and some shared Python paths are defined. When the virtual environment is activated, whatever you install with `pip` or `easy_install` will be put in and used by the site packages of the virtual environment, and not the global site packages of your Python installation.

To install the latest Django 3.0.x in your virtual environment, type the following command:

```
(env)$ pip install "Django~=3.0.0"
```

See also

- The *Creating a project file structure* recipe
- The *Working with Docker containers for Django, Gunicorn, Nginx, and PostgreSQL* recipe
- The *Deploying on Apache with mod_wsgi for the staging environment* recipe in Chapter 12, *Deployment*
- The *Deploying on Apache with mod_wsgi for the production environment* recipe in Chapter 12, *Deployment*
- The *Deploying on Nginx and Gunicorn for the staging environment* recipe in Chapter 12, *Deployment*
- The *Deploying on Nginx and Gunicorn for the production environment* recipe in Chapter 12, *Deployment*

Creating a project file structure

A consistent file structure for your projects makes you well organized and more productive. When you have the basic workflow defined, you can get stuck into the business logic more quickly and create awesome projects.

Getting ready

If you haven't done it yet, create a ~/projects directory, where you will keep all your Django projects (you can read about this in the *Working with a virtual environment* recipe).

Then, create a directory for your specific project—for example, myproject_website. Start the virtual environment in an env directory there. Activate it and install Django there, as described in the previous recipe. We would suggest adding a commands directory for local shell scripts that are related to the project, a db_backups directory for database dumps, a mockups directory for website design files, and, most importantly, an src directory for your Django project.

How to do it...

Follow these steps to create a file structure for your project:

1. With the virtual environment activated, go to the src directory and start a new Django project, as follows:

   (env)$ django-admin.py startproject myproject

   The executed command will create a directory called myproject, with project files inside. This directory will contain a Python module, also called myproject. For clarity and convenience, we will rename the top-level directory as django-myproject. It is the directory that you will put under version control, and so it will have a .git or similarly named subdirectory.

2. In the django-myproject directory, create a README.md file to describe your project to the new developdjango-admin.py startproject myprojecters.

3. The django-myproject directory will also contain the following:

   - Your project's Python package, named myproject.
   - Your project's pip requirements with the Django framework and other external dependencies (read about this in the *Handling project dependencies with pip* recipe).
   - The project license in a LICENSE file. If your project is open source, you can choose one of the most popular licenses from https://choosealicense.com.

4. In your project's root, `django-myproject`, create the following:

- A `media` directory for project uploads
- A `static` directory for collected static files
- A `locale` directory for project translations
- An `externals` directory for external dependencies that are included in this project when you can't use the pip requirements

5. The `myproject` directory should contain these directories and files:

- The `apps` directory where you will put all your in-house Django apps for the project. It is recommended that you have one app called `core` or `utils` for the projects' shared functionality.
- The `settings` directory for your project settings (read about this in the *Configuring settings for development, testing, staging, and production environments* recipe).
- The `site_static` directory for project-specific static files.
- The `templates` directory for the project's HTML templates.
- The `urls.py` file for the project's URL configuration.
- The `wsgi.py` file for the project's web server configuration.

6. In your `site_static` directory, create the `site` directory as a namespace for site-specific static files. Then, we will divide the static files between the categorized subdirectories within it. For instance, see the following:

- `scss` for Sass files (optional)
- `css` for the generated minified **Cascading Style Sheets** (CSS)
- `img` for styling images, favicons, and logos
- `js` for the project's JavaScriptdjango-admin.py startproject myproject
- `vendor` for any third-party module combining all types of files, such as the TinyMCE rich-text editor

7. Besides the `site` directory, the `site_static` directory might also contain overwritten static directories of third-party apps—for example, it might contain `cms`, which overwrites the static files from Django CMS. To generate the CSS files from Sass and minify the JavaScript files, you can use the CodeKit (https://codekitapp.com/) or Prepros (https://prepros.io/) applications with a graphical user interface.

8. Put your templates that are separated by the apps in your `templates` directory. If a template file represents a page (for example, `change_item.html` or `item_list.html`), then put it directly in the app's template directory. If the template is included in another template (for example, `similar_items.html`), put it in the `includes` subdirectory. Also, your templates directory can contain a directory called `utils` for globally reusable snippets, such as pagination and the language chooser.

How it works...

The whole file structure for a complete project will look similar to the following:

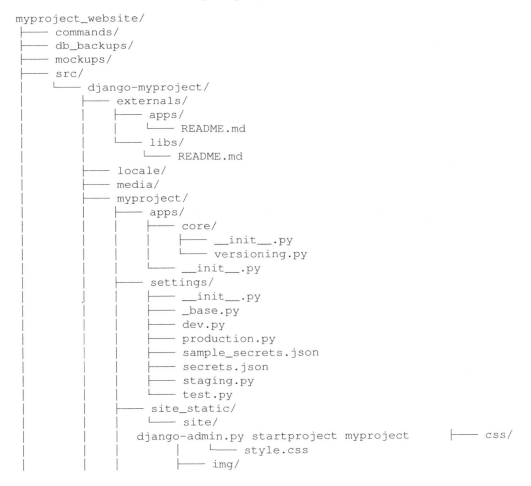

```
myproject_website/
├──── commands/
├──── db_backups/
├──── mockups/
├──── src/
│     └──── django-myproject/
│          ├──── externals/
│          │    ├──── apps/
│          │    │    └──── README.md
│          │    └──── libs/
│          │         └──── README.md
│          ├──── locale/
│          ├──── media/
│          ├──── myproject/
│          │    ├──── apps/
│          │    │    ├──── core/
│          │    │    │    ├──── __init__.py
│          │    │    │    └──── versioning.py
│          │    │    └──── __init__.py
│          │    ├──── settings/
│          │    │    ├──── __init__.py
│          │    │    ├──── _base.py
│          │    │    ├──── dev.py
│          │    │    ├──── production.py
│          │    │    ├──── sample_secrets.json
│          │    │    ├──── secrets.json
│          │    │    ├──── staging.py
│          │    │    └──── test.py
│          │    ├──── site_static/
│          │    │    └──── site/
django-admin.py startproject myproject        ├──── css/
                        │    └──── style.css
                        ├──── img/
```

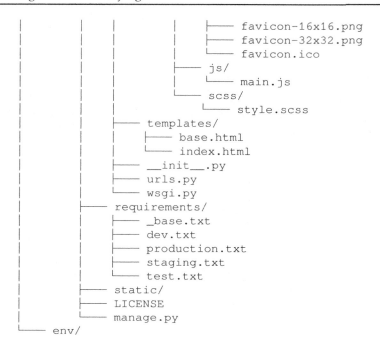

```
|           |           |                   |           ├──── favicon-16x16.png
|           |           |                   |           ├──── favicon-32x32.png
|           |           |                   |           └──── favicon.ico
|           |           |                   ├──── js/
|           |           |                   |           └──── main.js
|           |           |                   └──── scss/
|           |           |                               └──── style.scss
|           |           ├──── templates/
|           |           |           ├──── base.html
|           |           |           └──── index.html
|           |           ├──── __init__.py
|           |           ├──── urls.py
|           |           └──── wsgi.py
|           ├──── requirements/
|           |           ├──── _base.txt
|           |           ├──── dev.txt
|           |           ├──── production.txt
|           |           ├──── staging.txt
|           |           └──── test.txt
|           ├──── static/
|           ├──── LICENSE
|           └──── manage.py
└──── env/
```

There's more...

To speed up the creation of a project in the way we just described, you can use the project's boilerplate from `https://github.com/archatas/django-myproject`. After downloading the code, perform a global search and replace `myproject` with a meaningful name for your project, and you should be good to go.

See also

- The *Handling project dependencies with pip* recipe
- The *Including external dependencies in your project* recipe
- The *Configuring settings for development, testing, staging, and production environments* recipe
- The *Deploying on Apache with mod_wsgi for the staging environment* recipe in Chapter 12, *Deployment*

- The *Deploying on Apache with mod_wsgi for the production environment* recipe in `Chapter 12`, *Deployment*
- The *Deploying on Nginx and Gunicorn for the staging environment* recipe in `Chapter 12`, *Deployment*
- The *Deploying on Nginx and Gunicorn for the production environment* recipe in `Chapter 12`, *Deployment*

Handling project dependencies with pip

The most convenient tool to install and manage Python packages is pip. Rather than installing the packages one by one, it is possible to define a list of packages that you want to install as the contents of a text file. We can pass the text file into the pip tool, which will then handle the installation of all packages in the list automatically. An added benefit to this approach is that the package list can be stored in version control.

Generally speaking, it is ideal and often sufficient to have a single requirements file that directly matches your production environment. You can change versions or add and remove dependencies on a development machine and then manage them through version control. This way, going from one set of dependencies (and associated code changes) to another can be as simple as switching branches.

In some cases, environments differ enough that you will need to have at least two different instances of your project:

- The development environment, where you create new features
- The public website environment, which is usually called the production environment in a hosted server

There might be development environments for other developers, or special tools that are needed during development but that are unnecessary in production. You might also have a testing and staging environment in order to test the project locally and in a public website-like setup.

For good maintainability, you should be able to install the required Python modules for development, testing, staging, and production environments. Some of the modules will be shared and some of them will be specific to a subset of the environments. In this recipe, we will learn how to organize the project dependencies for multiple environments and manage them with pip.

Getting ready

Before using this recipe, you need to have a Django project ready with pip installed and a virtual environment activated. For more information on how to do this, read the *Working with a virtual environment* recipe.

How to do it...

Execute the following steps one by one to prepare pip requirements for your virtual environment Django project:

1. Let's go to the Django project that you have under version control and create a requirements directory with the following text files:

   - _base.txt for shared modules
   - dev.txt for the development environment
   - test.txt for the testing environment
   - staging.txt for the staging environment
   - production.txt for production

2. Edit _base.txt and add the Python modules that are shared in all environments, line by line:

   ```
   # requirements/_base.txt
   Django~=3.0.4
   djangorestframework
   -e git://github.com/omab/python-social-
   auth.git@6b1e301c79#egg=python-social-auth
   ```

3. If the requirements of a specific environment are the same as in _base.txt, add the line including _base.txt in the requirements file of that environment, as shown in the following example:

   ```
   # requirements/production.txt
   -r _base.txt
   ```

4. If there are specific requirements for an environment, add them after the `_base.txt` inclusion, as shown in the following code:

```
# requirements/dev.txt
-r _base.txt
coverage
django-debug-toolbar
selenium
```

5. You can run the following command in a virtual environment in order to install all of the required dependencies for the development environment (or an analogous command for other environments), as follows:

```
(env)$ pip install -r requirements/dev.txt
```

How it works...

The preceding `pip install` command, whether it is executed explicitly in a virtual environment or at the global level, downloads and installs all of your project dependencies from `requirements/_base.txt` and `requirements/dev.txt`. As you can see, you can specify a version of the module that you need for the Django framework and even directly install it from a specific commit at the Git repository, as is done for `python-social-auth` in our example.

When you have many dependencies in your project, it is good practice to stick to a narrow range of release versions for Python module release versions. Then you can have greater confidence that the project integrity will not be broken because of updates in your dependencies, which might contain conflicts or backward incompatibility. This is particularly important when deploying your project or handing it off to a new developer.

If you have already manually installed the project requirements with pip one by one, you can generate the `requirements/_base.txt` file using the following command within your virtual environment:

```
(env)$ pip freeze > requirements/_base.txt
```

There's more...

If you want to keep things simple and are sure that, for all environments, you will be using the same dependencies, you can use just one file for your requirements named `requirements.txt`, generated by definition, as shown in the following:

```
(env)$ pip freeze > requirements.txt
```

To install the modules in a new virtual environment, simply use the following command:

```
(env)$ pip install -r requirements.txt
```

If you need to install a Python library from another version control system, or on a local path, then you can learn more about pip from the official documentation at `https://pip.pypa.io/en/stable/user_guide/`.

Another approach to managing Python dependencies that is getting more and more popular is Pipenv. You can get it and learn about it at `https://github.com/pypa/pipenv`.

See also

- The *Working with a virtual environment* recipe
- The *Working with Docker containers for Django, Gunicorn, Nginx, and PostgreSQL* recipe
- The *Including external dependencies in your project* recipe
- The *Configuring settings for development, testing, staging, and production environments* recipe

Configuring settings for development, testing, staging, and production environments

As noted earlier, you will be creating new features in the development environment, testing them in the testing environment, and then putting the website onto a staging server to let other people try the new features. Then, the website will be deployed to the production server for public access. Each of these environments can have specific settings, and you will learn how to organize them in this recipe.

Getting ready

In a Django project, we'll create settings for each environment: development, testing, staging, and production.

How to do it...

Follow these steps to configure the project settings:

1. In the `myproject` directory, create a `settings` Python module with the following files:

    - `__init__.py` makes the settings directory a Python module.
    - `_base.py` for shared settings
    - `dev.py` for development settings
    - `test.py` for testing settings
    - `staging.py` for staging settings
    - `production.py` for production settings

2. Copy the contents of `settings.py`, which was automatically created when you started a new Django project, to `settings/_base.py`. Then, delete `settings.py`.

3. Change the `BASE_DIR` in the `settings/_base.py` to point one level up. It should first look as follows:

    ```
    BASE_DIR =
    os.path.dirname(os.path.dirname(os.path.abspath(__file__)))
    ```

    After changing it, it should look like the following:

    ```
    BASE_DIR = os.path.dirname(
        os.path.dirname(os.path.dirname(os.path.abspath(__file__)))
    )
    ```

4. If the settings of an environment are the same as the shared settings, then just import everything from `_base.py` there, as follows:

    ```
    # myproject/settings/production.py
    from ._base import *
    ```

5. Apply the settings that you want to attach or overwrite for your specific environment in the other files—for example, the development environment settings should go to dev.py, as shown in the following code snippet:

```
# myproject/settings/dev.py
from ._base import *
EMAIL_BACKEND = "django.core.mail.backends.console.EmailBackend"
```

6. Modify the manage.py and myproject/wsgi.py files to use one of the environment settings by default by changing the following line:

```
os.environ.setdefault('DJANGO_SETTINGS_MODULE',
'myproject.settings')
```

7. You should change this line to the following:

```
os.environ.setdefault('DJANGO_SETTINGS_MODULE',
'myproject.settings.production')
```

How it works...

By default, the Django management commands use the settings from myproject/settings.py. Using the method that is defined in this recipe, we can keep all of the required nonsensitive settings for all environments under version control in the config directory. On the other hand, the settings.py file itself would be ignored by version control and will only contain the settings that are necessary for the current development, testing, staging, or production environments.

 For each environment, it is recommended that you set the DJANGO_SETTINGS_MODULE environment variable individually, either in PyCharm settings, the env/bin/activate script, or in .bash_profile.

See also

- The *Working with Docker containers for Django, Gunicorn, Nginx, and PostgreSQL* recipe
- The *Handling sensitive settings* recipe
- The *Defining relative paths in the settings* recipe
- The *Creating a Git ignore file* recipe

Defining relative paths in the settings

Django requires you to define different file paths in the settings, such as the root of your media, the root of your static files, the path to templates, and the path to translation files. For each developer of your project, the paths may differ as the virtual environment can be set up anywhere and the user might be working on macOS, Linux, or Windows. Even when your project is wrapped in a Docker container, it reduces the maintainability and portability to define absolute paths. In any case, there is a way to define these paths dynamically so that they are relative to your Django project directory.

Getting ready

Have a Django project started and open `settings/_base.py`.

How to do it...

Modify your path-related settings accordingly, instead of hardcoding the paths to your local directories, as follows:

```python
# settings/_base.py
import os
BASE_DIR = os.path.dirname(
    os.path.dirname(os.path.dirname(os.path.abspath(__file__)))
)
# ...
TEMPLATES = [{
    # ...
    DIRS: [
        os.path.join(BASE_DIR, 'myproject', 'templates'),
    ],
    # ...
}]
# ...
LOCALE_PATHS = [
    os.path.join(BASE_DIR, 'locale'),
]
# ...
STATICFILES_DIRS = [
    os.path.join(BASE_DIR, 'myproject', 'site_static'),
]
STATIC_ROOT = os.path.join(BASE_DIR, 'static')
MEDIA_ROOT = os.path.join(BASE_DIR, 'media')
```

How it works...

By default, Django settings include a BASE_DIR value, which is an absolute path to the directory containing manage.py (usually one level higher than the settings.py file or two levels higher than settings/_base.py). Then, we set all of the paths relative to BASE_DIR using the os.path.join() function.

Based on the directory layout we set down in the *Creating a project file structure* recipe, we would insert 'myproject' as an intermediary path segment for some of the previous examples since the associated folders were created within this.

See also

- The *Creating a project file structure* recipe
- The *Working with Docker containers for Django, Gunicorn, Nginx, and PostgreSQL* recipe
- The *Including external dependencies in your project* recipe

Handling sensitive settings

When working when configuring a Django project, you will surely deal with some sensitive information, such as passwords and API keys. It is not recommended that you put that information under version control. There are two main ways to store that information: in environment variables and in separate untracked files. In this recipe, we will explore both cases.

Getting ready

Most of the settings for a project will be shared across all environments and saved in version control. These can be defined directly within the settings files; however, there will be some settings that are specific to the environment of the project instance or that are sensitive and require additional security, such as database or email settings. We will expose these using environment variables.

How to do it...

To read sensitive settings from the environment variables, perform these steps:

1. At the beginning of settings/_base.py, define the get_secret() function as
   follows:

   ```
   # settings/_base.py
   import os
   from django.core.exceptions import ImproperlyConfigured

   def get_secret(setting):
       """Get the secret variable or return explicit exception."""
       try:
           return os.environ[setting]
       except KeyError:
           error_msg = f'Set the {setting} environment variable'
           raise ImproperlyConfigured(error_msg)
   ```

2. Then, whenever you need to define a sensitive value, use the get_secret()
   function, as shown in the following example:

   ```
   SECRET_KEY = get_secret('DJANGO_SECRET_KEY')

   DATABASES = {
       'default': {
           'ENGINE': 'django.db.backends.postgresql_psycopg2',
           'NAME': get_secret('DATABASE_NAME'),
           'USER': get_secret('DATABASE_USER'),
           'PASSWORD': get_secret('DATABASE_PASSWORD'),
           'HOST': 'db',
           'PORT': '5432',
       }
   }
   ```

How it works...

If you run a Django management command without the environment variable set, you will
see an error raised with a message, such as **Set the DJANGO_SECRET_KEY environment
variable**.

You can set the environment variables in the PyCharm configuration, remote server configuration consoles, in the env/bin/activate script, .bash_profile, or directly in the Terminal like this:

```
$ export DJANGO_SECRET_KEY="change-this-to-50-characters-long-random-
  string"
$ export DATABASE_NAME="myproject"
$ export DATABASE_USER="myproject"
$ export DATABASE_PASSWORD="change-this-to-database-password"
```

Note that you should use the get_secret() function for all passwords, API keys, and any other sensitive information that you need in your Django project configuration.

There's more...

Instead of environment variables, you can also use text files with sensitive information that won't be tracked under version control. They can be YAML, INI, CSV, or JSON files, placed somewhere on the hard disk. For example, for a JSON file, you would have the get_secret() function, like this:

```
# settings/_base.py
import os
import json


with open(os.path.join(os.path.dirname(__file__), 'secrets.json'), 'r')
 as f:
    secrets = json.loads(f.read())


def get_secret(setting):
    """Get the secret variable or return explicit exception."""
    try:
        return secrets[setting]
    except KeyError:
        error_msg = f'Set the {setting} secret variable'
        raise ImproperlyConfigured(error_msg)
```

This reads a secrets.json file from the settings directory and expects it to have at least the following structure:

```
{
    "DATABASE_NAME": "myproject",
    "DATABASE_USER": "myproject",
```

```
    "DATABASE_PASSWORD":  "change-this-to-database-password",
    "DJANGO_SECRET_KEY":  "change-this-to-50-characters-long-random-string"
}
```

Make sure that the `secrets.json` file is ignored from the version control, but for convenience, you can create `sample_secrets.json` with empty values and put it under version control:

```
{
    "DATABASE_NAME":  "",
    "DATABASE_USER":  "",
    "DATABASE_PASSWORD":  "",
    "DJANGO_SECRET_KEY":  "change-this-to-50-characters-long-random-string"
}
```

See also

- The *Creating a project file structure* recipe
- The *Working with Docker containers for Django, Gunicorn, Nginx, and PostgreSQL* recipe

Including external dependencies in your project

Sometimes, you can't install an external dependency with pip and have to include it directly within your project, such as in the following cases:

- When you have a patched third-party app where you yourself fixed a bug or added a feature that did not get accepted by project owners
- When you need to use private apps that are not accessible at the **Python Package Index (PyPI)** or public version control repositories
- When you need to use legacy versions of dependencies that are not available at PyPI anymore

Including external dependencies in your project ensures that whenever a developer upgrades the dependent modules, all of the other developers will receive the upgraded version in the next update from the version control system.

Getting ready

You should start with a Django project under a virtual environment.

How to do it...

Execute the following steps one by one for a virtual environment project:

1. If you haven't done so already, create an `externals` directory under your Django project directory, `django-myproject`.

2. Then, create the `libs` and `apps` directories under it. The `libs` directory is for the Python modules that are required by your project—for example, Boto, Requests, Twython, and Whoosh. The `apps` directory is for third-party Django apps—for example, Django CMS, Django Haystack, and django-storages.
   We highly recommend that you create `README.md` files in the `libs` and `apps` directories, where you mention what each module is for, what the used version or revision is, and where it is taken from.

3. The directory structure should look something similar to the following:

```
externals/
├── apps/
│   ├── cms/
│   ├── haystack/
│   ├── storages/
│   └── README.md
└── libs/
    ├── boto/
    ├── requests/
    ├── twython/
    └── README.md
```

4. The next step is to put the external libraries and apps under the Python path so that they are recognized as if they were installed. This can be done by adding the following code in the settings:

```python
# settings/_base.py
import os
import sys
BASE_DIR = os.path.dirname(
    os.path.dirname(os.path.dirname(os.path.abspath(__file__)))
)
EXTERNAL_BASE = os.path.join(BASE_DIR, "externals")
EXTERNAL_LIBS_PATH = os.path.join(EXTERNAL_BASE, "libs")
```

```
EXTERNAL_APPS_PATH = os.path.join(EXTERNAL_BASE, "apps")
sys.path = ["", EXTERNAL_LIBS_PATH, EXTERNAL_APPS_PATH] + sys.path
```

How it works...

A module is meant to be under the Python path if you can run Python and import that module. One of the ways to put a module under the Python path is to modify the `sys.path` variable before importing a module that is in an unusual location. The value of `sys.path`, as specified by the settings file, is a list of directories starting with an empty string for the current directory, followed by the directories in the project, and finally the globally shared directories of the Python installation. You can see the value of `sys.path` in the Python shell, as follows:

```
(env)$ python manage.py shell
>>> import sys
>>> sys.path
```

When trying to import a module, Python searches for the module in this list and returns the first result that is found.

Therefore, we first define the `BASE_DIR` variable, which is the absolute path of `django-myproject` or three levels higher than `myproject/settings/_base.py`. Then, we define the `EXTERNAL_LIBS_PATH` and `EXTERNAL_APPS_PATH` variables, which are relative to `BASE_DIR`. Lastly, we modify the `sys.path` property, adding new paths to the beginning of the list. Note that we also add an empty string as the first path to search, which means that the current directory of any module should always be checked first before checking other Python paths.

This way of including external libraries doesn't work cross-platform with the Python packages that have C language bindings—for example, `lxml`. For such dependencies, we would recommend using the pip requirements that were introduced in the *Handling project dependencies with pip* recipe.

See also

- The *Creating a project file structure* recipe
- The *Working with Docker containers for Django, Gunicorn, Nginx, and PostgreSQL* recipe

- The *Handling project dependencies with pip* recipe
- The *Defining relative paths in the settings* recipe
- The *Using the Django shell* recipe in Chapter 10, *Bells and Whistles*

Setting up STATIC_URL dynamically

If you set STATIC_URL to a static value, then each time you update a CSS file, a JavaScript file, or an image, you and your website visitors will need to clear the browser cache in order to see the changes. There is a trick to work around clearing the browser's cache. It is to have the timestamp of the latest changes shown in STATIC_URL. Whenever the code is updated, the visitor's browser will force the loading of all new static files.

In this recipe, we will see how to put a timestamp in STATIC_URL for Git users.

Getting ready

Make sure that your project is under Git version control and that you have BASE_DIR defined in your settings, as shown in the *Defining relative paths in the settings* recipe.

How to do it...

The procedure to put the Git timestamp in the STATIC_URL setting consists of the following two steps:

1. If you haven't done so yet, create the myproject.apps.core app in your Django project. You should also create a versioning.py file there:

```
# versioning.py
import subprocess
from datetime import datetime


def get_git_changeset_timestamp(absolute_path):
    repo_dir = absolute_path
    git_log = subprocess.Popen(
        "git log --pretty=format:%ct --quiet -1 HEAD",
        stdout=subprocess.PIPE,
        stderr=subprocess.PIPE,
        shell=True,
        cwd=repo_dir,
```

```
                    universal_newlines=True,
    )

    timestamp = git_log.communicate()[0]
    try:
        timestamp = datetime.utcfromtimestamp(int(timestamp))
    except ValueError:
        # Fallback to current timestamp
        return datetime.now().strftime('%Y%m%d%H%M%S')
    changeset_timestamp = timestamp.strftime('%Y%m%d%H%M%S')
    return changeset_timestamp
```

2. Import the newly created `get_git_changeset_timestamp()` function in the settings and use it for the `STATIC_URL` path, as follows:

```
# settings/_base.py
from myproject.apps.core.versioning import
get_git_changeset_timestamp
# ...
timestamp = get_git_changeset_timestamp(BASE_DIR)
STATIC_URL = f'/static/{timestamp}/'
```

How it works...

The `get_git_changeset_timestamp()` function takes the `absolute_path` directory as a parameter and calls the `git log` shell command with the parameters to show the Unix timestamp of the HEAD revision in the directory. We pass `BASE_DIR` to the function, as we are sure that it is under version control. The timestamp is parsed, converted to a string consisting of the year, month, day, hour, minutes, and seconds returned, and is then included in the definition of the `STATIC_URL`.

There's more...

This method works only if each of your environments contains the full Git repository of the project—in some cases, for example, when you use Heroku or Docker for deployments—you don't have access to a Git repository and the `git log` command in the remote servers. In order to have the `STATIC_URL` with a dynamic fragment, you have to read the timestamp from a text file—for example, `myproject/settings/last-modified.txt`—that should be updated with each commit.

In this case, your settings would contain the following lines:

```python
# settings/_base.py
with open(os.path.join(BASE_DIR, 'myproject', 'settings', 'last-update.txt'), 'r') as f:
    timestamp = f.readline().strip()

STATIC_URL = f'/static/{timestamp}/'
```

You can make your Git repository update `last-modified.txt` with a pre-commit hook. This is an executable bash script that should be called `pre-commit` and placed under `django-myproject/.git/hooks/`:

```python
# django-myproject/.git/hooks/pre-commit
#!/usr/bin/env python
from subprocess import check_output, CalledProcessError
import os
from datetime import datetime


def root():
    ''' returns the absolute path of the repository root '''
    try:
        base = check_output(['git', 'rev-parse', '--show-toplevel'])
    except CalledProcessError:
        raise IOError('Current working directory is not a git repository')
    return base.decode('utf-8').strip()


def abspath(relpath):
    ''' returns the absolute path for a path given relative to the root of
        the git repository
    '''
    return os.path.join(root(), relpath)


def add_to_git(file_path):
    ''' adds a file to git '''
    try:
        base = check_output(['git', 'add', file_path])
    except CalledProcessError:
        raise IOError('Current working directory is not a git repository')
    return base.decode('utf-8').strip()


def main():
    file_path = abspath("myproject/settings/last-update.txt")

    with open(file_path, 'w') as f:
        f.write(datetime.now().strftime("%Y%m%d%H%M%S"))
```

```
        add_to_git(file_path)

if __name__ == '__main__':
        main()
```

This script will update `last-modified.txt` whenever you commit to the Git repository and will add that file to the Git index.

See also

- The *Creating the Git ignore file* recipe

Setting UTF-8 as the default encoding for the MySQL configuration

MySQL describes itself as the most popular open source database. In this recipe, we will tell you how to set UTF-8 as the default encoding for it. Note that if you don't set this encoding in the database configuration, you might get into a situation where LATIN1 is used by default with your UTF-8-encoded data. This will lead to database errors whenever symbols such as € are used. This recipe will also save you from the difficulties of converting the database data from LATIN1 to UTF-8, especially when you have some tables encoded in LATIN1 and others in UTF-8.

Getting ready

Make sure that the MySQL database management system and the **mysqlclient** Python module are installed and that you are using the MySQL engine in your project's settings.

How to do it...

Open the `/etc/mysql/my.cnf` MySQL configuration file in your favorite editor and ensure that the following settings are set in the `[client]`, `[mysql]`, and `[mysqld]` sections, as follows:

```
# /etc/mysql/my.cnf
[client]
default-character-set = utf8
```

```
[mysql]
default-character-set = utf8

[mysqld]
collation-server = utf8_unicode_ci
init-connect = 'SET NAMES utf8'
character-set-server = utf8
```

If any of the sections don't exist, create them in the file. If the sections already exist, add these settings to the existing configurations, and then restart MySQL in your command-line tool, as follows:

```
$ /etc/init.d/mysql restart
```

How it works...

Now, whenever you create a new MySQL database, the databases and all of their tables will be set in UTF-8 encoding by default. Don't forget to set this up on all computers on which your project is developed or published.

There's more...

In PostgreSQL, the default server encoding is already UTF-8, but if you want to explicitly create a PostgreSQL database with UTF-8 encoding, then you can do that with the following command:

```
$ createdb --encoding=UTF8 --locale=en_US.UTF-8 --template=template0
myproject
```

See also

- The *Creating a project file structure* recipe
- The *Working with Docker containers for Django, Gunicorn, Nginx, and PostgreSQL* recipe

Creating the Git ignore file

Git is the most popular distributed version control system, and you are probably already using it for your Django project. Although you are tracking file changes for most of your files, it's recommended that you keep some specific files and folders out of version control. Usually, caches, compiled code, log files, and hidden system files should not be tracked in the Git repository.

Getting ready

Make sure that your Django project is under Git version control.

How to do it...

Using your favorite text editor, create a `.gitignore` file at the root of your Django project and put the following files and directories there:

```
# .gitignore
### Python template
# Byte-compiled / optimized / DLL files
__pycache__/
*.py[cod]
*$py.class

# Installer logs
pip-log.txt
pip-delete-this-directory.txt

# Unit test / coverage reports
htmlcov/
.tox/
.nox/
.coverage
.coverage.*
.cache
nosetests.xml
coverage.xml
*.cover
.hypothesis/
.pytest_cache/

# Translations
*.mo
```

```
*.pot

# Django stuff:
*.log
db.sqlite3

# Sphinx documentation
docs/_build/

# IPython
profile_default/
ipython_config.py

# Environments
env/

# Media and Static directories
/media/
!/media/.gitkeep

/static/
!/static/.gitkeep

# Secrets
secrets.json
```

How it works...

The .gitignore file specifies patterns that should intentionally be untracked by the Git version control system. The .gitignore file that we created in this recipe will ignore the Python-compiled files, local settings, collected static files, and media directory with the uploaded files.

Note that we have exceptional syntax with exclamation marks for media and static files:

```
/media/
!/media/.gitkeep
```

This tells Git to ignore the /media/ directory but keep the /media/.gitkeep file tracked under version control. As Git version control tracks files, but not directories, we use .gitkeep to make sure that the media directory will be created in each environment, but not tracked.

See also

- The *Creating a project file structure* recipe
- The *Working with Docker containers for Django, Gunicorn, Nginx, and PostgreSQL* recipe

Deleting Python-compiled files

When you run your project for the first time, Python compiles all of your *.py code in bytecode-compiled files, *.pyc, which are used later for execution. Normally, when you change the *.py files, *.pyc is recompiled; however, sometimes when you switch branches or move the directories, you need to clean up the compiled files manually.

Getting ready

Use your favorite editor and edit or create a .bash_profile file in your home directory.

How to do it...

1. Add this alias at the end of .bash_profile, as follows:

```
# ~/.bash_profile
alias delpyc='
find . -name "*.py[co]" -delete
find . -type d -name "__pycache__" -delete'
```

2. Now, to clean the Python-compiled files, go to your project directory and type the following command on the command line:

```
(env)$ delpyc
```

How it works...

At first, we create a Unix alias that searches for the *.pyc and *.pyo files and __pycache__ directories and deletes them in the current directory, as well as its children. The .bash_profile file is executed when you start a new session in the command-line tool.

There's more...

If you want to avoid creating Python-compiled files altogether, you can set an environment variable, `PYTHONDONTWRITEBYTECODE=1`, in your `.bash_profile`, `env/bin/activate` script, or PyCharm configuration.

See also

- The *Creating the Git ignore file* recipe

Respecting the import order in Python files

When you create the Python modules, it is good practice to stay consistent with the structure in the files. This makes it easier for both you and other developers to read the code. This recipe will show you how to structure your imports.

Getting ready

Create a virtual environment and create a Django project in it.

How to do it...

Use the following structure for each Python file that you are creating. Categorize the imports into sections, as follows:

```
# System libraries
import os
import re
from datetime import datetime

# Third-party libraries
import boto
from PIL import Image

# Django modules
from django.db import models
from django.conf import settings

# Django apps
```

```
from cms.models import Page

# Current-app modules
from .models import NewsArticle
from . import app_settings
```

How it works...

We have five main categories for the imports, as follows:

- **System libraries** for packages in the default installation of Python
- **Third-party libraries** for the additional installed Python packages
- **Django modules** for different modules from the Django framework
- **Django apps** for third-party and local apps
- **Current-app modules** for relative imports from the current app

There's more...

When coding in Python and Django, use the official style guide for Python code, PEP 8. You can find it at https://www.python.org/dev/peps/pep-0008/.

See also

- The *Handling project dependencies with pip* recipe
- The *Including external dependencies in your project* recipe

Creating an app configuration

Django projects consist of multiple Python modules called applications (or, more commonly, apps) that combine different modular functionalities. Each app can have models, views, forms, URL configurations, management commands, migrations, signals, tests, context processors, middlewares, and so on. The Django framework has an application registry, where all apps and models are collected and later used for configuration and introspection. Since Django 1.7, metainformation about apps can be saved in the AppConfig instance for each app. Let's create a sample magazine app to take a look at how to use the app configuration there.

Getting ready

You can create a Django app either by calling the `startapp` management command or by creating the app module manually:

```
(env)$ cd myproject/apps/
(env)$ django-admin.py startapp magazine
```

With your `magazine` app created, add a `NewsArticle` model to `models.py`, create administration for the model in `admin.py`, and put `"myproject.apps.magazine"` in `INSTALLED_APPS` in the settings. If you are not yet familiar with these tasks, study the official Django tutorial at `https://docs.djangoproject.com/en/3.0/intro/tutorial01/`.

How to do it...

Follow these steps to create and use the app configuration:

1. Modify the `apps.py` file and insert the following content into it, as follows:

```python
# myproject/apps/magazine/apps.py
from django.apps import AppConfig
from django.utils.translation import gettext_lazy as _


class MagazineAppConfig(AppConfig):
    name = "myproject.apps.magazine"
    verbose_name = _("Magazine")

    def ready(self):
        from . import signals
```

2. Edit the `__init__.py` file in the `magazine` module to contain the following content:

```python
# myproject/apps/magazine/__init__.py
default_app_config = \
"myproject.apps.magazine.apps.MagazineAppConfig"
```

3. Let's create a `signals.py` file and add some signal handlers there:

```
# myproject/apps/magazine/signals.py
from django.db.models.signals import post_save, post_delete
from django.dispatch import receiver
from django.conf import settings

from .models import NewsArticle

@receiver(post_save, sender=NewsArticle)
def news_save_handler(sender, **kwargs):
    if settings.DEBUG:
        print(f"{kwargs['instance']} saved.")


@receiver(post_delete, sender=NewsArticle)
def news_delete_handler(sender, **kwargs):
    if settings.DEBUG:
        print(f"{kwargs['instance']} deleted.")
```

How it works...

When you run an HTTP server or invoke a management command, `django.setup()` is called. It loads the settings, sets up logging, and prepares the app registry. This registry is initialized in three steps. Django first imports the configurations for each item from `INSTALLED_APPS` in the settings. These items can point to app names or configurations directly—for example, `"myproject.apps.magazine"` or `"myproject.apps.magazine.apps.MagazineAppConfig"`.

Django then tries to import `models.py` from each app in `INSTALLED_APPS` and collect all of the models.

Finally, Django runs the `ready()` method for each app configuration. This method presents a good point in the development process to register signal handlers, if you have any. The `ready()` method is optional.

In our example, the `MagazineAppConfig` class sets the configuration for the `magazine` app. The `name` parameter defines the module of the current app. The `verbose_name` parameter defines a human name that is used in the Django model administration, where models are presented and grouped by apps. The `ready()` method imports and activates the signal handlers that, when in DEBUG mode, print in the terminal that a `NewsArticle` object was saved or deleted.

There's more...

After calling `django.setup()`, you can load the app configurations and models from the registry as follows:

```
>>> from django.apps import apps as django_apps
>>> magazine_app_config = django_apps.get_app_config("magazine")
>>> magazine_app_config
<MagazineAppConfig: magazine>
>>> magazine_app_config.models_module
<module 'magazine.models' from
'/path/to/myproject/apps/magazine/models.py'>
>>> NewsArticle = django_apps.get_model("magazine", "NewsArticle")
>>> NewsArticle
<class 'magazine.models.NewsArticle'>
```

You can read more about app configuration in the official Django documentation at `https://docs.djangoproject.com/en/2.2/ref/applications/`.

See also

- The *Working with a virtual environment* recipe
- The *Working with Docker containers for Django, Gunicorn, Nginx, and PostgreSQL* recipe
- The *Defining overwritable app settings* recipe
- `Chapter 6`, *Model Administration*

Defining overwritable app settings

This recipe will show you how to define settings for your app that can then be overwritten in your project's settings file. This is especially useful for reusable apps that you can customize by adding a configuration.

Getting ready

Follow the steps in the *Getting ready* in the *Creating app configuration* recipe to create your Django app.

How to do it...

1. Define your app settings using the `getattr()` pattern in `models.py` if you just have one or two settings, or in the `app_settings.py` file if the settings are extensive and you want to organize them better:

```python
# myproject/apps/magazine/app_settings.py
from django.conf import settings
from django.utils.translation import gettext_lazy as _

# Example:
SETTING_1 = getattr(settings, "MAGAZINE_SETTING_1", "default
value")

MEANING_OF_LIFE = getattr(settings, "MAGAZINE_MEANING_OF_LIFE", 42)

ARTICLE_THEME_CHOICES = getattr(
    settings,
    "MAGAZINE_ARTICLE_THEME_CHOICES",
    [
        ('futurism', _("Futurism")),
        ('nostalgia', _("Nostalgia")),
        ('sustainability', _("Sustainability")),
        ('wonder', _("Wonder")),
    ]
)
```

2. `models.py` will contain the `NewsArticle` model, like this:

```python
# myproject/apps/magazine/models.py
from django.db import models
from django.utils.translation import gettext_lazy as _


class NewsArticle(models.Model):
    created_at = models.DateTimeField(_("Created at"),
     auto_now_add=True)
    title = models.CharField(_("Title"), max_length=255)
    body = models.TextField(_("Body"))
    theme = models.CharField(_("Theme"), max_length=20)

    class Meta:
        verbose_name = _("News Article")
        verbose_name_plural = _("News Articles")

    def __str__(self):
        return self.title
```

3. Next, in `admin.py`, we will import and use the settings from `app_settings.py`, as follows:

```python
# myproject/apps/magazine/admin.py
from django import forms
from django.contrib import admin

from .models import NewsArticle

from .app_settings import ARTICLE_THEME_CHOICES


class NewsArticleModelForm(forms.ModelForm):
    theme = forms.ChoiceField(
        label=NewsArticle._meta.get_field("theme").verbose_name,
        choices=ARTICLE_THEME_CHOICES,
        required=not NewsArticle._meta.get_field("theme").blank,
    )
    class Meta:
        fields = "__all__"


@admin.register(NewsArticle)
class NewsArticleAdmin(admin.ModelAdmin):
    form = NewsArticleModelForm
```

4. If you want to overwrite the `ARTICLE_THEME_CHOICES` settings for a given project, you should add `MAGAZINE_ARTICLE_THEME_CHOICES` in the project settings:

```python
# myproject/settings/_base.py
from django.utils.translation import gettext_lazy as _
# ...
MAGAZINE_ARTICLE_THEME_CHOICES = [
    ('futurism', _("Futurism")),
    ('nostalgia', _("Nostalgia")),
    ('sustainability', _("Sustainability")),
    ('wonder', _("Wonder")),
    ('positivity', _("Positivity")),
    ('solutions', _("Solutions")),
    ('science', _("Science")),
]
```

How it works...

The `getattr(object, attribute_name[, default_value])` Python function tries to get the `attribute_name` attribute from `object` and returns `default_value` if it is not found. We try to read different settings from the Django project settings module or, if they don't exist there, the default values are used.

Note that we could have defined the `choices` for the `theme` field in `models.py`, but instead we created a custom `ModelForm` in administration and set the choices there. This was done to avoid the creation of new database migrations whenever the `ARTICLE_THEME_CHOICES` is changed.

See also

- The *Creating app configuration* recipe
- `Chapter 6`, *Model Administration*

Working with Docker containers for Django, Gunicorn, Nginx, and PostgreSQL

Django projects depend not only on Python requirements, but also on many system requirements, such as a web server, database, server cache, and mail server. When developing a Django project, you need to ensure that all environments and all developers will have all the same requirements installed. One way to keep those dependencies in sync is to use Docker. With Docker, you can have different versions of the database, web, or other servers required individually for each project.

Docker is a system for creating configured, customized virtual machines called containers. It allows us to duplicate the setup of any production environment precisely. Docker containers are created from so-called Docker images. Images consist of layers (or instructions) on how to build the container. There can be an image for PostgreSQL, an image for Redis, an image for Memcached, and a custom image for your Django project, and all those images can be combined into accompanying containers with Docker Compose.

In this recipe, we will use a project boilerplate to set up a Django project with a PostgreSQL database, served by Nginx and Gunicorn, and manage all of them with Docker Compose.

Getting ready

First, you will need to install the Docker Engine, following the instructions at `https://www.docker.com/get-started`. This usually includes the Compose tool, which makes it possible to manage systems that require multiple containers, ideal for a fully isolated Django project. If it is needed separately, installation details for Compose are available at `https://docs.docker.com/compose/install/`.

How to do it...

Let's explore the Django and Docker boilerplate:

1. Download the code from `https://github.com/archatas/django_docker` to your computer to the `~/projects/django_docker` directory, for example.

 If you choose another directory, for example, `myproject_docker`, then you will have to do a global search and replace `django_docker` with `myproject_docker`.

2. Open the `docker-compose.yml` file. There are three containers that need to be created: `nginx`, `gunicorn`, and `db`. Don't worry if it looks complicated; we'll describe it in detail later:

```
# docker-compose.yml
version: "3.7"

services:
  nginx:
    image: nginx:latest
    ports:
      - "80:80"
    volumes:
      - ./config/nginx/conf.d:/etc/nginx/conf.d
      - static_volume:/home/myproject/static
      - media_volume:/home/myproject/media
    depends_on:
      - gunicorn

  gunicorn:
    build:
      context: .
      args:
        PIP_REQUIREMENTS: "${PIP_REQUIREMENTS}"
```

```
command: bash -c "/home/myproject/env/bin/gunicorn --workers 3
--bind 0.0.0.0:8000 myproject.wsgi:application"
depends_on:
  - db
volumes:
  - static_volume:/home/myproject/static
  - media_volume:/home/myproject/media
expose:
  - "8000"
environment:
  DJANGO_SETTINGS_MODULE: "${DJANGO_SETTINGS_MODULE}"
  DJANGO_SECRET_KEY: "${DJANGO_SECRET_KEY}"
  DATABASE_NAME: "${DATABASE_NAME}"
  DATABASE_USER: "${DATABASE_USER}"
  DATABASE_PASSWORD: "${DATABASE_PASSWORD}"
  EMAIL_HOST: "${EMAIL_HOST}"
  EMAIL_PORT: "${EMAIL_PORT}"
  EMAIL_HOST_USER: "${EMAIL_HOST_USER}"
  EMAIL_HOST_PASSWORD: "${EMAIL_HOST_PASSWORD}"

db:
  image: postgres:latest
  restart: always
  environment:
    POSTGRES_DB: "${DATABASE_NAME}"
    POSTGRES_USER: "${DATABASE_USER}"
    POSTGRES_PASSWORD: "${DATABASE_PASSWORD}"
  ports:
    - 5432
  volumes:
    - postgres_data:/var/lib/postgresql/data/

volumes:
  postgres_data:
  static_volume:
  media_volume:
```

3. Open and read through the `Dockerfile` file. These are the layers (or instructions) that are needed to create the `gunicorn` container:

```
# Dockerfile
# pull official base image
FROM python:3.8

# accept arguments
ARG PIP_REQUIREMENTS=production.txt
```

```
# set environment variables
ENV PYTHONDONTWRITEBYTECODE 1
ENV PYTHONUNBUFFERED 1

# install dependencies
RUN pip install --upgrade pip setuptools

# create user for the Django project
RUN useradd -ms /bin/bash myproject

# set current user
USER myproject

# set work directory
WORKDIR /home/myproject

# create and activate virtual environment
RUN python3 -m venv env

# copy and install pip requirements
COPY --chown=myproject ./src/myproject/requirements
/home/myproject/requirements/
RUN ./env/bin/pip3 install -r
/home/myproject/requirements/${PIP_REQUIREMENTS}

# copy Django project files
COPY --chown=myproject ./src/myproject /home/myproject/
```

4. Copy the `build_dev_example.sh` script to `build_dev.sh` and edit its content. These are environment variables to pass to the `docker-compose` script:

```
# build_dev.sh
#!/usr/bin/env bash
DJANGO_SETTINGS_MODULE=myproject.settings.dev \
DJANGO_SECRET_KEY="change-this-to-50-characters-long-
 random-string" \
DATABASE_NAME=myproject \
DATABASE_USER=myproject \
DATABASE_PASSWORD="change-this-too" \
PIP_REQUIREMENTS=dev.txt \
docker-compose up --detach --build
```

5. In a command-line tool, add execution permissions to `build_dev.sh` and run it to build the containers:

```
$ chmod +x build_dev.sh
$ ./build_dev.sh
```

6. If you now go to `http://0.0.0.0/en/`, you should see a **Hello, World!** page there.
When navigating to `http://0.0.0.0/en/admin/`, you should see the following:

```
OperationalError at /en/admin/
 FATAL: role "myproject" does not exist
```

This means that you have to create the database user and the database in the Docker container.

7. Let's SSH to the `db` container and create the database user, password, and the database itself in the Docker container:

```
$ docker exec -it django_docker_db_1 bash
/# su - postgres
/$ createuser --createdb --password myproject
/$ createdb --username myproject myproject
```

When asked, enter the same password for the database as in the `build_dev.sh` script.

Press [*Ctrl + D*] twice to log out of the PostgreSQL user and Docker container.

If you now go to `http://0.0.0.0/en/admin/`, you should see the following:

```
ProgrammingError at /en/admin/ relation "django_session" does not
exist LINE 1: ...ession_data", "django_session"."expire_date" FROM
"django_se...
```

This means that you have to run migrations to create the database schema.

8. SSH into the `gunicorn` container and run the necessary Django management commands:

```
$ docker exec -it django_docker_gunicorn_1 bash
$ source env/bin/activate
(env)$ python manage.py migrate
(env)$ python manage.py collectstatic
(env)$ python manage.py createsuperuser
```

Answer all the questions that are asked by the management commands.

Press [*Ctrl + D*] twice to log out of the Docker container.

If you now navigate to `http://0.0.0.0/en/admin/`, you should see the Django administration, where you can log in with the super user's credentials that you have just created.

9. Create analogous scripts, `build_test.sh`, `build_staging.sh`, and `build_production.sh`, where only the environment variables differ.

How it works...

The structure of the code in the boilerplate is similar to the one in a virtual environment. The project source files are in the `src` directory. We have the `git-hooks` directory for the pre-commit hook that is used to track the last modification date and the `config` directory for the configurations of the services used in the containers:

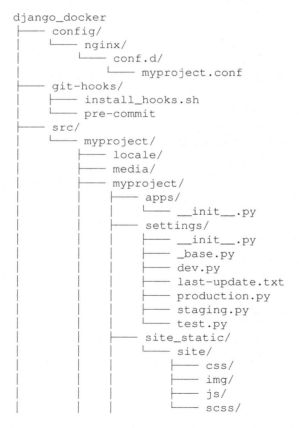

```
django_docker
├── config/
│   └── nginx/
│       └── conf.d/
│           └── myproject.conf
├── git-hooks/
│   ├── install_hooks.sh
│   └── pre-commit
├── src/
│   └── myproject/
│       ├── locale/
│       ├── media/
│       ├── myproject/
│       │   ├── apps/
│       │   │   └── __init__.py
│       │   ├── settings/
│       │   │   ├── __init__.py
│       │   │   ├── _base.py
│       │   │   ├── dev.py
│       │   │   ├── last-update.txt
│       │   │   ├── production.py
│       │   │   ├── staging.py
│       │   │   └── test.py
│       │   ├── site_static/
│       │   │   └── site/
│       │   │       ├── css/
│       │   │       ├── img/
│       │   │       ├── js/
│       │   │       └── scss/
```

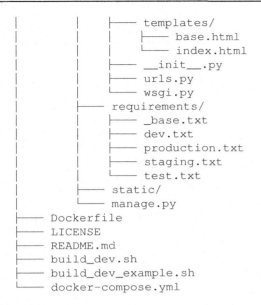

```
|        |       |        ├── templates/
|        |       |        |        ├── base.html
|        |       |        |        └── index.html
|        |       |        ├── __init__.py
|        |       |        ├── urls.py
|        |       |        └── wsgi.py
|        |       ├── requirements/
|        |       |        ├── _base.txt
|        |       |        ├── dev.txt
|        |       |        ├── production.txt
|        |       |        ├── staging.txt
|        |       |        └── test.txt
|        ├── static/
|        └── manage.py
├── Dockerfile
├── LICENSE
├── README.md
├── build_dev.sh
├── build_dev_example.sh
└── docker-compose.yml
```

The main Docker-related configurations are at `docker-compose.yml` and `Dockerfile`. Docker Compose is a wrapper around Docker's command-line API. The `build_dev.sh` script builds and runs the Django project under the Gunicorn WSGI HTTP server at port `8000`, Nginx at port `80` (serving static and media files and proxying other requests to Gunicorn), and the PostgreSQL database at port `5432`.

In the `docker-compose.yml` file, the creation of three Docker containers is requested:

- `nginx` for the Nginx web server
- `gunicorn` for the Django project with the Gunicorn web server
- `db` for the PostgreSQL database

The `nginx` and `db` containers will be created from the official images located at `https://hub.docker.com`. They have specific configuration parameters, such as the ports they are running on, environment variables, dependencies on other containers, and volumes.

Docker volumes are specific directories that stay untouched when you rebuild the Docker containers. Volumes need to be defined for the database data files, media, static, and the like.

The `gunicorn` container will be built from the instructions at the `Dockerfile`, defined by the build context in the `docker-compose.yml` file. Let's examine each layer (or instruction) there:

- The `gunicorn` container will be based on the `python:3.7` image
- It will take `PIP_REQUIREMENTS` as an argument from the `docker-compose.yml` file
- It will set environment variables for the container
- It will install and upgrade pip, setuptools, and virtualenv
- It will create a system user named `myproject` for the Django project
- It will set `myproject` as the current user
- It will set the home directory of the `myproject` user as the current working directory
- It will create a virtual environment there
- It will copy pip requirements from the base computer to the Docker container
- It will install the pip requirements for the current environment defined by the `PIP_REQUIREMENTS` variable
- It will copy the source of the entire Django project

The content of `config/nginx/conf.d/myproject.conf` will be saved under `/etc/nginx/conf.d/` in the `nginx` container. This is the configuration of the Nginx web server telling it to listen to port `80` (the default HTTP port) and forward requests to the Gunicorn server on port `8000`, except for requests asking for static or media content:

```
#/etc/nginx/conf.d/myproject.conf
upstream myproject {
    server django_docker_gunicorn_1:8000;
}

server {
    listen 80;

    location / {
        proxy_pass http://myproject;
        proxy_set_header X-Forwarded-For $proxy_add_x_forwarded_for;
        proxy_set_header Host $host;
        proxy_redirect off;
    }

    rewrite "/static/\d+/(.*)" /static/$1 last;

    location /static/ {
```

```
        alias /home/myproject/static/;
    }

    location /media/ {
        alias /home/myproject/media/;
    }
}
```

You can learn more about Nginx and Gunicorn configurations in the *Deploying on Nginx and Gunicorn for the staging environment* and *Deploying on Nginx and Gunicorn for the production environment* recipes in `Chapter 12`, *Deployment*.

There's more...

You can destroy Docker containers with the `docker-compose down` command and rebuild them with your build script:

```
$ docker-compose down
$ ./build_dev.sh
```

If something is not working as expected, you can inspect the logs with the `docker-compose logs` command:

```
$ docker-compose logs nginx
$ docker-compose logs gunicorn
$ docker-compose logs db
```

To connect to any of the containers via SSH, you should use one of the following:

```
$ docker exec -it django_docker_gunicorn_1 bash
$ docker exec -it django_docker_nginx_1 bash
$ docker exec -it django_docker_db_1 bash
```

You can copy files and directories to and from volumes on Docker containers using the `docker cp` command:

```
$ docker cp ~/avatar.png django_docker_gunicorn_1:/home/myproject/media/
$ docker cp django_docker_gunicorn_1:/home/myproject/media ~/Desktop/
```

If you want to get better a understanding of Docker and Docker Compose, check out the official documentation at `https://docs.docker.com/`, and specifically `https://docs.docker.com/compose/`.

See also

- The *Creating a project file structure* recipe
- The *Deploying on Apache with mod_wsgi for the staging environment* recipe in Chapter 12, *Deployment*
- The *Deploying on Apache with mod_wsgi for the production environment* recipe in Chapter 12, *Deployment*
- The *Deploying on Nginx and Gunicorn for the staging environment* recipe in Chapter 12, *Deployment*
- The *Deploying on Nginx and Gunicorn for the production environment* recipe in Chapter 12, *Deployment*

Models and Database Structure 2

In this chapter, we will cover the following topics:

- Using model mixins
- Creating a model mixin with URL-related methods
- Creating a model mixin to handle creation and modification dates
- Creating a model mixin to take care of meta tags
- Creating a model mixin to handle generic relations
- Handling multilingual fields
- Working with model translation tables
- Avoiding circular dependencies
- Adding database constraints
- Using migrations
- Changing a foreign key to the many-to-many field

Introduction

When you start a new app, the first thing that you do is create the models that represent your database structure. We are assuming that you have already created Django apps, or, at the very least, have read and understood the official Django tutorial. In this chapter, you will see a few interesting techniques that will make your database structure consistent across the different apps in your project. Then, you will see how to handle the internationalization of the data in your database. After that, you will learn how to avoid circular dependencies in your models and how to set database constraints. At the end of the chapter, you will see how to use migrations to change your database structure during the process of development.

Technical requirements

To work with the code in this book, you will need the latest stable version of Python, the MySQL or PostgreSQL database, and a Django project with a virtual environment.

You can find all the code for this chapter in the `ch02` directory in the GitHub repository at: `https://github.com/PacktPublishing/Django-3-Web-Development-Cookbook-Fourth-Edition`.

Using model mixins

In object-oriented languages, such as Python, a mixin class can be viewed as an interface with implemented features. When a model extends a mixin, it implements the interface and includes all of its fields, attributes, properties, and methods. The mixins in Django models can be used when you want to reuse the generic functionalities in different models multiple times. The model mixins in Django are abstract base model classes. We will explore them in the next few recipes.

Getting ready

First, you will need to create reusable mixins. A good place to keep your model mixins is in a `myproject.apps.core` app. If you create a reusable app that you will share with others, keep the model mixins in the reusable app itself, possibly in a `base.py` file.

How to do it...

Open the `models.py` file of any Django app that you want to use mixins with, and type the following code:

```
# myproject/apps/ideas/models.py
from django.db import models
from django.urls import reverse
from django.utils.translation import gettext_lazy as _

from myproject.apps.core.models import (
    CreationModificationDateBase,
    MetaTagsBase,
    UrlBase,
)
```

```
class Idea(CreationModificationDateBase, MetaTagsBase, UrlBase):
    title = models.CharField(
        _("Title"),
        max_length=200,
    )
    content = models.TextField(
        _("Content"),
    )
    # other fields...

    class Meta:
        verbose_name = _("Idea")
        verbose_name_plural = _("Ideas")

    def __str__(self):
        return self.title

    def get_url_path(self):
        return reverse("idea_details", kwargs={
            "idea_id": str(self.pk),
        })
```

How it works...

Django's model inheritance supports three types of inheritance: abstract base classes, multi-table inheritance, and proxy models. Model mixins are abstract model classes, in that we define them by using an abstract `Meta` class, with specified fields, properties, and methods. When you create a model such as `Idea`, as shown in the preceding example, it inherits all of the features from `CreationModificationDateMixin`, `MetaTagsMixin`, and `UrlMixin`. All of the fields of these abstract classes are saved in the same database table as the fields of the extending model. In the following recipes, you will learn how to define your model mixins.

There's more...

In normal Python class inheritance, if there is more than one base class, and all of them implement a specific method, and you call that method on the instance of a child class, only the method from the first parent class will be called, as in the following example:

```
>>> class A(object):
... def test(self):
...     print("A.test() called")
...
```

```
>>> class B(object):
... def test(self):
...     print("B.test() called")
...

>>> class C(object):
... def test(self):
...     print("C.test() called")
...

>>> class D(A, B, C):
... def test(self):
...     super().test()
...     print("D.test() called")

>>> d = D()
>>> d.test()
A.test() called
D.test() called
```

This is the same for Django model base classes; however, there is one special exception.

The Django framework does some magic with metaclasses that calls the `save()` and `delete()` methods from each of the base classes.

That means that you can confidently do pre-save, post-save, pre-delete, and post-delete manipulations for specific fields defined specifically in the mixin by overwriting the `save()` and `delete()` methods.

To learn more about the different types of model inheritance, refer to the official Django documentation, available at `https://docs.djangoproject.com/en/2.2/topics/db/models/#model-inheritance`.

See also

- The *Creating a model mixin with URL-related methods* recipe
- The *Creating a model mixin to handle creation and modification dates* recipe
- The *Creating a model mixin to take care of meta tags* recipe

Creating a model mixin with URL-related methods

For every model that has its own distinct detail page, it is good practice to define the `get_absolute_url()` method. This method can be used in templates and also in the Django admin site to preview the saved object. However, `get_absolute_url()` is ambiguous, as it returns the URL path instead of the full URL.

In this recipe, we will look at how to create a model mixin that provides simplified support for model-specific URLs. This mixin will enable you to do the following:

- Allow you to define either the URL path or the full URL in your model
- Generate the other URL automatically, based on the one that you defined
- Define the `get_absolute_url()` method behind the scenes

Getting ready

If you haven't yet done so, create the `myproject.apps.core` app where you will store your model mixins. Then, create a `models.py` file in the core package. Alternatively, if you create a reusable app, put the mixins in a `base.py` file in that app.

How to do it...

Execute the following steps, one by one:

1. Add the following content to the `models.py` file of your `core` app:

```python
# myproject/apps/core/models.py
from urllib.parse import urlparse, urlunparse
from django.conf import settings
from django.db import models

class UrlBase(models.Model):
    """
    A replacement for get_absolute_url()
    Models extending this mixin should have either get_url or
     get_url_path implemented.
    """
    class Meta:
        abstract = True
```

```
def get_url(self):
    if hasattr(self.get_url_path, "dont_recurse"):
        raise NotImplementedError
    try:
        path = self.get_url_path()
    except NotImplementedError:
        raise
    return settings.WEBSITE_URL + path
get_url.dont_recurse = True

def get_url_path(self):
    if hasattr(self.get_url, "dont_recurse"):
        raise NotImplementedError
    try:
        url = self.get_url()
    except NotImplementedError:
        raise
    bits = urlparse(url)
    return urlunparse(("", "") + bits[2:])
get_url_path.dont_recurse = True

def get_absolute_url(self):
    return self.get_url()
```

2. Add the WEBSITE_URL setting without a trailing slash to the dev, test, staging, and production settings. For example, for the development environment this will be as follows:

```
# myproject/settings/dev.py
from ._base import *

DEBUG = True
WEBSITE_URL = "http://127.0.0.1:8000"  # without trailing slash
```

3. To use the mixin in your app, import the mixin from the core app, inherit the mixin in your model class, and define the get_url_path() method, as follows:

```
# myproject/apps/ideas/models.py
from django.db import models
from django.urls import reverse
from django.utils.translation import gettext_lazy as _

from myproject.apps.core.models import UrlBase

class Idea(UrlBase):
    # fields, attributes, properties and methods...

    def get_url_path(self):
```

```
return reverse("idea_details", kwargs={
    "idea_id": str(self.pk),
})
```

How it works...

The `UrlBase` class is an abstract model that has three methods, as follows:

- `get_url()` retrieves the full URL of the object.
- `get_url_path()` retrieves the absolute path of the object.
- `get_absolute_url()` mimics the `get_url_path()` method.

The `get_url()` and `get_url_path()` methods are expected to be overwritten in the extended model class, for example, `Idea`. You can define `get_url()`, and `get_url_path()` will strip it to the path. Alternatively, you can define `get_url_path()`, and `get_url()` will prepend the website URL to the beginning of the path.

 The rule of thumb is to always overwrite the `get_url_path()` method.

In the templates, use `get_url_path()` when you need a link to an object on the same website, as follows:

```
<a href="{{ idea.get_url_path }}">{{ idea.title }}</a>
```

Use `get_url()` for links in external communication, such as in emails, RSS feeds, or APIs; an example is as follows:

```
<a href="{{ idea.get_url }}">{{ idea.title }}</a>
```

The default `get_absolute_url()` method will be used in the Django model administration for the **View on site** functionality, and might also be used by some third-party Django apps.

There's more...

In general, don't use incremental primary keys in the URLs, because it is not safe to expose them to the end user: the total amount of items would be visible, and it would be too easy to navigate through different items by just changing the URL path.

You can use the primary keys in the URLs for the detail pages only if they are **Universal Unique Identifiers** (**UUIDs**) or generated random strings. Otherwise, create and use a slug field, as follows:

```
class Idea(UrlBase):
    slug = models.SlugField(_("Slug for URLs"), max_length=50)
```

See also

- The *Using model mixins* recipe
- The *Creating a model mixin to handle creation and modification dates* recipe
- The *Creating a model mixin to take care of meta tags* recipe
- The *Creating a model mixin to handle generic relations* recipe
- The *Configuring settings for development, testing, staging, and production environments* recipe, in `Chapter 1`, *Getting Started with Django 3.0*

Creating a model mixin to handle creation and modification dates

It is common to include timestamps in your models for the creation and modification of your model instances. In this recipe, you will learn how to create a simple model mixin that saves the creation and modification dates and times for your model. Using such a mixin will ensure that all of the models use the same field names for the timestamps, and have the same behaviors.

Getting ready

If you haven't yet done so, create the `myproject.apps.core` package to save your mixins. Then, create the `models.py` file in the core package.

How to do it...

Open the `models.py` file in your `myprojects.apps.core` package, and insert the following content there:

```python
# myproject/apps/core/models.py
from django.db import models
from django.utils.translation import gettext_lazy as _


class CreationModificationDateBase(models.Model):
    """
    Abstract base class with a creation and modification date and time
    """

    created = models.DateTimeField(
        _("Creation Date and Time"),
        auto_now_add=True,
    )

    modified = models.DateTimeField(
        _("Modification Date and Time"),
        auto_now=True,
    )

    class Meta:
        abstract = True
```

How it works...

The `CreationModificationDateMixin` class is an abstract model, which means that extending model classes will create all of the fields in the same database table—that is, there will be no one-to-one relationships that make the table more complex to handle.

This mixin has two date-time fields, `created` and `modified`. With the `auto_now_add` and `auto_now` attributes, the timestamps will be saved automatically when saving a model instance. The fields will automatically get the `editable=False` attribute, and thus will be hidden in administration forms. If `USE_TZ` is set to `True` in the settings (which is the default and recommended), time-zone-aware timestamps will be used. Otherwise, time-zone-naive timestamps will be used. Timezone-aware timestamps are saved in the **Coordinated Universal Time (UTC)** time zone in the database and converted to the default time zone of the project when reading or writing them. Time-zone-naive timestamps are saved in the local time zone of the project in the database; they are not practical to use in general, because they make time management between time zones more complicated.

To make use of this mixin, we just have to import it and extend our model, as follows:

```python
# myproject/apps/ideas/models.py
from django.db import models

from myproject.apps.core.models import CreationModificationDateBase

class Idea(CreationModificationDateBase):
    # other fields, attributes, properties, and methods...
```

See also

- The *Using model mixins* recipe
- The *Creating a model mixin to take care of meta tags* recipe
- The *Creating a model mixin to handle generic relations* recipe

Creating a model mixin to take care of meta tags

When you optimize your site for search engines, you not only have to use semantic markup for each page, but you also have to include appropriate meta tags. For maximum flexibility, it helps to have a way to define content for common meta tags, specific to objects that have their own detail pages on your website. In this recipe, we will look at how to create a model mixin for the fields and methods related to the keyword, description, author, and copyright meta tags.

Getting ready

As detailed in the previous recipes, make sure that you have the myproject.apps.core package for your mixins. Also, create a directory structure, templates/utils/includes/, under the package, and inside of that, create a meta.html file to store the basic meta tag markup.

How to do it...

Let's create our model mixin:

1. Make sure to add "myproject.apps.core" to INSTALLED_APPS in the settings, because we want to take the templates directory into account for this module.

2. Add the following basic meta tag markup to meta_field.html:

```
{# templates/core/includes/meta_field.html #}
<meta name="{{ name }}" content="{{ content }}" />
```

3. Open the models.py file from the core package in your favorite editor, and add the following content:

```python
# myproject/apps/core/models.py
from django.conf import settings
from django.db import models
from django.utils.translation import gettext_lazy as _
from django.utils.safestring import mark_safe
from django.template.loader import render_to_string


class MetaTagsBase(models.Model):
    """
    Abstract base class for generating meta tags
    """
    meta_keywords = models.CharField(
        _("Keywords"),
        max_length=255,
        blank=True,
        help_text=_("Separate keywords with commas."),
    )
    meta_description = models.CharField(
        _("Description"),
        max_length=255,
        blank=True,
    )
    meta_author = models.CharField(
        _("Author"),
        max_length=255,
        blank=True,
    )
    meta_copyright = models.CharField(
        _("Copyright"),
        max_length=255,
        blank=True,
    )
```

```
class Meta:
    abstract = True

def get_meta_field(self, name, content):
    tag = ""
    if name and content:
        tag = render_to_string("core/includes/meta_field.html",
        {
            "name": name,
            "content": content,
        })
    return mark_safe(tag)

def get_meta_keywords(self):
    return self.get_meta_field("keywords", self.meta_keywords)

def get_meta_description(self):
    return self.get_meta_field("description",
     self.meta_description)

def get_meta_author(self):
    return self.get_meta_field("author", self.meta_author)

def get_meta_copyright(self):
    return self.get_meta_field("copyright",
     self.meta_copyright)

def get_meta_tags(self):
    return mark_safe("\n".join((
        self.get_meta_keywords(),
        self.get_meta_description(),
        self.get_meta_author(),
        self.get_meta_copyright(),
    )))
```

How it works...

This mixin adds four fields to the model that extends from it: `meta_keywords`, `meta_description`, `meta_author`, and `meta_copyright`. The corresponding `get_*()` methods, used to render the associated meta tags, are also added. Each of these passes the name and appropriate field content to the core `get_meta_field()` method, which uses this input to return rendered markup based on the `meta_field.html` template. Finally, a shortcut `get_meta_tags()` method is provided to generate the combined markup for all of the available metadata at once.

If you use this mixin in a model, such as `Idea`, which is shown in the *Using model mixins* recipe at the start of this chapter, you can put the following in the HEAD section of your `detail` page template to render all of the meta tags at once, as follows:

```
{% block meta_tags %}
{{ block.super }}
{{ idea.get_meta_tags }}
{% endblock %}
```

Here, a `meta_tags` block has been defined in a parent template, and this snippet shows how the child template redefines the block, including the content from the parent first as `block.super`, and extending it with our additional tags from the `idea` object. You could also render only a specific meta tag by using something like the following: `{{ idea.get_meta_description }}`.

As you may have noticed from the `models.py` code, the rendered meta tags are marked as safe – that is, they are not escaped, and we don't need to use the `safe` template filter. Only the values that come from the database are escaped, in order to guarantee that the final HTML is well formed. The database data in `meta_keywords` and other fields will automatically be escaped when we call `render_to_string()` for the `meta_field.html` template, because that template does not specify `{% autoescape off %}` in its content.

See also

- The *Using model mixins* recipe
- The *Creating a model mixin to handle creation and modification dates* recipe
- The *Creating a model mixin to handle generic relations* recipe
- The *Arranging the base.html template* recipe in `Chapter 4`, *Templates and JavaScript*

Creating a model mixin to handle generic relations

Aside from normal database relationships, such as a foreign-key relationship or a many-to-many relationship, Django has a mechanism to relate a model to an instance of any other model. This concept is called generic relations. For each generic relation, we save the content type of the related model as well as the ID of the instance of that model.

In this recipe, we will look at how to abstract the creation of generic relations in the model mixins.

Getting ready

For this recipe to work, you will need to have the `contenttypes` app installed. It should be in the `INSTALLED_APPS` list in the settings, by default, as shown in the following code:

```python
# myproject/settings/_base.py

INSTALLED_APPS = [
    # contributed
    "django.contrib.admin",
    "django.contrib.auth",
    "django.contrib.contenttypes",
    "django.contrib.sessions",
    "django.contrib.messages",
    "django.contrib.staticfiles",
    # third-party
    # ...
    # local
    "myproject.apps.core",
    "myproject.apps.categories",
    "myproject.apps.ideas",
]
```

Again, make sure that you have already created the `myproject.apps.core` app for your model mixins.

How to do it...

To create and use a mixin for generic relations follow these steps:

1. Open the `models.py` file in the core package in a text editor, and insert the following content there:

```python
# myproject/apps/core/models.py
from django.db import models
from django.utils.translation import gettext_lazy as _
from django.contrib.contenttypes.models import ContentType
from django.contrib.contenttypes.fields import GenericForeignKey
from django.core.exceptions import FieldError


def object_relation_base_factory(
        prefix=None,
        prefix_verbose=None,
        add_related_name=False,
        limit_content_type_choices_to=None,
        is_required=False):
    """
    Returns a mixin class for generic foreign keys using
    "Content type - object ID" with dynamic field names.
    This function is just a class generator.

    Parameters:
    prefix:             a prefix, which is added in front of
                        the fields
    prefix_verbose:     a verbose name of the prefix, used to
                        generate a title for the field column
                        of the content object in the Admin
    add_related_name:   a boolean value indicating, that a
                        related name for the generated content
                        type foreign key should be added. This
                        value should be true, if you use more
                        than one ObjectRelationBase in your
                        model.

    The model fields are created using this naming scheme:
        <<prefix>>_content_type
        <<prefix>>_object_id
        <<prefix>>_content_object
    """
    p = ""
    if prefix:
        p = f"{prefix}_"
```

```
prefix_verbose = prefix_verbose or _("Related object")
limit_content_type_choices_to = limit_content_type_choices_to
  or {}

content_type_field = f"{p}content_type"
object_id_field = f"{p}object_id"
content_object_field = f"{p}content_object"

class TheClass(models.Model):
    class Meta:
        abstract = True

if add_related_name:
    if not prefix:
        raise FieldError("if add_related_name is set to "
                         "True, a prefix must be given")
    related_name = prefix
else:
    related_name = None

optional = not is_required

ct_verbose_name = _(f"{prefix_verbose}'s type (model)")

content_type = models.ForeignKey(
    ContentType,
    verbose_name=ct_verbose_name,
    related_name=related_name,
    blank=optional,
    null=optional,
    help_text=_("Please select the type (model) "
                "for the relation, you want to build."),
    limit_choices_to=limit_content_type_choices_to,
    on_delete=models.CASCADE)

fk_verbose_name = prefix_verbose

object_id = models.CharField(
    fk_verbose_name,
    blank=optional,
    null=False,
    help_text=_("Please enter the ID of the related object."),
    max_length=255,
    default="")  # for migrations

content_object = GenericForeignKey(
    ct_field=content_type_field,
    fk_field=object_id_field)
```

```
TheClass.add_to_class(content_type_field, content_type)
TheClass.add_to_class(object_id_field, object_id)
TheClass.add_to_class(content_object_field, content_object)

return TheClass
```

2. The following code snippet is an example of how to use two generic relationships in your app (put this code in ideas/models.py):

```python
# myproject/apps/ideas/models.py
from django.db import models
from django.utils.translation import gettext_lazy as _

from myproject.apps.core.models import (
    object_relation_base_factory as generic_relation,
)


FavoriteObjectBase = generic_relation(
    is_required=True,
)


OwnerBase = generic_relation(
    prefix="owner",
    prefix_verbose=_("Owner"),
    is_required=True,
    add_related_name=True,
    limit_content_type_choices_to={
        "model__in": (
            "user",
            "group",
        )
    }
)


class Like(FavoriteObjectBase, OwnerBase):
    class Meta:
        verbose_name = _("Like")
        verbose_name_plural = _("Likes")

    def __str__(self):
        return _("{owner} likes {object}").format(
            owner=self.owner_content_object,
            object=self.content_object
        )
```

How it works...

As you can see, this snippet is more complex than the previous ones.

The `object_relation_base_factory` function, which we have aliased to `generic_relation`, for short, in our import, is not a mixin itself; it is a function that generates a model mixin – that is, an abstract model class to extend from. The dynamically created mixin adds the `content_type` and `object_id` fields and the `content_object` generic foreign key that points to the related instance.

Why can't we just define a simple model mixin with these three attributes? A dynamically generated abstract class allows us to have prefixes for each field name; therefore, we can have more than one generic relation in the same model. For example, the `Like` model, which was shown previously, will have the `content_type`, `object_id`, and `content_object` fields for the favorite object, and `owner_content_type`, `owner_object_id`, and `owner_content_object` for the one (user or group) that liked the object.

The `object_relation_base_factory` function, which we have aliased to `generic_relation` for short, adds the possibility to limit the content type choices by the `limit_content_type_choices_to` parameter. The preceding example limits the choices for `owner_content_type` to only the content types of the `User` and `Group` models.

See also

- The *Creating a model mixin with URL-related methods* recipe
- The *Creating a model mixin to handle creation and modification dates* recipe
- The *Creating a model mixin to take care of meta tags* recipe
- The *Implementing the Like widget* recipe in `Chapter 4`, *Templates and JavaScript*

Handling multilingual fields

Django uses the internationalization mechanism to translate verbose strings in the code and templates. But it's up to the developer to decide how to implement the multilingual content in the models. We'll show you a couple of ways for how to implement multilingual models directly in your project. The first approach will be using language-specific fields in your model.

This approach has the following features:

- It is straightforward to define multilingual fields in the model.
- It is simple to use the multilingual fields in database queries.
- You can use contributed administration to edit models with the multilingual fields, without additional modifications.
- If you need to, you can effortlessly show all of the translations of an object in the same template.
- After changing the amount of languages in the settings, you will need to create and run migrations for all multilingual models.

Getting ready

Have you created the `myproject.apps.core` package used in the preceding recipes of this chapter? You will now need a new `model_fields.py` file within the `core` app, for the custom model fields.

How to do it...

Execute the following steps to define the multilingual character field and multilingual text field:

1. Open the `model_fields.py` file, and create the base multilingual field, as follows:

```python
# myproject/apps/core/model_fields.py
from django.conf import settings
from django.db import models
from django.utils.translation import get_language
from django.utils import translation

class MultilingualField(models.Field):
    SUPPORTED_FIELD_TYPES = [models.CharField, models.TextField]

    def __init__(self, verbose_name=None, **kwargs):
        self.localized_field_model = None
        for model in MultilingualField.SUPPORTED_FIELD_TYPES:
            if issubclass(self.__class__, model):
                self.localized_field_model = model
        self._blank = kwargs.get("blank", False)
        self._editable = kwargs.get("editable", True)
        super().__init__(verbose_name, **kwargs)
```

```
@staticmethod
def localized_field_name(name, lang_code):
    lang_code_safe = lang_code.replace("-", "_")
    return f"{name}_{lang_code_safe}"

def get_localized_field(self, lang_code, lang_name):
    _blank = (self._blank
              if lang_code == settings.LANGUAGE_CODE
              else True)
    localized_field = self.localized_field_model(
        f"{self.verbose_name} ({lang_name})",
        name=self.name,
        primary_key=self.primary_key,
        max_length=self.max_length,
        unique=self.unique,
        blank=_blank,
        null=False, # we ignore the null argument!
        db_index=self.db_index,
        default=self.default or "",
        editable=self._editable,
        serialize=self.serialize,
        choices=self.choices,
        help_text=self.help_text,
        db_column=None,
        db_tablespace=self.db_tablespace)
    return localized_field

def contribute_to_class(self, cls, name,
                        private_only=False,
                        virtual_only=False):
    def translated_value(self):
        language = get_language()
        val = self.__dict__.get(
            MultilingualField.localized_field_name(
                name, language))
        if not val:
            val = self.__dict__.get(
                MultilingualField.localized_field_name(
                    name, settings.LANGUAGE_CODE))
        return val

    # generate language-specific fields dynamically
    if not cls._meta.abstract:
        if self.localized_field_model:
            for lang_code, lang_name in settings.LANGUAGES:
                localized_field = self.get_localized_field(
                    lang_code, lang_name)
                localized_field.contribute_to_class(
```

```
                        cls,
                        MultilingualField.localized_field_name(
                            name, lang_code))

                setattr(cls, name, property(translated_value))
            else:
                super().contribute_to_class(
                    cls, name, private_only, virtual_only)
```

2. In the same file, subclass the base field for character and text field forms, as follows:

```
class MultilingualCharField(models.CharField, MultilingualField):
    pass

class MultilingualTextField(models.TextField, MultilingualField):
    pass
```

3. Create an `admin.py` file in the core app, and add the following content:

```
# myproject/apps/core/admin.py
from django.conf import settings

def get_multilingual_field_names(field_name):
    lang_code_underscored = settings.LANGUAGE_CODE.replace("-",
    "_")
    field_names = [f"{field_name}_{lang_code_underscored}"]
    for lang_code, lang_name in settings.LANGUAGES:
        if lang_code != settings.LANGUAGE_CODE:
            lang_code_underscored = lang_code.replace("-", "_")
            field_names.append(
                f"{field_name}_{lang_code_underscored}"
            )
    return field_names
```

Now, we'll consider an example of how to use the multilingual fields in your app, as follows:

1. First, set multiple languages in the settings for your project. Let's say, our website will support all official languages of the European Union, with English being the default language:

```
# myproject/settings/_base.py
LANGUAGE_CODE = "en"

# All official languages of European Union
LANGUAGES = [
```

```
        ("bg", "Bulgarian"),      ("hr", "Croatian"),
        ("cs", "Czech"),          ("da", "Danish"),
        ("nl", "Dutch"),          ("en", "English"),
        ("et", "Estonian"),       ("fi", "Finnish"),
        ("fr", "French"),         ("de", "German"),
        ("el", "Greek"),          ("hu", "Hungarian"),
        ("ga", "Irish"),          ("it", "Italian"),
        ("lv", "Latvian"),        ("lt", "Lithuanian"),
        ("mt", "Maltese"),        ("pl", "Polish"),
        ("pt", "Portuguese"),     ("ro", "Romanian"),
        ("sk", "Slovak"),         ("sl", "Slovene"),
        ("es", "Spanish"),        ("sv", "Swedish"),
    ]
```

2. Then, open the `models.py` file from the `myproject.apps.ideas` app, and create the multilingual fields for the `Idea` model, as follows:

```python
# myproject/apps/ideas/models.py
from django.db import models
from django.utils.translation import gettext_lazy as _

from myproject.apps.core.model_fields import (
    MultilingualCharField,
    MultilingualTextField,
)


class Idea(models.Model):
    title = MultilingualCharField(
        _("Title"),
        max_length=200,
    )
    content = MultilingualTextField(
        _("Content"),
    )

    class Meta:
        verbose_name = _("Idea")
        verbose_name_plural = _("Ideas")

    def __str__(self):
        return self.title
```

3. Create an `admin.py` file for the `ideas` app:

```
# myproject/apps/ideas/admin.py
from django.contrib import admin
from django.utils.translation import gettext_lazy as _

from myproject.apps.core.admin import get_multilingual_field_names

from .models import Idea

@admin.register(Idea)
class IdeaAdmin(admin.ModelAdmin):
    fieldsets = [
        (_("Title and Content"), {
            "fields": get_multilingual_field_names("title") +
                      get_multilingual_field_names("content")
        }),
    ]
```

How it works...

The example of `Idea` will generate a model that is similar to the following:

```
class Idea(models.Model):
    title_bg = models.CharField(
        _("Title (Bulgarian)"),
        max_length=200,
    )
    title_hr = models.CharField(
        _("Title (Croatian)"),
        max_length=200,
    )
    # titles for other languages...
    title_sv = models.CharField(
        _("Title (Swedish)"),
        max_length=200,
    )

    content_bg = MultilingualTextField(
        _("Content (Bulgarian)"),
    )
    content_hr = MultilingualTextField(
        _("Content (Croatian)"),
    )
    # content for other languages...
    content_sv = MultilingualTextField(
```

```
            _("Content (Swedish)"),
    )

    class Meta:
        verbose_name = _("Idea")
        verbose_name_plural = _("Ideas")

    def __str__(self):
        return self.title
```

If there were any language codes with a dash, like "de-ch" for Swiss German, the fields for those languages would be replaced with underscores, like `title_de_ch` and `content_de_ch`.

In addition to the generated language-specific fields, there will be two properties – `title` and `content` – that will return the corresponding field in the currently active language. These will fall back to the default language if no localized field content is available.

The `MultilingualCharField` and `MultilingualTextField` fields will juggle the model fields dynamically, depending on your LANGUAGES setting. They will overwrite the `contribute_to_class()` method that is used when the Django framework creates the model classes. The multilingual fields dynamically add character or text fields for each language of the project. You'll need to create a database migration to add the appropriate fields in the database. Also, the properties are created to return the translated value of the currently active language or the main language, by default.

In the administration, `get_multilingual_field_names()` will return a list of language-specific field names, starting with one of the default languages and then proceeding with the other languages from the LANGUAGES setting.

Here are a couple of examples of how you might use the multilingual fields in templates and views.

If you have the following code in the template, it will show the text in the currently active language, let's say Lithuanian, and will fall back to English if the translation doesn't exist:

```
<h1>{{ idea.title }}</h1>
<div>{{ idea.content|urlize|linebreaks }}</div>
```

If you want to have your QuerySet ordered by the translated titles, you can define it as follows:

```
>>> lang_code = input("Enter language code: ")
>>> lang_code_underscored = lang_code.replace("-", "_")
>>> qs = Idea.objects.order_by(f"title_{lang_code_underscored}")
```

See also

- The *Working with model translation tables* recipe
- The *Using migrations* recipe
- Chapter 6, *Model Administration*

Working with model translation tables

The second approach to handling multilingual content in the database involves using model translation tables for each multilingual model.

The features of this approach are as follows:

- You can use contributed administration to edit translations as inlines.
- After changing the amount of languages in the settings, no migrations or other further actions are necessary.
- You can effortlessly show the translation of the current language in the template, but it would be more difficult to show several translations in specific languages on the same page.
- You have to know and use a specific pattern described in this recipe for creating model translations.
- It's not that simple to use this approach for database queries, but, as you will see, it's still possible.

Getting ready

Once again, we will start with the myprojects.apps.core app.

How to do it...

Execute the following steps to prepare for multilingual models:

1. In the core app, create model_fields.py with the following content:

```
# myproject/apps/core/model_fields.py
from django.conf import settings
from django.utils.translation import get_language
from django.utils import translation
```

```
class TranslatedField(object):
    def __init__(self, field_name):
        self.field_name = field_name

    def __get__(self, instance, owner):
        lang_code = translation.get_language()
        if lang_code == settings.LANGUAGE_CODE:
            # The fields of the default language are in the main
                model
            return getattr(instance, self.field_name)
        else:
            # The fields of the other languages are in the
                translation
            # model, but falls back to the main model
            translations = instance.translations.filter(
                language=lang_code,
            ).first() or instance
            return getattr(translations, self.field_name)
```

2. Add the `admin.py` file to the `core` app with the following content:

```
# myproject/apps/core/admin.py
from django import forms
from django.conf import settings
from django.utils.translation import gettext_lazy as _

class LanguageChoicesForm(forms.ModelForm):
    def __init__(self, *args, **kwargs):
        LANGUAGES_EXCEPT_THE_DEFAULT = [
            (lang_code, lang_name)
            for lang_code, lang_name in settings.LANGUAGES
            if lang_code != settings.LANGUAGE_CODE
        ]
        super().__init__(*args, **kwargs)
        self.fields["language"] = forms.ChoiceField(
            label=_("Language"),
            choices=LANGUAGES_EXCEPT_THE_DEFAULT,
            required=True,
        )
```

Now let's implement the multilingual models:

1. First, set multiple languages in the settings for your project. Let's say, our website will support all official languages of European Union with English being the default language:

```
# myproject/settings/_base.py
LANGUAGE_CODE = "en"
```

```
# All official languages of European Union
LANGUAGES = [
    ("bg", "Bulgarian"),      ("hr", "Croatian"),
    ("cs", "Czech"),          ("da", "Danish"),
    ("nl", "Dutch"),          ("en", "English"),
    ("et", "Estonian"),       ("fi", "Finnish"),
    ("fr", "French"),         ("de", "German"),
    ("el", "Greek"),          ("hu", "Hungarian"),
    ("ga", "Irish"),          ("it", "Italian"),
    ("lv", "Latvian"),        ("lt", "Lithuanian"),
    ("mt", "Maltese"),        ("pl", "Polish"),
    ("pt", "Portuguese"),     ("ro", "Romanian"),
    ("sk", "Slovak"),         ("sl", "Slovene"),
    ("es", "Spanish"),        ("sv", "Swedish"),
]
```

2. Then, let's create the `Idea` and `IdeaTranslations` models:

```
# myproject/apps/ideas/models.py
from django.db import models
from django.conf import settings
from django.utils.translation import gettext_lazy as _

from myproject.apps.core.model_fields import TranslatedField


class Idea(models.Model):
    title = models.CharField(
        _("Title"),
        max_length=200,
    )
    content = models.TextField(
        _("Content"),
    )
    translated_title = TranslatedField("title")
    translated_content = TranslatedField("content")

    class Meta:
        verbose_name = _("Idea")
        verbose_name_plural = _("Ideas")

    def __str__(self):
        return self.title


class IdeaTranslations(models.Model):
    idea = models.ForeignKey(
        Idea,
```

```
                verbose_name=_("Idea"),
                on_delete=models.CASCADE,
                related_name="translations",
            )
            language = models.CharField(_("Language"), max_length=7)

            title = models.CharField(
                _("Title"),
                max_length=200,
            )
            content = models.TextField(
                _("Content"),
            )

            class Meta:
                verbose_name = _("Idea Translations")
                verbose_name_plural = _("Idea Translations")
                ordering = ["language"]
                unique_together = [["idea", "language"]]

            def __str__(self):
                return self.title
```

3. Last, create the `admin.py` for the `ideas` app as follows:

```
# myproject/apps/ideas/admin.py
from django.contrib import admin
from django.utils.translation import gettext_lazy as _

from myproject.apps.core.admin import LanguageChoicesForm

from .models import Idea, IdeaTranslations


class IdeaTranslationsForm(LanguageChoicesForm):
    class Meta:
        model = IdeaTranslations
        fields = "__all__"


class IdeaTranslationsInline(admin.StackedInline):
    form = IdeaTranslationsForm
    model = IdeaTranslations
    extra = 0


@admin.register(Idea)
class IdeaAdmin(admin.ModelAdmin):
```

```
inlines = [IdeaTranslationsInline]

fieldsets = [
    (_("Title and Content"), {
        "fields": ["title", "content"]
    }),
]
```

How it works...

We keep the language-specific fields of the default language in the Idea model itself. The translations for each language are in the IdeaTranslations model, which will be listed in the administration as an inline translation. IdeaTranslations don't have the language choices at the model for a reason – we don't want to create migrations every time a new language is added or some language is removed. Instead, the language choices are set in the administration form, also making sure that the default language is skipped or not available for selection in the list. The language choices are restricted using the LanguageChoicesForm class.

To get a specific field in the current language, you would use the fields defined as TranslatedField. In the template, that would look like the following:

```
<h1>{{ idea.translated_title }}</h1>
<div>{{ idea.translated_content|urlize|linebreaks }}</div>
```

To order items by a translated title in a specific language, you would use the annotate() method as follows:

```
>>> from django.conf import settings
>>> from django.db import models
>>> lang_code = input("Enter language code: ")

>>> if lang_code == settings.LANGUAGE_CODE:
...     qs = Idea.objects.annotate(
...         title_translation=models.F("title"),
...         content_translation=models.F("content"),
...     )
... else:
...     qs = Idea.objects.filter(
...         translations__language=lang_code,
...     ).annotate(
...         title_translation=models.F("translations__title"),
...         content_translation=models.F("translations__content"),
...     )
```

```
>>> qs = qs.order_by("title_translation")

>>> for idea in qs:
...     print(idea.title_translation)
```

In this example, we prompt for a language code in the Django shell. If the language is the default one, we store the `title` and `content` as the `title_translation` and the `content_translation` from the `Idea` model. If there is another language chosen, we read the `title` and `content` as `title_translation` and `content_translation` from the `IdeaTranslations` model with the chosen language.

Afterward, we can filter or order `QuerySet` by `title_translation` or `content_translation`.

See also

- The *Handling multilingual fields* recipe
- `Chapter 6`, *Model Administration*

Avoiding circular dependencies

When developing Django models, it is very important to avoid circular dependencies especially in the `models.py` files. Circular dependencies are imports in different Python modules from each other. You should never cross-import from the different `models.py` files, because that causes serious stability issues. Instead, if you have interdependencies, you should use the actions described in this recipe.

Getting ready

Let's work with `categories` and `ideas` apps to illustrate how to deal with cross dependencies.

How to do it...

Follow these practices when working with models that use models from other apps:

1. For foreign keys and many-to-many relationships with models from other apps, use the "`<app_label>`.`<model>`" declaration instead of importing the model. In Django this works with `ForeignKey`, `OneToOneField`, and `ManyToManyField`, for example:

```python
# myproject/apps/ideas/models.py
from django.db import models
from django.conf import settings
from django.utils.translation import gettext_lazy as _


class Idea(models.Model):
    author = models.ForeignKey(
        settings.AUTH_USER_MODEL,
        verbose_name=_("Author"),
        on_delete=models.SET_NULL,
        blank=True,
        null=True,
    )
    category = models.ForeignKey(
        "categories.Category",
        verbose_name=_("Category"),
        blank=True,
        null=True,
        on_delete=models.SET_NULL,
    )
    # other fields, attributes, properties and methods...
```

Here, `settings.AUTH_USER_MODEL` is a setting with a value such as "`auth.User`":

2. If you need to access a model from another app in a method, import that model inside the method instead of at the module level, for example, as follows:

```python
# myproject/apps/categories/models.py
from django.db import models
from django.utils.translation import gettext_lazy as _


class Category(models.Model):
    # fields, attributes, properties, and methods...

    def get_ideas_without_this_category(self):
        from myproject.apps.ideas.models import Idea
        return Idea.objects.exclude(category=self)
```

3. If you use model inheritance, for example, for model mixins, keep the base classes in a separate app and place them before other apps that would use them in INSTALLED_APPS, as follows:

```
# myproject/settings/_base.py

INSTALLED_APPS = [
    # contributed
    "django.contrib.admin",
    "django.contrib.auth",
    "django.contrib.contenttypes",
    "django.contrib.sessions",
    "django.contrib.messages",
    "django.contrib.staticfiles",
    # third-party
    # ...
    # local
    "myproject.apps.core",
    "myproject.apps.categories",
    "myproject.apps.ideas",
]
```

Here the ideas app will use the model mixins from the core app as follows:

```
# myproject/apps/ideas/models.py
from django.db import models
from django.conf import settings
from django.utils.translation import gettext_lazy as _

from myproject.apps.core.models import (
    CreationModificationDateBase,
    MetaTagsBase,
    UrlBase,
)

class Idea(CreationModificationDateBase, MetaTagsBase, UrlBase):
    # fields, attributes, properties, and methods...
```

See also

- The *Configuring settings for development, testing, staging, and production environments* recipe in Chapter 1, *Getting Started with Django 3.0*
- The *Respecting the import order in Python files* recipe in Chapter 1, *Getting Started with Django 3.0*

- The *Using model mixins* recipe
- The *Changing the foreign key to the many-to-many field* recipe

Adding database constraints

For better database integrity, it's common to define database constraints, telling some fields to be bound to fields of other database tables, making some fields unique or not null. For advanced database constraints, such as making the fields unique with a condition or setting specific conditions for the values of some fields, Django has special classes: `UniqueConstraint` and `CheckConstraint`. In this recipe, you will see a practical example of how to use them.

Getting ready

Let's start with the `ideas` app and the `Idea` model that will have at least `title` and `author` fields.

How to do it...

Set the database constraints in the `Meta` class of the `Idea` model as follows:

```python
# myproject/apps/ideas/models.py
from django.db import models
from django.utils.translation import gettext_lazy as _


class Idea(models.Model):
    author = models.ForeignKey(
        settings.AUTH_USER_MODEL,
        verbose_name=_("Author"),
        on_delete=models.SET_NULL,
        blank=True,
        null=True,
        related_name="authored_ideas",
    )
    title = models.CharField(
        _("Title"),
        max_length=200,
    )

    class Meta:
```

```
            verbose_name = _("Idea")
            verbose_name_plural = _("Ideas")
            constraints = [
                models.UniqueConstraint(
                    fields=["title"],
                    condition=~models.Q(author=None),
                    name="unique_titles_for_each_author",
                ),
                models.CheckConstraint(
                    check=models.Q(
                        title__iregex=r"^\S.*\S$"
                        # starts with non-whitespace,
                        # ends with non-whitespace,
                        # anything in the middle
                    ),
                    name="title_has_no_leading_and_trailing_whitespaces",
                )
            ]
```

How it works...

We define two constraints in the database.

The first one, `UniqueConstraint`, tells the titles to be unique for each author. If the author is not set, the titles can be repeated. To check if the author is set we use the negated lookup: `~models.Q(author=None)`. Note that in Django, the ~ operator for lookups is equivalent to the `exclude()` method of a QuerySet, so these QuerySets are equivalent:

```
    ideas_with_authors = Idea.objects.exclude(author=None)
    ideas_with_authors2 = Idea.objects.filter(~models.Q(author=None))
```

The second constraint, `CheckConstraint`, checks if the title doesn't start and end with a whitespace. For that, we use a regular expression lookup.

There's more...

Database constraints don't affect form validation. They will just raise `django.db.utils.IntegrityError` if any data doesn't pass its conditions when saving entries to the database.

If you want to have data validated at the forms, you have to implement the validation in addition yourself, for example, in the `clean()` method of the model. That would look like this for the `Idea` model:

```python
# myproject/apps/ideas/models.py
from django.db import models
from django.conf import settings
from django.core.exceptions import ValidationError
from django.utils.translation import gettext_lazy as _


class Idea(models.Model):
    author = models.ForeignKey(
        settings.AUTH_USER_MODEL,
        verbose_name=_("Author"),
        on_delete=models.SET_NULL,
        blank=True,
        null=True,
        related_name="authored_ideas2",
    )
    title = models.CharField(
        _("Title"),
        max_length=200,
    )

    # other fields and attributes...

    class Meta:
        verbose_name = _("Idea")
        verbose_name_plural = _("Ideas")
        constraints = [
            models.UniqueConstraint(
                fields=["title"],
                condition=~models.Q(author=None),
                name="unique_titles_for_each_author2",
            ),
            models.CheckConstraint(
                check=models.Q(
                    title__iregex=r"^\S.*\S$"
                    # starts with non-whitespace,
                    # ends with non-whitespace,
                    # anything in the middle
                ),
                name="title_has_no_leading_and_trailing_whitespaces2",
            )
        ]

    def clean(self):
```

```
import re
if self.author and Idea.objects.exclude(pk=self.pk).filter(
    author=self.author,
    title=self.title,
).exists():
    raise ValidationError(
        _("Each idea of the same user should have a unique title.")
    )
if not re.match(r"^\S.*\S$", self.title):
    raise ValidationError(
        _("The title cannot start or end with a whitespace.")
    )

# other properties and methods...
```

See also

- Chapter 3, *Forms and Views*
- The *Using database query expressions* recipe in Chapter 10, *Bells and Whistles*

Using migrations

In Agile software development, requirements for the project evolve and get updated from time to time in the process of development. As development happens iteratively, you will have to perform database schema changes along the way. With Django migrations, you don't have to change the database tables and fields manually, as most of it is done automatically, using the command-line interface.

Getting ready

Activate your virtual environment in the command-line tool, and change the active directory to your project's directory.

How to do it...

To create the database migrations, take a look at the following steps:

1. When you create models in your new `categories` or `ideas` app, you have to create an initial migration that will create the database tables for your app. This can be done by using the following command:

   ```
   (env)$ python manage.py makemigrations ideas
   ```

2. The first time that you want to create all of the tables for your project, run the following command:

   ```
   (env)$ python manage.py migrate
   ```

   Run this command when you want to execute the new migrations for all of your apps.

3. If you want to execute the migrations for a specific app, run the following command:

   ```
   (env)$ python manage.py migrate ideas
   ```

4. If you make some changes in the database schema, you will have to create a migration for that schema. For example, if we add a new subtitle field to the idea model, we can create the migration by using the following command:

   ```
   (env)$ python manage.py makemigrations --name=subtitle_added ideas
   ```

   However, the `--name=subtitle_added` field can be skipped because in most cases Django generates fairly self-explanatory default names.

5. Sometimes, you may have to add to or change data in the existing schema in bulk, which can be done with a data migration, instead of a schema migration. To create a data migration that modifies the data in the database table, we can use the following command:

   ```
   (env)$ python manage.py makemigrations --name=populate_subtitle \
   > --empty ideas
   ```

   The `--empty` parameter tells Django to create a skeleton data migration, which you have to modify to perform the necessary data manipulation before applying it. For data migrations, setting the name is recommended.

6. To list all of the available applied and unapplied migrations, run the following command:

```
(env)$ python manage.py showmigrations
```

The applied migrations will be listed with an **[X]** prefix. The unapplied ones will be listed with a **[ ]** prefix.

7. To list all of the available migrations for a specific app, run the same command, but pass the app name, as follows:

```
(env)$ python manage.py showmigrations ideas
```

How it works...

Django migrations are instruction files for the database migration mechanism. The instruction files inform us about which database tables to create or remove, which fields to add or remove, and which data to insert, update, or delete. Also they define which migrations are dependent on which other migrations.

There are two types of migrations in Django. One is schema migration, and the other is data migration. Schema migration should be created when you add new models, or add or remove fields. Data migration should be used when you want to fill the database with some values or massively delete values from the database. Data migrations should be created by using a command in the command-line tool, and then coded in the migration file.

The migrations for each app are saved in their `migrations` directories. The first migration will usually be called `0001_initial.py`, and the other migrations in our example app will be called `0002_subtitle_added.py` and `0003_populate_subtitle.py`. Each migration gets a number prefix that is automatically incremented. For each migration that is executed, there is an entry that is saved in the `django_migrations` database table.

It is possible to migrate back and forth by specifying the number of the migration to which we want to migrate, as shown in the following command:

```
(env)$ python manage.py migrate ideas 0002
```

To unmigrate all migrations of the app including the initial migration, run the following:

```
(env)$ python manage.py migrate ideas zero
```

Unmigrating requires each migration to have both a forward and a backward action. Ideally, the backward action would undo exactly the changes made by the forward action. However, in some cases such a change would be unrecoverable, such as when the forward action has removed a column from the schema, because it will have destroyed data. In such a case, the backward action might restore the schema, but the data would remain lost forever, or else there might not be a backward action at all.

 Do not commit your migrations to version control until you have tested the forward and backward migration process and you are sure that they will work well in other developments and public website environments.

There's more...

Learn more about writing database migrations in the official *How To* guide, found at https://docs.djangoproject.com/en/2.2/howto/writing-migrations/.

See also

- The *Working with a virtual environment* recipe in Chapter 1, *Getting Started with Django 3.0*
- The *Working with Docker containers for Django, Gunicorn, Nginx, and PostgreSQL* recipe in Chapter 1, *Getting Started with Django 3.0*
- The *Handling project dependencies with pip* receipe in Chapter 1, *Getting Started with Django 3.0*
- The *Including external dependencies in your project* recipe in Chapter 1, *Getting Started with Django 3.0*
- The *Changing a foreign key to the many-to-many field* recipe

Changing a foreign key to the many-to-many field

This recipe is a practical example of how to change a many-to-one relation to a many-to-many relation, while preserving the already existing data. We will use both schema and data migrations in this situation.

Getting ready

Let's suppose that you have the Idea model, with a foreign key pointing to the Category model.

1. Let's define the Category model in the categories app, as follows:

```python
# myproject/apps/categories/models.py
from django.db import models
from django.utils.translation import gettext_lazy as _

from myproject.apps.core.model_fields import MultilingualCharField


class Category(models.Model):
    title = MultilingualCharField(
        _("Title"),
        max_length=200,
    )

    class Meta:
        verbose_name = _("Category")
        verbose_name_plural = _("Categories")

    def __str__(self):
        return self.title
```

2. Let's define the Idea model in the ideas app, as follows:

```python
# myproject/apps/ideas/models.py
from django.db import models
from django.conf import settings
from django.utils.translation import gettext_lazy as _

from myproject.apps.core.model_fields import (
    MultilingualCharField,
    MultilingualTextField,
```

```
    )

class Idea(models.Model):
    title = MultilingualCharField(
        _("Title"),
        max_length=200,
    )
    content = MultilingualTextField(
        _("Content"),
    )
    category = models.ForeignKey(
        "categories.Category",
        verbose_name=_("Category"),
        blank=True,
        null=True,
        on_delete=models.SET_NULL,
        related_name="category_ideas",
    )

    class Meta:
        verbose_name = _("Idea")
        verbose_name_plural = _("Ideas")

    def __str__(self):
        return self.title
```

3. Create and execute initial migrations by using the following commands:

```
(env)$ python manage.py makemigrations categories
(env)$ python manage.py makemigrations ideas
(env)$ python manage.py migrate
```

How to do it...

The following steps will show you how to switch from a foreign key relation to a many-to-many relation, while preserving the already existing data:

1. Add a new many-to-many field, called `categories`, as follows:

```
# myproject/apps/ideas/models.py
from django.db import models
from django.conf import settings
from django.utils.translation import gettext_lazy as _

from myproject.apps.core.model_fields import (
    MultilingualCharField,
```

```
            MultilingualTextField,
    )

class Idea(models.Model):
    title = MultilingualCharField(
        _("Title"),
        max_length=200,
    )
    content = MultilingualTextField(
        _("Content"),
    )
    category = models.ForeignKey(
        "categories.Category",
        verbose_name=_("Category"),
        blank=True,
        null=True,
        on_delete=models.SET_NULL,
        related_name="category_ideas",
    )
    categories = models.ManyToManyField(
        "categories.Category",
        verbose_name=_("Categories"),
        blank=True,
        related_name="ideas",
    )

    class Meta:
        verbose_name = _("Idea")
        verbose_name_plural = _("Ideas")

    def __str__(self):
        return self.title
```

2. Create and run a schema migration, in order to add the new relationship to the database, as shown in the following code snippet:

```
(env)$ python manage.py makemigrations ideas
(env)$ python manage.py migrate ideas
```

3. Create a data migration to copy the categories from the foreign key to the many-to-many field, as follows:

```
(env)$ python manage.py makemigrations --empty \
> --name=copy_categories ideas
```

4. Open the newly created migration file (`0003_copy_categories.py`), and define the forward migration instructions, as shown in the following code snippet:

```
# myproject/apps/ideas/migrations/0003_copy_categories.py
from django.db import migrations


def copy_categories(apps, schema_editor):
    Idea = apps.get_model("ideas", "Idea")
    for idea in Idea.objects.all():
        if idea.category:
            idea.categories.add(idea.category)


class Migration(migrations.Migration):

    dependencies = [
        ('ideas', '0002_idea_categories'),
    ]

    operations = [
        migrations.RunPython(copy_categories),
    ]
```

5. Run the new data migration, as follows:

```
(env)$ python manage.py migrate ideas
```

6. Delete the foreign key `category` field in the `models.py` file, leaving only the new `categories` many-to-many field, as follows:

```
# myproject/apps/ideas/models.py
from django.db import models
from django.conf import settings
from django.utils.translation import gettext_lazy as _

from myproject.apps.core.model_fields import (
    MultilingualCharField,
    MultilingualTextField,
)

class Idea(models.Model):
    title = MultilingualCharField(
        _("Title"),
        max_length=200,
    )
    content = MultilingualTextField(
```

```
        _("Content"),
    )

    categories = models.ManyToManyField(
        "categories.Category",
        verbose_name=_("Categories"),
        blank=True,
        related_name="ideas",
    )

    class Meta:
        verbose_name = _("Idea")
        verbose_name_plural = _("Ideas")

    def __str__(self):
        return self.title
```

7. Create and run a schema migration, in order to delete the `Categories` field from the database table, as follows:

```
(env)$ python manage.py makemigrations ideas
(env)$ python manage.py migrate ideas
```

How it works...

At first, we add a new many-to-many field to the `Idea` model, and a migration is generated to update the database accordingly. Then, we create a data migration that will copy the existing relations from the foreign key `category` to the new many-to-many `categories`. Lastly, we remove the foreign key field from the model, and update the database once more.

There's more...

Our data migration currently includes only the forward action, copying the foreign key category as the first related item in the new categories relationship. Although we did not elaborate here, in a real-world scenario it would be best to include the reverse operation as well. This could be accomplished by copying the first related item back to the `category` foreign key. Unfortunately, any `Idea` object with multiple categories would lose extra data.

See also

- The *Using migrations* recipe
- The *Handling multilingual fields* recipe
- The *Working with model translation tables* recipe
- The *Avoiding circular dependencies* recipe

3

Forms and Views

In this chapter, we will cover the following topics:

- Creating an app with CRUDL functions
- Saving the author of a model instance
- Uploading images
- Creating a form layout with custom templates
- Creating a form layout with django-crispy-forms
- Working with formsets
- Filtering object lists
- Managing paginated lists
- Composing class-based views
- Providing Open Graph and Twitter Card data
- Providing schema.org vocabularies
- Generating PDF documents
- Implementing a multilingual search with Haystack and Whoosh
- Implementing a multilingual search with Elasticsearch DSL

Introduction

While a database structure is defined in models, views provide the endpoints necessary to show content to users or to let them enter new and updated data. In this chapter, we will focus on views for managing forms, the list view, and views generating alternative outputs to HTML. In the simplest examples, we will leave the creation of URL rules and templates up to you.

Technical requirements

To work with the code of this chapter, as before, you will need the latest stable version of Python, MySQL, or a PostgreSQL database, and a Django project with a virtual environment. Some recipes will require specific Python dependencies. In addition, for generating PDF documents, you will need the `cairo`, `pango`, `gdk-pixbuf`, and `libffi` libraries. For searches, you will need an Elasticsearch server. You will get more details about them later in the corresponding recipes.

Most of the templates in this chapter will use the Bootstrap 4 CSS framework for a nicer look and feel.

You can find all of the code for this chapter in the `ch03` directory of the GitHub repository at: `https://github.com/PacktPublishing/Django-3-Web-Development-Cookbook-Fourth-Edition`.

Creating an app with CRUDL functions

In computer science, the **CRUDL** acronym stands for **Create**, **Read**, **Update**, **Delete**, and **List** functions. Many Django projects with interactive functionality will need you to implement all of those functions to manage data on the website. In this recipe, we will see how to create URLs and views for these basic functions.

Getting ready

Let's create a new app called `ideas` and put it in `INSTALLED_APPS` in the settings. Create the following `Idea` model with an `IdeaTranslations` model for translations inside of that app:

```python
# myproject/apps/idea/models.py
import uuid

from django.db import models
from django.urls import reverse
from django.conf import settings
from django.utils.translation import gettext_lazy as _

from myproject.apps.core.model_fields import TranslatedField
from myproject.apps.core.models import (
    CreationModificationDateBase, UrlBase
)
```

```
RATING_CHOICES = (
    (1, "★☆☆☆☆"),
    (2, "★★☆☆☆"),
    (3, "★★★☆☆"),
    (4, "★★★★☆"),
    (5, "★★★★★"),
)


class Idea(CreationModificationDateBase, UrlBase):
    uuid = models.UUIDField(
        primary_key=True, default=uuid.uuid4, editable=False
    )
    author = models.ForeignKey(
        settings.AUTH_USER_MODEL,
        verbose_name=_("Author"),
        on_delete=models.SET_NULL,
        blank=True,
        null=True,
        related_name="authored_ideas",
    )
    title = models.CharField(_("Title"), max_length=200)
    content = models.TextField(_("Content"))

    categories = models.ManyToManyField(
        "categories.Category",
        verbose_name=_("Categories"),
        related_name="category_ideas",
    )
    rating = models.PositiveIntegerField(
        _("Rating"), choices=RATING_CHOICES, blank=True, null=True
    )
    translated_title = TranslatedField("title")
    translated_content = TranslatedField("content")

    class Meta:
        verbose_name = _("Idea")
        verbose_name_plural = _("Ideas")

    def __str__(self):
        return self.title

    def get_url_path(self):
        return reverse("ideas:idea_detail", kwargs={"pk": self.pk})


class IdeaTranslations(models.Model):
    idea = models.ForeignKey(
```

```
        Idea,
        verbose_name=_("Idea"),
        on_delete=models.CASCADE,
        related_name="translations",
    )
    language = models.CharField(_("Language"), max_length=7)

    title = models.CharField(_("Title"), max_length=200)
    content = models.TextField(_("Content"))

    class Meta:
        verbose_name = _("Idea Translations")
        verbose_name_plural = _("Idea Translations")
        ordering = ["language"]
        unique_together = [["idea", "language"]]

    def __str__(self):
        return self.title
```

We are using several concepts here from the previous chapter: we inherit from model mixins and utilize a model translation table. Read more about that in the *Using model mixins* and the *Working with model translation tables* recipes. We are going to use the ideas app and these models for all of the recipes in this chapter.

In addition, create an analogous categories app with the Category and CategoryTranslations models:

```
# myproject/apps/categories/models.py
from django.db import models
from django.utils.translation import gettext_lazy as _

from myproject.apps.core.model_fields import TranslatedField


class Category(models.Model):
    title = models.CharField(_("Title"), max_length=200)

    translated_title = TranslatedField("title")

    class Meta:
        verbose_name = _("Category")
        verbose_name_plural = _("Categories")

    def __str__(self):
        return self.title
```

```
class CategoryTranslations(models.Model):
    category = models.ForeignKey(
        Category,
        verbose_name=_("Category"),
        on_delete=models.CASCADE,
        related_name="translations",
    )
    language = models.CharField(_("Language"), max_length=7)

    title = models.CharField(_("Title"), max_length=200)

    class Meta:
        verbose_name = _("Category Translations")
        verbose_name_plural = _("Category Translations")
        ordering = ["language"]
        unique_together = [["category", "language"]]

    def __str__(self):
        return self.title
```

How to do it...

The CRUDL functionality in Django consists of forms, views, and URL rules. Let's create them:

1. Add a new forms.py file to the ideas app with the model form for adding and changing the instances of your Idea model:

   ```
   # myprojects/apps/ideas/forms.py
   from django import forms
   from .models import Idea

   class IdeaForm(forms.ModelForm):
       class Meta:
           model = Idea
           fields = "__all__"
   ```

2. Add a new views.py file to the ideas app with the views to manipulate the Idea model:

   ```
   # myproject/apps/ideas/views.py
   from django.contrib.auth.decorators import login_required
   from django.shortcuts import render, redirect, get_object_or_404
   from django.views.generic import ListView, DetailView

   from .forms import IdeaForm
   ```

```python
from .models import Idea


class IdeaList(ListView):
    model = Idea


class IdeaDetail(DetailView):
    model = Idea
    context_object_name = "idea"


@login_required
def add_or_change_idea(request, pk=None):
    idea = None
    if pk:
        idea = get_object_or_404(Idea, pk=pk)

    if request.method == "POST":
        form = IdeaForm(
            data=request.POST,
            files=request.FILES,
            instance=idea
        )

        if form.is_valid():
            idea = form.save()
            return redirect("ideas:idea_detail", pk=idea.pk)
    else:
        form = IdeaForm(instance=idea)

    context = {"idea": idea, "form": form}
    return render(request, "ideas/idea_form.html", context)


@login_required
def delete_idea(request, pk):
    idea = get_object_or_404(Idea, pk=pk)
    if request.method == "POST":
        idea.delete()
        return redirect("ideas:idea_list")
    context = {"idea": idea}
    return render(request, "ideas/idea_deleting_confirmation.html",
context)
```

3. Create the `urls.py` file in the `ideas` app with the URL rules:

```
# myproject/apps/ideas/urls.py
from django.urls import path

from .views import (
    IdeaList,
    IdeaDetail,
    add_or_change_idea,
    delete_idea,
)

urlpatterns = [
    path("", IdeaList.as_view(), name="idea_list"),
    path("add/", add_or_change_idea, name="add_idea"),
    path("<uuid:pk>/", IdeaDetail.as_view(), name="idea_detail"),
    path("<uuid:pk>/change/", add_or_change_idea,
      name="change_idea"),
    path("<uuid:pk>/delete/", delete_idea, name="delete_idea"),
]
```

4. Now, let's plug in these URL rules to the project's URL configuration. We will
   also include the accounts' URL rules from the Django-contributed `auth` app, so
   that our `@login_required` decorator works properly:

```
# myproject/urls.py
from django.contrib import admin
from django.conf.urls.i18n import i18n_patterns
from django.urls import include, path
from django.conf import settings
from django.conf.urls.static import static
from django.shortcuts import redirect


urlpatterns = i18n_patterns(
    path("", lambda request: redirect("ideas:idea_list")),
    path("admin/", admin.site.urls),
    path("accounts/", include("django.contrib.auth.urls")),
    path("ideas/", include(("myproject.apps.ideas.urls", "ideas"),
      namespace="ideas")),
)
urlpatterns += static(settings.STATIC_URL,
document_root=settings.STATIC_ROOT)
urlpatterns += static("/media/", document_root=settings.MEDIA_ROOT)
```

5. You should now be able to create the following templates:

- `registration/login.html` with a form to log in
- `ideas/idea_list.html` with a list of ideas
- `ideas/idea_detail.html` with the details about an idea
- `ideas/idea_form.html` with a form to add or change an idea
- `ideas/idea_deleting_confirmation.html` with an empty form to confirm idea deletion

In the templates, you can address the URLs of the `ideas` app via the namespace and path names as follows:

```
{% load i18n %}
<a href="{% url 'ideas:change_idea' pk=idea.pk %}">{% trans "Change this idea" %}</a>
<a href="{% url 'ideas:add_idea' %}">{% trans "Add idea" %}</a>
```

If you get stuck or want to save time, check the corresponding templates in the code files for this book, which you can find at https://github.com/PacktPublishing/Django-3-Web-Development-Cookbook-Fourth-Edition/tree/master/ch03/myproject_virtualenv/src/django-myproject/myproject/templates/ideas.

How it works...

In this example, we are using a UUID field for the primary key of the `Idea` model. With this ID, each idea has an un-guessable unique URL. Alternatively, you can use slug fields for URLs, but then you have to make sure that each slug is populated and is unique throughout the website.

It is not recommended to use the default incremental IDs for URLs, for security reasons: users can figure out how many items you have in the database and try to access the next or previous item, although they might not have permission to do that.

In our example, we are using generic class-based views for the listing and reading ideas and function-based views for creating, updating, and deleting them. The views that change the records in the database require authenticated users with the `@login_required` decorator. It would be also perfectly fine to use class-based views or function-based views for all CRUDL functions.

After successfully adding or changing an idea, the user will be redirected to the detail view. After deleting an idea, the user will be redirected to the list view.

There's more...

In addition, you can use the Django messages framework to display success messages at the top of the page after each successful addition, change, or delete.

You can read about them in the official documentation at: `https://docs.djangoproject.com/en/2.2/ref/contrib/messages/`.

See also

- The *Using model mixins* recipe in `Chapter 2`, *Models and Database Structure*
- The *Working with model translation tables* recipe in `Chapter 2`, *Models and Database Structure*
- The *Saving the author of a model instance* recipe
- The *Arranging the base.html template* recipe in `Chapter 4`, *Templates and JavaScript*

Saving the author of a model instance

The first argument of every Django view is the `HttpRequest` object, which by convention is named `request`. It contains metadata about the request sent from a browser or other client, including such items as the current language code, user data, cookies, and session. By default, forms that are used by views accept the GET or POST data, files, initial data, and other parameters; however, they do not inherently have access to the `HttpRequest` object. In some cases, it is useful to additionally pass `HttpRequest` to the form, especially when you want to filter out the choices of form fields based on other request data or handle saving something such as the current user or IP in the form.

In this recipe, we will see an example of a form where, for added or changed ideas, the current user is saved as an author.

Getting ready

We will build upon the example in the previous recipe.

How to do it...

To complete this recipe, execute the following two steps:

1. Modify the `IdeaForm` model form as follows:

```python
# myprojects/apps/ideas/forms.py
from django import forms
from .models import Idea

class IdeaForm(forms.ModelForm):
    class Meta:
        model = Idea
        exclude = ["author"]

    def __init__(self, request, *args, **kwargs):
        self.request = request
        super().__init__(*args, **kwargs)

    def save(self, commit=True):
        instance = super().save(commit=False)
        instance.author = self.request.user
        if commit:
            instance.save()
            self.save_m2m()
        return instance
```

2. Modify the view to add or change the ideas:

```python
# myproject/apps/ideas/views.py
from django.contrib.auth.decorators import login_required
from django.shortcuts import render, redirect, get_object_or_404

from .forms import IdeaForm
from .models import Idea


@login_required
def add_or_change_idea(request, pk=None):
    idea = None
    if pk:
        idea = get_object_or_404(Idea, pk=pk)
```

```
if request.method == "POST":
    form = IdeaForm(request, data=request.POST,
      files=request.FILES, instance=idea)
    if form.is_valid():
        idea = form.save()
        return redirect("ideas:idea_detail", pk=idea.pk)
else:
    form = IdeaForm(request, instance=idea)

context = {"idea": idea, "form": form}
return render(request, "ideas/idea_form.html", context)
```

How it works...

Let's take a look at the form. At first, we exclude the `author` field from the form because we want to handle it programatically. We overwrite the `__init__()` method to accept `HttpRequest` as the first parameter and store it in the form. The `save()` method of a model form handles the saving of the model. The `commit` parameter tells the model form to save the instance immediately or otherwise to create and populate the instance, but not save it yet. In our case, we get the instance without saving it, then assign the author from the current user. Finally, we save the instance if `commit` is `True`. We will call the dynamically added `save_m2m()` method of the form to save many-to-many relations, for example, categories.

In the view, we just pass the `request` variable to the form as the first parameter.

See also

- The *Creating an app with CRUDL functions* recipe
- The *Uploading images* recipe

Uploading images

In this recipe, we will take a look at the easiest way to handle image uploads. We will add a `picture` field to the `Idea` model, and we will create image versions of different dimensions for different purposes.

Getting ready

For images with image versions, we will need the `Pillow` and `django-imagekit` libraries. Let's install them with `pip` in your virtual environment (and include them in `requirements/_base.txt`):

```
(env)$ pip install Pillow
(env)$ pip install django-imagekit==4.0.2
```

Then, add `"imagekit"` to INSTALLED_APPS in the settings.

How to do it...

Execute these steps to complete the recipe:

1. Modify the `Idea` model to add a `picture` field and image version specifications:

```python
# myproject/apps/ideas/models.py
import contextlib
import os

from imagekit.models import ImageSpecField
from pilkit.processors import ResizeToFill

from django.db import models
from django.utils.translation import gettext_lazy as _
from django.utils.timezone import now as timezone_now

from myproject.apps.core.models import
(CreationModificationDateBase, UrlBase)


def upload_to(instance, filename):
    now = timezone_now()
    base, extension = os.path.splitext(filename)
    extension = extension.lower()
    return f"ideas/{now:%Y/%m}/{instance.pk}{extension}"


class Idea(CreationModificationDateBase, UrlBase):
    # attributes and fields...
    picture = models.ImageField(
        _("Picture"), upload_to=upload_to
    )
    picture_social = ImageSpecField(
        source="picture",
```

```
            processors=[ResizeToFill(1024, 512)],
            format="JPEG",
            options={"quality": 100},
        )
    picture_large = ImageSpecField(
            source="picture",
            processors=[ResizeToFill(800, 400)],
            format="PNG"
        )
    picture_thumbnail = ImageSpecField(
            source="picture",
            processors=[ResizeToFill(728, 250)],
            format="PNG"
        )
    # other fields, properties, and  methods...

    def delete(self, *args, **kwargs):
        from django.core.files.storage import default_storage
        if self.picture:
            with contextlib.suppress(FileNotFoundError):
                default_storage.delete(
                    self.picture_social.path
                )
                default_storage.delete(
                    self.picture_large.path
                )
                default_storage.delete(
                    self.picture_thumbnail.path
                )
            self.picture.delete()
        super().delete(*args, **kwargs)
```

2. Create a model form, `IdeaForm`, for the `Idea` model in `forms.py`, just like we did in the previous recipes.

3. In the view for adding or changing ideas, make sure to post `request.FILES` beside `request.POST` to the form:

```
# myproject/apps/ideas/views.py
from django.contrib.auth.decorators import login_required
from django.shortcuts import (render, redirect, get_object_or_404)
from django.conf import settings

from .forms import IdeaForm
from .models import Idea


@login_required
```

```
def add_or_change_idea(request, pk=None):
    idea = None
    if pk:
        idea = get_object_or_404(Idea, pk=pk)
    if request.method == "POST":
        form = IdeaForm(
            request,
            data=request.POST,
            files=request.FILES,
            instance=idea,
        )
        if form.is_valid():
            idea = form.save()
            return redirect("ideas:idea_detail", pk=idea.pk)
    else:
        form = IdeaForm(request, instance=idea)

    context = {"idea": idea, "form": form}
    return render(request, "ideas/idea_form.html", context)
```

4. In the template, make sure to have encoding type set to `"multipart/form-data"`, as follows:

```
<form action="{{ request.path }}" method="post"
enctype="multipart/form-data">{% csrf_token %}
{{ form.as_p }}
<button type="submit">{% trans "Save" %}</button>
</form>
```

If you are using `django-crispy-form` as described in the *Creating a form layout with django-crispy-forms* recipe, the `enctype` attribute will be added to the form automatically.

How it works...

Django model forms are created dynamically from models. They provide the specified fields from the model so you don't need to redefine them manually in the form. In the preceding example, we created a model form for the `Idea` model. When we save the form, the form knows how to save each field in the database, as well as how to upload the files and save them in the media directory.

The `upload_to()` function in our example is used for saving the image to a specific directory and defining its name such that it wouldn't clash with filenames for other model instances. Each file will be saved under a path such as `ideas/2020/01/0422c6fe-b725-4576-8703-e2a9d9270986.jpg`, which consists of the year and month of the upload and the primary key of the `Idea` instance.

 Some filesystems (such as FAT32 and NTFS) have a limited amount of files available per directory; therefore, it is a good practice to divide them into directories by upload date, alphabet, or other criteria.

We are creating three image versions using `ImageSpecField` from django-imagekit:

- `picture_social` is used for social sharing.
- `picture_large` is used for the detail view.
- `picture_thumbnail` is used for the list view.

Image versions are not linked in the database but just saved in the default file storage under a file path such as `CACHE/images/ideas/2020/01/0422c6fe-b725-4576-8703-e2a9d9270986/`.

In the template, you can use the original or a specific image version, as follows:

```
<img src="{{ idea.picture.url }}" alt="" />
<img src="{{ idea.picture_large.url }}" alt="" />
```

At the end of the `Idea` model definition, we overwrite the `delete()` method to delete the image versions and the picture from the disk just before deleting the instance of `Idea` itself.

See also

- The *Creating a form layout with django-crispy-forms* recipe
- The *Arranging the base.html template* recipe in `Chapter 4, Templates and JavaScript`
- The *Providing responsive images* recipe in `Chapter 4, Templates and JavaScript`

Creating a form layout with custom templates

In earlier versions of Django, all form rendering was handled exclusively in Python code, but since Django 1.11, template-based form widget rendering has been introduced. In this recipe, we will examine how to use custom templates for form widgets. We are going to use the Django administration form to illustrate how the custom widget templates can improve the usability of the fields.

Getting ready

Let's create the default Django administration for the `Idea` model and its translations:

```python
# myproject/apps/ideas/admin.py
from django import forms
from django.contrib import admin
from django.utils.translation import gettext_lazy as _

from myproject.apps.core.admin import LanguageChoicesForm

from .models import Idea, IdeaTranslations


class IdeaTranslationsForm(LanguageChoicesForm):
    class Meta:
        model = IdeaTranslations
        fields = "__all__"


class IdeaTranslationsInline(admin.StackedInline):
    form = IdeaTranslationsForm
    model = IdeaTranslations
    extra = 0


@admin.register(Idea)
class IdeaAdmin(admin.ModelAdmin):
    inlines = [IdeaTranslationsInline]

    fieldsets = [
        (_("Author and Category"), {"fields": ["author", "categories"]}),
```

```
        (_("Title and Content"), {"fields": ["title", "content",
        "picture"]}),
        (_("Ratings"), {"fields": ["rating"]}),
    ]
```

If you access the administration form for the ideas, it will look like this:

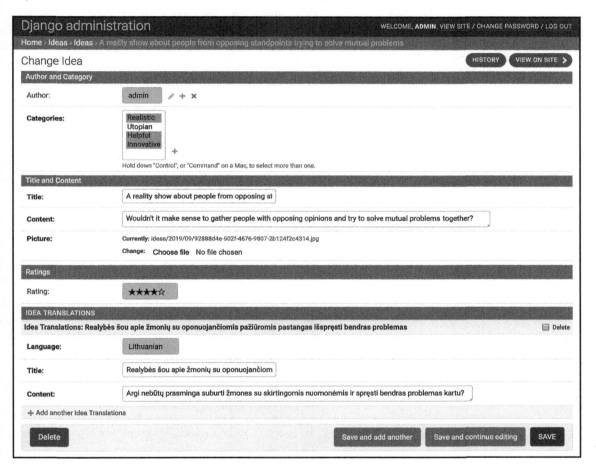

How to do it...

To complete the recipe, follow these steps:

1. Ensure that the template system will be able to find customized templates by adding `"django.forms"` to INSTALLED_APPS, including the APP_DIRS flag as True at the templates configuration, and using the `"TemplatesSetting"` form renderer:

```python
# myproject/settings/_base.py
INSTALLED_APPS = [
    "django.contrib.admin",
    "django.contrib.auth",
    "django.contrib.contenttypes",
    "django.contrib.sessions",
    "django.contrib.messages",
    "django.contrib.staticfiles",
    "django.forms",
    # other apps...
]

TEMPLATES = [
    {
        "BACKEND":
        "django.template.backends.django.DjangoTemplates",
        "DIRS": [os.path.join(BASE_DIR, "myproject", "templates")],
        "APP_DIRS": True,
        "OPTIONS": {
            "context_processors": [
                "django.template.context_processors.debug",
                "django.template.context_processors.request",
                "django.contrib.auth.context_processors.auth",
                "django.contrib.messages.context_processors
                 .messages",
                "django.template.context_processors.media",
                "django.template.context_processors.static",
                "myproject.apps.core.context_processors
                 .website_url",
            ]
        },
    }
]

FORM_RENDERER = "django.forms.renderers.TemplatesSetting"
```

2. Edit the `admin.py` file as follows:

```python
# myproject/apps/ideas/admin.py
from django import forms
from django.contrib import admin
from django.utils.translation import gettext_lazy as _

from myproject.apps.core.admin import LanguageChoicesForm

from myproject.apps.categories.models import Category
from .models import Idea, IdeaTranslations


class IdeaTranslationsForm(LanguageChoicesForm):
    class Meta:
        model = IdeaTranslations
        fields = "__all__"


class IdeaTranslationsInline(admin.StackedInline):
    form = IdeaTranslationsForm
    model = IdeaTranslations
    extra = 0


class IdeaForm(forms.ModelForm):
    categories = forms.ModelMultipleChoiceField(
        label=_("Categories"),
        queryset=Category.objects.all(),
        widget=forms.CheckboxSelectMultiple(),
        required=True,
    )

    class Meta:
        model = Idea
        fields = "__all__"

    def __init__(self, *args, **kwargs):
        super().__init__(*args, **kwargs)

        self.fields[
            "picture"
        ].widget.template_name = "core/widgets/image.html"


@admin.register(Idea)
class IdeaAdmin(admin.ModelAdmin):
    form = IdeaForm
```

```
inlines = [IdeaTranslationsInline]

fieldsets = [
    (_("Author and Category"), {"fields": ["author",
     "categories"]}),
    (_("Title and Content"), {"fields": ["title", "content",
     "picture"]}),
    (_("Ratings"), {"fields": ["rating"]}),
]
```

3. Finally, create a template for your picture field:

```
{# core/widgets/image.html #}
{% load i18n %}

<div style="margin-left: 160px; padding-left: 10px;">
    {% if widget.is_initial %}
        <a href="{{ widget.value.url }}">
            <img src="{{ widget.value.url }}" width="624"
             height="auto" alt="" />
        </a>
        {% if not widget.required %}<br />
            {{ widget.clear_checkbox_label }}:
            <input type="checkbox" name="{{ widget.checkbox_name
             }}" id="{{ widget.checkbox_id }}">
        {% endif %}<br />
        {{ widget.input_text }}:
    {% endif %}
    <input type="{{ widget.type }}" name="{{ widget.name }}"{%
     include "django/forms/widgets/attrs.html" %}>
</div>
<div class="help">
    {% trans "Available formats are JPG, GIF, and PNG." %}
    {% trans "Minimal size is 800 x 800 px." %}
</div>
```

How it works...

If you look at the administration form for ideas now, you will see something like this:

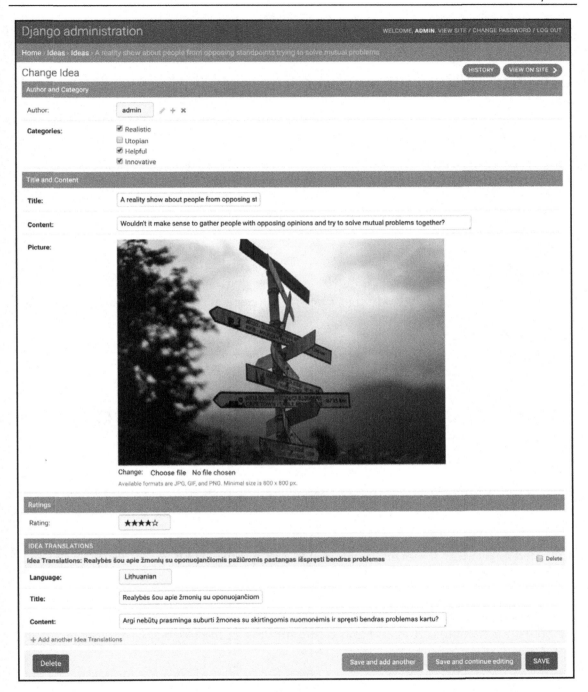

There are two changes here:

- The category selection is now using a widget with multiple checkboxes.
- The picture field is now rendered with a specific template, showing a preview of the image and help text with preferred file types and dimensions.

What we did here, was we overwrote the model form for the idea and modified the widget for the categories and the template for the picture field.

The default form renderer in Django is `"django.forms.renderers.DjangoTemplates"`, and it only searches for the templates in app directories. We changed it to `"django.forms.renderers.TemplatesSetting"` to also have a look in the templates under `DIRS` paths.

See also

- The *Working with model translation tables* recipe in `Chapter 2`, *Models and Database Structure*
- The *Uploading images* recipe
- The *Creating a form layout with django-crispy-forms* recipe

Creating a form layout with django-crispy-forms

The `django-crispy-forms` Django app allows you to build, customize, and reuse forms using one of the following CSS frameworks: Uni-Form, Bootstrap 3, Bootstrap 4, or Foundation. The use of `django-crispy-forms` is somewhat analogous to fieldsets in the Django contributed administration; however, it is more advanced and customizable. You define form layout in the Python code and need not worry about how each field is presented in HTML. Moreover, if you need to add specific HTML attributes or wrapping, you can easily do that too. All of the markup used by `django-crispy-forms` is located in templates that can be overwritten for specific needs.

In this recipe, we will create a nice layout for the frontend form to add or edit ideas using the Bootstrap 4, popular frontend framework for developing responsive, mobile-first web projects.

Getting ready

We will start with the `ideas` app that we created in this chapter. Next, we'll execute the following tasks one by one:

1. Make sure you have created a `base.html` template for your site. Learn more about this in the *Arranging the base.html template* recipe in `Chapter 4`, *Templates and JavaScript*.

2. Integrate the Bootstrap 4 frontend framework CSS and JS files from `https://getbootstrap.com/docs/4.3/getting-started/introduction/` into the `base.html` template.

3. Install `django-crispy-forms` in your virtual environment with `pip` (and include it in `requirements/_base.txt`):

   ```
   (env)$ pip install django-crispy-forms
   ```

4. Make sure that `"crispy_forms"` is added to `INSTALLED_APPS` in the settings, and then set `"bootstrap4"` as the template pack to be used in this project:

   ```
   # myproject/settings/_base.py
   INSTALLED_APPS = (
       # ...
       "crispy_forms",
       "ideas",
   )
   # ...
   CRISPY_TEMPLATE_PACK = "bootstrap4"
   ```

How to do it...

Follow these steps:

1. Let's modify the model form for the ideas:

   ```
   # myproject/apps/ideas/forms.py
   from django import forms
   from django.utils.translation import ugettext_lazy as _
   from django.conf import settings
   from django.db import models

   from crispy_forms import bootstrap, helper, layout

   from .models import Idea
   ```

```python
class IdeaForm(forms.ModelForm):
    class Meta:
        model = Idea
        exclude = ["author"]

    def __init__(self, request, *args, **kwargs):
        self.request = request
        super().__init__(*args, **kwargs)

        self.fields["categories"].widget = \
         forms.CheckboxSelectMultiple()

        title_field = layout.Field(
            "title", css_class="input-block-level"
        )
        content_field = layout.Field(
            "content", css_class="input-block-level", rows="3"
        )
        main_fieldset = layout.Fieldset(
            _("Main data"), title_field, content_field
        )

        picture_field = layout.Field(
            "picture", css_class="input-block-level"
        )
        format_html = layout.HTML(
            """{% include "ideas/includes
                /picture_guidelines.html" %}"""
        )

        picture_fieldset = layout.Fieldset(
            _("Picture"),
            picture_field,
            format_html,
            title=_("Image upload"),
            css_id="picture_fieldset",
        )

        categories_field = layout.Field(
            "categories", css_class="input-block-level"
        )
        categories_fieldset = layout.Fieldset(
            _("Categories"), categories_field,
            css_id="categories_fieldset"
        )

        submit_button = layout.Submit("save", _("Save"))
        actions = bootstrap.FormActions(submit_button)
```

```python
        self.helper = helper.FormHelper()
        self.helper.form_action = self.request.path
        self.helper.form_method = "POST"
        self.helper.layout = layout.Layout(
            main_fieldset,
            picture_fieldset,
            categories_fieldset,
            actions,
        )

    def save(self, commit=True):
        instance = super().save(commit=False)
        instance.author = self.request.user
        if commit:
            instance.save()
            self.save_m2m()
        return instance
```

2. Then, let's create the `picture_guidelines.html` template with the following content:

```
{# ideas/includes/picture_guidelines.html #}
{% load i18n %}
<p class="form-text text-muted">
    {% trans "Available formats are JPG, GIF, and PNG." %}
    {% trans "Minimal size is 800 × 800 px." %}
</p>
```

3. Finally, let's update the template for the form of ideas:

```
{# ideas/idea_form.html #}
{% extends "base.html" %}
{% load i18n crispy_forms_tags static %}

{% block content %}
    <a href="{% url "ideas:idea_list" %}">{% trans "List of
    ideas" %}</a>
    <h1>
        {% if idea %}
            {% blocktrans trimmed with
             title=idea.translated_title %}
                Change Idea "{{ title }}
            {% endblocktrans %}
        {% else %}
            {% trans "Add Idea" %}
        {% endif %}
```

```
            </h1>
            {% crispy form %}
{% endblock %}
```

How it works...

In the model form for ideas, we create a form helper with a layout consisting of a main fieldset, picture fieldset, categories fieldset, and submit button. Each fieldset consists of fields. Any fieldset, field, or button can have additional parameters that become the attributes of the field, for example, `rows="3"` or `placeholder=_("Please enter a title")`. For HTML `class` and `id` attributes, there are specific parameters, `css_class` and `css_id`.

The page with the idea form will look similar to the following:

List of ideas

Change Idea "A reality show about people from opposing standpoints trying to solve mutual problems"

Main data

Title*

A reality show about people from opposing standpoints trying to solve mutual problems

Content*

Wouldn't it make sense to gather people with opposing opinions and try to solve mutual problems together?

Picture

Picture*

Currently: ideas/2019/09/92888d4e-502f-4676-9807-2b124f2c4314.jpg

Change: **Choose file** No file chosen

Available formats are JPG, GIF, and PNG. Minimal size is 800 × 800 px.

Categories

Categories*

☑ Realistic
☐ Utopian
☑ Helpful
☑ Innovative

Save

Just like in the previous recipe, we modify the widget for the categories field and add additional help text for the picture field.

There's more...

For basic usage, the given example is more than necessary. However, if you need a specific markup for the forms in your project, you can still overwrite and modify templates of the `django-crispy-forms` app, as there is no markup hardcoded in the Python files, rather all of the generated markup is rendered through templates. Just copy the templates from the `django-crispy-forms` app to your project's template directory and change them as required.

See also

- The *Creating an app with CRUDL functions* recipe
- The *Creating a form layout with custom templates* recipe
- The *Filtering object lists* recipe
- The *Managing paginated lists* recipe
- The *Composing class-based views* recipe
- The *Arranging the base.html template* recipe in `Chapter 4`, *Templates and JavaScript*

Working with formsets

Besides normal or model forms, Django has a concept of formsets. These are sets of forms of the same type that allow us to create or change multiple instances at once. Django formsets can be enriched with JavaScript, which allows us to add them to a page dynamically. That's exactly what we will work on in this recipe. We will extend the form of ideas to allow adding translations to different languages on the same page.

Getting ready

Let's continue working on `IdeaForm` from the previous recipe, *Creating a form layout with django-crispy-forms*.

How to do it...

Follow these steps:

1. Let's modify the form layout for `IdeaForm`:

```python
# myproject/apps/ideas/forms.py
from django import forms
from django.utils.translation import ugettext_lazy as _
from django.conf import settings
from django.db import models

from crispy_forms import bootstrap, helper, layout

from .models import Idea, IdeaTranslations


class IdeaForm(forms.ModelForm):
    class Meta:
        model = Idea
        exclude = ["author"]

    def __init__(self, request, *args, **kwargs):
        self.request = request
        super().__init__(*args, **kwargs)

        self.fields["categories"].widget = \
         forms.CheckboxSelectMultiple()

        title_field = layout.Field(
            "title", css_class="input-block-level"
        )
        content_field = layout.Field(
            "content", css_class="input-block-level", rows="3"
        )
        main_fieldset = layout.Fieldset(
            _("Main data"), title_field, content_field
        )

        picture_field = layout.Field(
            "picture", css_class="input-block-level"
        )
        format_html = layout.HTML(
            """{% include "ideas/includes
                /picture_guidelines.html" %}"""
        )

        picture_fieldset = layout.Fieldset(
```

```
            _("Picture"),
            picture_field,
            format_html,
            title=_("Image upload"),
            css_id="picture_fieldset",
        )

        categories_field = layout.Field(
            "categories", css_class="input-block-level"
        )
        categories_fieldset = layout.Fieldset(
            _("Categories"), categories_field,
            css_id="categories_fieldset"
        )

        inline_translations = layout.HTML(
            """{% include "ideas/forms/translations.html" %}"""
        )

        submit_button = layout.Submit("save", _("Save"))
        actions = bootstrap.FormActions(submit_button)

        self.helper = helper.FormHelper()
        self.helper.form_action = self.request.path
        self.helper.form_method = "POST"
        self.helper.layout = layout.Layout(
            main_fieldset,
            inline_translations,
            picture_fieldset,
            categories_fieldset,
            actions,
        )

    def save(self, commit=True):
        instance = super().save(commit=False)
        instance.author = self.request.user
        if commit:
            instance.save()
            self.save_m2m()
        return instance
```

2. Then, let's add `IdeaTranslationsForm` at the end of the same file:

```python
class IdeaTranslationsForm(forms.ModelForm):
    language = forms.ChoiceField(
        label=_("Language"),
        choices=settings.LANGUAGES_EXCEPT_THE_DEFAULT,
        required=True,
    )

    class Meta:
        model = IdeaTranslations
        exclude = ["idea"]

    def __init__(self, request, *args, **kwargs):
        self.request = request
        super().__init__(*args, **kwargs)

        id_field = layout.Field("id")
        language_field = layout.Field(
            "language", css_class="input-block-level"
        )
        title_field = layout.Field(
            "title", css_class="input-block-level"
        )
        content_field = layout.Field(
            "content", css_class="input-block-level", rows="3"
        )
        delete_field = layout.Field("DELETE")
        main_fieldset = layout.Fieldset(
            _("Main data"),
            id_field,
            language_field,
            title_field,
            content_field,
            delete_field,
        )

        self.helper = helper.FormHelper()
        self.helper.form_tag = False
        self.helper.disable_csrf = True
        self.helper.layout = layout.Layout(main_fieldset)
```

3. Modify the view to add or change ideas, as follows:

```python
# myproject/apps/ideas/views.py
from django.contrib.auth.decorators import login_required
from django.shortcuts import render, redirect, get_object_or_404
from django.forms import modelformset_factory
from django.conf import settings

from .forms import IdeaForm, IdeaTranslationsForm
from .models import Idea, IdeaTranslations


@login_required
def add_or_change_idea(request, pk=None):
    idea = None
    if pk:
        idea = get_object_or_404(Idea, pk=pk)
    IdeaTranslationsFormSet = modelformset_factory(
        IdeaTranslations, form=IdeaTranslationsForm,
        extra=0, can_delete=True
    )
    if request.method == "POST":
        form = IdeaForm(request, data=request.POST,
         files=request.FILES, instance=idea)
        translations_formset = IdeaTranslationsFormSet(
            queryset=IdeaTranslations.objects.filter(idea=idea),
            data=request.POST,
            files=request.FILES,
            prefix="translations",
            form_kwargs={"request": request},
        )
        if form.is_valid() and translations_formset.is_valid():
            idea = form.save()
            translations = translations_formset.save(
                commit=False
            )
            for translation in translations:
                translation.idea = idea
                translation.save()
            translations_formset.save_m2m()
            for translation in
             translations_formset.deleted_objects:
                translation.delete()
            return redirect("ideas:idea_detail", pk=idea.pk)
    else:
        form = IdeaForm(request, instance=idea)
        translations_formset = IdeaTranslationsFormSet(
            queryset=IdeaTranslations.objects.filter(idea=idea),
```

```
                prefix="translations",
                form_kwargs={"request": request},
            )

        context = {
            "idea": idea,
            "form": form,
            "translations_formset": translations_formset
        }
        return render(request, "ideas/idea_form.html", context)
```

4. Then, let's edit the `idea_form.html` template and add a reference to the `inlines.js` script file at the end:

```
{# ideas/idea_form.html #}
{% extends "base.html" %}
{% load i18n crispy_forms_tags static %}

{% block content %}
    <a href="{% url "ideas:idea_list" %}">{% trans "List of
     ideas" %}</a>
    <h1>
        {% if idea %}
            {% blocktrans trimmed with
             title=idea.translated_title %}
                Change Idea "{{ title }}"
            {% endblocktrans %}
        {% else %}
            {% trans "Add Idea" %}
        {% endif %}
    </h1>
    {% crispy form %}
{% endblock %}

{% block js %}
    <script src="{% static 'site/js/inlines.js' %}"></script>
{% endblock %}
```

5. Create the template for the translation formsets:

```
{# ideas/forms/translations.html #}
{% load i18n crispy_forms_tags %}
<section id="translations_section" class="formset my-3">
    {{ translations_formset.management_form }}
    <h3>{% trans "Translations" %}</h3>
    <div class="formset-forms">
        {% for formset_form in translations_formset %}
            <div class="formset-form">
                {% crispy formset_form %}
            </div>
        {% endfor %}
    </div>
    <button type="button" class="btn btn-primary btn-sm
     add-inline-form">{% trans "Add translations to another
     language" %}</button>
    <div class="empty-form d-none">
        {% crispy translations_formset.empty_form %}
    </div>
</section>
```

6. Last but not least, add the JavaScript to manipulate the formsets:

```
/* site/js/inlines.js */
window.WIDGET_INIT_REGISTER = window.WIDGET_INIT_REGISTER || [];

$(function () {
    function reinit_widgets($formset_form) {
        $(window.WIDGET_INIT_REGISTER).each(function (index, func)
        {
            func($formset_form);
        });
    }

    function set_index_for_fields($formset_form, index) {
        $formset_form.find(':input').each(function () {
            var $field = $(this);
            if ($field.attr("id")) {
                $field.attr(
                    "id",
                    $field.attr("id").replace(/-__prefix__-/,
                    "-" + index + "-")
                );
            }
            if ($field.attr("name")) {
                $field.attr(
                    "name",
```

```
                                $field.attr("name").replace(
                                    /-__prefix__-/, "-" + index + "-"
                                )
                            );
                    }
                });
                $formset_form.find('label').each(function () {
                    var $field = $(this);
                    if ($field.attr("for")) {
                        $field.attr(
                            "for",
                            $field.attr("for").replace(
                                /-__prefix__-/, "-" + index + "-"
                            )
                        );
                    }
                });
                $formset_form.find('div').each(function () {
                    var $field = $(this);
                    if ($field.attr("id")) {
                        $field.attr(
                            "id",
                            $field.attr("id").replace(
                                /-__prefix__-/, "-" + index + "-"
                            )
                        );
                    }
                });
            }

            function add_delete_button($formset_form) {
                $formset_form.find('input:checkbox[id$=DELETE]')
                  .each(function () {
                    var $checkbox = $(this);
                    var $deleteLink = $(
                        '<button class="delete btn btn-sm
                          btn-danger mb-3">Remove</button>'
                    );
                    $formset_form.append($deleteLink);
                    $checkbox.closest('.form-group').hide();
                });

            }

            $('.add-inline-form').click(function (e) {
                e.preventDefault();
                var $formset = $(this).closest('.formset');
                var $total_forms = $formset.find('[id$="TOTAL_FORMS"]');
```

```
                    var $new_form = $formset.find('.empty-form')
                    .clone(true).attr("id", null);
                    $new_form.removeClass('empty-form d-none')
                    .addClass('formset-form');
                    set_index_for_fields($new_form,
                     parseInt($total_forms.val(), 10));
                    $formset.find('.formset-forms').append($new_form);
                    add_delete_button($new_form);
                    $total_forms.val(parseInt($total_forms.val(), 10) + 1);
                    reinit_widgets($new_form);
                });
                $('.formset-form').each(function () {
                    $formset_form = $(this);
                    add_delete_button($formset_form);
                    reinit_widgets($formset_form);
                });
                $(document).on('click', '.delete', function (e) {
                    e.preventDefault();
                    var $formset = $(this).closest('.formset-form');
                    var $checkbox =
                    $formset.find('input:checkbox[id$=DELETE]');
                    $checkbox.attr("checked", "checked");
                    $formset.hide();
                });
            });
```

How it works...

You might know about formsets from the Django model administration. Formsets are used there in the mechanism of inlines for child models having foreign keys to a parent model.

In this recipe, we added formsets to the idea form using `django-crispy-forms`. The result will look like this:

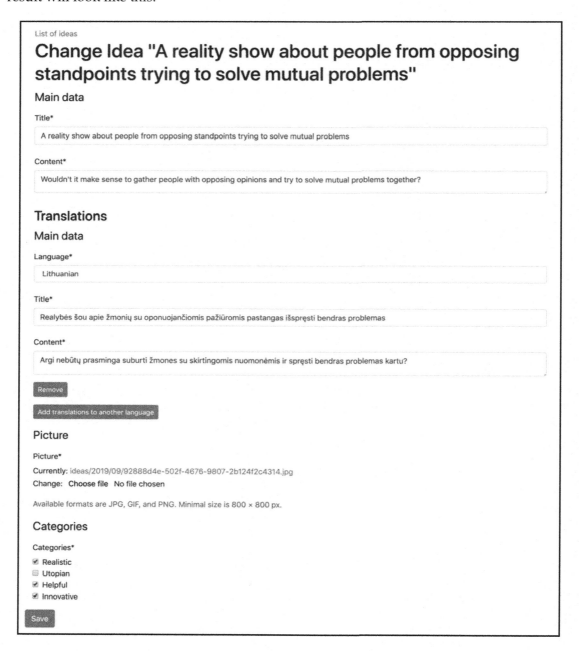

As you can see, we can insert the formsets not necessarily at the end of the form, but anywhere in between, where it makes sense. In our example, it makes sense to list out translations just after translatable fields.

The form layout for the translations forms has the main fieldset just like the layout of `IdeaForm`, but in addition, it has `id` and `DELETE` fields that are necessary for recognition of each model instance and the possibility to remove them from the list. The `DELETE` field is actually a checkbox that if checked, deletes the appropriate item from the database. Also, the form helper for the translation has `form_tag=False`, which doesn't generate the `<form>` tag, and `disable_csrf=True`, which doesn't include the CSRF token, because we have already defined these in the parent form, `IdeaForm`.

In the view, if the request is sent by the POST method and both the form and the formset are valid, then we save the form and create respective translation instances without saving them at first. This is done by the `commit=False` attribute. For each translation instance, we assign the idea and then save the translations to the database. Lastly, we check whether any forms in the formset were marked for deletion and delete them from the database.

In the `translations.html` template, we render each form in the formset and then we add an extra hidden empty form, which will be used by JavaScript to generate new forms of the formset to be added dynamically.

Each formset form has prefixes for all fields. For example, the `title` field of the first formset form will have an HTML field name, `"translations-0-title"`, and the `DELETE` field of the same formset form will have an HTML field name, `"translations-0-DELETE"`. The empty form has a word, `"__prefix__"`, instead of the index, for example, `"translations-__prefix__-title"`. This is abstracted at the Django level, but necessary to know for manipulating the formset forms with JavaScript.

The `inlines.js` JavaScript does a few things:

- For each existing formset form, it initializes its JavaScript-powered widgets (you could use tooltips, day or color pickers, maps, and so on) and creates a delete button, which is shown instead of the `DELETE` checkbox.
- When a delete button is clicked, it checks the `DELETE` checkbox and hides the formset form from the user.
- When the add button is clicked, it clones the empty form and replaces `"__prefix__"` with the next available index, adds the new form to the list, and initiates JavaScript-powered widgets.

There's more...

The JavaScript uses an array, `window.WIDGET_INIT_REGISTER`, which contains functions that should be called to initiate widgets with a given formset form. To register a new function in another JavaScript file, you can do the following:

```
/* site/js/main.js */
function apply_tooltips($formset_form) {
    $formset_form.find('[data-toggle="tooltip"]').tooltip();
}

/* register widget initialization for a formset form */
window.WIDGET_INIT_REGISTER = window.WIDGET_INIT_REGISTER || [];
window.WIDGET_INIT_REGISTER.push(apply_tooltips);
```

This will apply tooltip functionality for all occurrences in the formset forms where the tags in the markup have `data-toggle="tooltip"` and `title` attributes, as in this example:

```
<button data-toggle="tooltip" title="{% trans 'Remove this translation'
%}">{% trans "Remove" %}</button>
```

See also

- The *Creating a form layout with django-crispy-forms* recipe
- The *Arranging the base.html template* recipe in `Chapter 4`, *Templates and JavaScript*

Filtering object lists

In web development, besides views with forms, it is typical to have object-list views and detail views. List views can simply list objects that are ordered, for example, alphabetically or by creation date; however, that is not very user-friendly with huge amounts of data. For the best accessibility and convenience, you should be able to filter the content by all possible categories. In this recipe, we will see the pattern that is used to filter list views by any number of categories.

What we'll be creating is a list view of ideas that can be filtered by author, category, or rating. It will look similar to the following with Bootstrap 4 applied to it:

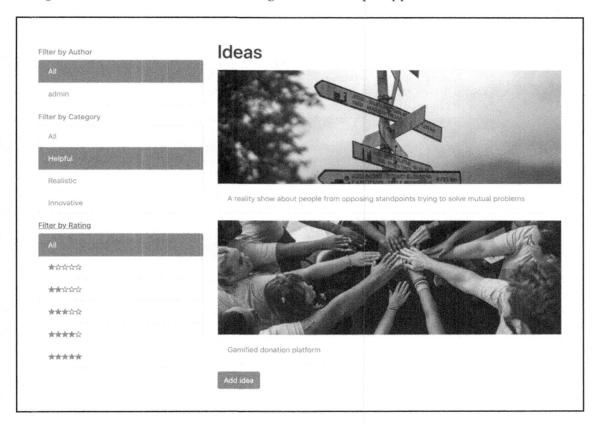

Getting ready

For the filtering example, we will use the `Idea` model with relation to the author and categories to filter by. It will also be possible to filter by ratings, which is `PositiveIntegerField` with choices. Let's use the ideas app with the models that we created in the previous recipes.

How to do it...

To complete the recipe, follow these steps:

1. Create `IdeaFilterForm` with all of the possible categories to filter by:

```python
# myproject/apps/ideas/forms.py
from django import forms
from django.utils.translation import ugettext_lazy as _
from django.db import models
from django.contrib.auth import get_user_model

from myproject.apps.categories.models import Category

from .models import RATING_CHOICES

User = get_user_model()


class IdeaFilterForm(forms.Form):
    author = forms.ModelChoiceField(
        label=_("Author"),
        required=False,
        queryset=User.objects.annotate(
            idea_count=models.Count("authored_ideas")
        ).filter(idea_count__gt=0),
    )
    category = forms.ModelChoiceField(
        label=_("Category"),
        required=False,
        queryset=Category.objects.annotate(
            idea_count=models.Count("category_ideas")
        ).filter(idea_count__gt=0),
    )
    rating = forms.ChoiceField(
        label=_("Rating"), required=False, choices=RATING_CHOICES
    )
```

2. Create the `idea_list` view to list filtered ideas:

```python
# myproject/apps/ideas/views.py
from django.shortcuts import render, redirect, get_object_or_404
from django.conf import settings

from .forms import IdeaFilterForm
from .models import Idea, RATING_CHOICES
```

```
PAGE_SIZE = getattr(settings, "PAGE_SIZE", 24)


def idea_list(request):
    qs = Idea.objects.order_by("title")
    form = IdeaFilterForm(data=request.GET)

    facets = {
        "selected": {},
        "categories": {
            "authors": form.fields["author"].queryset,
            "categories": form.fields["category"].queryset,
            "ratings": RATING_CHOICES,
        },
    }

    if form.is_valid():
        filters = (
            # query parameter, filter parameter
            ("author", "author"),
            ("category", "categories"),
            ("rating", "rating"),
        )
        qs = filter_facets(facets, qs, form, filters)

    context = {"form": form, "facets": facets, "object_list": qs}
    return render(request, "ideas/idea_list.html", context)
```

3. In the same file, add the helper function, `filter_facets()`:

```
def filter_facets(facets, qs, form, filters):
    for query_param, filter_param in filters:
        value = form.cleaned_data[query_param]
        if value:
            selected_value = value
            if query_param == "rating":
                rating = int(value)
                selected_value = (rating,
                  dict(RATING_CHOICES)[rating])
            facets["selected"][query_param] = selected_value
            filter_args = {filter_param: value}
            qs = qs.filter(**filter_args).distinct()
    return qs
```

4. If you haven't done so already, create a `base.html` template. You can do that according to the example provided in the *Arranging the base.html template* recipe in `Chapter 4`, *Templates and JavaScript*.

5. Create the `idea_list.html` template with the following content:

```
{# ideas/idea_list.html #}
{% extends "base.html" %}
{% load i18n utility_tags %}

{% block sidebar %}
    {% include "ideas/includes/filters.html" %}
{% endblock %}

{% block main %}
    <h1>{% trans "Ideas" %}</h1>
    {% if object_list %}
        {% for idea in object_list %}
            <a href="{{ idea.get_url_path }}" class="d-block my-3">
                <div class="card">
                    <img src="{{ idea.picture_thumbnail.url }}"
                    alt="" />
                    <div class="card-body">
                      <p class="card-text">{{ idea.translated_title
                      }}</p>
                    </div>
                </div>
            </a>
        {% endfor %}
    {% else %}
        <p>{% trans "There are no ideas yet." %}</p>
    {% endif %}
    <a href="{% url 'ideas:add_idea' %}" class="btn btn-primary">
    {% trans "Add idea" %}</a>
{% endblock %}
```

6. Then, let's create the template for the filters. This template uses the `{% modify_query %}` template tag, described in the *Creating a template tag to modify request query parameters* recipe in `Chapter 5`, *Custom Template Filters and Tags*, to generate URLs for the filters:

```
{# ideas/includes/filters.html #}
{% load i18n utility_tags %}
<div class="filters panel-group" id="accordion">
    {% with title=_('Author') selected=facets.selected.author %}
        <div class="panel panel-default my-3">
            {% include "misc/includes/filter_heading.html" with
            title=title %}
            <div id="collapse-{{ title|slugify }}"
                class="panel-collapse{% if not selected %}
                collapse{% endif %}">
```

```
                            <div class="panel-body"><div class="list-group">
                        {% include "misc/includes/filter_all.html" with
                         param="author" %}
                            {% for cat in facets.categories.authors %}
                                <a class="list-group-item
                                  {% if selected == cat %}
                                  active{% endif %}"
                                   href="{% modify_query "page"
                                    author=cat.pk %}">
                                      {{ cat }}</a>
                            {% endfor %}
                        </div></div>
                </div>
            </div>
    {% endwith %}
    {% with title=_('Category') selected=facets.selected
      .category %}
        <div class="panel panel-default my-3">
            {% include "misc/includes/filter_heading.html" with
               title=title %}
            <div id="collapse-{{ title|slugify }}"
                class="panel-collapse{% if not selected %}
                 collapse{% endif %}">
                <div class="panel-body"><div class="list-group">
                        {% include "misc/includes/filter_all.html" with
                         param="category" %}
                            {% for cat in facets.categories.categories %}
                                <a class="list-group-item
                                  {% if selected == cat %}
                                  active{% endif %}"
                                   href="{% modify_query "page"
                                    category=cat.pk %}">
                                      {{ cat }}</a>
                            {% endfor %}
                        </div></div>
                </div>
            </div>
    {% endwith %}
    {% with title=_('Rating') selected=facets.selected.rating %}
        <div class="panel panel-default my-3">
            {% include "misc/includes/filter_heading.html" with
               title=title %}
            <div id="collapse-{{ title|slugify }}"
                class="panel-collapse{% if not selected %}
                 collapse{% endif %}">
                <div class="panel-body"><div class="list-group">
                        {% include "misc/includes/filter_all.html" with
                         param="rating" %}
```

```
                {% for r_val, r_display in
                  facets.categories.ratings %}
                    <a class="list-group-item
                      {% if selected.0 == r_val %}
                      active{% endif %}"
                        href="{% modify_query "page"
                          rating=r_val %}">
                          {{ r_display }}</a>
                {% endfor %}
              </div></div>
          </div>
        </div>
    {% endwith %}
</div>
```

7. Each of the categories will follow a common pattern in the filters sidebar, so we can create and include templates with the common parts. First, we have the filter heading, corresponding to `misc/includes/filter_heading.html`, as in the following:

```
{# misc/includes/filter_heading.html #}
{% load i18n %}
<div class="panel-heading">
    <h6 class="panel-title">
        <a data-toggle="collapse" data-parent="#accordion"
            href="#collapse-{{ title|slugify }}">
            {% blocktrans trimmed %}
                Filter by {{ title }}
            {% endblocktrans %}
        </a>
    </h6>
</div>
```

8. And then each filter will contain a link to reset filtering for that category, represented by `misc/includes/filter_all.html` here. This template also uses the `{% modify_query %}` template tag, described in the *Creating a template tag to modify request query parameters* recipe in Chapter 5, *Custom Template Filters and Tags*:

```
{# misc/includes/filter_all.html #}
{% load i18n utility_tags %}
<a class="list-group-item {% if not selected %}active{% endif %}"
    href="{% modify_query "page" param %}">
    {% trans "All" %}
</a>
```

9. The idea list needs to be added to the URLs for the `ideas` app:

```
# myproject/apps/ideas/urls.py
from django.urls import path

from .views import idea_list

urlpatterns = [
    path("", idea_list, name="idea_list"),
    # other paths...
]
```

How it works...

We are using the `facets` dictionary that is passed to the template context to know which filters we have and which filters are selected. To look deeper, the `facets` dictionary consists of two sections: the `categories` dictionary and the `selected` dictionary. The `categories` dictionary contains QuerySets or choices of all filterable categories. The `selected` dictionary contains the currently selected values for each category. In `IdeaFilterForm`, we make sure that only those categories and authors are listed that have at least one idea.

In the view, we check whether the query parameters are valid in the form and then filter the QuerySet of objects based on the selected categories. Additionally, we set the selected values to the `facets` dictionary, which will be passed to the template.

In the template, for each categorization from the `facets` dictionary, we list all of the categories and mark the currently selected category as active. If nothing is selected for a given category, we mark the default "**All**" link as the active one.

See also

- The *Managing paginated lists* recipe
- The *Composing class-based views* recipe
- The *Arranging the base.html template* recipe in Chapter 4, *Templates and JavaScript*
- The *Creating a template tag to modify request query parameters* recipe in Chapter 5, *Custom Template Filters and Tags*

Managing paginated lists

If you have dynamically changing lists of objects or their count is greater than 24 or so, you will likely need pagination to provide a good user experience. Instead of the full QuerySet, pagination provides a specific number of items in the dataset that corresponds to the appropriate size for one page. We also display links to allow users to access the other pages making up the complete set of data. Django has classes to manage paginated data, and we will see how to use them in this recipe.

Getting ready

Let's start with the models, forms, and views of the `ideas` app from the *Filtering object lists* recipe.

How to do it...

To add pagination to the list view of the ideas, follow these steps:

1. Import the necessary pagination classes from Django into the `views.py` file. We will add pagination management to the `idea_list` view just after filtering. Also, we will slightly modify the context dictionary by assigning `page` to the `object_list` key:

```python
# myproject/apps/ideas/views.py
from django.shortcuts import render, redirect, get_object_or_404
from django.conf import settings
from django.core.paginator import (EmptyPage, PageNotAnInteger,
Paginator)

from .forms import IdeaFilterForm
from .models import Idea, RATING_CHOICES


PAGE_SIZE = getattr(settings, "PAGE_SIZE", 24)


def idea_list(request):
    qs = Idea.objects.order_by("title")
    form = IdeaFilterForm(data=request.GET)

    facets = {
        "selected": {},
```

```
                    "categories": {
                        "authors": form.fields["author"].queryset,
                        "categories": form.fields["category"].queryset,
                        "ratings": RATING_CHOICES,
                    },
                }

                if form.is_valid():
                    filters = (
                        # query parameter, filter parameter
                        ("author", "author"),
                        ("category", "categories"),
                        ("rating", "rating"),
                    )
                    qs = filter_facets(facets, qs, form, filters)

                paginator = Paginator(qs, PAGE_SIZE)
                page_number = request.GET.get("page")
                try:
                    page = paginator.page(page_number)
                except PageNotAnInteger:
                    # If page is not an integer, show first page.
                    page = paginator.page(1)
                except EmptyPage:
                    # If page is out of range, show last existing page.
                    page = paginator.page(paginator.num_pages)

                context = {
                    "form": form,
                    "facets": facets,
                    "object_list": page,
                }
                return render(request, "ideas/idea_list.html", context)
```

2. Modify the `idea_list.html` template as follows:

```
{# ideas/idea_list.html #}
{% extends "base.html" %}
{% load i18n utility_tags %}

{% block sidebar %}
    {% include "ideas/includes/filters.html" %}
{% endblock %}

{% block main %}
    <h1>{% trans "Ideas" %}</h1>
    {% if object_list %}
        {% for idea in object_list %}
```

```
                    <a href="{{ idea.get_url_path }}" class="d-block my-3">
                        <div class="card">
                            <img src="{{ idea.picture_thumbnail.url }}"
                             alt="" />
                            <div class="card-body">
                                <p class="card-text">{{ idea.translated_title
                                 }}</p>
                            </div>
                        </div>
                    </a>
                {% endfor %}
                {% include "misc/includes/pagination.html" %}
            {% else %}
                <p>{% trans "There are no ideas yet." %}</p>
            {% endif %}
            <a href="{% url 'ideas:add_idea' %}" class="btn btn-primary">
             {% trans "Add idea" %}</a>
        {% endblock %}
```

3. Create the pagination widget template:

```
{# misc/includes/pagination.html #}
{% load i18n utility_tags %}
{% if object_list.has_other_pages %}
    <nav aria-label="{% trans 'Page navigation' %}">

        <ul class="pagination">
            {% if object_list.has_previous %}
                <li class="page-item"><a class="page-link" href="{%
        modify_query page=object_list.previous_page_number %}">
                    {% trans "Previous" %}</a></li>
            {% else %}
                <li class="page-item disabled"><span class="page-
                  link">{% trans "Previous" %}</span></li>
            {% endif %}

            {% for page_number in object_list.paginator
             .page_range %}
                {% if page_number == object_list.number %}
                    <li class="page-item active">
                        <span class="page-link">{{ page_number }}
                            <span class="sr-only">{% trans
                             "(current)" %}</span>
                        </span>
                    </li>
                {% else %}
                    <li class="page-item">
                        <a class="page-link" href="{% modify_query
```

```
                           page=page_number %}">
                               {{ page_number }}</a>
                   </li>
               {% endif %}
           {% endfor %}

           {% if object_list.has_next %}
               <li class="page-item"><a class="page-link" href="{%
            modify_query page=object_list.next_page_number %}">
                       {% trans "Next" %}</a></li>
           {% else %}
               <li class="page-item disabled"><span class="page-
                   link">{% trans "Next" %}</span></li>
           {% endif %}
         </ul>
       </nav>
   {% endif %}
```

How it works...

When you look at the results in the browser, you will see the pagination controls, similar to the follo wing:

How do we achieve this? When QuerySet is filtered out, we will create a paginator object passing QuerySet and the maximal amount of items that we want to show per page, which is 24 here. Then, we will read the current page number from the query parameter, page. The next step is to retrieve the current page object from the paginator. If the page number is not an integer, we get the first page. If the number exceeds the number of possible pages, the last page is retrieved. The page object has methods and attributes necessary for the pagination widget shown in the preceding screenshot. Also, the page object acts like QuerySet so that we can iterate through it and get the items from the fraction of the page.

The snippet marked in the template creates a pagination widget with the markup for the Bootstrap 4 frontend framework. We show the pagination controls only if there are more pages than the current one. We have the links to the previous and next pages, and the list of all page numbers in the widget. The current page number is marked as active. To generate URLs for the links, we use the {% modify_query %} template tag, which will be described later in the *Creating a template tag to modify request query parameters* recipe in Chapter 5, *Custom Template Filters and Tags*.

See also

- The *Filtering object lists* recipe
- The *Composing class-based views* recipe
- The *Creating a template tag to modify request query parameters* recipe in `Chapter 5,` *Custom Template Filters and Tags*

Composing class-based views

Django views are callables that take requests and return responses. In addition to function-based views, Django provides an alternative way to define views as classes. This approach is useful when you want to create reusable modular views or combine views of the generic mixins. In this recipe, we will convert the previously shown function-based `idea_list` view into a class-based `IdeaListView` view.

Getting ready

Create the models, form, and template similar to the previous recipes, *Filtering object lists* and *Managing paginated lists*.

How to do it...

Follow these steps to execute the recipe:

1. Our class-based view, `IdeaListView`, will inherit the Django `View` class and override the `get()` method:

```python
# myproject/apps/ideas/views.py
from django.shortcuts import render, redirect, get_object_or_404
from django.conf import settings
from django.core.paginator import (EmptyPage, PageNotAnInteger,
Paginator)
from django.views.generic import View

from .forms import IdeaFilterForm
from .models import Idea, RATING_CHOICES

PAGE_SIZE = getattr(settings, "PAGE_SIZE", 24)
```

```python
class IdeaListView(View):
    form_class = IdeaFilterForm
    template_name = "ideas/idea_list.html"

    def get(self, request, *args, **kwargs):
        form = self.form_class(data=request.GET)
        qs, facets = self.get_queryset_and_facets(form)
        page = self.get_page(request, qs)
        context = {"form": form, "facets": facets,
         "object_list": page}
        return render(request, self.template_name, context)

    def get_queryset_and_facets(self, form):
        qs = Idea.objects.order_by("title")
        facets = {
            "selected": {},
            "categories": {
                "authors": form.fields["author"].queryset,
                "categories": form.fields["category"].queryset,
                "ratings": RATING_CHOICES,
            },
        }
        if form.is_valid():
            filters = (
                # query parameter, filter parameter
                ("author", "author"),
                ("category", "categories"),
                ("rating", "rating"),
            )
            qs = self.filter_facets(facets, qs, form, filters)
        return qs, facets

    @staticmethod
    def filter_facets(facets, qs, form, filters):
        for query_param, filter_param in filters:
            value = form.cleaned_data[query_param]
            if value:
                selected_value = value
                if query_param == "rating":
                    rating = int(value)
                    selected_value = (rating,
                     dict(RATING_CHOICES)[rating])
                facets["selected"][query_param] = selected_value
                filter_args = {filter_param: value}
                qs = qs.filter(**filter_args).distinct()
        return qs

    def get_page(self, request, qs):
```

```
paginator = Paginator(qs, PAGE_SIZE)
page_number = request.GET.get("page")
try:
    page = paginator.page(page_number)
except PageNotAnInteger:
    page = paginator.page(1)
except EmptyPage:
    page = paginator.page(paginator.num_pages)
return page
```

2. We will need to create a URL rule in the URL configuration using the class-based view. You may have added a rule previously for the function-based `idea_list` view, which would have been similar. To include a class-based view in the URL rules, use the `as_view()` method as follows:

```
# myproject/apps/ideas/urls.py
from django.urls import path

from .views import IdeaListView

urlpatterns = [
    path("", IdeaListView.as_view(), name="idea_list"),
    # other paths...
]
```

How it works...

The following are the things happening in the `get()` method, which is called for HTTP GET requests:

- First, we create the `form` object, passing the `request.GET` dictionary-like object to it. The `request.GET` object contains all of the query variables that are passed using the GET method.
- Then, the `form` object is passed to the `get_queryset_and_facets()` method, which returns the associated values via a tuple containing two elements: QuerySet and the `facets` dictionary respectively.
- The current request object and retrieved QuerySet are passed to the `get_page()` method, which returns the current page object.
- Lastly, we create a `context` dictionary and render the response.

If we needed to support it, we could also provide a `post()` method, which is called for HTTP POST requests.

There's more...

As you see, the `get()` and `get_page()` methods are largely generic, so we could create a generic `FilterableListView` class with these methods in the `core` app. Then, in any app that requires a filterable list, we could create a class-based view that extends `FilterableListView` to handle such scenarios. This extending class would define only the `form_class` and `template_name` attributes and the `get_queryset_and_facets()` method. Such modularity and extensibility represent two of the key benefits of how class-based views work.

See also

- The *Filtering object lists* recipe
- The *Managing paginated lists* recipe

Providing Open Graph and Twitter Card data

If you want the content of your website to be shared on social networks, you should at least implement Open Graph and Twitter Card meta tags. These meta tags define how the web page is represented in Facebook or Twitter feeds: what title and description will be shown, what image will be set, and what the URL is about. In this recipe, we will prepare the `idea_detail.html` template for social sharing.

Getting ready

Let's continue with the `ideas` app from previous recipes.

How to do it...

Follow these steps to complete the recipe:

1. Make sure to have the `Idea` model created with the picture field and picture version specifications. See the *Creating an app with CRUDL functions* and *Uploading images* recipes for more information.
2. Make sure to have a detail view ready for ideas. See the *Creating an app with CRUDL functions* recipe for information on how to do that.

3. Plug the detail view into the URL configuration. How to do that is described in the *Creating an app with CRUDL functions* recipe.

4. In the settings of your specific environment, define WEBSITE_URL and MEDIA_URL as full URLs of the media files, as in this example:

```
# myproject/settings/dev.py
from ._base import *

DEBUG = True
WEBSITE_URL = "http://127.0.0.1:8000"  # without trailing slash
MEDIA_URL = f"{WEBSITE_URL}/media/"
```

5. In the core app, create a context processor returning the WEBSITE_URL variable from the settings:

```
# myproject/apps/core/context_processors.py
from django.conf import settings

def website_url(request):
    return {
        "WEBSITE_URL": settings.WEBSITE_URL,
    }
```

6. Plug in the context processor in the settings:

```
# myproject/settings/_base.py
TEMPLATES = [
    {
        "BACKEND":
        "django.template.backends.django.DjangoTemplates",
        "DIRS": [os.path.join(BASE_DIR, "myproject", "templates")],
        "APP_DIRS": True,
        "OPTIONS": {
            "context_processors": [
                "django.template.context_processors.debug",
                "django.template.context_processors.request",
                "django.contrib.auth.context_processors.auth",
                "django.contrib.messages.context_processors
                 .messages",
                "django.template.context_processors.media",
                "django.template.context_processors.static",
                "myproject.apps.core.context_processors
                .website_url",
            ]
        },
    }
]
```

7. Create the `idea_detail.html` template with the following content:

```
{# ideas/idea_detail.html #}
{% extends "base.html" %}
{% load i18n %}

{% block meta_tags %}
    <meta property="og:type" content="website" />
    <meta property="og:url" content="{{ WEBSITE_URL }}
    {{ request.path }}" />
    <meta property="og:title" content="{{ idea.translated_title }}"
    />
    {% if idea.picture_social %}
        <meta property="og:image" content=
        "{{ idea.picture_social.url }}" />
        <!-- Next tags are optional but recommended -->
        <meta property="og:image:width" content=
        "{{ idea.picture_social.width }}" />
        <meta property="og:image:height" content=
        "{{ idea.picture_social.height }}" />
    {% endif %}
    <meta property="og:description" content=
    "{{ idea.translated_content }}" />
    <meta property="og:site_name" content="MyProject" />
    <meta property="og:locale" content="{{ LANGUAGE_CODE }}" />

    <meta name="twitter:card" content="summary_large_image">
    <meta name="twitter:site" content="@DjangoTricks">
    <meta name="twitter:creator" content="@archatas">
    <meta name="twitter:url" content="{{ WEBSITE_URL }}
    {{ request.path }}">
    <meta name="twitter:title" content=
    "{{ idea.translated_title }}">
    <meta name="twitter:description" content=
    "{{ idea.translated_content }}">
    {% if idea.picture_social %}
        <meta name="twitter:image" content=
        "{{ idea.picture_social.url }}">
    {% endif %}
{% endblock %}


{% block content %}
    <a href="{% url "ideas:idea_list" %}">
    {% trans "List of ideas" %}</a>
    <h1>
        {% blocktrans trimmed with title=idea.translated_title %}
            Idea "{{ title }}"
```

```
            {% endblocktrans %}
        </h1>
        <img src="{{ idea.picture_large.url }}" alt="" />
        {{ idea.translated_content|linebreaks|urlize }}
        <p>
            {% for category in idea.categories.all %}
                <span class="badge badge-pill badge-info">
                {{ category.translated_title }}</span>
            {% endfor %}
        </p>
        <a href="{% url 'ideas:change_idea' pk=idea.pk %}"
         class="btn btn-primary">{% trans "Change this idea" %}</a>
        <a href="{% url 'ideas:delete_idea' pk=idea.pk %}"
         class="btn btn-danger">{% trans "Delete this idea" %}</a>
    {% endblock %}
```

How it works...

Open Graph tags are meta tags with special names starting with `og:` and Twitter card tags are meta tags with special names starting with `twitter:`. These meta tags define the URL, title, description, and image of the current page, site name, author, and locale. It is important to provide full URLs there; the path alone would be not enough.

We use the `picture_social` image version which has the optimal dimensions for social networks: 1024 × 512 px.

You can validate your Open Graph implementation at `https://developers.facebook.com/tools/debug/sharing/`.

Twitter Card implementation can be validated at `https://cards-dev.twitter.com/validator`.

See also

- The *Creating an app with CRUDL functions* recipe
- The *Uploading images* recipe
- The *Providing schema.org vocabularies* recipe

Providing schema.org vocabularies

It is important to have semantic markup for **Search Engine Optimization** (**SEO**). But to improve search engine rankings even more, it is beneficial to provide structured data according to schema.org vocabularies. Many applications from Google, Microsoft, Pinterest, Yandex, and others use schema.org structures to create rich extensible experiences such as special consistent-looking cards in the search results for events, movies, authors, and so on.

There are several encodings, including RDFa, Microdata, and JSON-LD, that can be used to create schema.org vocabularies. In this recipe, we will prepare structured data for the Idea model in JSON-LD format, which is preferred and recommended by Google.

Getting ready

Let's install the django-json-ld package into your project's virtual environment (and include it in requirements/_base.txt):

```
(env)$ pip install django-json-ld==0.0.4
```

Put "django_json_ld" under INSTALLED_APPS in the settings:

```
# myproject/settings/_base.py
INSTALLED_APPS = [
    # other apps...
    "django_json_ld",
]
```

How to do it...

Follow these steps to complete the recipe:

1. Add the structured_data property with the following content to the Idea model:

   ```
   # myproject/apps/ideas/models.py
   from django.db import models
   from django.utils.translation import gettext_lazy as _

   from myproject.apps.core.models import (
   CreationModificationDateBase, UrlBase )


   class Idea(CreationModificationDateBase, UrlBase):
   ```

```python
# attributes, fields, properties, and methods...

@property
def structured_data(self):
    from django.utils.translation import get_language

    lang_code = get_language()
    data = {
        "@type": "CreativeWork",
        "name": self.translated_title,
        "description": self.translated_content,
        "inLanguage": lang_code,
    }
    if self.author:
        data["author"] = {
            "@type": "Person",
            "name": self.author.get_full_name() or
             self.author.username,
        }
    if self.picture:
        data["image"] = self.picture_social.url
    return data
```

2. Modify the `idea_detail.html` template:

```django
{# ideas/idea_detail.html #}
{% extends "base.html" %}
{% load i18n json_ld %}

{% block meta_tags %}
    {# Open Graph and Twitter Card meta tags here... #}

    {% render_json_ld idea.structured_data %}
{% endblock %}


{% block content %}
    <a href="{% url "ideas:idea_list" %}">
     {% trans "List of ideas" %}</a>
    <h1>
        {% blocktrans trimmed with title=idea.translated_title %}
            Idea "{{ title }}"
        {% endblocktrans %}
    </h1>
    <img src="{{ idea.picture_large.url }}" alt="" />
    {{ idea.translated_content|linebreaks|urlize }}
    <p>
        {% for category in idea.categories.all %}
```

```
                    <span class="badge badge-pill badge-info">
                        {{ category.translated_title }}</span>
                {% endfor %}
            </p>
            <a href="{% url 'ideas:change_idea' pk=idea.pk %}"
             class="btn btn-primary">{% trans "Change this idea" %}</a>
            <a href="{% url 'ideas:delete_idea' pk=idea.pk %}"
             class="btn btn-danger">{% trans "Delete this idea" %}</a>
        {% endblock %}
```

How it works...

The `{% render_json_ld %}` template tag will render the script tag similar to this:

```
<script type=application/ld+json>{"@type": "CreativeWork", "author":
{"@type": "Person", "name": "admin"}, "description": "Lots of African
countries have not enough water. Dig a water channel throughout Africa to
provide water to people who have no access to it.", "image":
"http://127.0.0.1:8000/media/CACHE/images/ideas/2019/09/b919eec5-c077-41f0-
afb4-35f221ab550c_bOFBDgv/9caa5e61fc832f65ff6382f3d482807a.jpg",
"inLanguage": "en", "name": "Dig a water channel throughout
Africa"}</script>
```

The `structured_data` property returns a nested dictionary according to the schema.org vocabularies that are well understood by most popular search engines.

You can decide which vocabularies to apply to your models by checking the official documentation at `https://schema.org/docs/schemas.html`.

See also

- The *Creating a model mixin to take care of meta tags* recipe in `Chapter 2`, *Models and Database Structure*
- The *Creating an app with CRUDL functions* recipe
- The *Uploading images* recipe
- The *Providing Open Graph and Twitter Card data* recipe

Generating PDF documents

Django views allow you to create much more than just HTML pages. You can create files of any type. For example, in the *Exposing settings in JavaScript* recipe in `Chapter 4`, *Templates and JavaScript*, our view provides its output as a JavaScript file rather than HTML. You can also create PDF documents for invoices, tickets, receipts, booking confirmations, and so on. In this recipe, we will show you how to generate handouts to print for each idea from the database. We are going to use the **WeasyPrint** library to make PDF documents out of HTML templates.

Getting ready

WeasyPrint depends on several libraries that you need to install on your computer. On macOS, you can install them with Homebrew using this command:

```
$ brew install python3 cairo pango gdk-pixbuf libffi
```

Then, you can install WeasyPrint itself in the virtual environment of your project. Also, include it in `requirements/_base.txt`:

```
(env)$ pip install WeasyPrint==48
```

For other operating systems, check the installation instructions at `https://weasyprint.readthedocs.io/en/latest/install.html`.

Also, we'll be using `django-qr-code` to generate a **QR code** linking back to the website for quick access. Let's also install it in the virtual environment (and include it in `requirements/_base.txt`):

```
(env)$ pip install django-qr-code==1.0.0
```

Add "`qr_code`" to `INSTALLED_APPS` in the settings:

```python
# myproject/settings/_base.py
INSTALLED_APPS = [
    # Django apps...
    "qr_code",
]
```

How to do it...

Follow these steps to complete the recipe:

1. Create the view that will generate the PDF document:

```python
# myproject/apps/ideas/views.py
from django.shortcuts import get_object_or_404
from .models import Idea


def idea_handout_pdf(request, pk):
    from django.template.loader import render_to_string
    from django.utils.timezone import now as timezone_now
    from django.utils.text import slugify
    from django.http import HttpResponse

    from weasyprint import HTML
    from weasyprint.fonts import FontConfiguration

    idea = get_object_or_404(Idea, pk=pk)
    context = {"idea": idea}
    html = render_to_string(
        "ideas/idea_handout_pdf.html", context
    )

    response = HttpResponse(content_type="application/pdf")
    response[
        "Content-Disposition"
    ] = "inline; filename={date}-{name}-handout.pdf".format(
        date=timezone_now().strftime("%Y-%m-%d"),
        name=slugify(idea.translated_title),
    )

    font_config = FontConfiguration()
    HTML(string=html).write_pdf(
        response, font_config=font_config
    )

    return response
```

2. Plug this view into the URL configuration:

```python
# myproject/apps/ideas/urls.py
from django.urls import path

from .views import idea_handout_pdf

urlpatterns = [
```

```
# URL configurations...
path(
    "<uuid:pk>/handout/",
    idea_handout_pdf,
    name="idea_handout",
),
]
```

3. Create a template for the PDF document:

```
{# ideas/idea_handout_pdf.html #}
{% extends "base_pdf.html" %}
{% load i18n qr_code %}

{% block content %}
    <h1 class="h3">{% trans "Handout" %}</h1>
    <h2 class="h1">{{ idea.translated_title }}</h2>
    <img src="{{ idea.picture_large.url }}" alt=""
     class="img-responsive w-100" />
    <div class="my-3">{{ idea.translated_content|linebreaks|
     urlize }}</div>
    <p>
        {% for category in idea.categories.all %}
            <span class="badge badge-pill badge-info">
             {{ category.translated_title }}</span>
        {% endfor %}
    </p>
    <h4>{% trans "See more information online:" %}</h4>
    {% qr_from_text idea.get_url size=20 border=0 as svg_code %}
    <img alt="" src="data:image/svg+xml,
     {{ svg_code|urlencode }}" />
    <p class="mt-3 text-break">{{ idea.get_url }}</p>
{% endblock %}
```

4. Also, create the `base_pdf.html` template:

```
{# base_pdf.html #}
<!doctype html>
{% load i18n static %}
<html lang="en">
<head>
    <!-- Required meta tags -->
    <meta charset="utf-8">
    <meta name="viewport" content="width=device-width,
     initial-scale=1, shrink-to-fit=no">

    <!-- Bootstrap CSS -->
    <link rel="stylesheet"
```

```
        href="https://stackpath.bootstrapcdn.com
          /bootstrap/4.3.1/css/bootstrap.min.css"
            integrity="sha384-
              ggOyR0iXCbMQv3Xipma34MD+dH/1fQ784/j6cY
              /iJTQUOhcWr7x9JvoRxT2MZw1T" crossorigin="anonymous">

    <title>{% trans "Hello, World!" %}</title>

    <style>
    @page {
        size: "A4";
        margin: 2.5cm 1.5cm 3.5cm 1.5cm;
    }
    footer {
        position: fixed;
        bottom: -2.5cm;
        width: 100%;
        text-align: center;
        font-size: 10pt;
    }
    footer img {
        height: 1.5cm;
    }
    </style>

    {% block meta_tags %}{% endblock %}
</head>
<body>
    <main class="container">
        {% block content %}
        {% endblock %}
    </main>
    <footer>
        <img alt="" src="data:image/svg+xml,
         {# url-encoded SVG logo goes here #}" />
        <br />
        {% trans "Printed from MyProject" %}
    </footer>
</body>
</html>
```

How it works...

WeasyPrint generates ready-to-print, pixel-perfect documents. Our example of a handout we could give out to an audience at presentations will look similar to this:

Handout

A reality show about people from opposing standpoints trying to solve mutual problems

Wouldn't it make sense to gather people with opposing opinions and try to solve mutual problems together?

  Realistic Helpful Innovative

See more information online:

http://127.0.0.1:8000/en/ideas/92888d4e-502f-4676-9807-2b124f2c4314/

Printed from MyProject

The layout of the document is defined in markup and CSS. WeasyPrint has its own rendering engine. Read more about supported features in the official documentation at: `https://weasyprint.readthedocs.io/en/latest/features.html`.

You can use SVG images, which will be saved as vector graphics, not bitmaps, and therefore will be crispier in the printout. Inline SVGs are not yet supported, but you can use `<img>` tags with a data source or external URL there. In our example, we use SVG images for the QR code and for the logo in the footer.

Let's get through the code of the view. We render the `idea_handout_pdf.html` template with the selected idea as an `html` string. Then, we create an `HttpResponse` object of PDF content type with the filename composed of the current date and slugified idea title. Then, we create WeasyPrint's HTML object with HTML content and write it to the response as if we would write to a file. In addition, we use the `FontConfiguration` object, which allows us to attach and use web fonts from CSS configuration in the layout. Lastly, we return the response object.

See also

- The *Creating an app with CRUDL functions* recipe
- The *Uploading images* recipe
- The *Exposing settings in JavaScript* recipe in `Chapter 4`, *Templates and JavaScript*

Implementing a multilingual search with Haystack and Whoosh

One of the main functionalities of content-driven websites is a full-text search. Haystack is a modular search API that supports the Solr, Elasticsearch, Whoosh, and Xapian search engines. For each model in your project that has to be findable in the search, you need to define an index that will read out the textual information from the models and place it into the backend. In this recipe, you will learn how to set up a search with Haystack and the Python-based Whoosh search engine for a multilingual website.

Getting ready

We are going to use the previously defined `categories` and `ideas` apps.

Make sure you have installed `django-haystack` and `Whoosh` in your virtual environment (and include them in `requirements/_base.txt`):

```
(env)$ pip install django-haystack==2.8.1
(env)$ pip install Whoosh==2.7.4
```

How to do it...

Let's set up a multilingual search with Haystack and Whoosh by executing the following steps:

1. Create a `search` app that will contain `MultilingualWhooshEngine` and search indexes for our ideas. The search engine will live in the `multilingual_whoosh_backend.py` file:

```
# myproject/apps/search/multilingual_whoosh_backend.py
from django.conf import settings
from django.utils import translation
from haystack.backends.whoosh_backend import (
    WhooshSearchBackend,
    WhooshSearchQuery,
    WhooshEngine,
)
from haystack import connections
from haystack.constants import DEFAULT_ALIAS


class MultilingualWhooshSearchBackend(WhooshSearchBackend):
    def update(self, index, iterable, commit=True,
      language_specific=False):
        if not language_specific and self.connection_alias ==
          "default":
            current_language = (translation.get_language() or
              settings.LANGUAGE_CODE)[
                :2
            ]
            for lang_code, lang_name in settings.LANGUAGES:
                lang_code_underscored = lang_code.replace("-", "_")
                using = f"default_{lang_code_underscored}"
                translation.activate(lang_code)
                backend = connections[using].get_backend()
```

```
                    backend.update(index, iterable, commit,
                        language_specific=True)
                translation.activate(current_language)
            elif language_specific:
                super().update(index, iterable, commit)


    class MultilingualWhooshSearchQuery(WhooshSearchQuery):
        def __init__(self, using=DEFAULT_ALIAS):
            lang_code_underscored =
            translation.get_language().replace("-", "_")
            using = f"default_{lang_code_underscored}"
            super().__init__(using=using)


    class MultilingualWhooshEngine(WhooshEngine):
        backend = MultilingualWhooshSearchBackend
        query = MultilingualWhooshSearchQuery
```

2. Let's create the search indexes, as follows:

```
# myproject/apps/search/search_indexes.py
from haystack import indexes

from myproject.apps.ideas.models import Idea


class IdeaIndex(indexes.SearchIndex, indexes.Indexable):
    text = indexes.CharField(document=True)

    def get_model(self):
        return Idea

    def index_queryset(self, using=None):
        """
        Used when the entire index for model is updated.
        """
        return self.get_model().objects.all()

    def prepare_text(self, idea):
        """
        Called for each language / backend
        """
        fields = [
            idea.translated_title, idea.translated_content
        ]
        fields += [
            category.translated_title
```

```
                  for category in idea.categories.all()
          ]
          return "\n".join(fields)
```

3. Configure the settings to use `MultilingualWhooshEngine`:

```python
# myproject/settings/_base.py
import os
BASE_DIR = os.path.dirname(os.path.dirname(os.path.dirname(
    os.path.abspath(__file__)
)))

#...

INSTALLED_APPS = [
    # contributed
    # ...
    # third-party
    # ...
    "haystack",
    # local
    "myproject.apps.core",
    "myproject.apps.categories",
    "myproject.apps.ideas",
    "myproject.apps.search",
]

LANGUAGE_CODE = "en"

# All official languages of European Union
LANGUAGES = [
    ("bg", "Bulgarian"),
    ("hr", "Croatian"),
    ("cs", "Czech"),
    ("da", "Danish"),
    ("nl", "Dutch"),
    ("en", "English"),
    ("et", "Estonian"),
    ("fi", "Finnish"),
    ("fr", "French"),
    ("de", "German"),
    ("el", "Greek"),
    ("hu", "Hungarian"),
    ("ga", "Irish"),
    ("it", "Italian"),
    ("lv", "Latvian"),
    ("lt", "Lithuanian"),
    ("mt", "Maltese"),
```

```
        ("pl", "Polish"),
        ("pt", "Portuguese"),
        ("ro", "Romanian"),
        ("sk", "Slovak"),
        ("sl", "Slovene"),
        ("es", "Spanish"),
        ("sv", "Swedish"),
    ]

HAYSTACK_CONNECTIONS = {}
for lang_code, lang_name in LANGUAGES:
  lang_code_underscored = lang_code.replace("-", "_")
  HAYSTACK_CONNECTIONS[f"default_{lang_code_underscored}"] = {
  "ENGINE":
  "myproject.apps.search.multilingual_whoosh_backend
   .MultilingualWhooshEngine",
  "PATH": os.path.join(BASE_DIR, "tmp",
   f"whoosh_index_{lang_code_underscored}"),
  }
  lang_code_underscored = LANGUAGE_CODE.replace("-", "_")
  HAYSTACK_CONNECTIONS["default"] = HAYSTACK_CONNECTIONS[
  f"default_{lang_code_underscored}"
  ]
```

4. Add a path to the URL rules:

```
# myproject/urls.py
from django.contrib import admin
from django.conf.urls.i18n import i18n_patterns
from django.urls import include, path
from django.conf import settings
from django.conf.urls.static import static
from django.shortcuts import redirect


urlpatterns = i18n_patterns(
    path("", lambda request: redirect("ideas:idea_list")),
    path("admin/", admin.site.urls),
    path("accounts/", include("django.contrib.auth.urls")),
    path("ideas/", include(("myproject.apps.ideas.urls", "ideas"),
    namespace="ideas")),
    path("search/", include("haystack.urls")),
)
urlpatterns += static(settings.STATIC_URL,
document_root=settings.STATIC_ROOT)
urlpatterns += static("/media/", document_root=settings.MEDIA_ROOT)
```

5. We will need a template for the search form and search results, as given here:

```
{# search/search.html #}
{% extends "base.html" %}
{% load i18n %}

{% block sidebar %}
    <form method="get" action="{{ request.path }}">
        <div class="well clearfix">
            {{ form.as_p }}
            <p class="pull-right">
                <button type="submit" class="btn btn-primary">
                {% trans "Search" %}</button>
            </p>
        </div>
    </form>
{% endblock %}

{% block main %}
    {% if query %}
        <h1>{% trans "Search Results" %}</h1>

        {% for result in page.object_list %}
            {% with idea=result.object %}
                <a href="{{ idea.get_url_path }}"
                class="d-block my-3">
                    <div class="card">
                        <img src="{{ idea.picture_thumbnail.url }}"
                        alt="" />
                        <div class="card-body">
                            <p class="card-text">
                            {{ idea.translated_title }}</p>
                        </div>
                    </div>
                </a>
            {% endwith %}
        {% empty %}
            <p>{% trans "No results found." %}</p>
        {% endfor %}

        {% include "misc/includes/pagination.html" with
        object_list=page %}
    {% endif %}
{% endblock %}
```

6. Add a pagination template at `misc/includes/pagination.html` just like in the *Managing paginated lists* recipe.

7. Call the `rebuild_index` management command to index the database data and prepare the full-text search to be used:

```
(env)$ python manage.py rebuild_index --noinput
```

How it works...

`MultilingualWhooshEngine` specifies two custom properties:

- `backend` points to `MultilingualWhooshSearchBackend`, which ensures that the items will be indexed for each language given in the LANGUAGES setting and put under the associated Haystack index location defined in HAYSTACK_CONNECTIONS.

- `query` references `MultilingualWhooshSearchQuery`, whose responsibility is to ensure that, when searching for keywords, the Haystack connection specific to the current language will be used.

Each index has a `text` field, where full text from a specific language of a model will be stored. The model for the index is determined by the `get_model()` method, the `index_queryset()` method defines what QuerySet to index, and the content to search within is defined as a newline-separated string in the `prepare_text()` method.

For the template, we have incorporated a few elements of Bootstrap 4 using the out-of-the-box rendering capabilities for forms. This might be enhanced using an approach such as explained in the *Creating a form layout with django-crispy-forms* recipe from earlier in this chapter.

The final search page will have the form in the sidebar and the search results in the main columns and will look similar to the following:

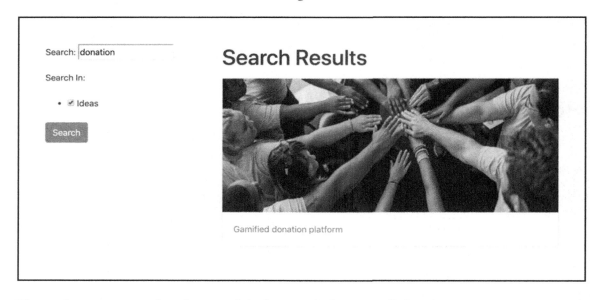

The easiest way to update the search index regularly is to call the `rebuild_index` management command, perhaps by a cron job every night. To learn about it, check the *Setting up cron jobs for regular tasks* recipe in `Chapter 13`, *Maintenance.*

See also

- The *Creating a form layout with django-crispy-forms* recipe
- The *Managing paginated lists* recipe
- The *Setting up cron jobs for regular tasks* recipe in `Chapter 13`, *Maintenance*

Implementing a multilingual search with Elasticsearch DSL

Haystack with Whoosh is a good stable search mechanism that requires just some Python modules, but for better performance, we recommend using Elasticsearch. In this recipe, we'll show you how to use it for a multilingual search.

Getting ready

To start with, let's install the Elasticsearch server. On macOS, you can do that with Homebrew:

```
$ brew install elasticsearch
```

At the time of writing, the latest stable version of Elasticsearch on Homebrew is 6.8.2.

Install `django-elasticsearch-dsl` in your virtual environment (and include it in `requirements/_base.txt`):

```
(env)$ pip install django-elasticsearch-dsl==6.4.1
```

 Note that it is important to install a matching `django-elasticsearch-dsl` version. Otherwise, you will get errors when trying to connect to the Elasticsearch server or building an index. You can see a version compatibility table at `https://github.com/sabricot/django-elasticsearch-dsl`.

How to do it...

Let's set up a multilingual search with Elasticsearch DSL by executing the following steps:

1. Modify the settings file and add `"django_elasticsearch_dsl"` to `INSTALLED_APPS` and set the `ELASTICSEARCH_DSL` setting as follows:

```python
# myproject/settings/_base.py

INSTALLED_APPS = [
    # other apps...
    "django_elasticsearch_dsl",
]

ELASTICSEARCH_DSL={
    'default': {
        'hosts': 'localhost:9200'
    },
}
```

2. In the `ideas` app, create a `documents.py` file with `IdeaDocument` for the idea search index, as follows:

```python
# myproject/apps/ideas/documents.py
from django.conf import settings
from django.utils.translation import get_language, activate
from django.db import models

from django_elasticsearch_dsl import fields
from django_elasticsearch_dsl.documents import (
    Document,
    model_field_class_to_field_class,
)
from django_elasticsearch_dsl.registries import registry

from myproject.apps.categories.models import Category
from .models import Idea

def _get_url_path(instance, language):
    current_language = get_language()
    activate(language)
    url_path = instance.get_url_path()
    activate(current_language)
    return url_path


@registry.register_document
class IdeaDocument(Document):
    author = fields.NestedField(
        properties={
            "first_name": fields.StringField(),
            "last_name": fields.StringField(),
            "username": fields.StringField(),
            "pk": fields.IntegerField(),
        },
        include_in_root=True,
    )
    title_bg = fields.StringField()
    title_hr = fields.StringField()
    # other title_* fields for each language in the LANGUAGES
        setting...
    content_bg = fields.StringField()
    content_hr = fields.StringField()
    # other content_* fields for each language in the LANGUAGES
        setting...

    picture_thumbnail_url = fields.StringField()
```

```python
categories = fields.NestedField(
    properties=dict(
        pk=fields.IntegerField(),
        title_bg=fields.StringField(),
        title_hr=fields.StringField(),
        # other title_* definitions for each language in the
            LANGUAGES setting...
    ),
    include_in_root=True,
)

url_path_bg = fields.StringField()
url_path_hr = fields.StringField()
# other url_path_* fields for each language in the LANGUAGES
    setting...

class Index:
    name = "ideas"
    settings = {"number_of_shards": 1, "number_of_replicas": 0}

class Django:
    model = Idea
    # The fields of the model you want to be indexed in
        Elasticsearch
    fields = ["uuid", "rating"]
    related_models = [Category]

def get_instances_from_related(self, related_instance):
    if isinstance(related_instance, Category):
        category = related_instance
        return category.category_ideas.all()
```

3. Add `prepare_*` methods to `IdeaDocument` to prepare data for the index:

```python
def prepare(self, instance):
    lang_code_underscored = settings.LANGUAGE_CODE.replace
    ("-", "_")
    setattr(instance, f"title_{lang_code_underscored}",
     instance.title)
    setattr(instance, f"content_{lang_code_underscored}",
     instance.content)
    setattr(
        instance,
        f"url_path_{lang_code_underscored}",
        _get_url_path(instance=instance,
            language=settings.LANGUAGE_CODE),
    )
    for lang_code, lang_name in
```

```python
        settings.LANGUAGES_EXCEPT_THE_DEFAULT:
            lang_code_underscored = lang_code.replace("-", "_")
            setattr(instance, f"title_{lang_code_underscored}",
             "")
            setattr(instance, f"content_{lang_code_underscored}",
             "")
            translations = instance.translations.filter(language=
            lang_code).first()
            if translations:
                setattr(instance, f"title_{lang_code_underscored}",
                 translations.title)
                setattr(
                    instance, f"content_{lang_code_underscored}",
                     translations.content
                )
            setattr(
                instance,
                f"url_path_{lang_code_underscored}",
                _get_url_path(instance=instance,
                 language=lang_code),
            )
        data = super().prepare(instance=instance)
        return data

    def prepare_picture_thumbnail_url(self, instance):
        if not instance.picture:
            return ""
        return instance.picture_thumbnail.url

    def prepare_author(self, instance):
        author = instance.author
        if not author:
            return []
        author_dict = {
            "pk": author.pk,
            "first_name": author.first_name,
            "last_name": author.last_name,
            "username": author.username,
        }
        return [author_dict]

    def prepare_categories(self, instance):
        categories = []
        for category in instance.categories.all():
            category_dict = {"pk": category.pk}
            lang_code_underscored =
             settings.LANGUAGE_CODE.replace("-", "_")
            category_dict[f"title_{lang_code_underscored}"] =
```

```
            category.title
        for lang_code, lang_name in
         settings.LANGUAGES_EXCEPT_THE_DEFAULT:
            lang_code_underscored = lang_code.replace("-", "_")
            category_dict[f"title_{lang_code_underscored}"] =
             ""
            translations =
             category.translations.filter(language=
              lang_code).first()
            if translations:
                category_dict[f"title_{lang_code_underscored}"]
                = translations.title
        categories.append(category_dict)
    return categories
```

4. Add some properties and methods to `IdeaDocument` to return translated content from the indexed documents:

```python
@property
def translated_title(self):
    lang_code_underscored = get_language().replace("-", "_")
    return getattr(self, f"title_{lang_code_underscored}", "")

@property
def translated_content(self):
    lang_code_underscored = get_language().replace("-", "_")
    return getattr(self, f"content_{lang_code_underscored}",
     "")

def get_url_path(self):
    lang_code_underscored = get_language().replace("-", "_")
    return getattr(self, f"url_path_{lang_code_underscored}",
     "")

def get_categories(self):
    lang_code_underscored = get_language().replace("-", "_")
    return [
        dict(
            translated_title=category_dict[f"title_{lang_
             code_underscored}"],
            **category_dict,
        )
        for category_dict in self.categories
    ]
```

5. One more thing to do in the `documents.py` file is to monkey-patch the `UUIDField` mappings because, by default, it is not yet supported by Django Elasticsearch DSL. To do that, insert this line just after the imports section:

```
model_field_class_to_field_class[models.UUIDField] =
fields.TextField
```

6. Create `IdeaSearchForm` under `forms.py` in your `ideas` app:

```
# myproject/apps/ideas/forms.py
from django import forms
from django.utils.translation import ugettext_lazy as _

from crispy_forms import helper, layout


class IdeaSearchForm(forms.Form):
    q = forms.CharField(label=_("Search for"), required=False)

    def __init__(self, request, *args, **kwargs):
        self.request = request
        super().__init__(*args, **kwargs)

        self.helper = helper.FormHelper()
        self.helper.form_action = self.request.path
        self.helper.form_method = "GET"
        self.helper.layout = layout.Layout(
            layout.Field("q", css_class="input-block-level"),
            layout.Submit("search", _("Search")),
        )
```

7. Add the view for searching with Elasticsearch:

```
# myproject/apps/ideas/views.py
from django.shortcuts import render
from django.conf import settings
from django.core.paginator import EmptyPage, PageNotAnInteger,
Paginator
from django.utils.functional import LazyObject

from .forms import IdeaSearchForm


PAGE_SIZE = getattr(settings, "PAGE_SIZE", 24)


class SearchResults(LazyObject):
    def __init__(self, search_object):
```

```python
        self._wrapped = search_object

    def __len__(self):
        return self._wrapped.count()

    def __getitem__(self, index):
        search_results = self._wrapped[index]
        if isinstance(index, slice):
            search_results = list(search_results)
        return search_results


def search_with_elasticsearch(request):
    from .documents import IdeaDocument
    from elasticsearch_dsl.query import Q

    form = IdeaSearchForm(request, data=request.GET)

    search = IdeaDocument.search()

    if form.is_valid():
        value = form.cleaned_data["q"]
        lang_code_underscored = request.LANGUAGE_CODE.replace("-",
         "_")
        search = search.query(
            Q("match_phrase", **{f"title_{
             lang_code_underscored}":
             value})
            | Q("match_phrase", **{f"content_{
               lang_code_underscored}": value})
            | Q(
                "nested",
                path="categories",
                query=Q(
                    "match_phrase",
                    **{f"categories__title_{
                     lang_code_underscored}": value},
                ),
            )
        )
    search_results = SearchResults(search)

    paginator = Paginator(search_results, PAGE_SIZE)
    page_number = request.GET.get("page")
    try:
        page = paginator.page(page_number)
    except PageNotAnInteger:
        # If page is not an integer, show first page.
```

```
                page = paginator.page(1)
            except EmptyPage:
                # If page is out of range, show last existing page.
                page = paginator.page(paginator.num_pages)

            context = {"form": form, "object_list": page}
            return render(request, "ideas/idea_search.html", context)
```

8. Create an `idea_search.html` template for the search form and search results:

```
{# ideas/idea_search.html #}
{% extends "base.html" %}
{% load i18n crispy_forms_tags %}

{% block sidebar %}
    {% crispy form %}
{% endblock %}

{% block main %}
    <h1>{% trans "Search Results" %}</h1>
    {% if object_list %}
        {% for idea in object_list %}
            <a href="{{ idea.get_url_path }}" class="d-block my-3">
                <div class="card">
                    <img src="{{ idea.picture_thumbnail_url }}"
                        alt="" />
                    <div class="card-body">
                        <p class="card-text">{{ idea.translated_title
                            }}</p>
                    </div>
                </div>
            </a>
        {% endfor %}
        {% include "misc/includes/pagination.html" %}
    {% else %}
        <p>{% trans "No ideas found." %}</p>
    {% endif %}
{% endblock %}
```

9. Add a pagination template at `misc/includes/pagination.html` just like in the *Managing paginated lists* recipe.

10. Call the `search_index --rebuild` management command to index the database data and prepare the full-text search to be used:

```
(env)$ python manage.py search_index --rebuild
```

How it works...

Django Elasticsearch DSL documents are similar to model forms. There you define which fields of the model to save to the index that later will be used for the search queries. In our `IdeaDocument` example, we are saving the UUID, rating, author, categories, titles, contents, and URL paths in all languages and a picture thumbnail URL. The `Index` class defines the settings of the Elasticsearch index for this document. The `Django` class defines where to populate the index fields from. There is the `related_models` setting that tells after which model changes to also update this index. In our case, it is a `Category` model. Note that with `django-elasticsearch-dsl`, the indexes will be updated automatically whenever the models are saved. That is done using signals.

The `get_instances_from_related()` method tells how to retrieve the `Idea` model instances when a `Category` instance is changed.

The `prepare()` and `prepare_*()` methods of `IdeaDocument` tell where to take the data from and how to save the data for specific fields. For example, we are reading the data for `title_lt` from the `title` field of the `IdeaTranslations` model where the `language` field equals `"lt"`.

The last properties and methods of the `IdeaDocument` are there to use for retrieval of information from the index in the currently active language.

Then, we have a view with the search form. There is a query field in the form called `q`. When it is submitted, we are searching for the queried word in the title, content, or category's title field of the current language. Then, we wrap the search results with a lazily evaluated `SearchResults` class, so that we could use it with the default Django paginator.

The template of the view will have the search form in the sidebar and the search results in the main column, and it will look something like this:

See also

- The *Creating an app with CRUDL functions* recipe
- The *Implementing a multilingual search with Haystack and Whoosh* recipe
- The *Creating a form layout with django-crispy-forms* recipe
- The *Managing paginated lists* recipe

4
Templates and JavaScript

In this chapter, we will cover the following topics:

- Arranging the base.html template
- Using Django Sekizai
- Exposing settings in JavaScript
- Using HTML5 data attributes
- Providing responsive images(env)$ python manage.py migrate ideas zero
- Implementing a continuous scrolling
- Opening object details in a modal dialog
- Implementing the Like widget
- Uploading images via Ajax

Introduction

Static websites are useful for static content, such as traditional documentation, online books, and tutorials; however, today, most interactive web apps and platforms must have dynamic components if they want to stand out and give visitors the best user experience. In this chapter, you will learn how to use JavaScript and CSS together with Django templates. We will use the Bootstrap 4 frontend framework for responsive layouts and the jQuery JavaScript framework for productive scripting.

Technical requirements

As before, to work with the code of this chapter, you will need the latest stable version of Python, MySQL, or PostgreSQL database and a Django project with a virtual environment. Some recipes will require specific Python dependencies. Some of them will require additional JavaScript libraries. You will see the requirements of each recipe later in the chapter.

You can find all the code for this chapter at the `ch04` directory of the GitHub repository at https://github.com/PacktPublishing/Django-3-Web-Development-Cookbook-Fourth-Edition.

Arranging the base.html template

When you start working on templates, one of the first things to do is create the `base.html` boilerplate, which will be extended by most of the page templates in your project. In this recipe, we will demonstrate how to create such a template for multilingual HTML5 websites, with responsiveness in mind.

 Responsive websites are those that provide the same base content to all devices, styled appropriately to the viewport, whether the visitor uses desktop browsers, tablets, or phones. This differs from adaptive websites, where the server attempts to determine the device type based on the user agent, then provides entirely different content, markup, and even functionality depending on how that user agent is categorized.

Getting ready

Create the `templates` directory in your project and set the template directories in the settings to include it, as shown here:

```python
# myproject/settings/_base.py
TEMPLATES = [
    {
        "BACKEND": "django.template.backends.django.DjangoTemplates",
        "DIRS": [os.path.join(BASE_DIR, "myproject", "templates")],
        "APP_DIRS": True,
        "OPTIONS": {
            "context_processors": [
```

```
                "django.template.context_processors.debug",
                "django.template.context_processors.request",
                "django.contrib.auth.context_processors.auth",
                "django.contrib.messages.context_processors.messages",
                "django.template.context_processors.media",
                "django.template.context_processors.static",
            ]
        },
    }
]
```

How to do it...

Go through the following steps:

1. In the root directory of your templates, create a `base.html` file with the
   following content:

```
{# base.html #}
<!doctype html>
{% load i18n static %}
<html lang="en">
<head>
    <meta charset="utf-8" />
    <meta name="viewport" content="width=device-width, initial-
      scale=1, shrink-to-fit=no" />
    <title>{% block head_title %}{% endblock %}</title>
    {% include "misc/includes/favicons.html" %}
    {% block meta_tags %}{% endblock %}

    <link rel="stylesheet"
          href="https://stackpath.bootstrapcdn.com/bootstrap
            /4.3.1/css/bootstrap.min.css"
          integrity="sha384-ggOyR0iXCbMQv3Xipma34MD+dH/1fQ784
            /j6cY/iJTQUOhcWr7x9JvoRxT2MZw1T"
          crossorigin="anonymous" />
    <link rel="stylesheet"
          href="{% static 'site/css/style.css' %}"
          crossorigin="anonymous" />

    {% block css %}{% endblock %}
    {% block extra_head %}{% endblock %}
</head>
<body>
    {% include "misc/includes/header.html" %}
    <div class="container my-5">
```

```
                    {% block content %}
                        <div class="row">
                            <div class="col-lg-4">{% block sidebar %}
                             {% endblock %}</div>
                            <div class="col-lg-8">{% block main %}
                             {% endblock %}</div>
                        </div>
                    {% endblock %}
                </div>
                {% include "misc/includes/footer.html" %}
                <script src="https://code.jquery.com/jquery-3.4.1.min.js"
                        crossorigin="anonymous"></script>
                <script src="https://cdnjs.cloudflare.com/ajax/libs/popper.js
                  /1.14.7/umd/popper.min.js"
                        integrity="sha384-UO2eT0CpHqdSJQ6hJty5KVphtPhzWj
                          9W01clHTMGa3JDZwrnQq4sF86dIHNDz0W1"
                        crossorigin="anonymous"></script>
                <script src="https://stackpath.bootstrapcdn.com/bootstrap
                  /4.3.1/js/bootstrap.min.js"
                        integrity="sha384-JjSmVgyd0p3pXB1rRibZUAYoIIy6OrQ6Vrj
                          IEaFf/nJGzIxFDsf4x0xIM+B07jRM"
                        crossorigin="anonymous"></script>
                {% block js %}{% endblock %}
                {% block extra_body %}{% endblock %}
            </body>
            </html>
```

2. Under `misc/includes`, create a template including all the versions of the favicon:

```
{# misc/includes/favicon.html #}
{% load static %}
<link rel="icon" type="image/png" href="{% static
'site/img/favicon-32x32.png' %}" sizes="32x32"/>
<link rel="icon" type="image/png" href="{% static
'site/img/favicon-16x16.png' %}" sizes="16x16"/>
```

A favicon is a small image that we usually see in the browser tabs, tiles of recently visited websites, and shortcuts on the desktop. You can use one of the online generators to generate different versions of the favicon from a logo for different use cases, browsers, and platforms. Our favorite favicon generators are https://favicomatic.com/ and https://realfavicongenerator.net/.

3. Create the templates `misc/includes/header.html`
   and `misc/includes/footer.html` with your website's header and footer. For
   now, you can just create empty files there.

How it works...

The base template contains the `<head>` and `<body>` sections of the HTML document, with
all the details that are reused on each page of the website. Depending on the web design
requirements, you can have additional base templates for different layouts. For example,
we can add the `base_simple.html` file, which has the same HTML `<head>` section and a
very minimalistic `<body>` section, and this can be used for the login screen, password reset,
or other simple pages. You can have separate base templates for other layouts as well, such
as single-column, two-column, and three-column layouts, where each extends `base.html`
and overwrites the blocks as needed.

Let's look into the details of the `base.html` template that we defined earlier. Here are the
details for the `<head>` section:

- We define UTF-8 as the default encoding to support multilingual content.
- Then, we have the viewport definition that will scale the website in the browser
  to use the full width. This is necessary for small-screen devices that will get
  specific screen layouts created with the Bootstrap frontend framework.
- Of course, there's a customizable website title that is used in the browser tabs and
  search results of search engines.
- Then we have a block for meta tags, that can be used for **search engine
  optimization (SEO)**, Open Graph, and Twitter Cards.
- Then we include favicons of different formats and sizes.
- We include the default Bootstrap and custom website styles. We load the
  Bootstrap CSS, as we want to have responsive layouts, and this will also
  normalize the basic styling for all elements for consistency across browsers.
- And lastly, we have extensible blocks for meta tags, style sheets, and whatever
  else might be necessary for the `<head>` section.

Here are the details for the `<body>` section:

- Firstly, we include the header of the website. That's where you can put your
  logo, website title, and main navigation.
- Then, we have the main container containing a content block placeholder, which
  is to be filled by extending the templates.

- Inside the container, there is the `content` block, which contains the `sidebar` and `main` blocks. In child templates, when we need a layout with a sidebar. We will overwrite the `sidebar` and `main` blocks, but, when we need the full-width content, we will overwrite the `content` block.
- Then, we include the footer of the website. That's where you can have copyright information and links to important meta pages, such as privacy policy, terms of use, contact form, and others.
- We then load the jQuery and Bootstrap scripts. Extensible JavaScript blocks are included here at the end of the `<body>` following the best practices for page-load performance, much like those for the style sheets included in the `<head>`.
- Lastly, we have blocks for additional JavaScript and extra HTML, such as HTML templates for JavaScript or hidden modal dialogs, which we will explore later in this chapter.

The base template that we created is, by no means, a static unchangeable template. You can modify the markup structure, or add the elements you need to it—for example, a template block for body attributes, a snippet for Google Analytics code, common JavaScript files, the Apple touch icon for iPhone bookmarks, Open Graph meta tags, Twitter Card tags, schema.org attributes, and so on. You may also want to define other blocks, depending on the requirements of your project, and maybe even wrap the whole content of the body so that you can overwrite it in a child template.

See also

- The *Using Django Sekizai* recipe
- The *Exposing settings in JavaScript* recipe

Using Django Sekizai

In Django templates, normally you would use template inheritance to overwrite blocks from parent templates to include styles or scripts to the HTML document. This means that every main template of each view should be aware of all content that is inside; however, sometimes it is much more convenient to let the included templates decide what styles and scripts to load. It is possible to do this with Django Sekizai, which we will use in this recipe.

Getting ready

Before we begin with the recipe, follow these steps to get ready:

1. Install `django-classy-tags` and `django-sekizai` to your virtual environment (and add them to the `requirements/_base.txt`):

   ```
   (env)$ pip install -e
   git+https://github.com/divio/django-classy-tags.git@4c94d0354eca160
   0ad2ead9c3c151ad57af398a4#egg=django-classy-tags
   (env)$ pip install django-sekizai==1.0.0
   ```

2. Then add `sekizai` to the installed apps in the settings:

   ```python
   # myproject/settings/_base.py
   INSTALLED_APPS = [
       # ...
       "sekizai",
       # ...
   ]
   ```

3. Next, add the `sekizai` context processor to the template configuration in the settings:

   ```python
   # myproject/settings/_base.py
   TEMPLATES = [
       {
           "BACKEND":
           "django.template.backends.django.DjangoTemplates",
           "DIRS": [os.path.join(BASE_DIR, "myproject", "templates")],
           "APP_DIRS": True,
           "OPTIONS": {
               "context_processors": [
                   "django.template.context_processors.debug",
                   "django.template.context_processors.request",
                   "django.contrib.auth.context_processors.auth",
                   "django.contrib.messages.context_processors
                    .messages",
                   "django.template.context_processors.media",
                   "django.template.context_processors.static",
                   "sekizai.context_processors.sekizai",
               ]
           },
       }
   ]
   ```

How to do it...

Go through the following steps to complete the recipe:

1. At the beginning of the `base.html` template, load the `sekizai_tags` library:

```
{# base.html #}
<!doctype html>
{% load i18n static sekizai_tags %}
```

2. In the same file, at the end of the `<head>` section, add the template tag `{% render_block "css" %}` as follows:

```
{% block css %}{% endblock %}
{% render_block "css" %}
{% block extra_head %}{% endblock %}
</head>
```

3. Then, at the end of the `<body>` section, add the template tag `{% render_block "js" %}` as follows:

```
{% block js %}{% endblock %}
{% render_block "js" %}
{% block extra_body %}{% endblock %}
</body>
```

4. Now, in any included template, when you want to add some styling or JavaScript, use the `{% addtoblock %}` template tags as follows:

```
{% load static sekizai_tags %}

<div>Sample widget</div>

{% addtoblock "css" %}
<link rel="stylesheet" href="{% static 'site/css/sample-widget.css' %}"/>
{% endaddtoblock %}

{% addtoblock "js" %}
<script src="{% static 'site/js/sample-widget.js' %}"></script>
{% endaddtoblock %}
```

How it works...

Django Sekizai works with the templates included by the {% include %} template tag, custom template tags that are rendered with templates, or templates for form widgets. The {% addtoblock %} template tags define the Sekizai block that we want to add HTML content to.

When you add something to a Sekizai block, django-sekizai takes care of including it there only once. This means that you can have multiple included widgets of the same type, but their CSS and JavaScript will only be loaded and executed once.

See also

- The *Implementing the Like widget* recipe
- The *Uploading images via Ajax* recipe

Exposing settings in JavaScript

Django projects have their configuration set in the settings files, such as myproject/settings/dev.py for the development environment; we described this in the *Configuring settings for development, testing, staging, and production environments* recipe in Chapter 1, *Getting Started with Django 3.0*. Some of these configuration values may also be useful for functionality in the browser, and so they will also need to be set in JavaScript. We want a single location to define our project settings, so, in this recipe, we will see how we can pass some configuration values from the Django server to the browser.

Getting ready

Make sure that you have the request context processor included in the TEMPLATES['OPTIONS']['context_processors'] setting, as follows:

```
# myproject/settings/_base.py
TEMPLATES = [
    {
        "BACKEND": "django.template.backends.django.DjangoTemplates",
        "DIRS": [os.path.join(BASE_DIR, "myproject", "templates")],
        "APP_DIRS": True,
        "OPTIONS": {
            "context_processors": [
```

```
                     "django.template.context_processors.debug",
                     "django.template.context_processors.request",
                     "django.contrib.auth.context_processors.auth",
                     "django.contrib.messages.context_processors.messages",
                     "django.template.context_processors.media",
                     "django.template.context_processors.static",
                     "sekizai.context_processors.sekizai",
                 ]
            },
        }
    ]
```

You should also create the `core` app, if you haven't done so already, and place it under `INSTALLED_APPS` in the settings:

```
INSTALLED_APPS = [
    # ...
    "myproject.apps.core",
    # ...
]
```

How to do it...

Follow these steps to create and include the JavaScript settings:

1. In the `views.py` of your `core` app, create a `js_settings()` view that returns a response of the JavaScript content type, as shown in the following code:

```
# myproject/apps/core/views.py
import json
from django.http import HttpResponse
from django.template import Template, Context
from django.views.decorators.cache import cache_page
from django.conf import settings

JS_SETTINGS_TEMPLATE = """
window.settings = JSON.parse('{{ json_data|escapejs }}');
"""

@cache_page(60 * 15)
def js_settings(request):
    data = {
        "MEDIA_URL": settings.MEDIA_URL,
        "STATIC_URL": settings.STATIC_URL,
        "DEBUG": settings.DEBUG,
        "LANGUAGES": settings.LANGUAGES,
```

```
            "DEFAULT_LANGUAGE_CODE": settings.LANGUAGE_CODE,
            "CURRENT_LANGUAGE_CODE": request.LANGUAGE_CODE,
    }
    json_data = json.dumps(data)
    template = Template(JS_SETTINGS_TEMPLATE)
    context = Context({"json_data": json_data})
    response = HttpResponse(
        content=template.render(context),
        content_type="application/javascript; charset=UTF-8",
    )
    return response
```

2. Plug in this view into the URL configuration:

```
# myproject/urls.py
from django.conf.urls.i18n import i18n_patterns
from django.urls import include, path
from django.conf import settings
from django.conf.urls.static import static

from myproject.apps.core import views as core_views


urlpatterns = i18n_patterns(
    # other URL configuration rules...
    path("js-settings/", core_views.js_settings,
     name="js_settings"),
)

urlpatterns += static(settings.STATIC_URL,
document_root=settings.STATIC_ROOT)
urlpatterns += static("/media/", document_root=settings.MEDIA_ROOT)
```

3. Load the JavaScript-based view in the frontend by adding it at the end of the `base.html` template:

```
{# base.html #}

    {# ... #}

    <script src="{% url 'js_settings' %}"></script>
    {% block js %}{% endblock %}
    {% render_block "js" %}
    {% block extra_body %}{% endblock %}
</body>
</html>
```

4. Now we can access the specified settings in any JavaScript file as follows:

```
if (window.settings.DEBUG) {
    console.warn('The website is running in DEBUG mode!');
}
```

How it works...

In the `js_settings` view, we built a dictionary of settings that we want to pass to the browser, converted the dictionary to JSON, and rendered a template for a JavaScript file that parses the JSON and assigns the result to the `window.settings` variable. By converting a dictionary to a JSON string and parsing it in the JavaScript file, we can be sure that we won't have any problems with trailing commas after the last element—that's allowed in Python, but invalid in JavaScript.

The rendered JavaScript file will look like this:

```
# http://127.0.0.1:8000/en/js-settings/
window.settings = JSON.parse('{\u0022MEDIA_URL\u0022:
\u0022http://127.0.0.1:8000/media/\u0022, \u0022STATIC_URL\u0022:
\u0022/static/20191001004640/\u0022, \u0022DEBUG\u0022: true,
\u0022LANGUAGES\u0022: [[\u0022bg\u0022, \u0022Bulgarian\u0022],
[\u0022hr\u0022, \u0022Croatian\u0022], [\u0022cs\u0022,
\u0022Czech\u0022], [\u0022da\u0022, \u0022Danish\u0022], [\u0022nl\u0022,
\u0022Dutch\u0022], [\u0022en\u0022, \u0022English\u0022], [\u0022et\u0022,
\u0022Estonian\u0022], [\u0022fi\u0022, \u0022Finnish\u0022],
[\u0022fr\u0022, \u0022French\u0022], [\u0022de\u0022, \u0022German\u0022],
[\u0022el\u0022, \u0022Greek\u0022], [\u0022hu\u0022,
\u0022Hungarian\u0022], [\u0022ga\u0022, \u0022Irish\u0022],
[\u0022it\u0022, \u0022Italian\u0022], [\u0022lv\u0022,
\u0022Latvian\u0022], [\u0022lt\u0022, \u0022Lithuanian\u0022],
[\u0022mt\u0022, \u0022Maltese\u0022], [\u0022pl\u0022,
\u0022Polish\u0022], [\u0022pt\u0022, \u0022Portuguese\u0022],
[\u0022ro\u0022, \u0022Romanian\u0022], [\u0022sk\u0022,
\u0022Slovak\u0022], [\u0022sl\u0022, \u0022Slovene\u0022],
[\u0022es\u0022, \u0022Spanish\u0022], [\u0022sv\u0022,
\u0022Swedish\u0022]], \u0022DEFAULT_LANGUAGE_CODE\u0022: \u0022en\u0022,
\u0022CURRENT_LANGUAGE_CODE\u0022: \u0022en\u0022}');
```

See also

- The *Configuring settings for development, testing, staging, and production environments* recipe in `Chapter 1`, *Getting Started with Django 3.0*
- The *Arranging the base.html template* recipe
- The *Using HTML5 data attributes* recipe

Using HTML5 data attributes

HTML5 introduces `data-*` attributes for passing data about a specific HTML element from the webserver to JavaScript and CSS. In this recipe, we will see a way to attach data efficiently from Django to custom HTML5 data attributes and then describe how to read the data from JavaScript with a practical example: we will render a Google Map with a marker at a specified geographical position; when we click on the marker, we will display the address in an information window.

Getting ready

To get ready, follow these steps:

1. Use a PostgreSQL database with a PostGIS extension for this and the following chapters. To see how to install the PostGIS extension, look at the official documentation at `https://docs.djangoproject.com/en/2.2/ref/contrib/gis/install/postgis/`.

2. Make sure that you use the `postgis` database backend for the Django project:

```python
# myproject/settings/_base.py
DATABASES = {
    "default": {
        "ENGINE": "django.contrib.gis.db.backends.postgis",
        "NAME": get_secret("DATABASE_NAME"),
        "USER": get_secret("DATABASE_USER"),
        "PASSWORD": get_secret("DATABASE_PASSWORD"),
        "HOST": "localhost",
        "PORT": "5432",
    }
}
```

3. Create a `locations` app with a `Location` model. It will contain a UUID primary key, character fields for the name, street address, city, country, and postal code, a PostGIS-related `Geoposition` field, and the `Description` text field:

```python
# myproject/apps/locations/models.py
import uuid
from collections import namedtuple
from django.contrib.gis.db import models
from django.urls import reverse
from django.conf import settings
from django.utils.translation import gettext_lazy as _
from myproject.apps.core.models import (
    CreationModificationDateBase, UrlBase
)

COUNTRY_CHOICES = getattr(settings, "COUNTRY_CHOICES", [])

Geoposition = namedtuple("Geoposition", ["longitude", "latitude"])

class Location(CreationModificationDateBase, UrlBase):
    uuid = models.UUIDField(primary_key=True, default=None,
      editable=False)
    name = models.CharField(_("Name"), max_length=200)
    description = models.TextField(_("Description"))
    street_address = models.CharField(_("Street address"),
      max_length=255, blank=True)
    street_address2 = models.CharField(
        _("Street address (2nd line)"), max_length=255, blank=True
    )
    postal_code = models.CharField(_("Postal code"),
      max_length=255, blank=True)
    city = models.CharField(_("City"), max_length=255,
      blank=True)
    country = models.CharField(
        _("Country"), choices=COUNTRY_CHOICES, max_length=255,
            blank=True
    )
    geoposition = models.PointField(blank=True, null=True)

    class Meta:
        verbose_name = _("Location")
        verbose_name_plural = _("Locations")

    def __str__(self):
        return self.name
```

```
def get_url_path(self):
    return reverse("locations:location_detail", kwargs={"pk":
     self.pk})
```

4. Overwrite the `save()` method to generate a unique UUID field value when creating a location:

```
def save(self, *args, **kwargs):
    if self.pk is None:
        self.pk = uuid.uuid4()
    super().save(*args, **kwargs)
```

5. Create methods to get the full address of the location in one string:

```
def get_field_value(self, field_name):
    if isinstance(field_name, str):
        value = getattr(self, field_name)
        if callable(value):
            value = value()
        return value
    elif isinstance(field_name, (list, tuple)):
        field_names = field_name
        values = []
        for field_name in field_names:
            value = self.get_field_value(field_name)
            if value:
                values.append(value)
        return " ".join(values)
    return ""

def get_full_address(self):
    field_names = [
        "name",
        "street_address",
        "street_address",
        ("postal_code", "city"),
        "get_country_display",
    ]
    full_address = []
    for field_name in field_names:
        value = self.get_field_value(field_name)
        if value:
            full_address.append(value)
    return ", ".join(full_address)
```

6. Create functions to get or set the geoposition by `latitude` and `longitude`—in the database, `geoposition` is saved as a `Point` field. We can use these functions in the Django shell, forms, management commands, data migrations, and elsewhere:

```python
def get_geoposition(self):
    if not self.geoposition:
        return None
    return Geoposition(
        self.geoposition.coords[0], self.geoposition.coords[1]
    )

def set_geoposition(self, longitude, latitude):
    from django.contrib.gis.geos import Point
    self.geoposition = Point(longitude, latitude, srid=4326)
```

7. Remember to make and run migrations for the app after updating the model.
8. Create a model administration to add and change locations. Instead of the standard `ModelAdmin`, we will be using `OSMGeoAdmin` from the `gis` app. It will render a map to set `geoposition` using `OpenStreetMap`, which can be found at `https://www.openstreetmap.org`:

```python
# myproject/apps/locations/admin.py
from django.contrib.gis import admin
from .models import Location

@admin.register(Location)
class LocationAdmin(admin.OSMGeoAdmin):
    pass
```

9. Add some locations in the administration for further usage.

We will use and evolve this `locations` app in further recipes too.

How to do it...

Go through the following steps:

1. Register for the Google Maps API key. You can learn how and where to do this at the Google developers' documentation at `https://developers.google.com/maps/documentation/javascript/get-api-key`.

2. Add the Google Maps API key to the secrets and then read it out in the settings:

```
# myproject/settings/_base.py
# ...
GOOGLE_MAPS_API_KEY = get_secret("GOOGLE_MAPS_API_KEY")
```

3. At the core app, create a context processor to expose GOOGLE_MAPS_API_KEY to the templates:

```
# myproject/apps/core/context_processors.py
from django.conf import settings

def google_maps(request):
    return {
        "GOOGLE_MAPS_API_KEY": settings.GOOGLE_MAPS_API_KEY,
    }
```

4. Refer to this context processor in the template settings:

```
# myproject/settings/_base.py
TEMPLATES = [
    {
        "BACKEND":
        "django.template.backends.django.DjangoTemplates",
        "DIRS": [os.path.join(BASE_DIR, "myproject", "templates")],
        "APP_DIRS": True,
        "OPTIONS": {
            "context_processors": [
                "django.template.context_processors.debug",
                "django.template.context_processors.request",
                "django.contrib.auth.context_processors.auth",
                "django.contrib.messages.context_processors
                 .messages",
                "django.template.context_processors.media",
                "django.template.context_processors.static",
                "sekizai.context_processors.sekizai",
                "myproject.apps.core.context_processors
                 .google_maps",
            ]
        },
    }
]
```

5. Create the list and detail views for the locations:

```
# myproject/apps/locations/views.py
from django.views.generic import ListView, DetailView
from .models import Location
```

```
class LocationList(ListView):
    model = Location
    paginate_by = 10

class LocationDetail(DetailView):
    model = Location
    context_object_name = "location"
```

6. Create the URL configuration for the `locations` app:

```
# myproject/apps/locations/urls.py
from django.urls import path
from .views import LocationList, LocationDetail

urlpatterns = [
    path("", LocationList.as_view(), name="location_list"),
    path("<uuid:pk>/", LocationDetail.as_view(),
      name="location_detail"),
]
```

7. Include the URLs of the locations in the project's URL configuration:

```
# myproject/urls.py
from django.contrib import admin
from django.conf.urls.i18n import i18n_patterns
from django.urls import include, path
from django.conf import settings
from django.conf.urls.static import static
from django.shortcuts import redirect

from myproject.apps.core import views as core_views


urlpatterns = i18n_patterns(
    path("", lambda request: redirect("locations:location_list")),
    path("admin/", admin.site.urls),
    path("accounts/", include("django.contrib.auth.urls")),
    path("locations/", include(("myproject.apps.locations.urls",
    "locations"), namespace="locations")),
    path("js-settings/", core_views.js_settings,
      name="js_settings"),
)
urlpatterns += static(settings.STATIC_URL,
document_root=settings.STATIC_ROOT)
urlpatterns += static("/media/", document_root=settings.MEDIA_ROOT)
```

8. It is time to create the template for the location list and location detail views. The location list will be as simple as possible for now; we only need it to be able to browse the locations and get to the location detail views.

```
{# locations/location_list.html #}
{% extends "base.html" %}
{% load i18n %}

{% block content %}
    <h1>{% trans "Interesting Locations" %}</h1>
    {% if object_list %}
        <ul>
            {% for location in object_list %}
                <li><a href="{{ location.get_url_path }}">
                    {{ location.name }}
                </a></li>
            {% endfor %}
        </ul>
    {% else %}
        <p>{% trans "There are no locations yet." %}</p>
    {% endif %}
{% endblock %}
```

9. Next, let's create a template for the location details by extending the `base.html` and overwriting the `content` block:

```
{# locations/location_detail.html #}
{% extends "base.html" %}
{% load i18n static %}

{% block content %}
    <a href="{% url "locations:location_list" %}">{% trans
     "Interesting Locations" %}</a>
    <h1 class="map-title">{{ location.name }}</h1>
    <div class="my-3">
        {{ location.description|linebreaks|urlize }}
    </div>
    {% with geoposition=location.get_geoposition %}
<div id="map" class="mb-3"
data-latitude="{{ geoposition.latitude|stringformat:"f" }}"
data-longitude="{{ geoposition.longitude|stringformat:"f" }}"
data-address="{{ location.get_full_address }}"></div>
    {% endwith %}
{% endblock %}
```

10. Also in the same template, overwrite the `js` block:

```
{% block js %}
 <script src="{% static 'site/js/location_detail.js' %}"></script>
 <script async defer src="https://maps-api-
  ssl.google.com/maps/api/js?key={{ GOOGLE_MAPS_API_KEY
}}&callback=Location.init"></script>
{% endblock %}
```

11. As well as the templates, we need the JavaScript file that will read out the HTML5 data attributes and use them to render a map with a marker on it:

```
/* site_static/site/js/location_detail.js */
(function(window) {
    "use strict";

    function Location() {
        this.case = document.getElementById("map");
        if (this.case) {
            this.getCoordinates();
            this.getAddress();
            this.getMap();
            this.getMarker();
            this.getInfoWindow();
        }
    }

    Location.prototype.getCoordinates = function() {
        this.coords = {
            lat: parseFloat(this.case.getAttribute("data-
                latitude")),
            lng: parseFloat(this.case.getAttribute("data-
                longitude"))
        };
    };

    Location.prototype.getAddress = function() {
        this.address = this.case.getAttribute("data-address");
    };

    Location.prototype.getMap = function() {
        this.map = new google.maps.Map(this.case, {
            zoom: 15,
            center: this.coords
        });
    };

    Location.prototype.getMarker = function() {
```

```
        this.marker = new google.maps.Marker({
            position: this.coords,
            map: this.map
        });
    };

    Location.prototype.getInfoWindow = function() {
        var self = this;
        var wrap = this.case.parentNode;
        var title = wrap.querySelector(".map-title").textContent;

        this.infoWindow = new google.maps.InfoWindow({
            content: "<h3>"+title+"</h3><p>"+this.address+"</p>"
        });

        this.marker.addListener("click", function() {
            self.infoWindow.open(self.map, self.marker);
        });
    };

    var instance;
    Location.init = function() {
        // called by Google Maps service automatically once loaded
        // but is designed so that Location is a singleton
        if (!instance) {
            instance = new Location();
        }
    };

    // expose in the global namespace
    window.Location = Location;
}(window));
```

12. For the map to be displayed nicely, we need to set some CSS, as shown in the
    following code:

```
/* site_static/site/css/style.css */
#map {
    box-sizing: padding-box;
    height: 0;
    padding-bottom: calc(9 / 16 * 100%); /* 16:9 aspect ratio */
    width: 100%;
}
@media screen and (max-width: 480px) {
    #map {
        display: none; /* hide on mobile devices (esp. portrait) */
    }
}
```

How it works...

If you run a local development server and browse to the detail view for a location, you will navigate to a page with a map and a marker. When you click on the marker, a popup will open with address information. This will look as follows:

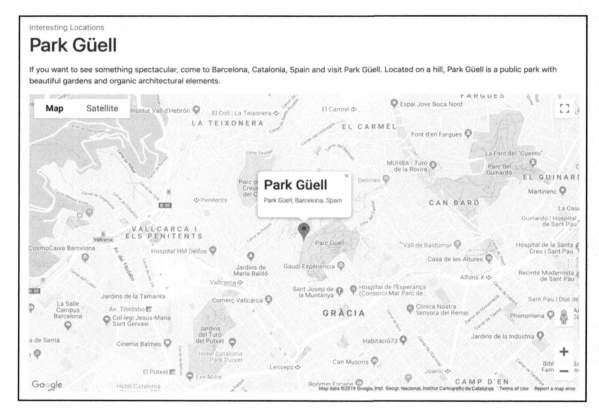

Since scrolling in maps on mobile devices can be problematic because of scroll-within-scroll issues, we have opted to hide the map on small screens (less than or equal to 480 px width) so that when we resize the screen down, the map eventually becomes invisible, as in the following:

Interesting Locations

Park Güell

If you want to see something spectacular, come to Barcelona, Catalonia, Spain and visit Park Güell. Located on a hill, Park Güell is a public park with beautiful gardens and organic architectural elements.

Let's take a look at the code. In the first few steps, we added the Google Maps API key and exposed it to all the templates. Then we created views to browse locations and plugged them into the URL configuration. Then we created the list and detail templates.

The `template_name` default for a `DetailView` comes from the lowercase version of the model's name, plus `detail`; hence; our template was named `location_detail.html`. If we wanted to use a different template, we could specify a `template_name` property for the view. In the same way, the `template_name` default for a `ListView` comes from the lowercase version of the model's name, plus `list`, so it is named `location_list.html`.

In the detail template, we had the location title and description followed by a `<div>` element with the `id="map"`, as well as the `data-latitude`, `data-longitude`, and `data-address` custom attributes. These made up the `content` block elements. Two `<script>` tags were added to the `js` block that came at the end of the `<body>`—one being the `location_detail.js` described next and the other being the Google Maps API script, to which we have passed our Maps API key and the name of the callback to invoke when the API loads.

In the JavaScript file, we created a `Location` class using a prototype function. This function has a static `init()` method, which was given as the callback to the Google Maps API. When `init()` is called, the constructor is invoked to create a new singleton `Location` instance. In the constructor function, a series of steps are taken to set up the map and its features:

1. First, the map case (container) is found by its ID. Only if that element is found, do we continue.
2. Next, we find the geographic coordinates using the `data-latitude` and `data-longitude` attributes, storing them in a dictionary as the location's `coords`. This object is in the form understood by the Google Maps API and will be used later.
3. The `data-address` is read next and stored directly as the address property of the location.
4. From here, we start building things out, beginning with the map. To ensure that the location will be visible, we set the center using the `coords` pulled from data attributes earlier.
5. A marker makes the location obvious on the map, positioned using the same `coords`.
6. Finally, we build up an information window, which is a type of pop-up bubble that can be displayed directly on the map using the API. In addition to the address that we retrieved earlier, we look for the location title based on the `.map-title` class that it was given in the template. This is added as an `<h1>` heading to the window, followed by the address as a `<p>` paragraph. To allow the window to be displayed, we add a click event listener to the marker that will open the window.

See also

- The *Exposing settings in JavaScript* recipe
- The *Arranging the base.html template* recipe
- The *Providing responsive images* recipe
- The *Opening object details in a modal dialog* recipe
- The *Inserting a map into a change form* recipe in `Chapter 6`, *Model Administration*

Providing responsive images

As responsive websites became the norm, many performance issues have arisen when it comes to providing identical content to both mobile devices and desktop computers. One very easy way to reduce the load time of a responsive site on small devices is to provide smaller images. This is where the `srcset` and `sizes` attributes, key components of responsive images, come into play.

Getting ready

Let's start with the `locations` app that was used in the previous recipe.

How to do it...

Go through the following steps to add the responsive images:

1. First of all, let's install `django-imagekit` into your virtual environment and add it to the `requirements/_base.txt`. We'll be using it to resize original images to specific sizes:

    ```
    (env)$ pip install django-imagekit==4.0.2
    ```

2. Put the `"imagekit"` into the `INSTALLED_APPS` in the settings:

    ```
    # myproject/settings/_base.py
    INSTALLED_APPS = [
        # ...
        "imagekit",
        # ...
    ]
    ```

3. In the beginning of the `models.py` file, let's import some libraries that are used for image versions and define a function responsible for the directory and the filenames of picture files:

```
# myproject/apps/locations/models.py
import contextlib
import os
# ...
from imagekit.models import ImageSpecField
from pilkit.processors import ResizeToFill
# ...

def upload_to(instance, filename):
    now = timezone_now()
    base, extension = os.path.splitext(filename)
    extension = extension.lower()
    return f"locations/{now:%Y/%m}/{instance.pk}{extension}"
```

4. Now let's add a `picture` field to the `Location` model in the same file together with image version definitions:

```
class Location(CreationModificationDateBase, UrlBase):
    # ...
    picture = models.ImageField(_("Picture"), upload_to=upload_to)
    picture_desktop = ImageSpecField(
        source="picture",
        processors=[ResizeToFill(1200, 600)],
        format="JPEG",
        options={"quality": 100},
    )
    picture_tablet = ImageSpecField(
        source="picture", processors=[ResizeToFill(768, 384)],
        format="PNG"
    )
    picture_mobile = ImageSpecField(
        source="picture", processors=[ResizeToFill(640, 320)],
        format="PNG"
    )
```

5. Then, overwrite the `delete()` method for the `Location` model to delete the generated versions when the model instance is deleted:

```
def delete(self, *args, **kwargs):
    from django.core.files.storage import default_storage

    if self.picture:
        with contextlib.suppress(FileNotFoundError):
```

```
        default_storage.delete(self.picture_desktop.path)
        default_storage.delete(self.picture_tablet.path)
        default_storage.delete(self.picture_mobile.path)
    self.picture.delete()

    super().delete(*args, **kwargs)
```

6. Make and run migrations to add the new `picture` field to the database schema.

7. Update the location detail template to include the image:

```
{# locations/location_detail.html #}
{% extends "base.html" %}
{% load i18n static %}


{% block content %}
    <a href="{% url "locations:location_list" %}">{% trans
    "Interesting Locations" %}</a>
    <h1 class="map-title">{{ location.name }}</h1>
    {% if location.picture %}
        <picture class="img-fluid">
            <source
                media="(max-width: 480px)"
                srcset="{{ location.picture_mobile.url }}" />
            <source
                media="(max-width: 768px)"
                srcset="{{ location.picture_tablet.url }}" />
            <img
                src="{{ location.picture_desktop.url }}"
                alt="{{ location.name }}"
                class="img-fluid"
            />
        </picture>
    {% endif %}
    {# ... #}
{% endblock %}

{% block js %}
    {# ... #}
{% endblock %}
```

8. Finally, add some images for locations in the administration.

How it works...

Responsive images are powerful and, at their base, are concerned with providing different images based on media rules that indicate the features of the displays upon which each image will be shown. The first thing we did here was to add the `django-imagekit` app, which makes it possible to generate the different images that are needed on the fly.

Obviously, we also will need the original image source, so in our `Location` model, we added an image field called `picture`. In the `upload_to()` function, we built the upload path and filename out of the current year and month, the UUID of the location, and the same file extension as the uploaded file. We also defined the image version specifications there as follows:

- `picture_desktop` will have the dimensions of 1,200 x 600 and will be used for the desktop layout
- `picture_tablet` will have the dimensions of 768 x 384 and will be used for tablet
- `picture_mobile` will have the dimensions of 640 x 320 and will be used for smartphones

In the `delete()` method of the location, we check whether the `picture` field has any value and then try to delete it and its image versions before deleting the location itself. We use the `contextlib.suppress(FileNotFoundError)` to silently ignore any errors if a file was not found on the disk.

The most interesting work happens in the template. When a location picture exists, we construct our `<picture>` element. On the surface, this is basically a container. In fact, it could have nothing inside of it besides the default `<img>` tag that appears at the end in our template, though that would not be very useful. In addition to the default image, we generate thumbnails for other widths—480 px and 768 px—and these are then used to build additional `<source>` elements. Each `<source>` element has the `media` rule with the conditions under which to select an image from the `srcset` attribute value. In our case, we only provide one image for each `<source>`. The location detail page will now include the image above the map and should look something like this:

Interesting Locations

Park Güell

If you want to see something spectacular, come to Barcelona, Catalonia, Spain and visit Park Güell. Located on a hill, Park Güell is a public park with beautiful gardens and organic architectural elements.

When the browser loads this markup, it follows a series of steps to determine which image to load:

- The `media` rules for each `<source>` are inspected in turn, checking to see whether any one of them matches the current viewport
- When a rule matches, the `srcset` is read and the appropriate image URL is loaded and displayed
- If no rules match, then the `src` of the final, default image is loaded

As a result, smaller images will be loaded on smaller viewports. For example, here we can see that the smallest image was loaded for a viewport only 375 px wide:

For browsers that cannot understand the `<picture>` and `<source>` tags at all, the default image can still be loaded, as it is nothing more than a normal `<img>` tag.

There's more...

You can use responsive images not only to provide targeted image sizes, but also to differentiate pixel density, and to provide images that are curated explicitly for the design at any given viewport size. This is known as art direction. If you are interested in learning more, the **Mozilla Developer Network (MDN)** has a thorough article on the topic, available at `https://developer.mozilla.org/en-US/docs/Learn/HTML/Multimedia_and_embedding/Responsive_images`.

See also

- The *Arranging the base.html template* recipe
- The *Using HTML5 data attributes* recipe
- The *Opening object details in a modal dialog* recipe
- The *Inserting a map into a change form* recipe in `Chapter 6`, *Model Administration*

Implementing a continuous scrolling

Social websites often have a feature called continuous scrolling, which is also known as infinite scrolling, as an alternative to pagination. Rather than having links to see additional sets of items separately, there are long lists of items, and, as you scroll down the page, new items are loaded and attached to the bottom automatically. In this recipe, we will see how to achieve such an effect with Django and the jScroll jQuery plugin.

 You can download the jScroll script and also find extensive documentation about the plugin from `https://jscroll.com/`.

Getting ready

We'll be reusing the `locations` app that we created in the previous recipes.

To have some more interesting data to show in the list view, let's add the `ratings` field to the `Location` model as follows:

```python
# myproject/apps/locations/models.py
# ...
RATING_CHOICES = ((1, "★☆☆☆☆"), (2, "★★☆☆☆"), (3, "★★★☆☆"), (4,
"★★★★☆"), (5, "★★★★★"))

class Location(CreationModificationDateBase, UrlBase):
    # ...
    rating = models.PositiveIntegerField(
        _("Rating"), choices=RATING_CHOICES, blank=True, null=True
    )

    # ...
    def get_rating_percentage(self):
        return self.rating * 20 if self.rating is not None else None
```

The `get_rating_percentage()` method will be necessary to return the rating as a percentage for the representation.

Don't forget to make and run migrations and then add some ratings for locations in the administration.

How to do it...

Go through the following steps to create a continuously scrolling page:

1. First, add enough locations in the administration. As you can see from the *Using HTML5 data attributes* recipe, we will be paginating the `LocationList` view by 10 items per page, so we will need at least 11 locations to see whether the continuous scroll works as expected.

2. Modify the template for the location list view as follows:

```html
{# locations/location_list.html #}
{% extends "base.html" %}
{% load i18n static utility_tags %}

{% block content %}
    <div class="row">
        <div class="col-lg-8">
            <h1>{% trans "Interesting Locations" %}</h1>
            {% if object_list %}
                <div class="item-list">
                    {% for location in object_list %}
```

```
                            <a href="{{ location.get_url_path }}"
                                class="item d-block my-3">
                                <div class="card">
                                    <div class="card-body">
                                        <div class="float-right">
                                            <div class="rating" aria-
                                                label="{% blocktrans with
                                                    stars=location.rating %}
                                                    {{ stars }} of 5 stars
                                                        {% endblocktrans %}">
                                                <span style="width:{{
                                                    location.get_rating
                                                    _percentage }}%"></span>
                                            </div>
                                        </div>
                                        <p class="card-text">{{
                                            location.name }}<br/>
                                            <small>{{ location.city }},
                                                {{location.get_country
                                                _display }}</small>
                                        </p>
                                    </div>
                                </div>
                            </a>
                    {% endfor %}
                    {% if page_obj.has_next %}
                        <div class="text-center">
                            <div class="loading-indicator"></div>
                        </div>
                        <p class="pagination">
                            <a class="next-page"
                                href="{% modify_query
                                page=page_obj.next_page_number %}">
                                    {% trans "More..." %}</a>
                        </p>
                    {% endif %}
                </div>
            {% else %}
                <p>{% trans "There are no locations yet." %}</p>
            {% endif %}
        </div>
        <div class="col-lg-4">
            {% include "locations/includes/navigation.html" %}
        </div>
    </div>
{% endblock %}
```

3. In the same template, overwrite the `css` and `js` blocks with the following markup:

```
{% block css %}
    <link rel="stylesheet" type="text/css"
        href="{% static 'site/css/rating.css' %}">
{% endblock %}

{% block js %}
    <script src="https://cdnjs.cloudflare.com/ajax
    /libs/jscroll/2.3.9/jquery.jscroll.min.js"></script>
    <script src="{% static 'site/js/list.js' %}"></script>
{% endblock %}
```

4. As a final step with this template, overwrite the `extra_body` block with the JavaScript template for the loading indicator:

```
{% block extra_body %}
    <script type="text/template" class="loader">
        <div class="text-center">
            <div class="loading-indicator"></div>
        </div>
    </script>
{% endblock %}
```

5. Create the page's navigation at `locations/includes/navigation.html`. For now, you can just create an empty file there.

6. The next step is to add JavaScript with the initialization of the continuous scroll widget:

```
/* site_static/site/js/list.js */
jQuery(function ($) {
    var $list = $('.item-list');
    var $loader = $('script[type="text/template"].loader');
    $list.jscroll({
        loadingHtml: $loader.html(),
        padding: 100,
        pagingSelector: '.pagination',
        nextSelector: 'a.next-page:last',
        contentSelector: '.item,.pagination'
    });
});
```

7. Finally, we'll add some CSS so that ratings can be displayed using user-friendly stars instead of just numbers:

```css
/* site_static/site/css/rating.css */
.rating {
  color: #c90;
  display: block;
  position: relative;
  margin: 0;
  padding: 0;
  white-space: nowrap;
}

.rating span {
  color: #fc0;
  display: block;
  position: absolute;
  overflow: hidden;
  top: 0;
  left: 0;
  bottom: 0;
  white-space: nowrap;
}

.rating span:before,
.rating span:after {
  display: block;
  position: absolute;
  overflow: hidden;
  left: 0;
  top: 0;
  bottom: 0;
}

.rating:before {
  content: "☆☆☆☆☆";
}

.rating span:after {
  content: "★★★★★";
}
```

8. In the main file for the main website style, add a style for the loading indicator:

```css
/* site_static/site/css/style.css */
/* ... */
.loading-indicator {
  display: inline-block;
  width: 45px;
  height: 45px;
}
.loading-indicator:after {
  content: "";
  display: block;
  width: 40px;
  height: 40px;
  border-radius: 50%;
  border: 5px solid rgba(0,0,0,.25);
  border-color: rgba(0,0,0,.25) transparent rgba(0,0,0,.25)
   transparent;
  animation: dual-ring 1.2s linear infinite;
}
@keyframes dual-ring {
  0% {
    transform: rotate(0deg);
  }
  100% {
    transform: rotate(360deg);
  }
}
```

How it works...

When you open the location list view in a browser, the predefined number of items set to `paginate_by` in the view (that is, 10) is shown on the page. As you scroll down, an additional page's worth of items and the next pagination link are loaded automatically and appended to the item container. The pagination link uses the `{% modify_query %}` custom template tag from the *Creating a template tag to modify request query parameters* recipe in Chapter 5, *Custom Template Filters and Tags* to generate an adjusted URL based on the current one, but pointing to the correct next page number. If you have a slower connection speed, then when you scroll to the bottom of the page, you will see a page like the following until the items of the next page are loaded and attached to the list:

Interesting Locations

Page navigation goes here...

Dancing House,
★★★★☆
Prague, Czechia

Park Güell,
★★★★☆
Barcelona, Spain

Three Crosses,
★★★★★
Vilnius, Lithuania

Vasa Museum,
★★★★★
Stockholm, Sweden

Gardens of the world,
★★★★★
Berlin, Germany

Raysko Praskalo,
★★★★★
Balkan Mountains, Bulgaria

Krka National Park,
★★★★★
Šibenik-Knin County, Croatia

Tivoli Gardens,
★★★★★
Copenhagen, Denmark

Temppeliaukio Church,
★★★★☆
Helsinki, Finland

La Géode,
★★★★☆
Paris, France

Scrolling down further, the second, third, and later pages of the items are loaded and attached at the bottom. This continues until there are no more pages left to load, which is signified by the lack of any further loaded pagination links in the final group.

We use the Cloudflare CDN URL to load the jScroll plugin here, but, if you opt to download a copy locally as a static file, then use a `{% static %}` lookup to add the script to the template.

Upon the initial page load, the element with the `item-list` CSS class, which contains the items and pagination links, will become a jScroll object through the code in the `list.js`. In fact, this implementation is generic enough that it could be used to enable continuous scrolling for any list display following a similar markup structure.

The following options are given to define its features:

- `loadingHtml`: This sets the markup that jScroll will inject at the end of the list while loading a new page of items. In our case, it is an animated loading indicator, and it is drawn from the HTML contained in a `<script type="text/template" />` tag directly in the markup. By giving this `type` attribute, the browser will not try to execute it as it would a normal JavaScript, and the content inside remains invisible to the user.
- `padding`: When the scroll position of the page is within this distance of the end of the scrolling area, a new page should be loaded. Here, we've set it at 100 pixels.
- `pagingSelector`: A CSS selector that indicates which HTML elements in the `object_list` are pagination links. These will be hidden in browsers where the jScroll plugin activates so that the continuous scroll can take over the loading of additional pages, but users in other browsers will still be able to navigate by clicking on the pagination normally.
- `nextSelector`: This CSS selector finds the HTML element(s) from which to read the URL of the next page.
- `contentSelector`: Another CSS selector. This specifies which HTML elements should be extracted from the Ajax-loaded content and added to the container.

The `rating.css` inserts Unicode star characters and overlaps the outlines with filled-in versions to create the rating effect. Using a width equivalent to the rating value's percentage of the maximum (5, in this case), the filled-in stars cover the right amount of space on top of the hollow ones, allowing for decimal ratings. In the markup, there is an `aria-label` attribute with the rating information for people using screen readers.

Finally, the CSS in the `style.css` file uses CSS animations to create a rotating loading indicator.

There's more...

We have a placeholder for navigation in the sidebar. Note that, with continuous scrolling, all the secondary navigation that you have after the list of items, should be positioned in the sidebar, rather than in the footer, because the visitor might never reach the end of the page.

See also

- The *Filtering object lists* recipe in Chapter 3, *Forms and Views*
- The *Managing paginated lists* recipe in Chapter 3, *Forms and Views*
- The *Composing class-based views* recipe in Chapter 3, *Forms and Views*
- The *Exposing settings in JavaScript* recipe
- The *Creating a template tag to modify request query parameters* recipe in Chapter 5, *Customizing Template Filters and Tags*

Opening object details in a modal dialog

In this recipe, we will create a list of links to the locations, which, when clicked, open a Bootstrap modal dialog with some information about the location and the **Learn more...** link, leading to the location detail page:

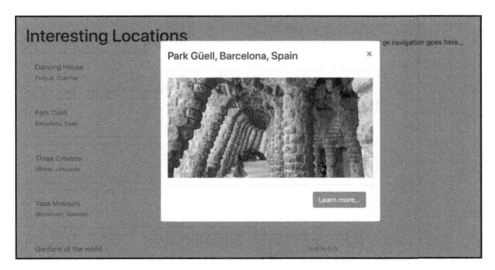

The content for the dialog will be loaded by Ajax. For visitors without JavaScript, the detail page will open immediately, without this intermediate step.

Getting ready

Let's start with the `locations` app that we created in the previous recipes.

Make sure that you have views, URL configuration, and templates for location listings and location details, just like we defined previously.

How to do it...

Execute these steps one by one to add the modal dialog as an intermediate step between the list view and the detail view:

1. First, in the URL configuration of the `locations` app, add a rule for the response of the modal dialog:

```python
# myproject/apps/locations/urls.py
from django.urls import path
from .views import LocationList, LocationDetail

urlpatterns = [
    path("", LocationList.as_view(), name="location_list"),
    path("add/", add_or_change_location, name="add_location"),
    path("<uuid:pk>/", LocationDetail.as_view(),
     name="location_detail"),
    path(
        "<uuid:pk>/modal/",
        LocationDetail.as_view(template_name=
         "locations/location_detail_modal.html"),
        name="location_detail_modal",
    ),
]
```

2. Create a template for the modal dialog:

```html
{# locations/location_detail_modal.html #}
{% load i18n %}
<p class="text-center">
    {% if location.picture %}
        <picture class="img-fluid">
            <source media="(max-width: 480px)"
                    srcset="{{ location.picture_mobile.url }}"/>
```

```
                <source media="(max-width: 768px)"
                        srcset="{{ location.picture_tablet.url }}"/>
                <img src="{{ location.picture_desktop.url }}"
                    alt="{{ location.name }}"
                    class="img-fluid"
                />
            </picture>
        {% endif %}
    </p>
    <div class="modal-footer text-right">
        <a href="{% url "locations:location_detail" pk=location.pk %}"
         class="btn btn-primary pull-right">
            {% trans "Learn more..." %}
        </a>
    </div>
</div>
```

3. In the template for the location list, update the links to the location details by adding custom data attributes:

```
{# locations/location_list.html #}
{# ... #}
<a href="{{ location.get_url_path }}"
    data-modal-title="{{ location.get_full_address }}"
    data-modal-url="{% url 'locations:location_detail_modal'
     pk=location.pk %}"
    class="item d-block my-3">
    {# ... #}
</a>
{# ... #}
```

4. In the same file, overwrite the extra_body content with the markup for the modal dialog:

```
{% block extra_body %}
    {# ... #}
    <div id="modal" class="modal fade" tabindex="-1" role="dialog"
        aria-hidden="true" aria-labelledby="modal_title">
        <div class="modal-dialog modal-dialog-centered"
            role="document">
            <div class="modal-content">
                <div class="modal-header">
                    <h4 id="modal_title"
                        class="modal-title"></h4>
                    <button type="button" class="close"
                            data-dismiss="modal"
                            aria-label="{% trans 'Close' %}">
                        <span aria-hidden="true">&times;</span>
                    </button>
```

```
                        </div>
                        <div class="modal-body"></div>
                    </div>
                </div>
            </div>
        {% endblock %}
```

5. Finally, modify the `list.js` file by adding a script to handle the opening and closing of the modal dialog:

```
/* site_static/js/list.js */
/* ... */
jQuery(function ($) {
    var $list = $('.item-list');
    var $modal = $('#modal');
    $modal.on('click', '.close', function (event) {
        $modal.modal('hide');
        // do something when dialog is closed...
    });
    $list.on('click', 'a.item', function (event) {
        var $link = $(this);
        var url = $link.data('modal-url');
        var title = $link.data('modal-title');
        if (url && title) {
            event.preventDefault();
            $('.modal-title', $modal).text(title);
            $('.modal-body', $modal).load(url, function () {
                $modal.on('shown.bs.modal', function () {
                    // do something when dialog is shown...
                }).modal('show');
            });
        }
    });
});
```

How it works...

If we go to the location's list view in a browser and click on one of the locations, we will see a modal dialog similar to the following:

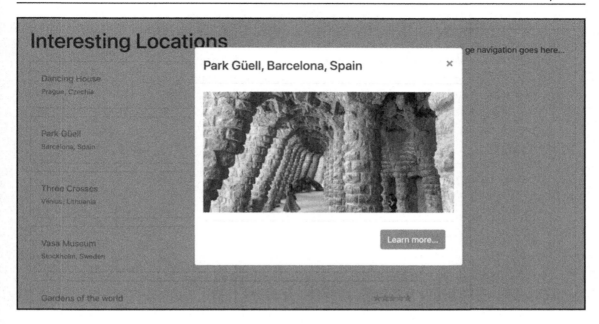

Let's examine how this all came together. The URL path named `location_detail_modal` points to the same location detail view, but uses a different template. The mentioned template just has a responsive image and a modal dialog footer with the link **Learn more...** leading to the normal detail page of the location. In the list view, we changed the link of a list item to include `data-modal-title` and `data-modal-url` attributes that will later be referred to by JavaScript. The first attribute stipulates that the full address should be used as the title. The second attribute stipulates the location from which the HTML for the body of the modal dialog should be taken. At the end of the list view, we have the markup for the Bootstrap 4 modal dialog. The dialog contains a header with the **Close** button and title, plus a content area for the main details. JavaScript should have been added via the `js` block.

In the JavaScript file, we used the jQuery framework to take advantage of shorter syntax and unified cross-browser functionality. When the page is loaded, we assign an event handler `on('click')` for the `.item-list` element. When any `a.item` is clicked, that event is delegated to this handler, which reads and stores the custom data attributes as the `url` and `title`. When these are extracted successfully, we prevent the original click action (navigation to the full detail page) and then set up the modal for display. We set the new title for the hidden dialog box and load the modal dialog's content to the `.modal-body` element over Ajax. Finally, the modal is shown to the visitor using the Bootstrap 4 `modal()` jQuery plugin.

If the JavaScript file were unable to process the URL of the modal dialog from the custom attribute, or, even worse, if the JavaScript in `list.js` failed to load or execute entirely, clicking on the location link would take the user to the detail page as usual. We have implemented our modal as a progressive enhancement so that the user experience is right, even in the face of failure.

See also

- The *Using HTML5 data attributes* recipe
- The *Providing responsive images* recipe
- The *Implementing a continuous scroll* recipe
- The *Implementing the Like widget* recipe

Implementing the Like widget

Websites in general, and most commonly those with a social component, often have integrated Facebook, Twitter, and Google+ widgets to like and share content. In this recipe, we will guide you through the building of a similar Django functionality that will save information in your database whenever a user likes something. You will be able to create specific views based on the things that people liked on your website. We will similarly create a Like widget with a two-state button and badge showing the number of total likes.

The following screenshot shows the inactive state, where you can click on a button to activate it:

The following screenshot shows the active state, where you can click on a button to deactivate it:

Changes in the state of the widget will be handled by Ajax calls.

Getting ready

First, create a `likes` app and add it to your `INSTALLED_APPS`. Then, set up a `Like` model, which has a foreign-key relation to the user who is liking something and a generic relationship to any object in the database. We will use `object_relation_base_factory`, which we defined in the *Creating a model mixin to handle generic relations* recipe in `Chapter 2`, *Models and Database Structure*. If you don't want to use the mixin, you can also define a generic relation in the following model yourself:

```python
# myproject/apps/likes/models.py
from django.db import models
from django.utils.translation import ugettext_lazy as _
from django.conf import settings

from myproject.apps.core.models import (
    CreationModificationDateBase,
    object_relation_base_factory,
)

LikeableObject = object_relation_base_factory(is_required=True)


class Like(CreationModificationDateBase, LikeableObject):
    class Meta:
        verbose_name = _("Like")
        verbose_name_plural = _("Likes")
        ordering = ("-created",)

    user = models.ForeignKey(settings.AUTH_USER_MODEL,
      on_delete=models.CASCADE)

    def __str__(self):
        return _("{user} likes {obj}").format(user=self.user,
          obj=self.content_object)
```

Also make sure that the `request` context processor is set in the settings. We also need authentication middleware in the settings for the currently logged-in user to be attached to the request:

```python
# myproject/settings/_base.py
# ...
MIDDLEWARE = [
    # ...
    "django.contrib.auth.middleware.AuthenticationMiddleware",
    # ...
]
```

```
TEMPLATES = [
    {
        # ...
        "OPTIONS": {
            "context_processors": [
                "django.template.context_processors.request",
                # ...
            ]
        },
    }
]
```

Remember to create and run a migration to set up the database accordingly for the new `Like` model.

How to do it...

Execute the following steps one by one:

1. In the `likes` app, create a `templatetags` directory with an empty `__init__.py` file to make it a Python module. Then, add the `likes_tags.py` file, where we'll define the `{% like_widget %}` template tag as follows:

```python
# myproject/apps/likes/templatetags/likes_tags.py
from django import template
from django.contrib.contenttypes.models import ContentType
from django.template.loader import render_to_string

from ..models import Like

register = template.Library()


# TAGS


class ObjectLikeWidget(template.Node):
    def __init__(self, var):
        self.var = var

    def render(self, context):
        liked_object = self.var.resolve(context)
        ct = ContentType.objects.get_for_model(liked_object)
        user = context["request"].user

        if not user.is_authenticated:
```

```
                return ""

            context.push(object=liked_object, content_type_id=ct.pk)
            output = render_to_string("likes/includes/widget.html",
             context.flatten())
            context.pop()
            return output


    @register.tag
    def like_widget(parser, token):
        try:
            tag_name, for_str, var_name = token.split_contents()
        except ValueError:
            tag_name = "%r" % token.contents.split()[0]
            raise template.TemplateSyntaxError(
                f"{tag_name} tag requires a following syntax: "
                f"{{% {tag_name} for <object> %}}"
            )
        var = template.Variable(var_name)
        return ObjectLikeWidget(var)
```

2. We'll also add filters in the same file to get the Like status for a user and the total number of Likes for a specified object:

```
# myproject/apps/likes/templatetags/likes_tags.py
# ...
# FILTERS

@register.filter
def liked_by(obj, user):
    ct = ContentType.objects.get_for_model(obj)
    liked = Like.objects.filter(user=user, content_type=ct,
object_id=obj.pk)
    return liked.count() > 0


@register.filter
def liked_count(obj):
    ct = ContentType.objects.get_for_model(obj)
    likes = Like.objects.filter(content_type=ct, object_id=obj.pk)
    return likes.count()
```

3. In the URL rules, we need a rule for a view that will handle the liking and unliking using Ajax:

```
# myproject/apps/likes/urls.py
from django.urls import path
from .views import json_set_like

urlpatterns = [
    path("<int:content_type_id>/<str:object_id>/",
        json_set_like,
        name="json_set_like")
]
```

4. Make sure that you map the URLs to the project as well:

```
# myproject/urls.py
from django.conf.urls.i18n import i18n_patterns
from django.urls import include, path

urlpatterns = i18n_patterns(
    # ...
    path("likes/", include(("myproject.apps.likes.urls", "likes"),
      namespace="likes")),
)
```

5. Then we need to define the view, as shown in the following code:

```
# myproject/apps/likes/views.py
from django.contrib.contenttypes.models import ContentType
from django.http import JsonResponse
from django.views.decorators.cache import never_cache
from django.views.decorators.csrf import csrf_exempt

from .models import Like
from .templatetags.likes_tags import liked_count


@never_cache
@csrf_exempt
def json_set_like(request, content_type_id, object_id):
    """
    Sets the object as a favorite for the current user
    """
    result = {
        "success": False,
    }
    if request.user.is_authenticated and request.method == "POST":
        content_type = ContentType.objects.get(id=content_type_id)
```

```
    obj = content_type.get_object_for_this_type(pk=object_id)

    like, is_created = Like.objects.get_or_create(
        content_type=ContentType.objects.get_for_model(obj),
        object_id=obj.pk,
        user=request.user)
    if not is_created:
        like.delete()

    result = {
        "success": True,
        "action": "add" if is_created else "remove",
        "count": liked_count(obj),
    }

    return JsonResponse(result)
```

6. In the template for the list or detail view of any object, we can add the template tag for the widget. Let's add the widget to the location detail that we created in the previous recipes, as follows:

```
{# locations/location_detail.html #}
{% extends "base.html" %}
{% load i18n static likes_tags %}


{% block content %}
    <a href="{% url "locations:location_list" %}">{% trans
     "Interesting Locations" %}</a>
    <div class="float-right">
        {% if request.user.is_authenticated %}
            {% like_widget for location %}
        {% endif %}
    </div>
    </div>
    <h1 class="map-title">{{ location.name }}</h1>
    {# ... #}
{% endblock %}
```

7. Then, we need a template for the widget, as shown in the following code:

```
{# likes/includes/widget.html #}
{% load i18n static likes_tags sekizai_tags %}
<p class="like-widget">
    <button type="button"
            class="like-button btn btn-primary{% if object|
            liked_by:request.user %} active{% endif %}"
            data-href="{% url "likes:json_set_like"
              content_type_id=content_type_id
```

```
                          object_id=object.pk %}"
                 data-remove-label="{% trans "Like" %}"
                 data-add-label="{% trans "Unlike" %}">
            {% if object|liked_by:request.user %}
                {% trans "Unlike" %}
            {% else %}
                {% trans "Like" %}
            {% endif %}
        </button>
        <span class="like-badge badge badge-secondary">
            {{ object|liked_count }}</span>
</p>
{% addtoblock "js" %}
<script src="{% static 'likes/js/widget.js' %}"></script>
{% endaddtoblock %}
```

8. Finally, we create JavaScript to handle the liking and unliking action in the
   browser, as follows:

```
/* myproject/apps/likes/static/likes/js/widget.js */
(function($) {
    $(document).on("click", ".like-button", function() {
        var $button = $(this);
        var $widget = $button.closest(".like-widget");
        var $badge = $widget.find(".like-badge");

        $.post($button.data("href"), function(data) {
            if (data.success) {
                var action = data.action; // "add" or "remove"
                var label = $button.data(action + "-label");

                $button[action + "Class"]("active");
                $button.html(label);

                $badge.html(data.count);
            }
        }, "json");
    });
}(jQuery));
```

How it works...

You can now use the {% like_widget for object %} template tag for any object in your website. It generates a widget that will show the Like state based on whether and how the current logged-in user has responded to the object.

The Like button has three custom HTML5 data attributes:

- data-href supplies a unique, object-specific URL to change the current state of the widget
- data-add-text is the translated text to be displayed when the Like association has been added (Unlike)
- data-remove-text is similarly the translated text for when the Like association has been removed (Like)

Using django-sekizai, we add the <script src="{% static 'likes/js/widget.js' %}"></script> to the page. Note that, if there were more than one Like widget on the page, we would just include the JavaScript once. And, if there were no Like widgets on the page, then the JavaScript wasn't included on the page at all.

In the JavaScript file, Like buttons are recognized by the like-button CSS class. An event listener, attached to the document, watches for click events from any such button found in the page, and then posts an Ajax call to the URL specified by the data-href attribute.

The specified view json_set_like accepts two parameters: the content type ID and the primary key of the liked object. The view checks whether a Like exists for the specified object, and if it does, the view removes it; otherwise, the Like object is added. As a result, the view returns a JSON response with the success status, the action that was taken for the Like object (add or remove), and the total count of Likes for the object across all users. Depending on the action that is returned, JavaScript will show an appropriate state for the button.

You can debug the Ajax responses in the browser's developer tools, generally in the **Network** tab. If any server errors occur while you are developing, and you have DEBUG turned on in your settings, you will see the error traceback in the preview of the response; otherwise, you will see the returned JSON, as shown in the following screenshot:

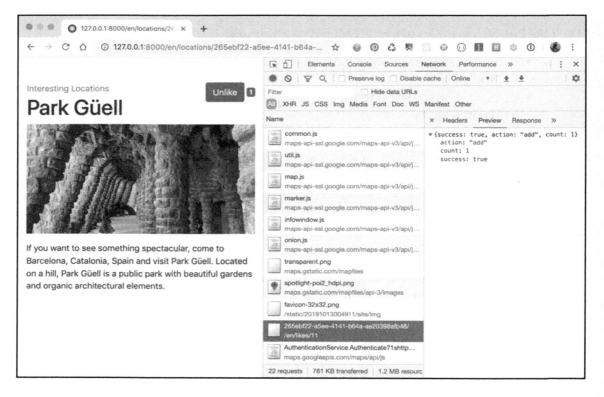

See also

- The *Using Django Sekizai* recipe
- The *Opening object details in a modal dialog* recipe
- The *Implementing a continuous scroll* recipe
- The *Uploading images by Ajax* recipe
- The *Creating a model mixin to handle generic relations* recipe in Chapter 2, *Models and Database Structure*
- Chapter 5, *Customizing Template Filters and Tags*

Uploading images via Ajax

With the default file input fields, it quickly becomes obvious that there is a lot we could do to improve the user experience:

- First, only the path to the selected file is displayed within the field, whereas people want to see what they have chosen right after selecting the file.
- Second, the file input itself is generally too narrow to show much of the path selected and reads from the left end. As a result, the filename is rarely visible within the field.
- Finally, if the form has validation errors, nobody wants to select the files again; the file should still be selected in the form with validation errors.

In this recipe, we will see how the file uploads could be improved.

Getting ready

Let's start with the `locations` app that we created in the previous recipes.

Our own JavaScript file will rely upon an external library–jQuery File Upload. You can download and extract the files from `https://github.com/blueimp/jQuery-File-Upload/tree/v10.2.0` and place them in `site_static/site/vendor/jQuery-File-Upload-10.2.0`. This utility also requires the `jquery.ui.widget.js` in turn, which is made available in a `vendor/` subdirectory alongside the other files. With that, we're ready to begin.

How to do it...

Let's define the form for the locations so that it can support Ajax uploads using the following steps:

1. Let's create a model form for the locations with the nonrequired `picture` field, a hidden `picture_path` field, and `latitude` and `longitude` fields for geoposition:

```
# myproject/apps/locations/forms.py
import os
from django import forms
from django.urls import reverse
from django.utils.translation import ugettext_lazy as _
from django.core.files.storage import default_storage
```

```
from crispy_forms import bootstrap, helper, layout
from .models import Location

class LocationForm(forms.ModelForm):
    picture = forms.ImageField(
        label=_("Picture"), max_length=255,
         widget=forms.FileInput(), required=False
    )
    picture_path = forms.CharField(
        max_length=255, widget=forms.HiddenInput(), required=False
    )
    latitude = forms.FloatField(
        label=_("Latitude"),
        help_text=_("Latitude (Lat.) is the angle between any point
        and the equator (north pole is at 90; south pole is at
        -90)."),
        required=False,
    )
    longitude = forms.FloatField(
        label=_("Longitude"),
        help_text=_("Longitude (Long.) is the angle east or west
        of an arbitrary point on Earth from Greenwich (UK),
        which is the international zero-longitude point
        (longitude=0 degrees). The anti-meridian of Greenwich is
        both 180 (direction to east) and -180 (direction to
        west)."),
        required=False,
    )
    class Meta:
        model = Location
        exclude = ["geoposition", "rating"]
```

2. In the __init__() method of this form, we will read out the geoposition from the model instance, and then define the django-crispy-forms layout for the form:

```
def __init__(self, request, *args, **kwargs):
    self.request = request
    super().__init__(*args, **kwargs)
    geoposition = self.instance.get_geoposition()
    if geoposition:
        self.fields["latitude"].initial = geoposition.latitude
        self.fields["longitude"].initial = geoposition.longitude

    name_field = layout.Field("name", css_class="input-block-
      level")
    description_field = layout.Field(
        "description", css_class="input-block-level", rows="3"
```

```
)
main_fieldset = layout.Fieldset(_("Main data"), name_field,
 description_field)

picture_field = layout.Field(
    "picture",
    data_url=reverse("upload_file"),
    template="core/includes/file_upload_field.html",
)
picture_path_field = layout.Field("picture_path")

picture_fieldset = layout.Fieldset(
    _("Picture"),
    picture_field,
    picture_path_field,
    title=_("Picture upload"),
    css_id="picture_fieldset",
)

street_address_field = layout.Field(
    "street_address", css_class="input-block-level"
)
street_address2_field = layout.Field(
    "street_address2", css_class="input-block-level"
)
postal_code_field = layout.Field("postal_code",
 css_class="input-block-level")
city_field = layout.Field("city", css_class="input-block-
 level")
country_field = layout.Field("country", css_class="input-
 block-level")
latitude_field = layout.Field("latitude", css_class="input-
 block-level")
longitude_field = layout.Field("longitude", css_class="input-
 block-level")
address_fieldset = layout.Fieldset(
    _("Address"),
    street_address_field,
    street_address2_field,
    postal_code_field,
    city_field,
    country_field,
    latitude_field,
    longitude_field,
)

submit_button = layout.Submit("save", _("Save"))
actions = bootstrap.FormActions(layout.Div(submit_button,
```

```
        css_class="col"))

    self.helper = helper.FormHelper()
    self.helper.form_action = self.request.path
    self.helper.form_method = "POST"
    self.helper.attrs = {"noValidate": "noValidate"}
    self.helper.layout = layout.Layout(main_fieldset,
     picture_fieldset, address_fieldset, actions)
```

3. Then we need to add the validation for the `picture` and `picture_path` fields to the same form:

```
def clean(self):
    cleaned_data = super().clean()
    picture_path = cleaned_data["picture_path"]
    if not self.instance.pk and not self.files.get("picture")
     and not picture_path:
        raise forms.ValidationError(_("Please choose an image."))
```

4. Lastly, we add the saving method to this form, which will take care of the saving of the image and geoposition:

```
def save(self, commit=True):
    instance = super().save(commit=False)
    picture_path = self.cleaned_data["picture_path"]
    if picture_path:
        temporary_image_path = os.path.join("temporary-uploads",
         picture_path)
        file_obj = default_storage.open(temporary_image_path)
        instance.picture.save(picture_path, file_obj, save=False)
        default_storage.delete(temporary_image_path)
    latitude = self.cleaned_data["latitude"]
    longitude = self.cleaned_data["longitude"]
    if latitude is not None and longitude is not None:
        instance.set_geoposition(longitude=longitude,
         latitude=latitude)
    if commit:
        instance.save()
        self.save_m2m()
    return instance
```

5. In addition to the previously defined views in the `locations` app, we'll add an `add_or_change_location` view, as shown in the following code:

```python
# myproject/apps/locations/views.py
from django.contrib.auth.decorators import login_required
from django.shortcuts import render, redirect, get_object_or_404

from .forms import LocationForm
from .models import Location

# ...

@login_required
def add_or_change_location(request, pk=None):
    location = None
    if pk:
        location = get_object_or_404(Location, pk=pk)
    if request.method == "POST":
        form = LocationForm(request, data=request.POST,
         files=request.FILES, instance=location)
        if form.is_valid():
            location = form.save()
            return redirect("locations:location_detail",
             pk=location.pk)
    else:
        form = LocationForm(request, instance=location)

    context = {"location": location, "form": form}
    return render(request, "locations/location_form.html", context)
```

6. Let's add this view to the URL configuration:

```python
# myproject/apps/locations/urls.py
from django.urls import path
from .views import add_or_change_location

urlpatterns = [
    # ...
    path("<uuid:pk>/change/", add_or_change_location,
     name="add_or_change_location"),
]
```

7. In the views of the `core` app, we will add a generic `upload_file` function to upload pictures that can be reused by other apps with a `picture` field:

```python
# myproject/apps/core/views.py
import os
from django.core.files.base import ContentFile
```

```
from django.core.files.storage import default_storage
from django.http import JsonResponse
from django.core.exceptions import SuspiciousOperation
from django.urls import reverse
from django.views.decorators.csrf import csrf_protect
from django.utils.translation import gettext_lazy as _
from django.conf import settings
# ...


@csrf_protect
def upload_file(request):
    status_code = 400
    data = {"files": [], "error": _("Bad request")}
    if request.method == "POST" and request.is_ajax() and "picture"
     in request.FILES:
        file_types = [f"image/{x}" for x in ["gif", "jpg", "jpeg",
         "png"]]
        file = request.FILES.get("picture")
        if file.content_type not in file_types:
            status_code = 405
            data["error"] = _("Invalid file format")
        else:
            upload_to = os.path.join("temporary-uploads",
             file.name)
            name = default_storage.save(upload_to,
             ContentFile(file.read()))
            file = default_storage.open(name)
            status_code = 200
            del data["error"]
            absolute_uploads_dir = os.path.join(
                settings.MEDIA_ROOT, "temporary-uploads"
            )
            file.filename = os.path.basename(file.name)
            data["files"].append(
                {
                    "name": file.filename,
                    "size": file.size,
                    "deleteType": "DELETE",
                    "deleteUrl": (
                        reverse("delete_file") +
                        f"?filename={file.filename}"
                    ),
                    "path": file.name[len(absolute_uploads_dir)
                     + 1 :],
                }
            )

    return JsonResponse(data, status=status_code)
```

8. We set the URL rules for the new upload view as follows:

```python
# myproject/urls.py
from django.urls import path
from myproject.apps.core import views as core_views

# ...

urlpatterns += [
    path(
        "upload-file/",
        core_views.upload_file,
        name="upload_file",
    ),
]
```

9. Now let's create a template for the location form as follows:

```html
{# locations/location_form.html #}
{% extends "base.html" %}
{% load i18n crispy_forms_tags %}

{% block content %}
    <div class="row">
        <div class="col-lg-8">
            <a href="{% url "locations:location_list" %}">{% trans
              "Interesting Locations" %}</a>
            <h1>
                {% if location %}
                    {% blocktrans trimmed with name=
                      location.name %}
                        Change Location "{{ name }}"
                    {% endblocktrans %}
                {% else %}
                    {% trans "Add Location" %}
                {% endif %}
            </h1>
            {% crispy form %}
        </div>
    </div>
{% endblock %}
```

10. We need a couple more templates. Create a custom template for the file upload field that will include the necessary CSS and JavaScript:

```
{# core/includes/file_upload_field.html #}
{% load i18n crispy_forms_field static sekizai_tags %}

{% include "core/includes/picture_preview.html" %}
<{% if tag %}{{ tag }}{% else %}div{% endif %} id="div_{{
field.auto_id }}"
class="form-group{% if 'form-horizontal' in form_class %} row{%
endif %}{% if wrapper_class %} {{ wrapper_class }}{% endif %}{% if
field.css_classes %} {{ field.css_classes }}{% endif %}">
   {% if field.label and form_show_labels %}
     <label for="{{ field.id_for_label }}"
            class="col-form-label {{ label_class }}{% if field
             .field.required %} requiredField{% endif %}">
       {{ field.label|safe }}{% if field.field.required %}<span
        class="asteriskField">*</span>{% endif %}
     </label>
   {% endif %}

   <div class="{{ field_class }}">
     <span class="btn btn-success fileinput-button">
        <span>{% trans "Upload File..." %}</span>
        {% crispy_field field %}
     </span>
     {% include 'bootstrap4/layout/help_text_and_errors.html' %}
     <p class="form-text text-muted">
        {% trans "Available formats are JPG, GIF, and PNG." %}
        {% trans "Minimal size is 800 x 800 px." %}
     </p>
   </div>
</{% if tag %}{{ tag }}{% else %}div{% endif %}>

{% addtoblock "css" %}
<link rel="stylesheet" href="{% static 'site/vendor/jQuery-File-
Upload-10.2.0/css/jquery.fileupload-ui.css' %}"/>
<link rel="stylesheet" href="{% static 'site/vendor/jQuery-File-
Upload-10.2.0/css/jquery.fileupload.css' %}"/>
{% endaddtoblock %}

{% addtoblock "js" %}
<script src="{% static 'site/vendor/jQuery-File-
Upload-10.2.0/js/vendor/jquery.ui.widget.js' %}"></script>
<script src="{% static 'site/vendor/jQuery-File-
Upload-10.2.0/js/jquery.iframe-transport.js' %}"></script>
<script src="{% static 'site/vendor/jQuery-File-
Upload-10.2.0/js/jquery.fileupload.js' %}"></script>
```

```
<script src="{% static 'site/js/picture_upload.js' %}"></script>
{% endaddtoblock %}
```

11. Next, let's create a template for the picture preview:

```
{# core/includes/picture_preview.html #}
<div id="picture_preview">
  {% if form.instance.picture %}
    <img src="{{ form.instance.picture.url }}" alt=""
     class="img-fluid"/>
  {% endif %}
</div>
<div id="progress" class="progress" style="visibility: hidden">
  <div class="progress-bar progress-bar-striped
   progress-bar-animated"
      role="progressbar"
      aria-valuenow="0"
      aria-valuemin="0"
      aria-valuemax="100"
      style="width: 0%"></div>
</div>
```

12. Finally, let's add the JavaScript that will handle picture uploads and previews:

```
/* site_static/site/js/picture_upload.js */
$(function() {
  $("#id_picture_path").each(function() {
    $picture_path = $(this);
    if ($picture_path.val()) {
      $("#picture_preview").html(
        '<img src="' +
          window.settings.MEDIA_URL +
          "temporary-uploads/" +
          $picture_path.val() +
          '" alt="" class="img-fluid" />'
      );
    }
  });
  $("#id_picture").fileupload({
    dataType: "json",
    add: function(e, data) {
      $("#progress").css("visibility", "visible");
      data.submit();
    },
    progressall: function(e, data) {
      var progress = parseInt((data.loaded / data.total) * 100,
       10);
      $("#progress .progress-bar")
```

```
            .attr("aria-valuenow", progress)
            .css("width", progress + "%");
        },
        done: function(e, data) {
          $.each(data.result.files, function(index, file) {
            $("#picture_preview").html(
              '<img src="' +
                window.settings.MEDIA_URL +
                "temporary-uploads/" +
                file.name +
                '" alt="" class="img-fluid" />'
            );
            $("#id_picture_path").val(file.name);
          });
          $("#progress").css("visibility", "hidden");
        }
      });
    });
```

How it works...

If the JavaScript fails to execute, then the form remains completely usable, but when the JavaScript runs properly, we get an enhanced form with the file field replaced by a simple button, as shown here:

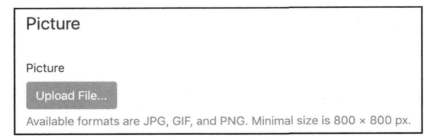

When an image is selected by clicking on the **Upload File...** button, the result in the browser will look similar to the following screenshot:

Clicking on the **Upload File...** the button triggers a file dialog that asks you to select a file, and, upon selection, it immediately starts the Ajax upload process. Then we see a preview of the image that has been attached. The preview picture is uploaded to a temporary directory and its filename is saved at the picture_path hidden field. When you submit the form, the form either saves the picture from this temporary location or from the picture field. The picture field will have a value if the form was submitted without JavaScript or if it failed to load the JavaScript. If there are any validation errors for the other fields after the page reload, then the preview image loaded is based on the picture_path.

Let's run through the steps to dig deeper into the process and see how it works.

In our model form for the `Location` model, we made the `picture` field nonrequired, although it is required at the model level. In addition, we added the `picture_path` field there, and then we expect either of those fields to be submitted to the form. In the `crispy-forms` layout, we defined a custom template for the `picture` field, `file_upload_field.html`. There, we set a preview image, upload progress bar, and custom help text with the allowed file formats and minimal dimensions. In the same template, we also attached the CSS and JavaScript files from the jQuery File Upload library and a custom script, `picture_upload.js`. The CSS files rendered the file upload field as a nice button. The JavaScript files are responsible for the Ajax-based file upload.

The `picture_upload.js` sent the selected file to the `upload_file` view. This view checked whether the file is of an image type and then tries to save it under the `temporary-uploads/` directory under the project's `MEDIA_ROOT`. The view returned a JSON with the details about a successful or unsuccessful file upload.

After a picture has been selected and uploaded and the form submitted, the `save()` method of `LocationForm` will be called. If the `picture_path` field value exists, a file will be taken from the temporary directory and copied to the `picture` field of the `Location` model. Then the picture at the temporary directory gets deleted and the `Location` instance is saved.

There's more...

We exclude the `geoposition` field from the model form and instead render the `latitude` and `longitude` fields for the geoposition data. The default geoposition's `PointField` is rendered as a `Leaflet.js` map with no possibilities to customize it. With the two `latitude` and `longitude` fields, we are flexible and can make use of the Google Maps API, Bing Maps API, or `Leaflet.js` to show them in a map, enter manually, or geocode them from the filled-in location address.

For convenience, we use two helper methods, `get_geoposition()` and `set_geoposition()`, which we defined earlier in the *Using HTML5 data attributes* recipe.

See also

- The *Using HTML5 data attributes* recipe
- The *Uploading images* recipe in `Chapter 3`, *Forms and Views*
- The *Opening object details in a modal dialog* recipe
- The *Implementing a continuous scroll* recipe
- The *Implementing the Like widget* recipe
- The *Making forms secure from cross-site request forgery (CSRF)* recipe in `Chapter 7`, *Security and Performance*

5
Custom Template Filters and Tags

In this chapter, we will cover the following recipes:

- Following conventions for your own template filters and tags
- Creating a template filter to show how many days have passed since a post was published
- Creating a template filter to extract the first media object
- Creating a template filter to humanize URLs
- Creating a template tag to include a template, if it exists
- Creating a template tag to load a QuerySet in a template
- Creating a template tag to parse content as a template
- Creating template tags to modify request query parameters

Introduction

Django has an extensive template system with features such as template inheritance, filters to change the representation of values, and tags for presentational logic. Moreover, Django allows you to add your own template filters and tags to your apps. Custom filters or tags should be located in a template-tag library file under the `templatetags` Python package in your app. Your template-tag library can then be loaded in any template with the `{% load %}` template tag. In this chapter, we will create several useful filters and tags that will give more control to template editors.

Technical requirements

For working with the code of this chapter, you will need the latest stable version of Python 3, the MySQL or PostgreSQL database, and a Django project with a virtual environment.

You can find all the code for this chapter at the `ch05` directory of the GitHub repository: `https://github.com/PacktPublishing/Django-3-Web-Development-Cookbook-Fourth-Edition`.

Following conventions for your own template filters and tags

Custom template filters and tags can be confusing and inconsistent if you don't have guidelines to follow. It is essential to have both handy and flexible template filters and tags that should serve template editors as much as possible. In this recipe, we will take a look at some conventions that you should use when enhancing the functionality of the Django template system:

1. Don't create or use custom template filters or tags when the logic for the page fits better in the view, context processors, or model methods. When your content is context-specific, such as a list of objects or an object-detail view, load the object in the view. If you need to show some content on nearly every page, create a context processor. Use custom methods of the model instead of template filters when you need to get some properties of an object that are not related to the context of the template.
2. Name the template-tag library with the `_tags` suffix. When your template-tag library is named differently than your app, you can avoid ambiguous package-importing problems.
3. In the newly created library, separate the filters from the tags—for example, using comments, as shown in the following code:

```
# myproject/apps/core/templatetags/utility_tags.py
from django import template

register = template.Library()

""" TAGS """

# Your tags go here...
```

```
""" FILTERS """

# Your filters go here...
```

4. When creating advanced custom template tags, make sure that their syntax is easy to remember by including the following constructs that can follow the tag name:

   - `for [app_name.model_name]`: Include this construct to use a specific model.
   - `using [template_name]`: Include this construct to use a template for the output of the template tag.
   - `limit [count]`: Include this construct to limit the results to a specific number.
   - `as [context_variable]`: Include this construct to store the results in a context variable that can be reused multiple times.

5. Try to avoid multiple values that are defined positionally in the template tags, unless they are self-explanatory. Otherwise, this will likely confuse template developers.

6. Make as many resolvable arguments as possible. Strings without quotes should be treated as context variables that need to be resolved, or as short words that remind you of the structure of the template-tag components.

Creating a template filter to show how many days have passed since a post was published

When talking about creation or modification dates, it is convenient to read a more human-readable time difference—for example, the blog entry was posted 3 days ago, the news article was published today, and the user last logged in yesterday. In this recipe, we will create a template filter named `date_since`, which converts dates to humanized time differences based on days, weeks, months, or years.

Getting ready

Create the `core` app, and put it under `INSTALLED_APPS` in the settings, if you haven't done so already. Then, create a `templatetags` Python package in this app (Python packages are directories with an empty `__init__.py` file).

How to do it...

Create a `utility_tags.py` file with the following content:

```python
# myproject/apps/core/templatetags/utility_tags.py
from datetime import datetime
from django import template
from django.utils import timezone
from django.utils.translation import ugettext_lazy as _

register = template.Library()


""" FILTERS """

DAYS_PER_YEAR = 365
DAYS_PER_MONTH = 30
DAYS_PER_WEEK = 7


@register.filter(is_safe=True)
def date_since(specific_date):
    """
    Returns a human-friendly difference between today and past_date
    (adapted from https://www.djangosnippets.org/snippets/116/)
    """
    today = timezone.now().date()
    if isinstance(specific_date, datetime):
        specific_date = specific_date.date()
    diff = today - specific_date
    diff_years = int(diff.days / DAYS_PER_YEAR)
    diff_months = int(diff.days / DAYS_PER_MONTH)
    diff_weeks = int(diff.days / DAYS_PER_WEEK)
    diff_map = [
        ("year", "years", diff_years,),
        ("month", "months", diff_months,),
        ("week", "weeks", diff_weeks,),
        ("day", "days", diff.days,),
    ]
```

```
for parts in diff_map:
    (interval, intervals, count,) = parts
    if count > 1:
        return _(f"{count} {intervals} ago")
    elif count == 1:
        return _("yesterday") \
            if interval == "day" \
            else _(f"last {interval}")
if diff.days == 0:
    return _("today")
else:
    # Date is in the future; return formatted date.
    return f"{specific_date:%B %d, %Y}"
```

How it works...

This filter used in a template, as shown in the following code, will render something similar to yesterday, last week, or 5 months ago:

```
{% load utility_tags %}
{{ object.published|date_since }}
```

You can apply this filter to values of the date and datetime types.

Each template-tag library has a register of template.Library type where filters and tags are collected. Django filters are functions registered by the @register.filter decorator. In this case, we pass the is_safe=True parameter to indicate that our filter will not introduce any unsafe HTML markup.

By default, the filter in the template system will be named the same as the function or another callable object. If you want, you can set a different name for the filter by passing the name to the decorator, as follows:

```
@register.filter(name="humanized_date_since", is_safe=True)
def date_since(value):
    # ...
```

The filter itself is fairly self-explanatory. At first, the current date is read. If the given value of the filter is of the datetime type, its date is extracted. Then, the difference between today and the extracted value is calculated based on the DAYS_PER_YEAR, DAYS_PER_MONTH, DAYS_PER_WEEK, or days intervals. Depending on the count, different string results are returned, falling back to displaying a formatted date if the value is in the future.

There's more...

If required, we could cover other stretches of time too, as in 20 minutes ago, 5 hours ago, or even 1 decade ago. To do so, we would add more intervals to the existing `diff_map` set, and to show the difference in time, we would need to operate on `datetime` values instead of `date` values.

See also

- The *Creating a template filter to extract the first media object* recipe
- The *Creating a template filter to humanize URLs* recipe

Creating a template filter to extract the first media object

Imagine that you are developing a blog overview page, and, for each post, you want to show images, music, or videos on that page, taken from the content. In such a case, you need to extract the `<figure>`, `<img>`, `<object>`, `<embed>`, `<video>`, `<audio>`, and `<iframe>` tags from the HTML content of the post, as stored on a field of the post model. In this recipe, we will see how to perform this using regular expressions in the `first_media` filter.

Getting ready

We will start with the `core` app that should be set in `INSTALLED_APPS` in the settings and should contain the `templatetags` package in this app.

How to do it...

In the `utility_tags.py` file, add the following content:

```
# myproject/apps/core/templatetags/utility_tags.py
import re
from django import template
from django.utils.safestring import mark_safe
```

```
register = template.Library()

""" FILTERS """

MEDIA_CLOSED_TAGS = "|".join([
    "figure", "object", "video", "audio", "iframe"])
MEDIA_SINGLE_TAGS = "|".join(["img", "embed"])
MEDIA_TAGS_REGEX = re.compile(
    r"<(?P<tag>" + MEDIA_CLOSED_TAGS + ")[\S\s]+?</(?P=tag)>|" +
    r"<(" + MEDIA_SINGLE_TAGS + ")[^>]+>",
    re.MULTILINE)


@register.filter
def first_media(content):
    """
    Returns the chunk of media-related markup from the html content
    """
    tag_match = MEDIA_TAGS_REGEX.search(content)
    media_tag = ""
    if tag_match:
        media_tag = tag_match.group()
    return mark_safe(media_tag)
```

How it works...

If the HTML content in the database is valid, and you put the following code in the template, it will retrieve the media tags from the content field of the object; otherwise, an empty string will be returned if no media is found:

```
{% load utility_tags %}
{{ object.content|first_media }}
```

Regular expressions are a powerful feature to search or replace patterns of text. At first, we define lists of all the supported media tag names, splitting them into groups for those that have both opening and closing tags (MEDIA_CLOSED_TAGS), and those that are self-closed (MEDIA_SINGLE_TAGS). From these lists, we generate the compiled regular expression as MEDIA_TAGS_REGEX. In this case, we search for all the possible media tags, allowing them to occur across multiple lines.

Let's see how this regular expression works, as follows:

- Alternating patterns are separated by the pipe (|) symbol.
- There are two groups within the patterns—first of all, those with both opening and closing normal tags (`<figure>`, `<object>`, `<video>`, `<audio>`, `<iframe>`, and `<picture>`), and then one final pattern for what are called self-closing or void tags (`<img>` and `<embed>`).
- For the possibly multiline normal tags, we will use the `[\S\s]+?` pattern that matches any symbol at least once; however, we do this as few times as possible until we find the string that goes after it.
- Therefore, `<figure[\S\s]+?</figure>` searches for the start of the `<figure>` tag and everything after it, until it finds the closing `</figure>` tag.
- Similarly, with the `[^>]+` pattern for self-closing tags, we search for any symbol except the right-angle bracket (possibly better known as a greater-than symbol—that is to say, >) at least once and as many times as possible, until we encounter such a bracket indicating the closure of the tag.

The `re.MULTILINE` flag ensures that matches can be found, even if they span multiple lines in the content. Then, in the filter, we perform a search using this regular-expression pattern. By default, in Django, the result of any filter will show the <, >, and & symbols escaped as the `&lt;`, `&gt;`, and `&amp;` entities, respectively. In this case, however, we use the `mark_safe()` function to indicate that the result is safe and HTML-ready, so that any content will be rendered without escaping. Because the originating content is user input, we do this instead of passing `is_safe=True` when registering the filter, as we need to explicitly certify that the markup is safe.

There's more...

If you are interested in regular expressions, you can learn more about them in the official Python documentation at `https://docs.python.org/3/library/re.html`.

See also

- The *Creating a template filter to show how many days have passed since a post was published* recipe
- The *Creating a template filter to humanize URLs* recipe

Creating a template filter to humanize URLs

Web users commonly recognize URLs without the protocol (http://) or trailing slash (/), and, similarly, they will enter URLs in this fashion in address fields. In this recipe, we will create a humanize_url filter that is used to present URLs to the user in a shorter format, truncating very long addresses, similar to what Twitter does with the links in tweets.

Getting ready

Similar to the previous recipes, we will start with the core app that should be set in INSTALLED_APPS in the settings, which contains the templatetags package in the app.

How to do it...

In the FILTERS section of the utility_tags.py template library in the core app, let's add the humanize_url filter and register it, as shown in the following code:

```python
# myproject/apps/core/templatetags/utility_tags.py
import re
from django import template

register = template.Library()

""" FILTERS """

@register.filter
def humanize_url(url, letter_count=40):
    """
    Returns a shortened human-readable URL
    """
    letter_count = int(letter_count)
    re_start = re.compile(r"^https?://")
    re_end = re.compile(r"/$")
    url = re_end.sub("", re_start.sub("", url))
    if len(url) > letter_count:
        url = f"{url[:letter_count - 1]}..."
    return url
```

How it works...

We can use the `humanize_url` filter in any template, as follows:

```
{% load utility_tags %}
<a href="{{ object.website }}" target="_blank">
    {{ object.website|humanize_url }}
</a>
<a href="{{ object.website }}" target="_blank">
    {{ object.website|humanize_url:30 }}
</a>
```

The filter uses regular expressions to remove the leading protocol and trailing slash, shortens the URL to the given amount of letters (40, by default), and adds an ellipsis to the end after truncating it if the full URL doesn't fit the specified letter count. For example, for the `https://docs.djangoproject.com/en/3.0/howto/custom-template-tags/` URL, the 40-character humanized version would be `docs.djangoproject.com/en/3.0/howto/cus...`.

See also

- The *Creating a template filter to show how many days have passed since a post was published* recipe
- The *Creating a template filter to extract the first media object* recipe
- The *Creating a template tag to include a template, if it exists* recipe

Creating a template tag to include a template, if it exists

Django provides the `{% include %}` template tag that allows one template to render and include another template. However, this template tag raises an error if you try to include a template that doesn't exist in the filesystem. In this recipe, we will create a `{% try_to_include %}` template tag that includes another template, if it exists, and fails silently by rendering as an empty string otherwise.

Getting ready

We will start again with the `core` app that is installed and ready for custom template tags.

How to do it...

Perform the following steps to create the `{% try_to_include %}` template tag:

1. First, let's create the function parsing the template-tag arguments, as follows:

```python
# myproject/apps/core/templatetags/utility_tags.py
from django import template
from django.template.loader import get_template

register = template.Library()


""" TAGS """

@register.tag
def try_to_include(parser, token):
    """
    Usage: {% try_to_include "some_template.html" %}

    This will fail silently if the template doesn't exist.
    If it does exist, it will be rendered with the current context.
    """
    try:
        tag_name, template_name = token.split_contents()
    except ValueError:
        tag_name = token.contents.split()[0]
        raise template.TemplateSyntaxError(
            f"{tag_name} tag requires a single argument")
    return IncludeNode(template_name)
```

2. Then, we need a custom `IncludeNode` class in the same file, extending from the base `template.Node`. Let's insert it just before the `try_to_include()` function, as follows:

```python
class IncludeNode(template.Node):
    def __init__(self, template_name):
        self.template_name = template.Variable(template_name)

    def render(self, context):
        try:
            # Loading the template and rendering it
```

```
            included_template = self.template_name.resolve(context)
            if isinstance(included_template, str):
                included_template = get_template(included_template)
            rendered_template = included_template.render(
                context.flatten()
            )
        except (template.TemplateDoesNotExist,
                template.VariableDoesNotExist,
                AttributeError):
            rendered_template = ""
        return rendered_template


@register.tag
def try_to_include(parser, token):
    # ...
```

How it works...

Advanced custom template tags consist of two things:

- A function that parses the arguments of the template tag
- The Node class that is responsible for the logic of the template tag as well as the output

The {% try_to_include %} template tag expects one argument— that is, template_name. Therefore, in the try_to_include() function, we try to assign the split contents of the token only to the tag_name variable (which is try_to_include) and the template_name variable. If this doesn't work, a TemplateSyntaxError is raised. The function returns the IncludeNode object, which gets the template_name field and stores it in a template Variable object for later use.

In the render() method of IncludeNode, we resolve the template_name variable. If a context variable was passed to the template tag, its value will be used here for template_name. If a quoted string was passed to the template tag, then the content within the quotes will be used for included_template, whereas a string corresponding to a context variable will be resolved into its string equivalent for the same.

Lastly, we will try to load the template, using the resolved `included_template` string, and render it with the current template context. If that doesn't work, an empty string is returned.

There are at least two situations where we could use this template tag:

- When including a template whose path is defined in a model, as follows:

```
{% load utility_tags %}
{% try_to_include object.template_path %}
```

- When including a template whose path is defined with the `{% with %}` template tag somewhere high in the template context variable's scope. This is especially useful when you need to create custom layouts for plugins in the placeholder of a template in Django CMS:

```
{# templates/cms/start_page.html #}
{% load cms_tags %}
{% with editorial_content_template_path=
"cms/plugins/editorial_content/start_page.html" %}
    {% placeholder "main_content" %}
{% endwith %}
```

Later, the placeholder can be filled with the `editorial_content` plugins, and the `editorial_content_template_path` context variable is then read and the template can be safely included, if available:

```
{# templates/cms/plugins/editorial_content.html #}
{% load utility_tags %}
{% if editorial_content_template_path %}
    {% try_to_include editorial_content_template_path %}
{% else %}
    <div>
        <!-- Some default presentation of
        editorial content plugin -->
    </div>
{% endif %}
```

There's more...

You can use the `{% try_to_include %}` tag in any combination with the default `{% include %}` tag to include the templates that extend other templates. This is beneficial for large-scale web platforms, where you have different kinds of lists in which complex items share the same structure as widgets but have a different source of data.

For example, in the artist list template, you can include the `artist_item` template, as follows:

```
{% load utility_tags %}
{% for object in object_list %}
    {% try_to_include "artists/includes/artist_item.html" %}
{% endfor %}
```

This template will extend from the item base, as follows:

```
{# templates/artists/includes/artist_item.html #}
{% extends "utils/includes/item_base.html" %}
{% block item_title %}
    {{ object.first_name }} {{ object.last_name }}
{% endblock %}
```

The item base defines the markup for any item and also includes a Like widget, as follows:

```
{# templates/utils/includes/item_base.html #}
{% load likes_tags %}
<h3>{% block item_title %}{% endblock %}</h3>
{% if request.user.is_authenticated %}
    {% like_widget for object %}
{% endif %}
```

See also

- The *Implementing the Like widget* recipe in Chapter 4, *Templates and JavaScript*
- The *Creating a template tag to load a QuerySet in a template* recipe
- The *Creating a template tag to parse content as a template* recipe
- The *Creating template tags to modify request query parameters* recipe

Creating a template tag to load a QuerySet in a template

Generally, the content that should be shown on a web page will be defined in the context by views. If the content is to be shown on every page, it is logical to create a context processor to make it available globally. Another situation is when you need to show additional content, such as the latest news or a random quote, on some pages—for example, the starting page or the details page of an object. In this case, you can load the necessary content with a custom {% load_objects %} template tag, which we will implement in this recipe.

Getting ready

Once again, we will start with the core app, which should be installed and ready for custom template tags.

In addition, to illustrate the concept, let's create a news app with an Article model, as follows:

```python
# myproject/apps/news/models.py
from django.db import models
from django.urls import reverse
from django.utils.translation import ugettext_lazy as _

from myproject.apps.core.models import CreationModificationDateBase, UrlBase


class ArticleManager(models.Manager):
    def random_published(self):
        return self.filter(
            publishing_status=self.model.PUBLISHING_STATUS_PUBLISHED,
        ).order_by("?")


class Article(CreationModificationDateBase, UrlBase):
    PUBLISHING_STATUS_DRAFT, PUBLISHING_STATUS_PUBLISHED = "d", "p"
    PUBLISHING_STATUS_CHOICES = (
        (PUBLISHING_STATUS_DRAFT, _("Draft")),
        (PUBLISHING_STATUS_PUBLISHED, _("Published")),
    )
    title = models.CharField(_("Title"), max_length=200)
    slug = models.SlugField(_("Slug"), max_length=200)
```

```
content = models.TextField(_("Content"))
publishing_status = models.CharField(
    _("Publishing status"),
    max_length=1,
    choices=PUBLISHING_STATUS_CHOICES,
    default=PUBLISHING_STATUS_DRAFT,
)

custom_manager = ArticleManager()

class Meta:
    verbose_name = _("Article")
    verbose_name_plural = _("Articles")

def __str__(self):
    return self.title

def get_url_path(self):
    return reverse("news:article_detail", kwargs={"slug": self.slug})
```

There, the interesting part is the `custom_manager` for the `Article` model. The manager can be used to list out random published articles.

Using the examples of the previous chapter, you can complete the app with URL configurations, views, templates, and administration setup. Then, add some articles to the database using the administration form.

How to do it...

An advanced custom template tag consists of a function that parses the arguments that are passed to the tag, and the `Node` class that renders the output of the tag or modifies the template context. Perform the following steps to create the `{% load_objects %}` template tag:

1. First, let's create the function that handles the parsing of the template-tag arguments, as follows:

```
# myproject/apps/core/templatetags/utility_tags.py
from django import template
from django.apps import apps

register = template.Library()


""" TAGS """
```

```python
@register.tag
def load_objects(parser, token):
    """
    Gets a queryset of objects of the model specified by app and
    model names

    Usage:
        {% load_objects [<manager>.]<method>
                        from <app_name>.<model_name>
                        [limit <amount>]
                        as <var_name> %}

    Examples:
        {% load_objects latest_published from people.Person
                        limit 3 as people %}
        {% load_objects site_objects.all from news.Article
                        as articles %}
        {% load_objects site_objects.all from news.Article
                        limit 3 as articles %}
    """
    limit_count = None
    try:
        (tag_name, manager_method,
         str_from, app_model,
         str_limit, limit_count,
         str_as, var_name) = token.split_contents()
    except ValueError:
        try:
            (tag_name, manager_method,
             str_from, app_model,
             str_as, var_name) = token.split_contents()
        except ValueError:
            tag_name = token.contents.split()[0]
            raise template.TemplateSyntaxError(
                f"{tag_name} tag requires the following syntax: "
                f"{{% {tag_name} [<manager>.]<method> from "
                "<app_name>.<model_name> [limit <amount>] "
                "as <var_name> %}")
    try:
        app_name, model_name = app_model.split(".")
    except ValueError:
        raise template.TemplateSyntaxError(
            "load_objects tag requires application name "
            "and model name, separated by a dot")
    model = apps.get_model(app_name, model_name)
    return ObjectsNode(
        model, manager_method, limit_count, var_name
    )
```

2. Then, we will create the custom `ObjectsNode` class in the same file, extending from the `template.Node` base. Let's insert it just before the `load_objects()` function, as shown in the following code:

```
class ObjectsNode(template.Node):
    def __init__(self, model, manager_method, limit, var_name):
        self.model = model
        self.manager_method = manager_method
        self.limit = template.Variable(limit) if limit else None
        self.var_name = var_name

    def render(self, context):
        if "." in self.manager_method:
            manager, method = self.manager_method.split(".")
        else:
            manager = "_default_manager"
            method = self.manager_method

        model_manager = getattr(self.model, manager)
        fallback_method = self.model._default_manager.none
        qs = getattr(model_manager, method, fallback_method)()
        limit = None
        if self.limit:
            try:
                limit = self.limit.resolve(context)
            except template.VariableDoesNotExist:
                limit = None
        context[self.var_name] = qs[:limit] if limit else qs
        return ""


@register.tag
def load_objects(parser, token):
    # ...
```

How it works...

The `{% load_objects %}` template tag loads a QuerySet defined by the method of the manager from a specified app and model, limits the result to the specified count, and saves the result to the given context variable.

The following code is a simple example of how to use the template tag that we have just created. It will load all news articles in any template, using the following snippet:

```
{% load utility_tags %}
{% load_objects all from news.Article as all_articles %}
<ul>
    {% for article in all_articles %}
        <li><a href="{{ article.get_url_path }}">
        {{ article.title }}</a></li>
    {% endfor %}
</ul>
```

This is using the `all()` method of the default `objects` manager of the `Article` model, and it will sort the articles by the `ordering` attribute defined in the `Meta` class of the model.

Next is an example that uses a custom manager with a custom method to query the objects from the database. A manager is an interface that provides the database query operations to models.

Each model has at least one manager called `objects`, by default. For our `Article` model, we added an extra manager called `custom_manager` with a method, `random_published()`. Here is how we can use it with our `{% load_objects %}` template tag to load one random published article:

```
{% load utility_tags %}
{% load_objects custom_manager.random_published from news.Article limit 1
as random_published_articles %}
<ul>
    {% for article in random_published_articles %}
        <li><a href="{{ article.get_url_path }}">
        {{ article.title }}</a></li>
    {% endfor %}
</ul>
```

Let's look at the code of the `{% load_objects %}` template tag. In the parsing function, there are two allowed forms for the tag—with or without a `limit`. The string is parsed, and if the format is recognized, the components of the template tag are passed to the `ObjectsNode` class.

In the `render()` method of the `Node` class, we check the manager's name and its method's name. If no manager is specified, `_default_manager` will be used. This is an automatic property of any model injected by Django and points to the first available `models.Manager()` instance. In most cases, `_default_manager` will be the `objects` manager. After that, we will call the method of the manager and fall back to an empty QuerySet if the method doesn't exist. If a `limit` is defined, we resolve the value of it and limit the QuerySet accordingly. Lastly, we will store the resulting QuerySet in the context variable, as given by `var_name`.

See also

- The *Creating a model mixin with URL-related methods* recipe in `Chapter 2`, *Models and Database Structure*
- The *Creating a model mixin to handle creation and modification dates* recipe in `Chapter 2`, *Models and Database Structure*
- The *Creating a template tag to include a template, if it exists* recipe
- The *Creating a template tag to parse content as a template* recipe
- The *Creating template tags to modify request query parameters* recipe

Creating a template tag to parse content as a template

In this recipe, we will create the `{% parse %}` template tag that will allow you to put template snippets in the database. This is valuable when you want to provide different content for authenticated and unauthenticated users, when you want to include a personalized salutation, or when you don't want to hardcode the media paths in the database.

Getting ready

As usual, we will start with the `core` app that should be installed and ready for custom template tags.

How to do it...

An advanced custom template tag consists of a function that parses the arguments that are passed to the tag, and a `Node` class that renders the output of the tag or modifies the template context. Perform the following steps to create the `{% parse %}` template tag:

1. First, let's create the function parsing the arguments of the template tag, as follows:

```python
# myproject/apps/core/templatetags/utility_tags.py
from django import template

register = template.Library()


""" TAGS """

@register.tag
def parse(parser, token):
    """
    Parses a value as a template and prints or saves to a variable

    Usage:
        {% parse <template_value> [as <variable>] %}

    Examples:
        {% parse object.description %}
        {% parse header as header %}
        {% parse "{{ MEDIA_URL }}js/" as js_url %}
    """
    bits = token.split_contents()
    tag_name = bits.pop(0)
    try:
        template_value = bits.pop(0)
        var_name = None
        if len(bits) >= 2:
            str_as, var_name = bits[:2]
    except ValueError:
        raise template.TemplateSyntaxError(
            f"{tag_name} tag requires the following syntax: "
            f"{{% {tag_name} <template_value> [as <variable>] %}}")
    return ParseNode(template_value, var_name)
```

2. Then, we will create the custom `ParseNode` class in the same file, extending from the base `template.Node`, as shown in the following code (place it just before the `parse()` function):

```python
class ParseNode(template.Node):
    def __init__(self, template_value, var_name):
        self.template_value = template.Variable(template_value)
        self.var_name = var_name

    def render(self, context):
        template_value = self.template_value.resolve(context)
        t = template.Template(template_value)
        context_vars = {}
        for d in list(context):
            for var, val in d.items():
                context_vars[var] = val
        req_context = template.RequestContext(
            context["request"], context_vars
        )
        result = t.render(req_context)
        if self.var_name:
            context[self.var_name] = result
            result = ""
        return result


@register.tag
def parse(parser, token):
    # ...
```

How it works...

The `{% parse %}` template tag allows you to parse a value as a template and render it immediately or store it in a context variable.

If we have an object with a description field, which can contain template variables or logic, we can parse and render it using the following code:

```
{% load utility_tags %}
{% parse object.description %}
```

It is also possible to define a value to parse using a quoted string, as shown in the following code:

```
{% load static utility_tags %}
{% get_static_prefix as STATIC_URL %}
{% parse "{{ STATIC_URL }}site/img/" as image_directory %}
<img src="{{ image_directory }}logo.svg" alt="Logo" />
```

Let's take a look at the code of the `{% parse %}` template tag. The parsing function checks the arguments of the template tag bit by bit. At first, we expect the parse name and the template value. If there are still more bits in the token, we expect the combination of an optional `as` word followed by the context variable name. The template value and the optional variable name are passed to the `ParseNode` class.

The `render()` method of that class first resolves the value of the template variable and creates a template object out of it. The `context_vars` are copied and a request context is generated, which the template renders. If the variable name is defined, the result is stored in it and an empty string is rendered; otherwise, the rendered template is shown immediately.

See also

- The *Creating a template tag to include a template, if it exists* recipe
- The *Creating a template tag to load a QuerySet in a template* recipe
- The *Creating template tags to modify request query parameters* recipe

Creating template tags to modify request query parameters

Django has a convenient and flexible system to create canonical and clean URLs just by adding regular-expression rules to the URL configuration files. However, there is a lack of built-in techniques to manage query parameters. Views such as search or filterable object lists need to accept query parameters to drill down through the filtered results using another parameter or to go to another page. In this recipe, we will create `{% modify_query %}`, `{% add_to_query %}`, and `{% remove_from_query %}` template tags, which let you add, change, or remove the parameters of the current query.

Getting ready

Once again, we start with the `core` app that should be set in
`INSTALLED_APPS` which contains the `templatetags` package.

Also, make sure that you have the `request` context processor added to the
`context_processors` list in the `TEMPLATES` settings under `OPTIONS`, as follows:

```python
# myproject/settings/_base.py
TEMPLATES = [
    {
        "BACKEND": "django.template.backends.django.DjangoTemplates",
        "DIRS": [os.path.join(BASE_DIR, "myproject", "templates")],
        "APP_DIRS": True,
        "OPTIONS": {
            "context_processors": [
                "django.template.context_processors.debug",
                "django.template.context_processors.request",
                "django.contrib.auth.context_processors.auth",
                "django.contrib.messages.context_processors.messages",
                "django.template.context_processors.media",
                "django.template.context_processors.static",
                "myproject.apps.core.context_processors.website_url",
            ]
        },
    }
]
```

How to do it...

For these template tags, we will be using the `@simple_tag` decorator that parses the
components and requires you to just define the rendering function, as follows:

1. First, let's add a helper method for putting together the query strings that each of
   our tags will output:

   ```python
   # myproject/apps/core/templatetags/utility_tags.py
   from urllib.parse import urlencode

   from django import template
   from django.utils.encoding import force_str
   from django.utils.safestring import mark_safe

   register = template.Library()
   ```

```
""" TAGS """

def construct_query_string(context, query_params):
    # empty values will be removed
    query_string = context["request"].path
    if len(query_params):
        encoded_params = urlencode([
            (key, force_str(value))
            for (key, value) in query_params if value
        ]).replace("&", "&amp;")
        query_string += f"?{encoded_params}"
    return mark_safe(query_string)
```

2. Then, we will create the `{% modify_query %}` template tag:

```
@register.simple_tag(takes_context=True)
def modify_query(context, *params_to_remove, **params_to_change):
    """Renders a link with modified current query parameters"""
    query_params = []
    for key, value_list in context["request"].GET.lists():
        if not key in params_to_remove:
            # don't add key-value pairs for params_to_remove
            if key in params_to_change:
                # update values for keys in params_to_change
                query_params.append((key, params_to_change[key]))
                params_to_change.pop(key)
            else:
                # leave existing parameters as they were
                # if not mentioned in the params_to_change
                for value in value_list:
                    query_params.append((key, value))
                    # attach new params
    for key, value in params_to_change.items():
        query_params.append((key, value))
    return construct_query_string(context, query_params)
```

3. Next, let's create the `{% add_to_query %}` template tag:

```
@register.simple_tag(takes_context=True)
def add_to_query(context, *params_to_remove, **params_to_add):
    """Renders a link with modified current query parameters"""
    query_params = []
    # go through current query params..
    for key, value_list in context["request"].GET.lists():
        if key not in params_to_remove:
            # don't add key-value pairs which already
            # exist in the query
            if (key in params_to_add
```

```
                        and params_to_add[key] in value_list):
                    params_to_add.pop(key)
            for value in value_list:
                    query_params.append((key, value))
        # add the rest key-value pairs
        for key, value in params_to_add.items():
            query_params.append((key, value))
        return construct_query_string(context, query_params)
```

4. Lastly, let's create the {% remove_from_query %} template tag:

```
@register.simple_tag(takes_context=True)
def remove_from_query(context, *args, **kwargs):
    """Renders a link with modified current query parameters"""
    query_params = []
    # go through current query params..
    for key, value_list in context["request"].GET.lists():
        # skip keys mentioned in the args
        if key not in args:
            for value in value_list:
                # skip key-value pairs mentioned in kwargs
                if not (key in kwargs and
                        str(value) == str(kwargs[key])):
                    query_params.append((key, value))
    return construct_query_string(context, query_params)
```

How it works...

All three created template tags behave similarly. At first, they read the current query parameters from the request.GET dictionary-like QueryDict object to a new list of (key, value) query_params tuples. Then, the values are updated depending on the positional arguments and keyword arguments. Lastly, the new query string is formed via the helper method defined first. In this process, all spaces and special characters are URL-encoded, and the ampersands connecting the query parameters are escaped. This new query string is returned to the template.

To read more about the QueryDict objects, refer to the official Django documentation
at https://docs.djangoproject.com/en/3.0/ref/request-response/#querydict-objects.

Let's take a look at an example of how the `{% modify_query %}` template tag can be used. Positional arguments in the template tag define which query parameters are to be removed, and the keyword arguments define which query parameters are to be updated in the current query. If the current URL is `http://127.0.0.1:8000/artists/?category=fine-art&page=5`, we can use the following template tag to render a link that goes to the next page:

```
{% load utility_tags %}
<a href="{% modify_query page=6 %}">6</a>
```

The following snippet is the output rendered using the preceding template tag:

```
<a href="/artists/?category=fine-art&amp;page=6">6</a>
```

We can also use the following example to render a link that resets pagination and goes to another category, `sculpture`, as follows:

```
{% load utility_tags %}
<a href="{% modify_query "page" category="sculpture" %}">
    Sculpture
</a>
```

So, the output rendered using the preceding template tag would be as shown in this snippet:

```
<a href="/artists/?category=sculpture">
    Sculpture
</a>
```

With the `{% add_to_query %}` template tag, you can add, step by step, the parameters with the same name. For example, if the current URL is `http://127.0.0.1:8000/artists/?category=fine-art`, you can add another category, `Sculpture`, with the help of the following snippet:

```
{% load utility_tags %}
<a href="{% add_to_query category="sculpture" %}">
    + Sculpture
</a>
```

This will be rendered in the template, as shown in the following snippet:

```
<a href="/artists/?category=fine-art&amp;category=sculpture">
    + Sculpture
</a>
```

Lastly, with the help of the `{% remove_from_query %}` template tag, you can remove, step by step, the parameters with the same name. For example, if the current URL is `http://127.0.0.1:8000/artists/?category=fine-art&category=sculpture`, you can remove the `Sculpture` category, with the help of the following snippet:

```
{% load utility_tags %}
<a href="{% remove_from_query category="sculpture" %}">
    - Sculpture
</a>
```

This will be rendered in the template as follows:

```
<a href="/artists/?category=fine-art">
    - Sculpture
</a>
```

See also

- The *Filtering object lists* recipe in Chapter 3, *Forms and Views*
- The *Creating a template tag to include a template, if it exists* recipe
- The *Creating a template tag to load a QuerySet in a template* recipe
- The *Creating a template tag to parse content as a template* recipe

Model Administration

6

In this chapter, we will cover the following topics:

- Customizing columns on the change list page
- Creating sortable inlines
- Creating admin actions
- Developing change list filters
- Changing the app label of a third-party app
- Creating a custom accounts app
- Getting user Gravatars
- Inserting a map into a change form

Introduction

The Django framework comes with a built-in administration system for your data models. With very little effort, you can set up filterable, searchable, and sortable lists in order to browse your models, and you can configure forms to add and manage data. In this chapter, we will go through the advanced techniques we can use to customize administration by developing some practical cases.

Technical requirements

To work with the code in this chapter, you will need the latest stable version of Python, a MySQL or PostgreSQL database, and a Django project with a virtual environment.

You can find all the code for this chapter in the `chapter 06` directory of this book's GitHub repository: `https://github.com/PacktPublishing/Django-3-Web-Development-Cookbook-Fourth-Edition`

Customizing columns on the change list page

The change list views in the default Django administration system provide an overview of all of the instances of the specific models. By default, the `list_display` model admin attribute controls the fields that are shown in different columns. Additionally, you can implement custom admin methods that will return the data from relations or display custom HTML. In this recipe, we will create a special function, for use with the `list_display` attribute, that shows an image in one of the columns of the list view. As a bonus, we will make one field directly editable in the list view by adding the `list_editable` setting.

Getting ready

For this recipe, we will need the `Pillow` and `django-imagekit` libraries. Let's install them in the virtual environment using the following commands:

```
(env)$ pip install Pillow
(env)$ pip install django-imagekit
```

Make sure that `django.contrib.admin` and `imagekit` are in `INSTALLED_APPS` in the settings:

```
# myproject/settings/_base.py
INSTALLED_APPS = [
    # ...
    "django.contrib.admin",
    "imagekit",
]
```

Then, hook up the admin site in the URL configuration, as follows:

```
# myproject/urls.py
from django.contrib import admin
from django.conf.urls.i18n import i18n_patterns
from django.urls import include, path

urlpatterns = i18n_patterns(
    # ...
    path("admin/", admin.site.urls),
)
```

Next, create a new `products` app and put it under `INSTALLED_APPS`. This app will contain the `Product` and `ProductPhoto` models. Here, one product might have multiple photos. For this example, we will also be using `UrlMixin`, which was defined in the *Creating a model mixin with URL-related methods* recipe in `Chapter 2`, *Models and Database Structure*.

Let's create the `Product` and `ProductPhoto` models in the `models.py` file as follows:

```python
# myproject/apps/products/models.py
import os

from django.urls import reverse, NoReverseMatch
from django.db import models
from django.utils.timezone import now as timezone_now
from django.utils.translation import ugettext_lazy as _

from ordered_model.models import OrderedModel

from myproject.apps.core.models import UrlBase


def product_photo_upload_to(instance, filename):
    now = timezone_now()
    slug = instance.product.slug
    base, ext = os.path.splitext(filename)
    return f"products/{slug}/{now:%Y%m%d%H%M%S}{ext.lower()}"


class Product(UrlBase):
    title = models.CharField(_("title"), max_length=200)
    slug = models.SlugField(_("slug"), max_length=200)
    description = models.TextField(_("description"), blank=True)
    price = models.DecimalField(
        _("price (EUR)"), max_digits=8, decimal_places=2,
        blank=True, null=True
    )

    class Meta:
        verbose_name = _("Product")
        verbose_name_plural = _("Products")

    def get_url_path(self):
        try:
            return reverse("product_detail", kwargs={"slug": self.slug})
        except NoReverseMatch:
            return ""

    def __str__(self):
```

```
                    return self.title


class ProductPhoto(models.Model):
    product = models.ForeignKey(Product, on_delete=models.CASCADE)
    photo = models.ImageField(_("photo"),
     upload_to=product_photo_upload_to)

    class Meta:
        verbose_name = _("Photo")
        verbose_name_plural = _("Photos")

    def __str__(self):
        return self.photo.name
```

How to do it...

In this recipe, we will create a simple administration for the Product model that will have instances of the ProductPhoto model attached to the product as inlines.

In the list_display property, we will include the first_photo() method of the model admin, which will be used to show the first photo from the many-to-one relationship. So, let's begin:

1. Let's create an admin.py file that contains the following content:

```
# myproject/apps/products/admin.py
from django.contrib import admin
from django.template.loader import render_to_string
from django.utils.html import mark_safe
from django.utils.translation import ugettext_lazy as _

from .models import Product, ProductPhoto


class ProductPhotoInline(admin.StackedInline):
    model = ProductPhoto
    extra = 0
    fields = ["photo"]
```

2. Then, in the same file, let's add the administration for the product:

```python
@admin.register(Product)
class ProductAdmin(admin.ModelAdmin):
    list_display = ["first_photo", "title", "has_description",
     "price"]
    list_display_links = ["first_photo", "title"]
    list_editable = ["price"]

    fieldsets = ((_("Product"), {"fields": ("title", "slug",
     "description", "price")}),)
    prepopulated_fields = {"slug": ("title",)}
    inlines = [ProductPhotoInline]

def first_photo(self, obj):
        project_photos = obj.productphoto_set.all()[:1]
        if project_photos.count() > 0:
        photo_preview = render_to_string(
            "admin/products/includes/photo-preview.html",
             {"photo": project_photos[0], "product": obj},
             )
            return mark_safe(photo_preview)
        return ""

    first_photo.short_description = _("Preview")

def has_description(self, obj):
return bool(obj.description)

    has_description.short_description = _("Has description?")
    has_description.admin_order_field = "description"
    has_description.boolean = True
```

3. Now, let's create the template that will be used to generate the photo-preview, as follows:

```
{# admin/products/includes/photo-preview.html #}
{% load imagekit %}
{% thumbnail "120x120" photo.photo -- alt=
 "{{ product.title }} preview" %}
```

How it works...

If you add a few products with photos and then look at the product administration list in the browser, it will look similar to the following screenshot:

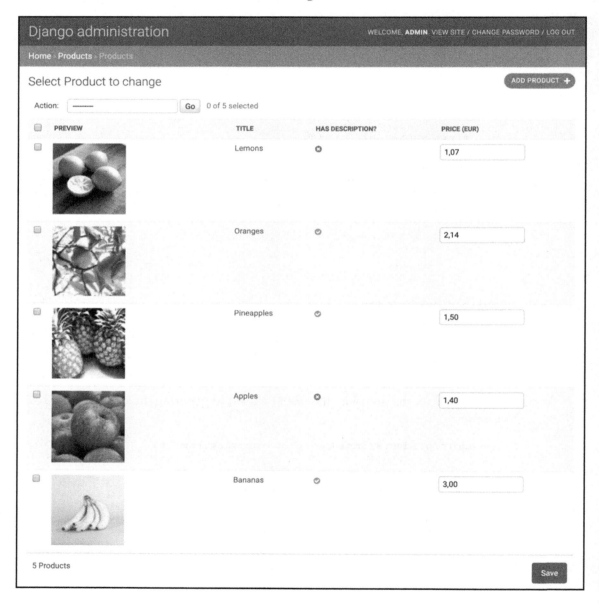

The `list_display` property is usually used to define the fields so that they're displayed in the administration list view; for example, **TITLE** and **PRICE** are fields of the `Product` model. Besides the normal field names, though, the `list_display` property also accepts the following:

- A function, or another callable
- The name of an attribute of the model admin class
- The name of an attribute of the model

When using callables in `list_display`, each one will get the model instance passed as the first argument. Therefore, in our example, we have defined the `get_photo()` method in the model admin class, which receives the `Product` instance as `obj`. The method tries to get the first `ProductPhoto` object from the many-to-one relationship, and, if it exists, it returns HTML generated from the include template with the `<img>` tag. By setting `list_display_links`, we make both the photo and the title linked to the admin change form for the `Product` model.

You can set several attributes for the callables that you use in `list_display`:

- The `short_description` attribute of the callable defines the **TITLE** shown at the top of the column.
- By default, the values that are returned by callables are not sortable in **administration**, but the `admin_order_field` attribute can be set to define which database field we should sort that generated column by. Optionally, you can prefix the field with a hyphen to indicate a reversed sort order.
- By setting `boolean = True`, you can show icons for the `True` or `False` values.

Finally, the **PRICE** field can be made editable if we include it in the `list_editable` setting. Since there are now editable fields, a **Save** button will appear at the bottom so that we can save the whole list of products.

See also

- The *Creating a model mixin with URL-related methods* recipe in `Chapter 2`, *Models and Database Structure*
- The *Creating admin actions* recipe
- The *Developing change list filters* recipe

Creating sortable inlines

You will want to sort most of the models in your database by creation date, happening date, or alphabetically. But sometimes, the user has to be able to show items in a custom sorting order. This applies to categories, image galleries, curated lists, and similar cases. In this recipe, we will show you how to use `django-ordered-model` to allow custom sorting in administration.

Getting ready

In this recipe, we will build upon the `products` app that we defined in the previous recipe. Follow these steps to get started:

1. Let's install `django-ordered-model` in our virtual environment:

```
(env)$ pip install django-ordered-model
```

2. Add `ordered_model` to `INSTALLED_APPS` in the settings.
3. Then, modify the `ProductPhoto` model from the previously defined `products` app, as follows:

```
# myproject/apps/products/models.py
from django.db import models
from django.utils.translation import ugettext_lazy as _

from ordered_model.models import OrderedModel

# ...

class ProductPhoto(OrderedModel):
    product = models.ForeignKey(Product, on_delete=models.CASCADE)
    photo = models.ImageField(_("photo"),
     upload_to=product_photo_upload_to)

order_with_respect_to = "product"

    class Meta(OrderedModel.Meta):
        verbose_name = _("Photo")
        verbose_name_plural = _("Photos")

def __str__(self):
return self.photo.name
```

The `OrderedModel` class introduces an `order` field. Make and run migrations to add the new `order` field for `ProductPhoto` to the database.

How to do it...

To set up sortable product photos, we'll need to modify the model administration for the `products` app. Let's get started:

1. Modify `ProductPhotoInline` in the admin file, as follows:

    ```python
    # myproject/apps/products/admin.py
    from django.contrib import admin
    from django.template.loader import render_to_string
    from django.utils.html import mark_safe
    from django.utils.translation import ugettext_lazy as _
    from ordered_model.admin import OrderedTabularInline, \
    OrderedInlineModelAdminMixin

    from .models import Product, ProductPhoto


    class ProductPhotoInline(OrderedTabularInline):
        model = ProductPhoto
        extra = 0
        fields = ("photo_preview", "photo", "order",
        "move_up_down_links")
        readonly_fields = ("photo_preview", "order",
        "move_up_down_links")
        ordering = ("order",)

        def get_photo_preview(self, obj):
            photo_preview = render_to_string(
                "admin/products/includes/photo-preview.html",
                {"photo": obj, "product": obj.product},
            )
            return mark_safe(photo_preview)

        get_photo_preview.short_description = _("Preview")
    ```

2. Then, modify `ProductAdmin` as follows:

    ```python
    @admin.register(Product)
    class ProductAdmin(OrderedInlineModelAdminMixin, admin.ModelAdmin):
        # ...
    ```

How it works...

If you open the **Change Product** form, you will see something like this:

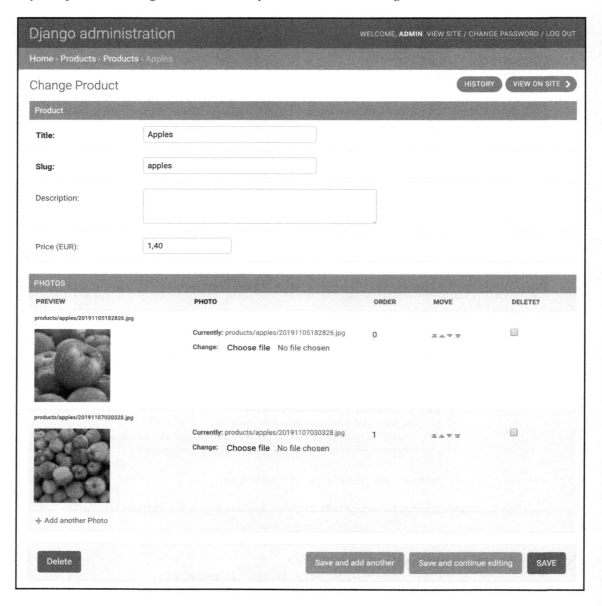

In the model, we set the `order_with_respect_to` attribute to ensure that ordering will be separate for each product instead of just ordering the whole list of product photos in general.

In **Django administration**, product photos can be edited by following the product details itself as tabular inlines. In the first column, we have a photo preview. We are generating it using the same `photo-preview.html` template that we used in the previous recipe. In the second column, there is a field for changing the photo. Then, there is a column for the **ORDER** field, followed by a column with arrow buttons so that we can reorder the photos manually next to it. The arrow buttons are coming from the `move_up_down_links` method. Finally, there is a column with a checkbox so that we can delete the inline.

The `readonly_fields` attribute tells Django that some fields or methods will be for reading only. If you want to use another method to display something in the change form, you have to put those methods in the `readonly_fields` list. In our case, `get_photo_preview` and `move_up_down_links` are such methods.

`move_up_down_links` is defined in `OrderedTabularInline`, which we are extending instead of `admin.StackedInline` or `admin.TabularInline`. This renders the arrow buttons so that they switch places in the product photos.

See also

- The *Customizing columns on the change list page* recipe
- The *Creating admin actions* recipe
- The *Developing change list filters* recipe

Creating admin actions

The Django administration system provides actions that we can execute for selected items in the list. One action is provided, by default, and it is used to delete selected instances. In this recipe, we will create an additional action for the list of the `Product` model, which will allow the administrators to export selected products to Excel spreadsheets.

Getting ready

We will start with the `products` app that we created in the previous recipes. Make sure that you have the `openpyxl` module installed in your virtual environment in order to create an Excel spreadsheet, as follows:

```
(env)$ pip install openpyxl
```

How to do it...

Admin actions are functions that take three arguments, as follows:

- The current `ModelAdmin` value
- The current `HttpRequest` value
- The `QuerySet` value, which contains the selected items

Perform the following steps to create a custom admin action to export a spreadsheet:

1. Create a `ColumnConfig` class for spreadsheet column configuration in the `admin.py` file of the `products` app, as follows:

```
# myproject/apps/products/admin.py
from openpyxl import Workbook
from openpyxl.styles import Alignment, NamedStyle, builtins
from openpyxl.styles.numbers import FORMAT_NUMBER
from openpyxl.writer.excel import save_virtual_workbook

from django.http.response import HttpResponse
from django.utils.translation import ugettext_lazy as _
from ordered_model.admin import OrderedTabularInline,
OrderedInlineModelAdminMixin

# other imports...

class ColumnConfig:
    def __init__(
            self,
            heading,
            width=None,
            heading_style="Headline 1",
            style="Normal Wrapped",
            number_format=None,
        ):
        self.heading = heading
```

```
        self.width = width
        self.heading_style = heading_style
        self.style = style
        self.number_format = number_format
```

2. Then, in the same file, create the `export_xlsx()` function:

```
def export_xlsx(modeladmin, request, queryset):
    wb = Workbook()
    ws = wb.active
    ws.title = "Products"

    number_alignment = Alignment(horizontal="right")
    wb.add_named_style(
        NamedStyle(
            "Identifier", alignment=number_alignment,
             number_format=FORMAT_NUMBER
        )
    )
    wb.add_named_style(
        NamedStyle("Normal Wrapped",
          alignment=Alignment(wrap_text=True))
    )

    column_config = {
        "A": ColumnConfig("ID", width=10, style="Identifier"),
        "B": ColumnConfig("Title", width=30),
        "C": ColumnConfig("Description", width=60),
        "D": ColumnConfig("Price", width=15, style="Currency",
            number_format="#,##0.00 €"),
        "E": ColumnConfig("Preview", width=100, style="Hyperlink"),
    }

    # Set up column widths, header values and styles
    for col, conf in column_config.items():
        ws.column_dimensions[col].width = conf.width

        column = ws[f"{col}1"]
        column.value = conf.heading
        column.style = conf.heading_style

    # Add products
    for obj in queryset.order_by("pk"):
        project_photos = obj.productphoto_set.all()[:1]
        url = ""
        if project_photos:
            url = project_photos[0].photo.url
```

```
                    data = [obj.pk, obj.title, obj.description, obj.price, url]
                    ws.append(data)

                    row = ws.max_row
                    for row_cells in ws.iter_cols(min_row=row, max_row=row):
                        for cell in row_cells:
                            conf = column_config[cell.column_letter]
                            cell.style = conf.style
                            if conf.number_format:
                                cell.number_format = conf.number_format

                mimetype = "application/vnd.openxmlformats-
                 officedocument.spreadsheetml.sheet"
                charset = "utf-8"
                response = HttpResponse(
                    content=save_virtual_workbook(wb),
                    content_type=f"{mimetype}; charset={charset}",
                    charset=charset,
                )
                response["Content-Disposition"] = "attachment;
                 filename=products.xlsx"
                return response

            export_xlsx.short_description = _("Export XLSX")
```

3. Then, add the `actions` setting to `ProductAdmin`, as follows:

```
@admin.register(Product)
class ProductAdmin(OrderedInlineModelAdminMixin, admin.ModelAdmin):
    # ...
    actions = [export_xlsx]
    # ...
```

How it works...

If you take a look at the product administration list page in the browser, you will see a new action called **Export XLSX**, along with the default **Delete selected Products** action, as shown in the following screenshot:

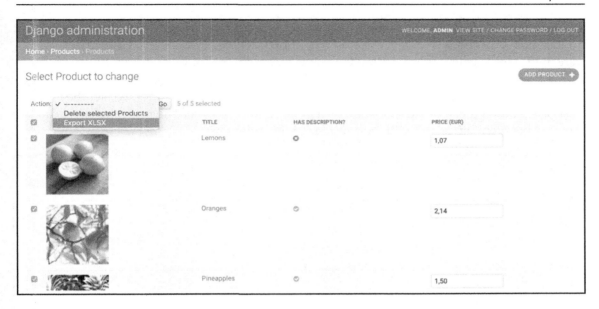

We use the `openpyxl` Python module to create an OpenOffice XML file that's compatible with Excel and other spreadsheet software.

First, a workbook is created, and the active worksheet is selected, for which we set the title to `Products`. Because there are common styles that we will want to use throughout the worksheet, these are set up as named styles so that they can be applied by name to each cell, as appropriate. These styles, the column headings, and the column widths are stored as `Config` objects, and a `column_config` dictionary maps column letter keys to the objects. This is then iterated over to set up the headers and column widths.

We use the `append()` method of the sheet to add the content for each of the selected products in `QuerySet`, ordered by ID, including the URL of the first photo for the product for when photos are available. The product data is then individually styled by iterating over each of the cells in the just-added row, once again referring to `column_config` to apply styles consistently.

By default, admin actions do something with `QuerySet` and redirect the administrator back to the change list page. However, for more complex actions, `HttpResponse` can be returned. The `export_xlsx()` function saves a virtual copy of the workbook to `HttpResponse`, with the content type and character set appropriate to the **Office Open XML (OOXML)** spreadsheet. Using the `Content-Disposition` header, we set the response so that it can be downloaded as a `products.xlsx` file. The resulting sheet can be opened in Open Office and will look similar to the following:

See also

- The *Customizing columns on the change list page* recipe
- The *Developing change list filters* recipe
- `Chapter 9`, *Importing and Exporting Data*

Developing change list filters

If you want administrators to be able to filter the change list by date, relation, or field choices, you have to use the `list_filter` property of the admin model. Additionally, there is the possibility of having custom-tailored filters. In this recipe, we will add a filter that allows us to select products by the number of photos attached to them.

Getting ready

Let's start with the `products` app that we created in the previous recipes.

How to do it...

Execute the following steps:

1. In the `admin.py` file, create a `PhotoFilter` class that extends from `SimpleListFilter`, as follows:

```
# myproject/apps/products/admin.py
from django.contrib import admin
from django.db import models
from django.utils.translation import ugettext_lazy as _

# other imports...

ZERO = "zero"
ONE = "one"
MANY = "many"


class PhotoFilter(admin.SimpleListFilter):
    # Human-readable title which will be displayed in the
    # right admin sidebar just above the filter options.
    title = _("photos")

    # Parameter for the filter that will be used in the
    # URL query.
    parameter_name = "photos"

    def lookups(self, request, model_admin):
        """
        Returns a list of tuples, akin to the values given for
        model field choices. The first element in each tuple is the
        coded value for the option that will appear in the URL
        query. The second element is the human-readable name for
        the option that will appear in the right sidebar.
        """
        return (
            (ZERO, _("Has no photos")),
            (ONE, _("Has one photo")),
            (MANY, _("Has more than one photo")),
        )

    def queryset(self, request, queryset):
        """
        Returns the filtered queryset based on the value
        provided in the query string and retrievable via
        `self.value()`.
```

```
"""
qs = queryset.annotate(num_photos=
  models.Count("productphoto"))

if self.value() == ZERO:
    qs = qs.filter(num_photos=0)
elif self.value() == ONE:
    qs = qs.filter(num_photos=1)
elif self.value() == MANY:
    qs = qs.filter(num_photos__gte=2)
return qs
```

2. Then, add a list filter to `ProductAdmin`, as shown in the following code:

```
@admin.register(Product)
class ProductAdmin(OrderedInlineModelAdminMixin, admin.ModelAdmin):
    # ...
    list_filter = [PhotoFilter]
    # ...
```

How it works...

The list filter, based on the custom field that we just created, will be shown in the sidebar of the product list, as follows:

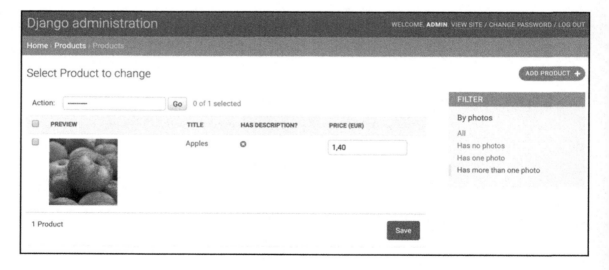

The `PhotoFilter` class has a translatable title and query parameter name as properties. It also has two methods, as follows:

- The `lookups()` method, which defines the choices of the filter
- The `queryset()` method, which defines how to filter `QuerySet` objects when a specific value is selected

In the `lookups()` method, we define three choices, as follows:

- There are **no photos**
- There is **one photo**
- There is **more than one photo** attached

In the `queryset()` method, we use the `annotate()` method of `QuerySet` to select the count of photos for each product. This count is then filtered according to the selected choice.

To learn more about aggregation functions, such as `annotate()`, refer to the official Django documentation at `https://docs.djangoproject.com/en/3.0/topics/db/aggregation/`.

See also

- The *Customizing columns on the change list page* recipe
- The *Creating admin actions* recipe
- The *Creating a custom accounts app* recipe

Changing the app label of a third-party app

The Django framework has a lot of third-party apps that you can use in your project. You can browse and compare most of them at `https://djangopackages.org/`. In this recipe, we will show you how to rename the label of the `python-social-auth` app in administration. Analogically, you will be able to change the label of any Django third-party app.

Getting ready

Follow the instructions at https://python-social-auth.readthedocs.io/en/latest/ configuration/django.html to install Python Social Auth into your project. Python Social Auth allows your users to log in with social network accounts or their Open ID. Once you've done this, the index page of the administration will look like this:

PYTHON SOCIAL AUTH		
Associations	+ Add	✎ Change
Nonces	+ Add	✎ Change
User social auths	+ Add	✎ Change

How to do it...

To begin, change the **PYTHON SOCIAL AUTH** label to something more user-friendly, such as SOCIAL **AUTHENTICATION**. Now, follow these steps:

1. Create an app called accounts. In the apps.py file there, add the following content:

```
# myproject/apps/accounts/apps.py
from django.apps import AppConfig
from django.utils.translation import ugettext_lazy as _


class AccountsConfig(AppConfig):
    name = "myproject.apps.accounts"
    verbose_name = _("Accounts")

    def ready(self):
        pass


class SocialDjangoConfig(AppConfig):
    name = "social_django"
    verbose_name = _("Social Authentication")
```

2. One of the steps of setting up Python Social Auth involved adding the "social_django" app to INSTALLED_APPS. Now, replace the app there with "myproject.apps.accounts.apps.SocialDjangoConfig":

```
# myproject/settings/_base.py
# ...
INSTALLED_APPS = [
    # ...
    #"social_django",
    "myproject.apps.accounts.apps.SocialDjangoConfig",
    # ...
]
```

How it works...

If you check the index page of administration, you will see something like this:

SOCIAL AUTHENTICATION		
Associations	+ Add	Change
Nonces	+ Add	Change
User social auths	+ Add	Change

The INSTALLED_APPS setting accepts either the path to an app or the path to app configuration. Instead of the default app path, we can pass an app configuration. There, we change the verbose name of the app and can even apply some signal handlers or do some other initial setup for the app.

See also

- The *Creating a custom accounts app* recipe
- The *Getting user Gravatars* recipe

Creating a custom accounts app

Django comes with a contributed `django.contrib.auth` app that's used for authentication. It allows users to log in with their username and password to be able to use administration features, for example. This app has been designed so that you can extend it with your own functionality. In this recipe, we will create a custom user and role models and will set administration for them. Instead of a username and password, you will be able to log in by email and password.

Getting ready

Create an `accounts` app and put this app under `INSTALLED_APPS`, in the settings:

```
# myproject/apps/_base.py
INSTALLED_APPS = [
    # ...
    "myproject.apps.accounts",
]
```

How to do it...

Follow these steps to overwrite the user and group models:

1. Create `models.py` in the `accounts` app with the following content:

   ```
   # myproject/apps/accounts/models.py
   import uuid

   from django.contrib.auth.base_user import BaseUserManager
   from django.db import models
   from django.contrib.auth.models import AbstractUser, Group
   from django.utils.translation import ugettext_lazy as _


   class Role(Group):
       class Meta:
           proxy = True
           verbose_name = _("Role")
           verbose_name_plural = _("Roles")

       def __str__(self):
           return self.name
   ```

```python
class UserManager(BaseUserManager):
    def create_user(self, username="", email="", password="",
     **extra_fields):
        if not email:
            raise ValueError("Enter an email address")
        email = self.normalize_email(email)
        user = self.model(username=username, email=email,
         **extra_fields)
        user.set_password(password)
        user.save(using=self._db)
        return user

    def create_superuser(self, username="", email="", password=""):
        user = self.create_user(email=email, password=password,
         username=username)
        user.is_superuser = True
        user.is_staff = True
        user.save(using=self._db)
        return user


class User(AbstractUser):
    uuid = models.UUIDField(primary_key=True, default=None,
     editable=False)
    # change username to non-editable non-required field
    username = models.CharField(
        _("username"), max_length=150, editable=False, blank=True
    )
    # change email to unique and required field
    email = models.EmailField(_("email address"), unique=True)

    USERNAME_FIELD = "email"
    REQUIRED_FIELDS = []

    objects = UserManager()

    def save(self, *args, **kwargs):
        if self.pk is None:
            self.pk = uuid.uuid4()
        super().save(*args, **kwargs)
```

2. Create the `admin.py` file in the `accounts` app with the administration configuration for the `User` model:

```python
# myproject/apps/accounts/admin.py
from django.contrib import admin
from django.contrib.auth.admin import UserAdmin, Group, GroupAdmin
from django.urls import reverse
from django.contrib.contenttypes.models import ContentType
from django.http import HttpResponse
from django.shortcuts import get_object_or_404, redirect
from django.utils.encoding import force_bytes
from django.utils.safestring import mark_safe
from django.utils.translation import ugettext_lazy as _
from django.contrib.auth.forms import UserCreationForm

from .helpers import download_avatar
from .models import User, Role


class MyUserCreationForm(UserCreationForm):
    def save(self, commit=True):
        user = super().save(commit=False)
        user.username = user.email
        user.set_password(self.cleaned_data["password1"])
        if commit:
            user.save()
        return user


@admin.register(User)
class MyUserAdmin(UserAdmin):
    save_on_top = True
    list_display = [
        "get_full_name",
        "is_active",
        "is_staff",
        "is_superuser",
    ]
    list_display_links = [
        "get_full_name",
    ]
    search_fields = ["email", "first_name", "last_name", "id",
     "username"]
    ordering = ["-is_superuser", "-is_staff", "last_name",
     "first_name"]

    fieldsets = [
        (None, {"fields": ("email", "password")}),
```

```
            (_("Personal info"), {"fields": ("first_name",
             "last_name")}),
            (
                _("Permissions"),
                {
                    "fields": (
                        "is_active",
                        "is_staff",
                        "is_superuser",
                        "groups",
                        "user_permissions",
                    )
                },
            ),
            (_("Important dates"), {"fields": ("last_login",
             "date_joined")}),
        ]
        add_fieldsets = (
            (None, {"classes": ("wide",), "fields": ("email",
             "password1", "password2")}),
        )
        add_form = MyUserCreationForm

        def get_full_name(self, obj):
            return obj.get_full_name()

        get_full_name.short_description = _("Full name")
```

3. In the same file, add configuration for the `Role` model:

```
        admin.site.unregister(Group)

        @admin.register(Role)
        class MyRoleAdmin(GroupAdmin):
            list_display = ("__str__", "display_users")
            save_on_top = True

            def display_users(self, obj):
                links = []
                for user in obj.user_set.all():
                    ct = ContentType.objects.get_for_model(user)
                    url = reverse(
                        "admin:{}_{}_change".format(ct.app_label,
                            ct.model), args=(user.pk,)
                    )
                    links.append(
                        """<a href="{}" target="_blank">{}</a>""".format(
                            url,
```

```
                              user.get_full_name() or user.username,
                )
            )
        return mark_safe(u"<br />".join(links))

    display_users.short_description = _("Users")
```

How it works...

The default user administration list looks similar to the following screenshot:

The default group administration list looks similar to the following screenshot:

In this recipe, we created two models:

- The `Role` model, which is a proxy for the `Group` model from the `django.contrib.auth` app. The `Role` model was created to rename the verbose name of `Group` to `Role`.
- The `User` model, which extends the same abstract `AbstractUser` class as the `User` model from `django.contrib.auth`. The `User` model was created to replace the primary key with `UUIDField` and to allow us to log in via email and password instead of username and password.

The admin classes, `MyUserAdmin` and `MyRoleAdmin`, extend the contributed `UserAdmin` and `GroupAdmin` classes and overwrite some of the properties. Then, we unregistered the existing administration classes for the `User` and `Group` models and registered the new, modified ones.

The following screenshot shows what the user administration looks like:

The modified user administration settings show more fields than the default settings in the list view, additional filters and ordering options, and **Submit** buttons at the top of the editing form.

In the change list of the new group administration settings, we will display those users who have been assigned to specific groups. In the browser, this will look similar to the following screenshot:

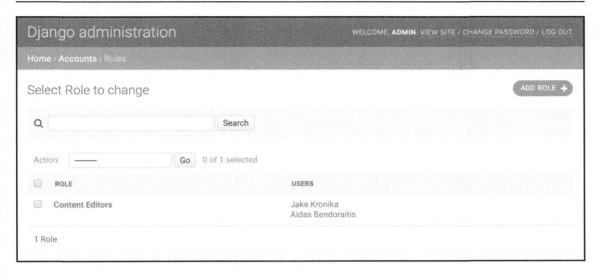

See also

- The *Customizing columns on the change list page* recipe
- The *Inserting a map into a change form* recipe

Getting user Gravatars

Now that we've started using a custom `User` model for authentication, we can enhance it even more by adding more useful fields. In this recipe, we will add an `avatar` field and the ability to download a user's avatar from the Gravatar service (https://en.gravatar.com/). The users of this service can upload avatars and assign them to their emails. By doing this, different comment systems and social platforms will be able to show those avatars from Gravatar based on the hashes of the user's emails.

Getting ready

Let's continue with the `accounts` app that we created in the previous recipes.

How to do it...

Follow these steps to enhance the `User` model in the `accounts` app:

1. Add the `avatar` field and `django-imagekit` thumbnail specification to the `User` model:

```python
# myproject/apps/accounts/models.py
import os

from imagekit.models import ImageSpecField
from pilkit.processors import ResizeToFill
from django.utils import timezone

# ...

def upload_to(instance, filename):
    now = timezone.now()
    filename_base, filename_ext = os.path.splitext(filename)
    return "users/{user_id}/{filename}{ext}".format(
        user_id=instance.pk,
        filename=now.strftime("%Y%m%d%H%M%S"),
        ext=filename_ext.lower(),
    )


class User(AbstractUser):
    # ...

    avatar = models.ImageField(_("Avatar"), upload_to=upload_to,
     blank=True)
    avatar_thumbnail = ImageSpecField(
        source="avatar",
        processors=[ResizeToFill(60, 60)],
        format="JPEG",
        options={"quality": 100},
    )

    # ...
```

2. Add some methods in order to download and show a Gravatar to the
   `MyUserAdmin` class:

```python
# myprojects/apps/accounts/admin.py
from django.contrib import admin
from django.contrib.auth.admin import UserAdmin, Group, GroupAdmin
from django.urls import reverse
from django.contrib.contenttypes.models import ContentType
from django.http import HttpResponse
from django.shortcuts import get_object_or_404
from django.utils.encoding import force_bytes
from django.utils.safestring import mark_safe
from django.utils.translation import ugettext_lazy as _
from django.contrib.auth.forms import UserCreationForm

from .helpers import download_avatar
from .models import User, Role


class MyUserCreationForm(UserCreationForm):
    def save(self, commit=True):
        user = super().save(commit=False)
        user.username = user.email
        user.set_password(self.cleaned_data["password1"])
        if commit:
            user.save()
        return user


@admin.register(User)
class MyUserAdmin(UserAdmin):
    save_on_top = True
    list_display = [
        "get_avatar",
        "get_full_name",
        "download_gravatar",
        "is_active",
        "is_staff",
        "is_superuser",
    ]
    list_display_links = [
        "get_avatar",
        "get_full_name",
    ]
    search_fields = ["email", "first_name", "last_name", "id",
     "username"]
    ordering = ["-is_superuser", "-is_staff", "last_name",
     "first_name"]
```

```python
    fieldsets = [
        (None, {"fields": ("email", "password")}),
        (_("Personal info"), {"fields": ("first_name",
         "last_name")}),
        (
            _("Permissions"),
            {
                "fields": (
                    "is_active",
                    "is_staff",
                    "is_superuser",
                    "groups",
                    "user_permissions",
                )
            },
        ),
        (_("Avatar"), {"fields": ("avatar",)}),
        (_("Important dates"), {"fields": ("last_login",
         "date_joined")}),
    ]
    add_fieldsets = (
        (None, {"classes": ("wide",), "fields": ("email",
         "password1", "password2")}),
    )
    add_form = MyUserCreationForm

    def get_full_name(self, obj):
        return obj.get_full_name()

    get_full_name.short_description = _("Full name")

    def get_avatar(self, obj):
        from django.template.loader import render_to_string
        html = render_to_string("admin/accounts
         /includes/avatar.html", context={
            "obj": obj
        })
        return mark_safe(html)

    get_avatar.short_description = _("Avatar")

    def download_gravatar(self, obj):
        from django.template.loader import render_to_string
        info = self.model._meta.app_label,
         self.model._meta.model_name
        gravatar_url = reverse("admin:%s_%s_download_gravatar" %
         info, args=[obj.pk])
        html = render_to_string("admin/accounts
```

```
        /includes/download_gravatar.html", context={
            "url": gravatar_url
        })
        return mark_safe(html)

    download_gravatar.short_description = _("Gravatar")

    def get_urls(self):
        from functools import update_wrapper
        from django.conf.urls import url

        def wrap(view):
            def wrapper(*args, **kwargs):
                return self.admin_site.admin_view(view)(*args,
                  **kwargs)

            wrapper.model_admin = self
            return update_wrapper(wrapper, view)

        info = self.model._meta.app_label,
         self.model._meta.model_name

        urlpatterns = [
            url(
                r"^(.+)/download-gravatar/$",
                wrap(self.download_gravatar_view),
                name="%s_%s_download_gravatar" % info,
            )
        ] + super().get_urls()

        return urlpatterns

    def download_gravatar_view(self, request, object_id):
        if request.method != "POST":
            return HttpResponse(
                "{} method not allowed.".format(request.method),
                status=405
            )
        from .models import User

        user = get_object_or_404(User, pk=object_id)
        import hashlib

        m = hashlib.md5()
        m.update(force_bytes(user.email))
        md5_hash = m.hexdigest()
        # d=404 ensures that 404 error is raised if gravatar is not
        # found instead of returning default placeholder
```

```
                url = "https://www.gravatar.com/avatar
                /{md5_hash}?s=800&d=404".format(
                    md5_hash=md5_hash
                )
                download_avatar(object_id, url)
                return HttpResponse("Gravatar downloaded.", status=200)
```

3. Add a `helpers.py` file to the `accounts` app with the following content:

```
# myproject/apps/accounts/helpers.py

def download_avatar(user_id, image_url):
    import tempfile
    import requests
    from django.contrib.auth import get_user_model
    from django.core.files import File

    response = requests.get(image_url, allow_redirects=True,
     stream=True)
    user = get_user_model().objects.get(pk=user_id)

    if user.avatar:  # delete the old avatar
        user.avatar.delete()

    if response.status_code != requests.codes.ok:
        user.save()
        return

    file_name = image_url.split("/")[-1]

    image_file = tempfile.NamedTemporaryFile()

    # Read the streamed image in sections
    for block in response.iter_content(1024 * 8):
        # If no more file then stop
        if not block:
            break
        # Write image block to temporary file
        image_file.write(block)

    user.avatar.save(file_name, File(image_file))
    user.save()
```

4. Create a template for the avatar in the administration file:

```
{# admin/accounts/includes/avatar.html #}
{% if obj.avatar %}
    <img src="{{ obj.avatar_thumbnail.url }}" alt=""
    width="30" height="30" />
{% endif %}
```

5. Create a template for the `button` to download `Gravatar`:

```
{# admin/accounts/includes/download_gravatar.html #}
{% load i18n %}
<button type="button" data-url="{{ url }}" class="button
js_download_gravatar download-gravatar">
    {% trans "Get Gravatar" %}
</button>
```

6. Finally, create a template for user change list administration with the JavaScript to handle mouse clicks on the **Get Gravatar** buttons:

```
{# admin/accounts/user/change_list.html #}
{% extends "admin/change_list.html" %}
{% load static %}

{% block footer %}
{{ block.super }}
<style nonce="{{ request.csp_nonce }}">
.button.download-gravatar {
    padding: 2px 10px;
}
</style>
<script nonce="{{ request.csp_nonce }}">
django.jQuery(function($) {
    $('.js_download_gravatar').on('click', function(e) {
        e.preventDefault();
        $.ajax({
            url: $(this).data('url'),
            cache: 'false',
            dataType: 'json',
            type: 'POST',
            data: {},
            beforeSend: function(xhr) {
                xhr.setRequestHeader('X-CSRFToken',
                '{{ csrf_token }}');
            }
        }).then(function(data) {
            console.log('Gravatar downloaded.');
```

```
                        document.location.reload(true);
            }, function(data) {
                console.log('There were problems downloading the
                    Gravatar.');
                document.location.reload(true);
            });
        })
    })

    </script>
    {% endblock %}
```

How it works...

If you look at the user change list administration now, you will see something like this:

The columns start with the user's **AVATAR**, then **FULL NAME**, and then a button to get the Gravatar. When a user clicks on the **Get Gravatar** button, a JavaScript `onclick` event handler makes a `POST` request to `download_gravatar_view`. This view creates a URL for the user's Gravatar, which is dependent on the MD5 hash of the user's email, and then calls a helper function to download an image for the user and link it to the `avatar` field.

There's more...

Gravatar images are quite small and relatively quick to download. If you were downloading bigger images from a different service, you could use Celery or Huey task queues to retrieve the images in the background. You can learn about Celery at `https://docs.celeryproject.org/en/latest/django/first-steps-with-django.html`, and about Huey at `https://huey.readthedocs.io/en/0.4.9/django.html`.

See also

- The *Changing the app label of a third-party app* recipe
- The *Creating a custom accounts app* recipe

Inserting a map into a change form

Google Maps offers a JavaScript API that we can use to insert maps into our websites. In this recipe, we will create a `locations` app with the `Location` model and extend the template of the change form in order to add a map where an administrator can find and mark the geographical coordinates of a location.

Getting ready

Register for a Google Maps API key and expose it to the templates, just like we did in the *Using HTML5 data attributes* recipe in `Chapter 4`, *Templates and JavaScript*. Note that for this recipe, in the Google Cloud Platform console, you will need to activate **Maps JavaScript API** and **Geocoding API**. For those APIs to function, you also need to set billing data.

We will continue by creating a `locations` app:

1. Put the app under INSTALLED_APPS in the settings:

```
# myproject/settings/_base.py
INSTALLED_APPS = [
    # ...
    "myproject.apps.locations",
]
```

2. Create a `Location` model there with a name, description, address, geographical coordinates, and picture, as follows:

```
# myproject/apps/locations/models.py
import os
import uuid
from collections import namedtuple

from django.contrib.gis.db import models
from django.urls import reverse
from django.conf import settings
from django.utils.translation import gettext_lazy as _
from django.utils.timezone import now as timezone_now

from myproject.apps.core.models import
CreationModificationDateBase, UrlBase

COUNTRY_CHOICES = getattr(settings, "COUNTRY_CHOICES", [])

Geoposition = namedtuple("Geoposition", ["longitude", "latitude"])


def upload_to(instance, filename):
    now = timezone_now()
    base, extension = os.path.splitext(filename)
    extension = extension.lower()
    return f"locations/{now:%Y/%m}/{instance.pk}{extension}"


class Location(CreationModificationDateBase, UrlBase):
    uuid = models.UUIDField(primary_key=True, default=None,
     editable=False)
    name = models.CharField(_("Name"), max_length=200)
    description = models.TextField(_("Description"))
    street_address = models.CharField(_("Street address"),
     max_length=255, blank=True)
    street_address2 = models.CharField(
        _("Street address (2nd line)"), max_length=255, blank=True
```

```
)
postal_code = models.CharField(_("Postal code"),
 max_length=255, blank=True)
city = models.CharField(_("City"), max_length=255, blank=True)
country = models.CharField(
    _("Country"), choices=COUNTRY_CHOICES, max_length=255,
     blank=True
)
geoposition = models.PointField(blank=True, null=True)
picture = models.ImageField(_("Picture"), upload_to=upload_to)

class Meta:
    verbose_name = _("Location")
    verbose_name_plural = _("Locations")

def __str__(self):
    return self.name

def get_url_path(self):
    return reverse("locations:location_detail",
     kwargs={"pk": self.pk})

def save(self, *args, **kwargs):
    if self.pk is None:
        self.pk = uuid.uuid4()
    super().save(*args, **kwargs)

def delete(self, *args, **kwargs):
    if self.picture:
        self.picture.delete()
    super().delete(*args, **kwargs)

def get_geoposition(self):
    if not self.geoposition:
        return None
    return Geoposition(self.geoposition.coords[0],
     self.geoposition.coords[1])

def set_geoposition(self, longitude, latitude):
    from django.contrib.gis.geos import Point
    self.geoposition = Point(longitude, latitude, srid=4326)
```

3. Next, we'll need to install the PostGIS extension for our PostgreSQL database. The easiest way to do that is to run the `dbshell` management command and execute the following command:

```
> CREATE EXTENSION postgis;
```

4. Now, create the default administration for the model with a geoposition (we will change this in the *How to do it...* section):

```
# myproject/apps/locations/admin.py
from django.contrib.gis import admin
from .models import Location


@admin.register(Location)
class LocationAdmin(admin.OSMGeoAdmin):
    pass
```

The default Django administration for geographical `Point` fields from the contributed `gis` module uses the `Leaflet.js` JavaScript mapping library. The tiles are obtained from Open Street Maps and the administration will look like this:

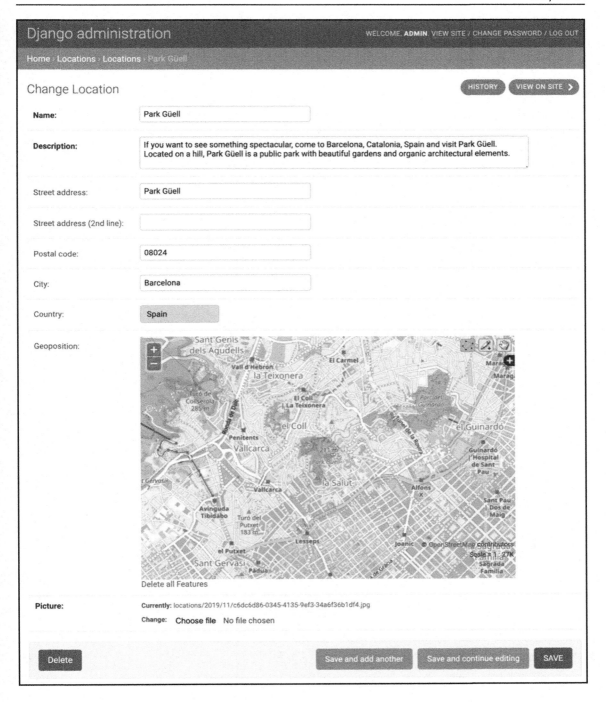

Note that in the default setup, you can't enter the longitude and latitude manually and there is no possibility to geocode the geoposition from the address information. We will implement that in this recipe.

How to do it...

The administration of the `Location` model will be combined from multiple files. Perform the following steps to create it:

1. Let's create the administration configuration for the `Location` model. Note that we are also creating a custom model form to create separate `latitude` and `longitude` fields:

```python
# myproject/apps/locations/admin.py
from django.contrib import admin
from django import forms
from django.conf import settings
from django.template.loader import render_to_string
from django.utils.translation import ugettext_lazy as _

from .models import Location

LATITUDE_DEFINITION = _(
    "Latitude (Lat.) is the angle between any point and the "
    "equator (north pole is at 90°; south pole is at -90°)."
)

LONGITUDE_DEFINITION = _(
    "Longitude (Long.) is the angle east or west of a point "
    "on Earth at Greenwich (UK), which is the international "
    "zero-longitude point (longitude = 0°). The anti-meridian "
    "of Greenwich (the opposite side of the planet) is both "
    "180° (to the east) and -180° (to the west)."
)


class LocationModelForm(forms.ModelForm):
    latitude = forms.FloatField(
        label=_("Latitude"), required=False,
        help_text=LATITUDE_DEFINITION
    )
    longitude = forms.FloatField(
        label=_("Longitude"), required=False,
        help_text=LONGITUDE_DEFINITION
    )
```

```python
    class Meta:
        model = Location
        exclude = ["geoposition"]

    def __init__(self, *args, **kwargs):
        super().__init__(*args, **kwargs)
        if self.instance:
            geoposition = self.instance.get_geoposition()
            if geoposition:
                self.fields["latitude"].initial = \
                geoposition.latitude
                self.fields["longitude"].initial = \
                geoposition.longitude

    def save(self, commit=True):
        cleaned_data = self.cleaned_data
        instance = super().save(commit=False)
        instance.set_geoposition(
            longitude=cleaned_data["longitude"],
            latitude=cleaned_data["latitude"],
        )
        if commit:
            instance.save()
            self.save_m2m()
        return instance


@admin.register(Location)
class LocationAdmin(admin.ModelAdmin):
    form = LocationModelForm
    save_on_top = True
    list_display = ("name", "street_address", "description")
    search_fields = ("name", "street_address", "description")

    def get_fieldsets(self, request, obj=None):
        map_html = render_to_string(
            "admin/locations/includes/map.html",
            {"MAPS_API_KEY": settings.GOOGLE_MAPS_API_KEY},
        )
        fieldsets = [
            (_("Main Data"), {"fields": ("name", "description")}),
            (
                _("Address"),
                {
                    "fields": (
                        "street_address",
                        "street_address2",
                        "postal_code",
```

```
                        "city",
                        "country",
                        "latitude",
                        "longitude",
                    )
                },
            ),
            (_("Map"), {"description": map_html, "fields": []}),
            (_("Image"), {"fields": ("picture",)}),
        ]
        return fieldsets
```

2. To create a custom change form template, add a new `change_form.html` file, under `admin/locations/location/`, to your templates directory. This template will extend from the default `admin/change_form.html` template, and will overwrite the `extrastyle` and `field_sets` blocks, as follows:

```
{# admin/locations/location/change_form.html #}
{% extends "admin/change_form.html" %}
{% load i18n static admin_modify admin_urls %}

{% block extrastyle %}
    {{ block.super }}
    <link rel="stylesheet" type="text/css"
        href="{% static 'site/css/location_map.css' %}" />
{% endblock %}

{% block field_sets %}
    {% for fieldset in adminform %}
        {% include "admin/includes/fieldset.html" %}
    {% endfor %}
    <script src="{% static 'site/js/location_change_form.js'
    %}"></script>
{% endblock %}
```

3. Then, we have to create the template for the map that will be inserted into the Map fieldset, as follows:

```
{# admin/locations/includes/map.html #}
{% load i18n %}
<div class="form-row map js_map">
    <div class="canvas">
        <!-- THE GMAPS WILL BE INSERTED HERE DYNAMICALLY -->
    </div>
    <ul class="locations js_locations"></ul>
    <div class="btn-group">
        <button type="button"
```

```
                        class="btn btn-default locate-address
                          js_locate_address">
                    {% trans "Locate address" %}
                </button>
                <button type="button"
                        class="btn btn-default remove-geo js_remove_geo">
                    {% trans "Remove from map" %}
                </button>
            </div>
    </div>
    <script src="https://maps-api-ssl.google.com/maps/api/js?key={{
    MAPS_API_KEY }}"></script>
```

4. Of course, the map won't be styled by default. Therefore, we will have to add some CSS, as shown in the following code:

```
/* site_static/site/css/location_map.css */
.map {
    box-sizing: border-box;
    width: 98%;
}
.map .canvas,
.map ul.locations,
.map .btn-group {
    margin: 1rem 0;
}
.map .canvas {
    border: 1px solid #000;
    box-sizing: padding-box;
    height: 0;
    padding-bottom: calc(9 / 16 * 100%); /* 16:9 aspect ratio */
    width: 100%;
}
.map .canvas:before {
    color: #eee;
    color: rgba(0, 0, 0, 0.1);
    content: "map";
    display: block;
    font-size: 5rem;
    line-height: 5rem;
    margin-top: -25%;
    padding-top: calc(50% - 2.5rem);
    text-align: center;
}
.map ul.locations {
    padding: 0;
}
.map ul.locations li {
```

```
    border-bottom: 1px solid #ccc;
    list-style: none;
}
.map ul.locations li:first-child {
    border-top: 1px solid #ccc;
}
.map .btn-group .btn.remove-geo {
    float: right;
}
```

5. Next, let's create a `location_change_form.js` JavaScript file. We don't want to pollute the environment with global variables. Therefore, we will start with a closure in order to make a private scope for variables and functions.
We will be using jQuery in this file (as jQuery comes with the contributed administration system and makes this easy and cross-browser), as follows:

```
/* site_static/site/js/location_change_form.js */
(function ($, undefined) {
    var gettext = window.gettext || function (val) {
        return val;
    };
    var $map, $foundLocations, $lat, $lng, $street, $street2,
        $city, $country, $postalCode, gMap, gMarker;
    // ...this is where all the further JavaScript functions go...
}(django.jQuery));
```

6. We will create JavaScript functions and add them to `location_change_form.js` one by one. The `getAddress4search()` function will collect the address string from the address fields that will be used later for geocoding, as follows:

```
function getAddress4search() {
    var sStreetAddress2 = $street2.val();
    if (sStreetAddress2) {
        sStreetAddress2 = " " + sStreetAddress2;
    }

    return [
        $street.val() + sStreetAddress2,
        $city.val(),
        $country.val(),
        $postalCode.val()
    ].join(", ");
}
```

7. The `updateMarker()` function will take the `latitude` and `longitude` arguments and draw or move a marker on the map. It will also make the marker draggable, as follows:

```
function updateMarker(lat, lng) {
    var point = new google.maps.LatLng(lat, lng);

    if (!gMarker) {
        gMarker = new google.maps.Marker({
            position: point,
            map: gMap
        });
    }

    gMarker.setPosition(point);
    gMap.panTo(point, 15);
    gMarker.setDraggable(true);

    google.maps.event.addListener(gMarker, "dragend",
        function() {
            var point = gMarker.getPosition();
            updateLatitudeAndLongitude(point.lat(), point.lng());
        }
    );
}
```

8. The `updateLatitudeAndLongitude()` function, as referenced in the preceding dragend event listener, takes the `latitude` and `longitude` arguments and updates the values for the fields with the `id_latitude` and `id_longitude` IDs, as follows:

```
function updateLatitudeAndLongitude(lat, lng) {
    var precision = 1000000;
    $lat.val(Math.round(lat * precision) / precision);
    $lng.val(Math.round(lng * precision) / precision);
}
```

9. The `autocompleteAddress()` function gets the results from Google Maps geocoding and lists them under the map in order to select the correct result. If there is only one result, it updates the geographical position and address fields, as follows:

```
function autocompleteAddress(results) {
    var $item = $('<li/>');
    var $link = $('<a href="#"/>');

    $foundLocations.html("");
```

```
        results = results || [];

    if (results.length) {
        results.forEach(function (result, i) {
            $link.clone()
                .html(result.formatted_address)
                .click(function (event) {
                    event.preventDefault();
                    updateAddressFields(result
                     .address_components);

                    var point = result.geometry.location;
                    updateLatitudeAndLongitude(
                        point.lat(), point.lng());
                    updateMarker(point.lat(), point.lng());
                    $foundLocations.hide();
                })
                .appendTo($item.clone()
                 .appendTo($foundLocations));
        });
        $link.clone()
            .html(gettext("None of the above"))
            .click(function(event) {
                event.preventDefault();
                $foundLocations.hide();
            })
            .appendTo($item.clone().appendTo($foundLocations));
        $foundLocations.show();
    } else {
        $foundLocations.hide();
    }
}
```

10. The `updateAddressFields()` function takes a nested dictionary, with the address components as an argument, and fills in all of the address fields, as follows:

```
function updateAddressFields(addressComponents) {
    var streetName, streetNumber;
    var typeActions = {
        "locality": function(obj) {
            $city.val(obj.long_name);
        },
        "street_number": function(obj) {
            streetNumber = obj.long_name;
        },
        "route": function(obj) {
            streetName = obj.long_name;
```

```
        },
        "postal_code": function(obj) {
            $postalCode.val(obj.long_name);
        },
        "country": function(obj) {
            $country.val(obj.short_name);
        }
    };

    addressComponents.forEach(function(component) {
        var action = typeActions[component.types[0]];
        if (typeof action === "function") {
            action(component);
        }
    });

    if (streetName) {
        var streetAddress = streetName;
        if (streetNumber) {
            streetAddress += " " + streetNumber;
        }
        $street.val(streetAddress);
    }
}
```

11. Finally, we have the initialization function, which is called when the page is loaded. It attaches the onclick event handlers to the buttons, creates a Google Map, and, initially, marks the geoposition that is defined in the latitude and longitude fields, as follows:

```
$(function(){
    $map = $(".map");

    $foundLocations = $map.find("ul.js_locations").hide();
    $lat = $("#id_latitude");
    $lng = $("#id_longitude");
    $street = $("#id_street_address");
    $street2 = $("#id_street_address2");
    $city = $("#id_city");
    $country = $("#id_country");
    $postalCode = $("#id_postal_code");

    $map.find("button.js_locate_address")
        .click(function(event) {
            var geocoder = new google.maps.Geocoder();
            geocoder.geocode(
                {address: getAddress4search()},
```

```
                        function (results, status) {
                            if (status === google.maps.GeocoderStatus.OK) {
                                autocompleteAddress(results);
                            } else {
                                autocompleteAddress(false);
                            }
                        }
                    );
                });

            $map.find("button.js_remove_geo")
                .click(function() {
                    $lat.val("");
                    $lng.val("");
                    gMarker.setMap(null);
                    gMarker = null;
                });

            gMap = new google.maps.Map($map.find(".canvas").get(0), {
                scrollwheel: false,
                zoom: 16,
                center: new google.maps.LatLng(51.511214, -0.119824),
                disableDoubleClickZoom: true
            });

            google.maps.event.addListener(gMap, "dblclick", function(event)
            {
                var lat = event.latLng.lat();
                var lng = event.latLng.lng();
                updateLatitudeAndLongitude(lat, lng);
                updateMarker(lat, lng);
            });

            if ($lat.val() && $lng.val()) {
                updateMarker($lat.val(), $lng.val());
            }
        });
```

How it works...

If you look at the **Change Location** form in the browser, you will see a **Map** shown in a fieldset, followed by the fieldset containing the address fields, as shown in the following screenshot:

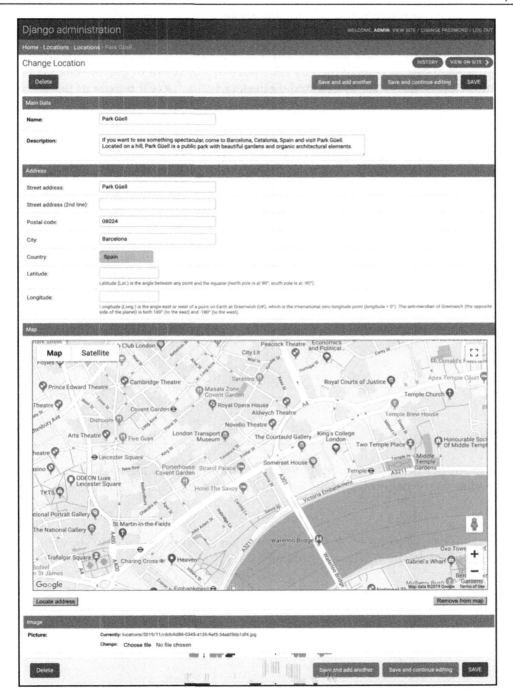

Under the map, there are two buttons: **Locate address** and **Remove from map**.

When you click on the **Locate address** button, the geocoding is called in order to search for the geographical coordinates of the entered address. The result of performing geocoding is one or more addresses listed in a nested dictionary format. We'll represent the addresses as a list of clickable links, as follows:

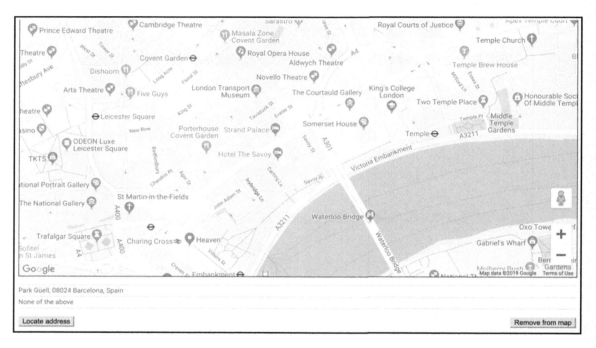

To view the structure of the nested dictionary in the console of the developer tools, put the following line at the beginning of the `autocompleteAddress()` function:

```
console.log(JSON.stringify(results, null, 4));
```

When you click on one of the selections, the marker appears on the map showing the exact geoposition of the location. The **Latitude** and **Longitude** fields will be filled in like so:

Then, the administrator can move the marker on the map by dragging and dropping it. Also, double-clicking anywhere on the map will update the geographical coordinates and the marker position.

Finally, if the **Remove from map** button is clicked, the geographical coordinates are cleaned and the marker is removed.

Administration uses a custom `LocationModelForm` that excludes the `geoposition` field, adds the `Latitude` and `Longitude` fields, and handles saving and loading their values.

See also

- `Chapter 4`, *Templates and JavaScript*

Security and Performance 7

In this chapter, we will cover the following recipes:

- Making forms secure from **Cross-Site Request Forgery (CSRF)**
- Making requests secure with **Content Security Policy (CSP)**
- Using django-admin-honeypot
- Implementing password validation
- Downloading authorized files
- Adding a dynamic watermark to images
- Authenticating with Auth0
- Caching the method return value
- Using Memcached to cache Django views
- Using Redis to cache Django views

Introduction

Software will never last if it inappropriately exposes sensitive information, makes the user suffer through interminable wait times, or requires extensive amounts of hardware. It is our responsibility as developers to make sure that applications are secure and performant. In this chapter, we will examine just some of the many ways we can keep our users (and yourself) safe while operating within Django applications. Then, we'll cover a few options for caching that can reduce processing and get data to users at a lower expense in terms of money and time.

Technical requirements

To work with the code in this chapter, you will need the latest stable version of Python, a MySQL or PostgreSQL database, and a Django project with a virtual environment.

You can find all the code for this chapter in the `ch07` directory of this book's GitHub repository at: `https://github.com/PacktPublishing/Django-3-Web-Development-Cookbook-Fourth-Edition`.

Making forms secure from Cross-Site Request Forgery (CSRF)

Without the proper precautions, malicious sites could potentially invoke requests against your website, which would result in undesired changes being made to your server. For example, they could affect a user's authentication or alter content without the user's consent. Django comes bundled with a system for preventing CSRF attacks such as these, and we'll review that in this recipe.

Getting ready

Start with the `ideas` app that we created in the *Creating an app with CRUDL functions* recipe in `Chapter 3`, *Forms and Views*.

How to do it...

To enable CSRF prevention in Django, follow these steps:

1. Make sure that `CsrfViewMiddleware` is included in your project settings, as shown here:

```python
# myproject/settings/_base.py
MIDDLEWARE = [
    "django.middleware.security.SecurityMiddleware",
    "django.contrib.sessions.middleware.SessionMiddleware",
    "django.middleware.common.CommonMiddleware",
    "django.middleware.csrf.CsrfViewMiddleware",
    "django.contrib.auth.middleware.AuthenticationMiddleware",
    "django.contrib.messages.middleware.MessageMiddleware",
    "django.middleware.clickjacking.XFrameOptionsMiddleware",
```

```
        "django.middleware.locale.LocaleMiddleware",
]
```

2. Make sure the form view is rendered using the request context. For example, in the existing `ideas` app, we have this:

```python
# myproject/apps/ideas/views.py
from django.contrib.auth.decorators import login_required
from django.shortcuts import render


@login_required
def add_or_change_idea(request, pk=None):
    # ...
    return render(request, "ideas/idea_form.html", context)
```

3. In the template for the form, make sure it uses the POST method and includes the `{% csrf_token %}` tag:

```django
{# ideas/idea_form.html #}
{% extends "base.html" %}
{% load i18n crispy_forms_tags static %}

{% block content %}
    <h1>
        {% if idea %}
            {% blocktrans trimmed with title=idea
             .translated_title %}
                Change Idea "{{ title }}"
            {% endblocktrans %}
        {% else %}
            {% trans "Add Idea" %}
        {% endif %}
    </h1>
    <form action="{{ request.path }}" method="post">
        {% csrf_token %}
        {{ form.as_p }}
        <p>
            <button type="submit">{% trans "Save" %}</button>
        </p>
    </form>
{% endblock %}
```

4. If you use `django-crispy-forms` for the form layout, the CSRF token will be included by default:

```
{# ideas/idea_form.html #}
{% extends "base.html" %}
{% load i18n crispy_forms_tags static %}

{% block content %}
    <h1>
        {% if idea %}
            {% blocktrans trimmed with title=idea
             .translated_title %}
                Change Idea "{{ title }}"
            {% endblocktrans %}
        {% else %}
            {% trans "Add Idea" %}
        {% endif %}
    </h1>
    {% crispy form %}
{% endblock %}
```

How it works...

Django uses a hidden field approach to prevent CSRF attacks. A token is generated on the server, based on a combination of request-specific and randomized information. Through `CsrfViewMiddleware`, this token is automatically made available via the request context. While it is not recommended to disable this middleware, it is possible to mark individual views to get the same behavior by applying the `@csrf_protect` decorator:

```
from django.views.decorators.csrf import csrf_protect

@csrf_protect
def my_protected_form_view():
    # ...
```

Similarly, we can exclude individual views from CSRF checks, even when the middleware is enabled, by using the `@csrf_exempt` decorator:

```
from django.views.decorators.csrf import csrf_exempt

@csrf_exempt
def my_unsecured_form_view():
    # ...
```

The built-in `{% csrf_token %}` tag generates the hidden input field that provides the token, as shown in the following example:

```
<input type="hidden" name="csrfmiddlewaretoken"
value="29sQH3UhogpseHH60eEaTq0xKen9TvbKe5lpT9xs30cR01dy5QVAtATWmAHvUZFk">
```

It is considered invalid to include the token for forms that submit requests using the GET, HEAD, OPTIONS, or TRACE methods, as any requests using those methods should not cause side effects in the first place. In most cases, web forms that require CSRF protection will be POST forms.

When a protected form using an unsafe method is submitted without the required token, Django's built-in form validation will recognize this and reject the request outright. Only those submissions containing a token with a valid value will be allowed to proceed. As a result, external sites will be unable to make changes to your server since they won't be able to know and include the currently valid token value.

There's more...

In many cases, it is desirable to enhance a form so that it can be submitted over Ajax. These also need to be protected using CSRF tokens, and while it is possible to inject the token as extra data in each request, using such an approach requires developers to remember to do so for each and every POST request. The alternative of using a CSRF token header exists and it makes things more efficient.

First, the token value needs to be retrieved, and how we do this depends on the value of the CSRF_USE_SESSIONS setting. When it is True, the token is stored in the session rather than a cookie, so we must use the `{% csrf_token %}` tag to include it in the DOM. Then, we can read that element to retrieve the data in JavaScript:

```
var input = document.querySelector('[name="csrfmiddlewaretoken"]');
var csrfToken = input && input.value;
```

When the CSRF_USE_SESSIONS setting is in the default False state, the preferred source of the token value is the csrftoken cookie. While it is possible to roll your own cookie manipulation methods, there are many utilities available that simplify this process. For example, we can extract the token easily by name using the **js-cookie** API, available at https://github.com/js-cookie/js-cookie, as shown here:

```
var csrfToken = Cookies.get('crsftoken');
```

Once the token has been extracted, it needs to be set as the CSRF token header value for `XmlHttpRequest`. Although this might be done separately for each request, doing so has the same drawbacks as adding the data to the request parameters for each request. Instead, we might use jQuery and its ability to attach data to all requests automatically before they are sent, like so:

```
var CSRF_SAFE_METHODS = ['GET', 'HEAD', 'OPTIONS', 'TRACE'];
$.ajaxSetup({
    beforeSend: function(xhr, settings) {
        if (CSRF_SAFE_METHODS.indexOf(settings.type) < 0
            && !this.crossDomain) {
            xhr.setRequestHeader("X-CSRFToken", csrfToken);
        }
    }
});
```

See also

- The *Creating an app with CRUDL functions* recipe in `Chapter 3`, *Forms and Views*
- The *Implementing password validation* recipe
- The *Downloading authorized files* recipe
- The *Authenticating with Auth0* recipe

Making requests secure with Content Security Policy (CSP)

Dynamic multi-user websites usually allow users to add all kinds of data from a wide variety of media types: images, videos, audios, HTML, JavaScript snippets, and so on. This opens up the potential of users adding malicious code to the website that could steal cookies or other personal information, call unwanted Ajax requests in the background, or do other harm. Modern browsers support an extra layer of security that whitelists the sources of your media resources. It is called CSP and in this recipe, we will show you how to use it within a Django website.

Getting ready

Let's start with an existing Django project; for example, the one containing the `ideas` app from `Chapter 3`, *Forms and Views*.

How to do it...

To protect your project with CSP, follow these steps:

1. Install `django-csp` into your virtual environment:

   ```
   (env)$ pip install django-csp==3.6
   ```

2. In the settings, add `CSPMiddleware`:

   ```python
   # myproject/settings/_base.py
   MIDDLEWARE = [
       "django.middleware.security.SecurityMiddleware",
       "django.contrib.sessions.middleware.SessionMiddleware",
       "django.middleware.common.CommonMiddleware",
       "django.middleware.csrf.CsrfViewMiddleware",
       "django.contrib.auth.middleware.AuthenticationMiddleware",
       "django.contrib.messages.middleware.MessageMiddleware",
       "django.middleware.clickjacking.XFrameOptionsMiddleware",
       "django.middleware.locale.LocaleMiddleware",
       "csp.middleware.CSPMiddleware",
   ]
   ```

3. In the same settings file, add the `django-csp` settings for whitelisting the
   sources of included media that you trust, for example, the CDN for jQuery and
   Bootstrap (you'll find a detailed explanation of this in the *How it works...* section):

   ```python
   # myproject/settings/_base.py
   CSP_DEFAULT_SRC = [
       "'self'",
       "https://stackpath.bootstrapcdn.com/",
   ]
   CSP_SCRIPT_SRC = [
       "'self'",
       "https://stackpath.bootstrapcdn.com/",
       "https://code.jquery.com/",
       "https://cdnjs.cloudflare.com/",
   ]
   CSP_IMG_SRC = ["*", "data:"]
   CSP_FRAME_SRC = ["*"]
   ```

4. If you have any inline scripts or styles anywhere in the templates, whitelist them using a cryptographic `nonce`, as follows:

```
<script nonce="{{ request.csp_nonce }}">
    window.settings = {
        STATIC_URL: '{{ STATIC_URL }}',
        MEDIA_URL: '{{ MEDIA_URL }}',
    }
</script>
```

How it works...

CSP directives can be added to the meta tags in the head section or the response headers:

- The `meta` tag syntax looks like this:

```
<meta http-equiv="Content-Security-Policy" content="img-src *
data:; default-src 'self' https://stackpath.bootstrapcdn.com/
'nonce-WWNu7EYqfTcVVZDs'; frame-src *; script-src 'self'
https://stackpath.bootstrapcdn.com/ https://code.jquery.com/
https://cdnjs.cloudflare.com/">
```

- Our chosen `django-csp` module uses **response headers** to create the list sources that you want to be loaded into the website. You can check the headers in the **Network** section of the browser's inspector, as follows:

```
Content-Security-Policy: img-src * data:; default-src 'self'
https://stackpath.bootstrapcdn.com/ 'nonce-WWNu7EYqfTcVVZDs';
frame-src *; script-src 'self' https://stackpath.bootstrapcdn.com/
https://code.jquery.com/ https://cdnjs.cloudflare.com/
```

CSP allows you to define resource types and allowed sources next to each other. The main directives that you can use are as follows:

- `default-src` is used as a fallback for all unset sources and is controlled in the Django settings by `CSP_DEFAULT_SRC`.
- `script-src` is used for `<script>` tags and is controlled in the Django settings by `CSP_DEFAULT_SRC`.
- `style-src` is used for the `<style>` and `<link rel="stylesheet">` tags and CSS `@import` statements, and is controlled by the `CSP_STYLE_SRC` setting.
- `img-src` is used for the `<img>` tags and is controlled by the `CSP_IMG_SRC` setting.

- `frame-src` is used for the `<frame>` and `<iframe>` tags and is controlled by the `CSP_FRAME_SRC` setting.
- `media-src` is used for the `<audio>`, `<video>`, and `<track>` tags and is controlled by the `CSP_MEDIA_SRC` setting.
- `font-src` is used for the web fonts and is controlled by the `CSP_FONT_SRC` setting.
- `connect-src` is used for the resources loaded by JavaScript and is controlled by the `CSP_CONNECT_SRC` setting.

 A full list of resource types and analogical settings can be found at `https://developer.mozilla.org/en-US/docs/Web/HTTP/Headers/Content-Security-Policy` and `https://django-csp.readthedocs.io/en/latest/configuration.html`, respectively.

The values for each directive can be one or more from the following list (the single quotes matter):

- `*`: Allow all sources
- `'none'`: Disallow all sources
- `'self'`: Allow sources from the same domain
- A protocol; for instance, `https:` or `data:`
- A domain; for instance, `example.com` or `*.example.com`
- A website URL, for instance, `https://example.com`
- `'unsafe-inline'`: Allow inline `<script>` or `<style>` tags
- `'unsafe-eval'`: Allow script execution with the `eval()` function
- `'nonce-<b64-value>'`: Allow specific tags by cryptographic nonces
- `'sha256-...'`: Allow resources by their source hashes

There is no general bulletproof way to configure `django-csp`. It's always a process of trial and error. However, here are our guidelines:

1. Start by adding the CSP for an existing working project. Premature restrictions will only make it more difficult to develop the website.
2. Check all the scripts, styles, fonts, and other static files that have been hardcoded into the templates and whitelist them.

3. Allow all sources for images, media, and frames if you allow media to be embedded into blog posts or other dynamic content, as follows:

```python
# myproject/settings/_base.py
CSP_IMG_SRC = ["*"]
CSP_MEDIA_SRC = ["*"]
CSP_FRAME_SRC = ["*"]
```

4. If you use inline scripts or styles, add `nonce="{{ request.csp_nonce }}"` to them.

5. Avoid `'unsafe-inline'` and `'unsafe-eval'` CSP values unless the only way to enter HTML into the website is by hardcoding it in the templates.

6. Browse through the website and search for any content that is not loading correctly. If you see a message like the following in the developer console, it means that the content was restricted by CSP:

Refused to execute inline script because it violates the following Content Security Policy directive: "script-src 'self' https://stackpath.bootstrapcdn.com/ https://code.jquery.com/ https://cdnjs.cloudflare.com/". Either the 'unsafe-inline' keyword, a hash ('sha256-P1v4zceJ/oPr/yp20lBqDnqynDQhHf76lljlXUxt7NI='), or a nonce ('nonce-...') is required to enable inline execution.

Errors like these usually occur because some third-party tools such as django-cms, Django Debug Toolbar, and Google Analytics are trying to include a resource through JavaScript. You can whitelist those resources with source hashes like the one we saw in the error message:
`'sha256-P1v4zceJ/oPr/yp20lBqDnqynDQhHf76lljlXUxt7NI='`.

7. If you develop modern **Progressive Web Apps (PWAs)**, consider checking the directives for the manifest and web workers controlled by the `CSP_MANIFEST_SRC` and `CSP_WORKER_SRC` settings.

See also

- The *Making forms secure from Cross Site Request Forgery (CSRF)* recipe

Using django-admin-honeypot

If you keep the default administration path for your Django website, you make it possible for hackers to perform brute-force attacks and try to log in with different passwords from their lists. There is an app called django-admin-honeypot that allows you to fake the login screen and detect those brute-force attacks. In this recipe, we'll learn how to use it.

Getting ready

We can start with any Django project that we want to secure. For example, you can extend the project from the previous recipe.

How to do it...

Follow these steps to set up django-admin-honeypot:

1. Install the module in your virtual environment:

   ```
   (env)$ pip install django-admin-honeypot==1.1.0
   ```

2. Add `"admin_honeypot"` to `INSTALLED_APPS` in your settings:

   ```python
   # myproject/settings/_base.py
   INSTALLED_APPS = (
       # ...
       "admin_honeypot",
   )
   ```

3. Modify the URL rules:

   ```python
   # myproject/urls.py
   from django.contrib import admin
   from django.conf.urls.i18n import i18n_patterns
   from django.urls import include, path

   urlpatterns = i18n_patterns(
       # ...
       path("admin/", include("admin_honeypot.urls",
       namespace="admin_honeypot")),
       path("management/", admin.site.urls),
   )
   ```

How it works...

If you go to the default administration URL, `http://127.0.0.1:8000/en/admin/`, you will see the login screen, but whatever you enter will be described as an invalid password:

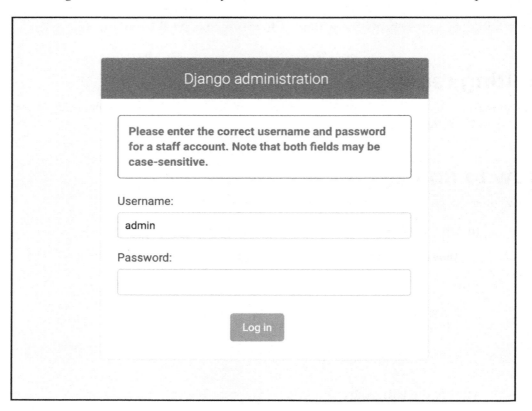

The real site's administration is now under `http://127.0.0.1:8000/en/management/`, where you can see the tracked logins from the honeypot.

There's more...

At the time of writing, django-admin-honeypot is not perfectly functioning with Django 3.0 – the administration interface escapes the HTML where it should render it safely. Until django-admin-honeypot is updated and a new release is available, we can fix it by making some changes, as follows:

1. Create an app called `admin_honeypot_fix` with the `admin.py` file that contains the following code:

```python
# myproject/apps/admin_honeypot_fix/admin.py
from django.contrib import admin

from admin_honeypot.admin import LoginAttemptAdmin
from admin_honeypot.models import LoginAttempt
from django.utils.safestring import mark_safe
from django.utils.translation import gettext_lazy as _

admin.site.unregister(LoginAttempt)


@admin.register(LoginAttempt)
class FixedLoginAttemptAdmin(LoginAttemptAdmin):
    def get_session_key(self, instance):
        return mark_safe('<a href="?session_key=
            %(key)s">%(key)s</a>' % {'key': instance.session_key})
    get_session_key.short_description = _('Session')

    def get_ip_address(self, instance):
        return mark_safe('<a href="?ip_address=%(ip)s">%(ip)s</a>'
            % {'ip': instance.ip_address})
    get_ip_address.short_description = _('IP Address')

    def get_path(self, instance):
        return mark_safe('<a href="?path=%(path)s">%(path)s</a>'
            % {'path': instance.path})
    get_path.short_description = _('URL')
```

2. In the same app, create an `apps.py` file with the new app configuration:

```python
# myproject/apps/admin_honeypot_fix/apps.py
from django.apps import AppConfig
from django.utils.translation import gettext_lazy as _

class AdminHoneypotConfig(AppConfig):
    name = "admin_honeypot"
    verbose_name = _("Admin Honeypot")
```

```
def ready(self):
    from .admin import FixedLoginAttemptAdmin
```

3. Replace `"admin_honeypot"` with the new app configuration
   in `INSTALLED_APPS` in the settings:

```
# myproject/settings/_base.py
INSTALLED_APPS = [
    # ...
    #"admin_honeypot",
    "myproject.apps.admin_honeypot_fix.apps.AdminHoneypotConfig",
]
```

The login attempts at the honeypot will now look like this:

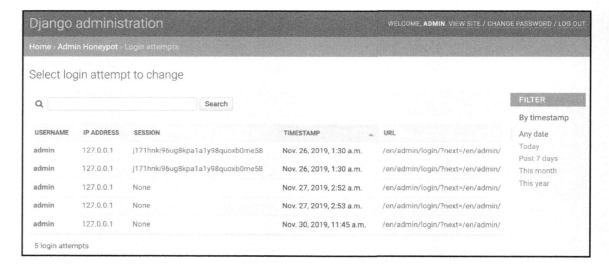

See also

- The *Implementing password validation* recipe
- The *Authenticating with Auth0* recipe

Implementing password validation

Among the items at the top of the list of software security failures is the choice of insecure passwords by users. In this recipe, we will learn how to enforce minimum password requirements through both built-in and custom password validators so that users are guided toward setting up more secure authentication.

Getting ready

Open the project's settings file and locate the AUTH_PASSWORD_VALIDATORS setting. Also, create a new auth_extra app containing a password_validation.py file.

How to do it...

Follow these steps to set up stronger password validation for your project:

1. Let's customize the settings for the validators that are included with Django by adding some options:

```
# myproject/settings/_base.py
AUTH_PASSWORD_VALIDATORS = [
    {
        "NAME": "django.contrib.auth.password_validation."
        "UserAttributeSimilarityValidator",
        "OPTIONS": {"max_similarity": 0.5},
    },
    {
        "NAME": "django.contrib.auth.password_validation."
        "MinimumLengthValidator",
        "OPTIONS": {"min_length": 12},
    },
    {"NAME": "django.contrib.auth.password_validation."
    "CommonPasswordValidator"},
    {"NAME": "django.contrib.auth.password_validation."
    "NumericPasswordValidator"},
]
```

2. Add the MaximumLengthValidator class to the password_validation.py file in the new auth_extra app, as follows:

```
# myproject/apps/auth_extra/password_validation.py
from django.core.exceptions import ValidationError
from django.utils.translation import gettext as _
```

```
class MaximumLengthValidator:
    def __init__(self, max_length=24):
        self.max_length = max_length

    def validate(self, password, user=None):
        if len(password) > self.max_length:
            raise ValidationError(
                self.get_help_text(pronoun="this"),
                code="password_too_long",
                params={'max_length': self.max_length},
            )

    def get_help_text(self, pronoun="your"):
        return _(f"{pronoun.capitalize()} password must contain "
                 f"no more than {self.max_length} characters")
```

3. In the same file, create the `SpecialCharacterInclusionValidator` class:

```
class SpecialCharacterInclusionValidator:
    DEFAULT_SPECIAL_CHARACTERS = ('$', '%', ':', '#', '!')

    def __init__(self, special_chars=DEFAULT_SPECIAL_CHARACTERS):
        self.special_chars = special_chars

    def validate(self, password, user=None):
        has_specials_chars = False
        for char in self.special_chars:
            if char in password:
                has_specials_chars = True
                break
        if not has_specials_chars:
            raise ValidationError(
                self.get_help_text(pronoun="this"),
                code="password_missing_special_chars"
            )

    def get_help_text(self, pronoun="your"):
        return _(f"{pronoun.capitalize()} password must contain at"
                 " least one of the following special characters: "
                 f"{', '.join(self.special_chars)}")
```

4. Then, add the new validators to the settings:

```
# myproject/settings/_base.py
from myproject.apps.auth_extra.password_validation import (
    SpecialCharacterInclusionValidator,
)
```

```
AUTH_PASSWORD_VALIDATORS = [
    {
        "NAME": "django.contrib.auth.password_validation."
        "UserAttributeSimilarityValidator",
        "OPTIONS": {"max_similarity": 0.5},
    },
    {
        "NAME": "django.contrib.auth.password_validation."
        "MinimumLengthValidator",
        "OPTIONS": {"min_length": 12},
    },
    {"NAME": "django.contrib.auth.password_validation."
    "CommonPasswordValidator"},
    {"NAME": "django.contrib.auth.password_validation."
    "NumericPasswordValidator"},
    {
        "NAME": "myproject.apps.auth_extra.password_validation."
        "MaximumLengthValidator",
        "OPTIONS": {"max_length": 32},
    },
    {
        "NAME": "myproject.apps.auth_extra.password_validation."
        "SpecialCharacterInclusionValidator",
        "OPTIONS": {
            "special_chars": ("{", "}", "^", "&")
            + SpecialCharacterInclusionValidator
              .DEFAULT_SPECIAL_CHARACTERS
        },
    },
]
```

How it works...

Django contains a set of default password validators:

- `UserAttributeSimilarityValidator` ensures that any password that's chosen is not too similar to certain attributes of the user. By default, the similarity ratio is set to `0.7` and the attributes that are checked are the username, first and last name, and email address. If any of these attributes contains multiple words, each word is checked independently.

- `MinimumLengthValidator` checks that the password that's entered is at least the minimum number of characters in length. By default, passwords must be eight or more characters long.
- `CommonPasswordValidator` refers to a file containing a list of passwords that are often used, and hence are insecure. The list Django uses by default contains 1,000 such passwords.
- `NumericPasswordValidator` verifies that the password that's entered is not made up entirely of numbers.

When you use the `startproject` management command to create a new project, these are added with their default options as the initial set of validators. In this recipe, we've shown how these options can be adjusted for our project needs, increasing the minimum length of passwords to 12 characters.

For `UserAttributeSimilarityValidator`, we have also reduced `max_similarity` to `0.5`, which means that passwords must differ more greatly from user attributes than the default.

Looking at `password_validation.py`, we have defined two new validators:

- `MaximumLengthValidator` is very similar to the built-in one for minimum length, ensuring that the password is no longer than the default of 24 characters
- `SpecialCharacterInclusionValidator` checks that one or more special characters – defined as the $, %, :, #, and ! symbols by default – are found within the given password

Each validator class has two required methods:

- The `validate()` method performs the actual checks against the `password` argument. Optionally, a second `user` argument will be passed when a user has been authenticated.
- We must also provide a `get_help_text()` method, which returns a string describing the validation requirements for the user.

Finally, we add the new validators to the settings in order to override the defaults to allow up to a 32-character maximum length for the password, and to be able to add the symbols {, }, ^, and & to the default special character list.

There's more...

The validators that are provided in `AUTH_PASSWORD_VALIDATORS` are executed automatically for the `createsuperuser` and `changepassword` management commands, as well as the built-in forms that are used to change or reset passwords. There will be times where you will want to use the same validation for custom password management code, though. Django provides functions for that level of integration and you can check the details in the contributed Django `auth` app in the `django.contrib.auth.password_validation` module.

See also

- The *Downloading authorized files* recipe
- The *Authenticating with Auth0* recipe

Downloading authorized files

Sometimes, you may only need to allow specific people to download intellectual property from your website. For example, music, videos, literature, or other artistic works should only be accessible to paid members. In this recipe, you will learn how to restrict image downloads only to authenticated users using the contributed Django auth app.

Getting ready

Let's start with the `ideas` app that we created in `Chapter 3`, *Forms and Views*.

How to do it...

Execute these steps one by one:

1. Create the view that will require authentication to download a file, as follows:

```python
# myproject/apps/ideas/views.py
import os

from django.contrib.auth.decorators import login_required
from django.http import FileResponse, HttpResponseNotFound
from django.shortcuts import get_object_or_404
```

```
from django.utils.text import slugify

from .models import Idea


@login_required
def download_idea_picture(request, pk):
    idea = get_object_or_404(Idea, pk=pk)
    if idea.picture:
        filename, extension =
        os.path.splitext(idea.picture.file.name)
        extension = extension[1:]  # remove the dot
        response = FileResponse(
            idea.picture.file, content_type=f"image/{extension}"
        )
        slug = slugify(idea.title)[:100]
        response["Content-Disposition"] = (
            "attachment; filename="
            f"{slug}.{extension}"
        )
    else:
        response = HttpResponseNotFound(
            content="Picture unavailable"
        )
    return response
```

2. Add the download view to the URL configuration:

```
# myproject/apps/ideas/urls.py
from django.urls import path

from .views import download_idea_picture

urlpatterns = [
    # ...
    path(
        "<uuid:pk>/download-picture/",
        download_idea_picture,
        name="download_idea_picture",
    ),
]
```

3. Set up the login view in our project URL configuration:

```
# myproject/urls.py
from django.conf.urls.i18n import i18n_patterns
from django.urls import include, path

urlpatterns = i18n_patterns(
    # ...
    path("accounts/", include("django.contrib.auth.urls")),
    path("ideas/", include(("myproject.apps.ideas.urls", "ideas"),
     namespace="ideas")),
)
```

4. Create a template for the login form, as shown in the following code:

```
{# registration/login.html #}
{% extends "base.html" %}
{% load i18n %}

{% block content %}
    <h1>{% trans "Login" %}</h1>
    <form action="{{ request.path }}" method="POST">
        {% csrf_token %}
        {{ form.as_p }}
        <button type="submit" class="btn btn-primary">{% trans
         "Log in" %}</button>
    </form>
{% endblock %}
```

5. In the template of idea details, add a link to the download:

```
{# ideas/idea_detail.html #}
{% extends "base.html" %}
{% load i18n %}

{% block content %}
...
    <a href="{% url 'ideas:download_idea_picture' pk=idea.pk %}"
    class="btn btn-primary">{% trans "Download picture" %}</a>
{% endblock %}
```

You should restrict users from bypassing Django and downloading restricted files directly. To do so, on an Apache web server, you can put a `.htaccess` file in the `media/ideas` directory by using the following content if you are running Apache 2.4:

```
# media/ideas/.htaccess
Require all denied
```

 When using `django-imagekit`, as shown in the examples throughout this book, the generated image versions will be stored and served from the `media/CACHE` directory, so our `.htaccess` configuration won't affect it.

How it works...

The `download_idea_picture` view streams the original uploaded picture from a specific idea. The `Content-Disposition` header that is set to `attachment` makes the file downloadable instead of being immediately shown in the browser. The filename for the file is also set in this header, and will be something similar to `gamified-donation-platform.jpg`. If the picture for an idea is unavailable, a 404 page will be shown with a very simple message: **Picture unavailable.**

The `@login_required` decorator will redirect the visitor to the login page if they try to access the downloadable file without being logged in. The login screen will look like this by default:

Login

Username: [   ]

Password: [   ]

[Log in]

See also

- The *Uploading images* recipe from `Chapter 3`, *Forms and Views*
- The *Creating a form layout with custom templates* recipe from `Chapter 3`, *Forms and Views*
- The *Creating a form layout with django-crispy-forms* recipe from `Chapter 3`, *Forms and Views*
- The *Arranging the base.html template* recipe from `Chapter 4`, *Templates and JavaScript*
- The *Implementing password validation* recipe
- The *Adding a dynamic watermark to images* recipe

Adding a dynamic watermark to images

Sometimes, it is desirable to allow users to see images, but keep them from being redistributed due to intellectual property and artistic rights. In this recipe, we will learn how to apply a watermark to images that are displayed on your site.

Getting ready

Let's start with the `core` and `ideas` apps that we created in the *Creating an app with CRUDL functions* recipe in `Chapter 3`, *Forms and Views*.

How to do it...

Follow these steps to apply a watermark to the displayed idea images:

1. If you haven't done so already, install `django-imagekit` into your virtual environment:

```
(env)$ pip install django-imagekit==4.0.2
```

2. Put "imagekit" into INSTALLED_APPS in the settings:

```python
# myproject/settings/_base.py
INSTALLED_APPS = [
    # ...
    "imagekit",
]
```

3. In the core app, create a file called processors.py with a WatermarkOverlay class, as follows:

```python
# myproject/apps/core/processors.py
from pilkit.lib import Image

class WatermarkOverlay(object):
    def __init__(self, watermark_image):
        self.watermark_image = watermark_image

    def process(self, img):
        original = img.convert('RGBA')
        overlay = Image.open(self.watermark_image)
        img = Image.alpha_composite(original,
        overlay).convert('RGB')
        return img
```

4. In the Idea model, add the watermarked_picture_large specification next to the picture field, as follows:

```python
# myproject/apps/ideas/models.py
import os

from imagekit.models import ImageSpecField
from pilkit.processors import ResizeToFill

from django.db import models
from django.conf import settings
from django.utils.translation import gettext_lazy as _
from django.utils.timezone import now as timezone_now

from myproject.apps.core.models import
CreationModificationDateBase, UrlBase
from myproject.apps.core.processors import WatermarkOverlay

def upload_to(instance, filename):
    now = timezone_now()
    base, extension = os.path.splitext(filename)
    extension = extension.lower()
    return f"ideas/{now:%Y/%m}/{instance.pk}{extension}"
```

```
class Idea(CreationModificationDateBase, UrlBase):
    # ...
    picture = models.ImageField(
        _("Picture"), upload_to=upload_to
    )
    watermarked_picture_large = ImageSpecField(
        source="picture",
        processors=[
            ResizeToFill(800, 400),
            WatermarkOverlay(
                watermark_image=os.path.join(settings.STATIC_ROOT,
                'site', 'img', 'watermark.png'),
            )
        ],
        format="PNG"
    )
```

5. Using a graphical program of your choice, create a semi-transparent PNG image with white text or a logo on a transparent background. Make it 800 x 400 px in size. Save the image as `site_static/site/img/watermark.png`. Here's what it might look like:

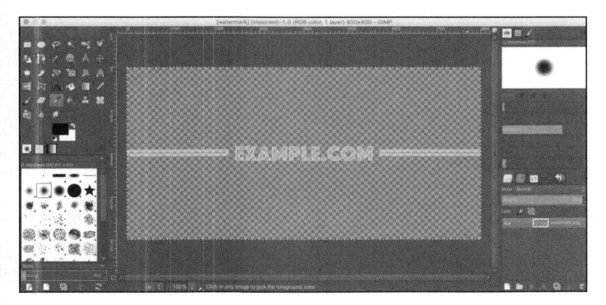

6. Run the `collectstatic` management command afterward:

```
(env)$ export DJANGO_SETTINGS_MODULE=myproject.settings.dev
(env)$ python manage.py collectstatic
```

7. Edit the idea detail template and add the watermarked image there, as follows:

```
{# ideas/idea_detail.html #}
{% extends "base.html" %}
{% load i18n %}

{% block content %}
    <a href="{% url "ideas:idea_list" %}">{% trans "List of ideas"
    %}</a>
    <h1>
        {% blocktrans trimmed with title=idea.translated_title %}
            Idea "{{ title }}"
        {% endblocktrans %}
    </h1>
    <img src="{{ idea.watermarked_picture_large.url }}" alt="" />
    {{ idea.translated_content|linebreaks|urlize }}
    <p>
        {% for category in idea.categories.all %}
            <span class="badge badge-pill badge-info">
            {{ category.translated_title }}</span>
        {% endfor %}
    </p>
    <a href="{% url 'ideas:download_idea_picture' pk=idea.pk %}"
     class="btn btn-primary">{% trans "Download picture" %}</a>
{% endblock %}
```

How it works...

If we navigate to the idea detail page, we should see the large image masked by our watermark, similar to this:

Let's examine how this was done. In the detail template, the `src` attribute for the `<img>` tag uses the idea's image specification, that is, `watermarked_picture_large`, to create a modified image that is then saved under the `media/CACHE/` directory and served from there.

The `django-imagekit` specifications use processors to modify images. Two processors are used there:

- `ResizeToFill` resizes the image to 800 × 400 px
- Our custom processor, `WatermarkOverlay`, applies the semi-transparent overlay to it

`django-imagekit` processors must have a `process()` method that takes the image from the previous processors and returns a new modified image. In our case, we compose the result from the original and the semi-transparent overlay.

See also

- The *Downloading authorized files* recipe

Authenticating with Auth0

As the number of services people interact with daily increases, so does the number of usernames and passwords that they need to remember. Beyond just that, each additional place where user information is stored is another place that it could be stolen from, in the event of a security breach. To help mitigate this, services such as **Auth0** allow you to centralize authentication services on a single, secure platform.

In addition to its support for username and password credentials, Auth0 has the ability to authenticate users via social platforms such as Google, Facebook, or Twitter. You could use passwordless login via single-time codes sent by SMS or email, and there is even enterprise-level support for different services. In this recipe, you'll learn how to connect an Auth0 application to Django and how to integrate it to handle user authentication.

Getting ready

If you haven't done so yet, create an Auth0 application at `https://auth0.com/` and configure it by following the instructions there. Two social connections are provided in the free plan, so we will activate Google and Twitter to log in with them. You can also try other services. Note that some of them require you to register an app and get API keys and secrets.

Next, we need to install `python-social-auth` and some other dependencies in the project. Include these dependencies in your `pip` requirements:

```
# requirements/_base.txt
social-auth-app-django~=3.1
python-jose~=3.0
python-dotenv~=0.9
```

 `social-auth-app-django` is a Django-specific package of the `python-social-auth` project that allows you to authenticate to your website using one of many social connections.

Install those dependencies with `pip` into your virtual environment.

How to do it...

To connect Auth0 to your Django project, follow these steps:

1. Add the social authentication app to `INSTALLED_APPS` in the settings file, like so:

```
# myproject/settings/_base.py
INSTALLED_APPS = [
    # ...
    "social_django",
]
```

2. Now, add the Auth0 settings required by the `social_django` app, which will be similar to the following:

```
# myproject/settings/_base.py
SOCIAL_AUTH_AUTH0_DOMAIN = get_secret("AUTH0_DOMAIN")
SOCIAL_AUTH_AUTH0_KEY = get_secret("AUTH0_KEY")
SOCIAL_AUTH_AUTH0_SECRET = get_secret("AUTH0_SECRET")
SOCIAL_AUTH_AUTH0_SCOPE = ["openid", "profile", "email"]
SOCIAL_AUTH_TRAILING_SLASH = False
```

Make sure that you define `AUTH0_DOMAIN`, `AUTH0_KEY`, and `AUTH0_SECRET` in your secrets or environment variables. The values for those variables can be found in the settings of your Auth0 app that you created in *Step 1* of this recipe's *Getting ready* section.

3. We need to create a backend for the Auth0 connection, as shown in the following example:

```
# myproject/apps/external_auth/backends.py
from urllib import request
from jose import jwt
from social_core.backends.oauth import BaseOAuth2

class Auth0(BaseOAuth2):
    """Auth0 OAuth authentication backend"""

    name = "auth0"
    SCOPE_SEPARATOR = " "
    ACCESS_TOKEN_METHOD = "POST"
    REDIRECT_STATE = False
    EXTRA_DATA = [("picture", "picture"), ("email", "email")]

    def authorization_url(self):
        return "https://" + self.setting("DOMAIN") + "/authorize"
```

```
        def access_token_url(self):
            return "https://" + self.setting("DOMAIN") + "/oauth/token"

        def get_user_id(self, details, response):
            """Return current user id."""
            return details["user_id"]

        def get_user_details(self, response):
            # Obtain JWT and the keys to validate the signature
            id_token = response.get("id_token")
            jwks = request.urlopen(
                "https://" + self.setting("DOMAIN") + "/.well-
                    known/jwks.json"
            )
            issuer = "https://" + self.setting("DOMAIN") + "/"
            audience = self.setting("KEY")   # CLIENT_ID
            payload = jwt.decode(
                id_token,
                jwks.read(),
                algorithms=["RS256"],
                audience=audience,
                issuer=issuer,
            )
            first_name, last_name = (payload.get("name") or
             " ").split(" ", 1)
            return {
                "username": payload.get("nickname") or "",
                "first_name": first_name,
                "last_name": last_name,
                "picture": payload.get("picture") or "",
                "user_id": payload.get("sub") or "",
                "email": payload.get("email") or "",
            }
```

4. Add the new backend to your AUTHENTICATION_BACKENDS setting, as shown in the following code:

```
# myproject/settings/_base.py
AUTHENTICATION_BACKENDS = {
    "myproject.apps.external_auth.backends.Auth0",
    "django.contrib.auth.backends.ModelBackend",
}
```

5. We want the social authentication user to be accessible from any template. Therefore, we'll create a context processor for it:

```python
# myproject/apps/external_auth/context_processors.py
def auth0(request):
    data = {}
    if request.user.is_authenticated:
        auth0_user = request.user.social_auth.filter(
            provider="auth0",
        ).first()
        data = {
            "auth0_user": auth0_user,
        }
    return data
```

6. Next, we need to register it in the settings:

```python
# myproject/settings/_base.py
TEMPLATES = [
    {
        "BACKEND":
        "django.template.backends.django.DjangoTemplates",
        "DIRS": [os.path.join(BASE_DIR, "myproject", "templates")],
        "APP_DIRS": True,
        "OPTIONS": {
            "context_processors": [
                "django.template.context_processors.debug",
                "django.template.context_processors.request",
                "django.contrib.auth.context_processors.auth",
                "django.contrib.messages.context_processors
                 .messages",
                "django.template.context_processors.media",
                "django.template.context_processors.static",
                "myproject.apps.core.context_processors
                 .website_url",
                "myproject.apps.external_auth
               .context_processors.auth0",
            ]
        },
    }
]
```

7. Now, let's create views for the index page, dashboard, and logout:

```python
# myproject/apps/external_auth/views.py
from urllib.parse import urlencode

from django.shortcuts import render, redirect
```

```python
from django.contrib.auth.decorators import login_required
from django.contrib.auth import logout as log_out
from django.conf import settings


def index(request):
    user = request.user
    if user.is_authenticated:
        return redirect(dashboard)
    else:
        return render(request, "index.html")


@login_required
def dashboard(request):
    return render(request, "dashboard.html")


def logout(request):
    log_out(request)
    return_to = urlencode({"returnTo":
     request.build_absolute_uri("/")})
    logout_url = "https://%s/v2/logout?client_id=%s&%s" % (
        settings.SOCIAL_AUTH_AUTH0_DOMAIN,
        settings.SOCIAL_AUTH_AUTH0_KEY,
        return_to,
    )
    return redirect(logout_url)
```

8. Create the index template, as follows:

```html
{# index.html #}
{% extends "base.html" %}
{% load i18n utility_tags %}

{% block content %}
<div class="login-box auth0-box before">
    <h3>{% trans "Please log in for the best user experience" %}</h3>
    <a class="btn btn-primary btn-lg" href="{% url "social:begin" backend="auth0" %}">{% trans "Log in" %}</a>
</div>
{% endblock %}
```

9. Create a dashboard template accordingly:

```
{# dashboard.html #}
{% extends "base.html" %}
{% load i18n %}

{% block content %}
    <div class="logged-in-box auth0-box logged-in">
        <img alt="{% trans 'Avatar' %}" src="{{
        auth0_user.extra_data.picture }}"
        width="50" height="50" />
        <h2>{% blocktrans with name=request.user
        .first_name %}Welcome, {{ name }}
        {% endblocktrans %}!</h2>

        <a class="btn btn-primary btn-logout" href="{% url
        "auth0_logout" %}">{% trans "Log out" %}</a>
    </div>
{% endblock %}
```

10. Update the URL rules:

```
# myproject/urls.py
from django.conf.urls.i18n import i18n_patterns
from django.urls import path, include

from myproject.apps.external_auth import views as
external_auth_views

urlpatterns = i18n_patterns(
    path("", external_auth_views.index, name="index"),
    path("dashboard/", external_auth_views.dashboard,
     name="dashboard"),
    path("logout/", external_auth_views.logout,
     name="auth0_logout"),
    path("", include("social_django.urls")),
    # ...
)
```

11. Finally, add the login URL settings:

```
LOGIN_URL = "/login/auth0"
LOGIN_REDIRECT_URL = "dashboard"
```

How it works...

If you point a browser to the index page of your project, you will see a link inviting you to log in. When you click on it, you will be redirected to the Auth0 authentication system, whose screen will look similar to the following:

This much is enabled out of the box by `python-social-auth`, an `Auth0` backend, by configuring its associated `SOCIAL_AUTH_*` settings.

Once a successful login has been completed, the Auth0 backend receives the data from the response and processes it. The associated data is attached to the user object associated with the request. In the dashboard view, which is reached as a result of authentication proceeding to `LOGIN_REDIRECT_URL`, user details are extracted and added to the template context. `dashboard.html` is then rendered. The result may look as follows:

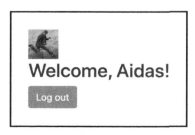

The logout button presented on the dashboard will proceed to log the user back out when pressed.

See also

- The *Implementing password validation* recipe
- The *Downloading authorized files* recipe

Caching the method return value

If you call a model method with heavy calculations or database queries multiple times in the request-response cycle, the performance of the view might become very slow. In this recipe, you will learn about a pattern that you can use to cache the return value of a method for later repetitive use. Note that we are not using the Django cache framework here, only what Python provides us by default.

Getting ready

Choose an app with a model that has a time-consuming method that will be used repetitively in the same request-response cycle.

How to do it...

Perform the following steps:

1. This is a pattern that you can use to cache a method return value of a model for repetitive use in views, forms, or templates, as follows:

```
class SomeModel(models.Model):
    def some_expensive_function(self):
        if not hasattr(self, "_expensive_value_cached"):
            # do some heavy calculations...
            # ... and save the result to result variable
            self._expensive_value_cached = result
        return self._expensive_value_cached
```

2. For example, let's create a `get_thumbnail_url()` method for the `ViralVideo` model. You will explore this in more detail later in the *Using database query expressions* recipe in `Chapter 10`, *Bells and Whistles*:

```python
# myproject/apps/viral_videos/models.py
import re
from django.db import models
from django.utils.translation import ugettext_lazy as _

from myproject.apps.core.models import
CreationModificationDateBase, UrlBase


class ViralVideo(CreationModificationDateBase, UrlBase):
    embed_code = models.TextField(
        _("YouTube embed code"),
        blank=True)

    # ...

    def get_thumbnail_url(self):
        if not hasattr(self, "_thumbnail_url_cached"):
            self._thumbnail_url_cached = ""
            url_pattern = re.compile(
                r'src="https://www.youtube.com/embed/([^"]+)"'
            )
            match = url_pattern.search(self.embed_code)
            if match:
                video_id = match.groups()[0]
                self._thumbnail_url_cached = (
                    f"https://img.youtube.com/vi/{video_id}/0.jpg"
                )
        return self._thumbnail_url_cached
```

How it works...

In this generic example, the method checks whether the `_expensive_value_cached` attribute exists for the model instance. If it doesn't exist, time-consuming calculations are performed and the result is assigned to this new attribute. At the end of the method, the cached value is returned. Of course, if you have several weighty methods, you will need to use different attribute names to save each calculated value.

You can now use something such as `{{ object.some_expensive_function }}` in the header and footer of a template, and the time-consuming calculations will be done just once.

In a template, you can also use the function in both the `{% if %}` condition and the output of the value, as follows:

```
{% if object.some_expensive_function %}
    <span class="special">
        {{ object.some_expensive_function }}
    </span>
{% endif %}
```

In the other example, we checked the thumbnail of a YouTube video by parsing the URL of the video's embed code, getting its ID, and then composing the URL of the thumbnail image. By doing this, you can use it in a template, as follows:

```
{% if video.get_thumbnail_url %}
    <figure>
        <img src="{{ video.get_thumbnail_url }}"
            alt="{{ video.title }}"
        />
        <figcaption>{{ video.title }}</figcaption>
    </figure>
{% endif %}
```

There's more...

The approach we have just described only works if the method is called without arguments so that the result will always be the same. But what if the input varies? Since Python 3.2, there is a decorator we can use to provide basic **Least Recently Used** (LRU) caching of method calls based on a hash of the arguments (at least those that are hashable).

For example, let's look at a contrived and trivial example with a function that takes in two values and returns the result of some expensive logic:

```
def busy_bee(a, b):
    # expensive logic
    return result
```

If we had such a function and wanted to provide a cache to store the results of some commonly used input variations, we could do so easily with the `@lru_cache` decorator from the `functools` package, as follows:

```python
from functools import lru_cache

@lru_cache(maxsize=100, typed=True)
def busy_bee(a, b):
    # expensive logic
    return result
```

Now, we have provided a caching mechanism that will store up to 100 results under the keys that we hashed from the input. The `typed` option was added in Python 3.3 and, by specifying `True`, we have made it so that a call that has a=1 and b=2 will be stored separately from one with a=1.0 and b=2.0. Depending on how the logic operates and what the return value is, such variation may or may not be appropriate.

 You can learn more about the `@lru_cache` decorator in the `functools` documentation at `https://docs.python.org/3/library/functools. html#functools.lru_cache`.

We could also use this decorator for the examples earlier in this recipe to simplify the code, as follows:

```python
# myproject/apps/viral_videos/models.py
from functools import lru_cache
# ...

class ViralVideo(CreationModificationDateMixin, UrlMixin):
    # ...
    @lru_cache
    def get_thumbnail_url(self):
        # ...
```

See also

- Chapter 4, *Templates and JavaScript*
- The *Using Memcached to cache Django views* recipe
- The *Using Redis to cache Django views* recipe

Using Memcached to cache Django views

Django allows us to speed up the request-response cycle by caching the most expensive parts, such as database queries or template rendering. The fastest and most reliable caching natively supported by Django is the memory-based cache server **Memcached**. In this recipe, you will learn how to use Memcached to cache a view for the `viral_videos` app. We'll explore this further in the *Using database query expressions* recipe in `Chapter 10`, *Bells and Whistles*.

Getting ready

There are several things we need to do in order to prepare caching for our Django project:

1. Let's install the `memcached` service. For example, the simplest way to do that on macOS is to use Homebrew:

   ```
   $ brew install memcached
   ```

2. Then, you can start, stop, or restart the Memcached service with these commands:

   ```
   $ brew services start memcached
   $ brew services stop memcached
   $ brew services restart memcached
   ```

    On other operating systems, you can install Memcached using apt-get, yum, or other default package management utilities. Another option is to compile it from the source, as mentioned at `https://memcached.org/downloads`.

3. Install Memcached Python bindings in your virtual environment, as follows:

   ```
   (env)$ pip install python-memcached==1.59
   ```

How to do it...

To integrate caching for your specific views, perform the following steps:

1. Set `CACHES` in the project settings, as follows:

   ```
   # myproject/settings/_base.py
   CACHES = {
   ```

```
    "memcached": {
        "BACKEND":
        "django.core.cache.backends.memcached.MemcachedCache",
        "LOCATION": get_secret("CACHE_LOCATION"),
        "TIMEOUT": 60,   # 1 minute
        "KEY_PREFIX": "myproject",
    },
}
CACHES["default"] = CACHES["memcached"]
```

2. Make sure that you have `CACHE_LOCATION` set to `"localhost:11211"` in your secrets or environment variables.

3. Modify the views of the `viral_videos` app, as follows:

```
# myproject/apps/viral_videos/views.py
from django.shortcuts import render
from django.views.decorators.cache import cache_page
from django.views.decorators.vary import vary_on_cookie


@vary_on_cookie
@cache_page(60)
def viral_video_detail(request, pk):
    # ...
    return render(
        request,
        "viral_videos/viral_video_detail.html",
        {'video': video}
    )
```

 If you follow the Redis setup in the next recipe, you'll see that there is no change whatsoever in the `views.py` file. This shows us that we can change the underlying caching mechanism at will without ever needing to modify the code that uses it.

How it works...

As you will see later in the *Using database query expressions* recipe in Chapter 10, *Bells and Whistles*, the detail view of the viral video shows the number of impressions by authenticated and anonymous users. If you access a viral video (such as at `http://127.0.0.1:8000/en/videos/1/`) and refresh the page a few times with caching enabled, you will notice that the number of impressions changes only once a minute. This is because each response is cached for 60 seconds for every user. We set caching for the view using the `@cache_page` decorator.

Memcached is a key-value store and it uses the full URL by default to generate the key for each cached page. When two visitors access the same page simultaneously, the first visitor's request would receive the page generated by the Python code, and the second one would get the same HTML code but from the Memcached server.

In our example, to ensure that each visitor gets treated separately, even if they access the same URL, we are using the `@vary_on_cookie` decorator. This decorator checks the uniqueness of the `Cookie` header in the HTTP request.

 You can learn more about Django's cache framework from the official documentation at `https://docs.djangoproject.com/en/3.0/topics/cache/`. Similarly, you can find out more about Memcached at `https://memcached.org/`.

See also

- The *Caching the method return value* recipe
- The *Using Redis to cache Django views* recipe
- The *Using database query expressions* recipe in `Chapter 10`, *Bells and Whistles*

Using Redis to cache Django views

Although Memcached is well established in the market as a caching mechanism, and well supported by Django, Redis is an alternate system that provides all the functionality of Memcached and more. Here, we'll revisit the process from the *Using Memcached to cache Django views* recipe and learn how to do the same using Redis instead.

Getting ready

There are several things we need to do in order to prepare caching for our Django project:

1. Let's install the Redis service. For example, the simplest way to do that on macOS is to use Homebrew:

   ```
   $ brew install redis
   ```

2. Then, you can start, stop, or restart the Redis service with these commands:

```
$ brew services start redis
$ brew services stop redis
$ brew services restart redis
```

 On other operating systems, you can install Redis using apt-get, yum, or other default package management utilities. Another option is to compile it from the source, as mentioned at `https://redis.io/download`.

3. Install the Redis cache backend for Django and its dependencies in your virtual environment, as follows:

```
(env)$ pip install redis==3.3.11
(env)$ pip install hiredis==1.0.1
(env)$ pip install django-redis-cache==2.1.0
```

How to do it...

To integrate caching for your specific views, perform the following steps:

1. Set CACHES in the project settings, as follows:

```
# myproject/settings/_base.py
CACHES = {
    "redis": {
        "BACKEND": "redis_cache.RedisCache",
        "LOCATION": [get_secret("CACHE_LOCATION")],
        "TIMEOUT": 60, # 1 minute
        "KEY_PREFIX": "myproject",
    },
}
CACHES["default"] = CACHES["redis"]
```

2. Make sure that you have CACHE_LOCATION set to "localhost:6379" in your secrets or environment variables.

3. Modify the views of the viral_videos app, as follows:

```
# myproject/apps/viral_videos/views.py
from django.shortcuts import render
from django.views.decorators.cache import cache_page
from django.views.decorators.vary import vary_on_cookie

@vary_on_cookie
```

```
@cache_page(60)
def viral_video_detail(request, pk):
    # ...
    return render(
        request,
        "viral_videos/viral_video_detail.html",
        {'video': video}
    )
```

 If you followed the Memcached setup from the previous recipe, you will see that there is no change whatsoever in the `views.py` here. This shows you that we can change the underlying caching mechanism at will without ever needing to modify the code that uses it.

How it works...

Just like with Memcached, we set caching for the view using the `@cache_page` decorator. So, each response is cached for 60 seconds for every user. A viral video detail view (such as the one at `http://127.0.0.1:8000/en/videos/1/`) shows the number of impressions by authenticated and anonymous users. With caching enabled, if you refresh the page a few times, you will notice that the number of impressions changes only once a minute.

Just like Memcached, Redis is a key-value store, and when used for caching, it generates the key for each cached page based on the full URL. When two visitors access the same page simultaneously, the first visitor's request would receive the page generated by the Python code, and the second one would get the same HTML code but from the Redis server.

In our example, to ensure that each visitor gets treated separately, even if they access the same URL, we are using the `@vary_on_cookie` decorator. This decorator checks the uniqueness of the `Cookie` header in the HTTP request.

 You can learn more about Django's cache framework from the official documentation at `https://docs.djangoproject.com/en/3.0/topics/cache/`. Similarly, you can find out more about Memcached at `https://redis.io/`.

There's more...

While Redis is able to handle caching in the same manner as Memcached, there is a multitude of additional options for the caching algorithm built right into the system. In addition to caching, Redis can also be used as a database or message store. It supports a variety of data structures, transactions, pub/sub, and automatic failover, among other things.

Through the django-redis-cache backend, Redis can also be configured as the session backend with almost no effort, like so:

```
# myproject/settings/_base.py
SESSION_ENGINE = "django.contrib.sessions.backends.cache"
SESSION_CACHE_ALIAS = "default"
```

See also

- The *Caching the method return value* recipe
- The *Using Memcached to cache Django views* recipe
- The *Using database query expressions* recipe in Chapter 10, *Bells and Whistles*

8
Hierarchical Structures

In this chapter, we will cover the following topics:

- Creating hierarchical categories with django-mptt
- Creating a category administration interface with django-mptt-admin
- Rendering categories in a template with django-mptt
- Using a single selection field to choose a category in forms with django-mptt
- Using a checkbox list to choose multiple categories in forms with django-mptt
- Creating hierarchical categories with django-treebeard
- Creating a basic category administration interface with django-treebeard

Introduction

Whether you build your own forum, threaded comments, or categorization system, there will be a moment when you need to save hierarchical structures in a database. Although the tables of relational databases (such as MySQL and PostgreSQL) are flat, there is a fast and effective way to store hierarchical structures. It is called **Modified Preorder Tree Traversal** (**MPTT**). MPTT allows you to read tree structures without recursive calls to the database.

Firstly, let's get familiar with the terminology of tree structures. A tree data structure is a nested collection of **nodes**, starting at the **root** node and with references to **child** nodes. There are restrictions: for instance, no node should reference back to create a loop and no reference should be duplicated. The following are some other terms to remember:

- A parent is any node that has references to child nodes.
- **Descendants** are nodes that can be reached by recursively traversing from a parent to its children. Therefore, a node's descendants will be its child, the child's children, and so on.

- **Ancestors** are nodes that can be reached by recursively traversing from a child to its parent. Therefore, a node's ancestors will be its parent, the parent's parent, and so on up to the root.
- **Siblings** are nodes with the same parent.
- A **leaf** is a node without children.

Now, I'll explain how MPTT works. Imagine laying out your tree horizontally with the root node at the top. Each node in the tree has left and right values. Imagine them as small left and right handles on the left- and right-hand sides of the node. Then, you walk (traverse) around the tree counterclockwise, starting from the root node, and mark each left or right value that you find with a number: 1, 2, 3, and so on. It will look similar to the following diagram:

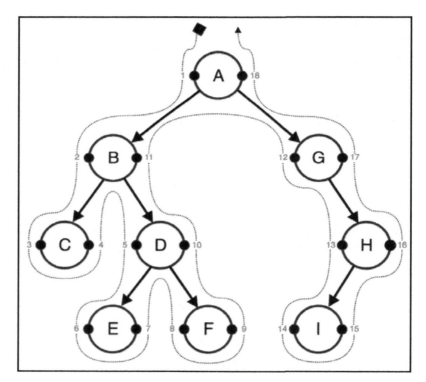

In the database table of this hierarchical structure, you have a title, left value, and right value for each node.

Now, if you want to get the **subtree** of the **B** node with **2** as the left value and **11** as the right value, you will have to select all of the nodes that have a left value between **2** and **11**. They are **C**, **D**, **E**, and **F**.

To get all of the **ancestors** of the **D** node with **5** as the left value and **10** as the right value, you have to select all of the nodes that have a left value that is less than **5** and a right value that is more than **10**. These would be **B** and **A**.

To get the number of the **descendants** for a node, you can use the following formula:

descendants = (right - left - 1) / 2

Therefore, the number of **descendants** for the **B** node can be calculated as shown in the following formula:

(11 - 2 - 1) / 2 = 4

If we want to attach the **E** node to the **C** node, we will have to update the left and right values only for the nodes of their first common ancestor, the **B** node. Then, the **C** node will still have **3** as the left value; the **E** node will get **4** as the left value and **5** as the right value; the right value of the **C** node will become **6**; the left value of the **D** node will become **7**; the left value of the **F** node will stay at **8**; the others will also remain the same.

Similarly, there are other tree-related operations with nodes in MPTT. It might be too complicated to manage all of this by yourself for every hierarchical structure in your project. Luckily, there is a Django app called `django-mptt` that has a long history of handling these algorithms and provides a straightforward API to handle the tree structures. Another app, `django-treebeard`, has also been tried and tested and gained additional traction as a powerful alternative when it replaced MPTT in django CMS 3.1. In this chapter, you will learn how to use these helper apps.

Technical requirements

You will need the latest stable version of Python 3, MySQL, or PostgreSQL and a Django project with a virtual environment.

You can find all of the code for this chapter at the `ch08` directory of the GitHub repository, at: `https://github.com/PacktPublishing/Django-3-Web-Development-Cookbook-Fourth-Edition`.

Creating hierarchical categories with django-mptt

To illustrate how to deal with MPTT, we will build on top of the `ideas` app from Chapter 3, *Forms and Views*. In our changes, we will replace the categories with a hierarchical `Category` model and update the `Idea` model to have a many-to-many relationship with the categories. Alternatively, you can create the app from fresh, using only the content shown here, to implement a very basic version of the `Idea` model from scratch.

Getting ready

To get started, perform the following steps:

1. Install `django-mptt` in your virtual environment using the following command:

   ```
   (env)$ pip install django-mptt==0.10.0
   ```

2. Create the `categories` and `ideas` apps if you have not done so already. Add those apps as well as `mptt` to `INSTALLED_APPS` in the settings, as follows:

   ```python
   # myproject/settings/_base.py
   INSTALLED_APPS = [
       # ...
       "mptt",
       # ...
       "myproject.apps.categories",
       "myproject.apps.ideas",
   ]
   ```

How to do it...

We will create a hierarchical Category model and tie it to the Idea model, which will have a many-to-many relationship with the categories, as follows:

1. Open the models.py file in the categories app and add a Category model that extends mptt.models.MPTTModel and CreationModificationDateBase, defined in Chapter 2, *Models and Database Structure*. In addition to the fields coming from the mixins, the Category model will need to have a parent field of the TreeForeignKey type and a title field:

```python
# myproject/apps/ideas/models.py
from django.db import models
from django.utils.translation import ugettext_lazy as _
from mptt.models import MPTTModel
from mptt.fields import TreeForeignKey

from myproject.apps.core.models import CreationModificationDateBase


class Category(MPTTModel, CreationModificationDateBase):
    parent = TreeForeignKey(
        "self", on_delete=models.CASCADE,
        blank=True, null=True, related_name="children"
    )
    title = models.CharField(_("Title"), max_length=200)

    class Meta:
        ordering = ["tree_id", "lft"]
        verbose_name = _("Category")
        verbose_name_plural = _("Categories")

    class MPTTMeta:
        order_insertion_by = ["title"]

    def __str__(self):
        return self.title
```

2. Update the `Idea` model to include the `categories` field of
   the `TreeManyToManyField` type:

```python
# myproject/apps/ideas/models.py
from django.utils.translation import gettext_lazy as _

from mptt.fields import TreeManyToManyField

from myproject.apps.core.models import
CreationModificationDateBase, UrlBase


class Idea(CreationModificationDateBase, UrlBase):
    # ...
    categories = TreeManyToManyField(
        "categories.Category",
        verbose_name=_("Categories"),
        related_name="category_ideas",
    )
```

3. Update your database by making migrations and running them:

```
(env)$ python manage.py makemigrations
(env)$ python manage.py migrate
```

How it works...

The `MPTTModel` mixin will add the `tree_id`, `lft`, `rght`, and `level` fields to the `Category` model:

- The `tree_id` field is used as you can have multiple trees in the database table. In fact, each root category is saved in a separate tree.
- The `lft` and `rght` fields store the left and right values used in the MPTT algorithms.
- The `level` field stores the node's depth in the tree. The root node will be level 0.

Through the `order_insertion_by` meta option specific to MPTT, we ensure that when new categories are added, they stay in alphabetical order by title.

Besides new fields, the `MPTTModel` mixin adds methods to navigate through the tree structure similar to how you navigate through DOM elements using JavaScript. These methods are as follows:

- If you want to access the ancestors of a category, use the following code. Here, the `ascending` parameter defines from which direction to read the nodes (the default is `False`), and the `include_self` parameter defines whether to include the category itself in `QuerySet` (the default is `False`):

  ```
  ancestor_categories = category.get_ancestors(
      ascending=False,
      include_self=False,
  )
  ```

- To just get the root category, use the following code:

  ```
  root = category.get_root()
  ```

- If you want to get the direct children of a category, use the following code:

  ```
  children = category.get_children()
  ```

- To get all of the descendants of a category, use the following code. Here, the `include_self` parameter again defines whether or not to include the category itself in `QuerySet`:

  ```
  descendants = category.get_descendants(include_self=False)
  ```

- If you want to get the descendant count without querying the database, use the following code:

  ```
  descendants_count = category.get_descendant_count()
  ```

- To get all siblings, call the following method:

  ```
  siblings = category.get_siblings(include_self=False)
  ```

Root categories are considered siblings of other root categories.

- To just get the previous and next siblings, call the following methods:

```
previous_sibling = category.get_previous_sibling()
next_sibling = category.get_next_sibling()
```

- Also, there are methods to check whether the category is root, child, or leaf, as follows:

```
category.is_root_node()
category.is_child_node()
category.is_leaf_node()
```

All of these methods can be used either in views, templates, or management commands. If you want to manipulate the tree structure, you can also use the `insert_at()` and `move_to()` methods. In this case, you can read about them and the tree manager methods at `https://django-mptt.readthedocs.io/en/stable/models.html`.

In the preceding models, we used `TreeForeignKey` and `TreeManyToManyField`. These are similar to `ForeignKey` and `ManyToManyField`, except that they show the choices indented in hierarchies in the administration interface.

Also, note that in the `Meta` class of the `Category` model, we order the categories by `tree_id` and then by the `lft` value to show the categories naturally in the tree structure.

See also

- The *Creating a model mixin to handle creation and modification dates* recipe in `Chapter 2`, *Models and Database Structure*
- The *Creating a category administration interface with django-mptt-admin* recipe

Creating a category administration interface with django-mptt-admin

The `django-mptt` app comes with a simple model administration mixin that allows you to create a tree structure and list it with indentation. To reorder trees, you need to either create this functionality yourself or use a third-party solution. One app that can help you to create a draggable administration interface for hierarchical models is `django-mptt-admin`. Let's take a look at it in this recipe.

Getting ready

First, set up the `categories` app as described in the previous, *Creating hierarchical categories with django-mptt* recipe. Then, we need to install the `django-mptt-admin` app by performing the following steps:

1. Install the app in your virtual environment using the following command:

   (env)$ pip install django-mptt-admin==0.7.2

2. Put it in `INSTALLED_APPS` in the settings, as follows:

   ```
   # myproject/settings/_base.py
   INSTALLED_APPS = [
       # ...
       "mptt",
       "django_mptt_admin",
   ]
   ```

3. Make sure that the static files for `django-mptt-admin` are available to your project:

   (env)$ python manage.py collectstatic

How to do it...

Create an `admin.py` file in which we will define the administration interface for the `Category` model. It will extend `DjangoMpttAdmin` instead of `admin.ModelAdmin`, as follows:

```
# myproject/apps/categories/admin.py
from django.contrib import admin
from django_mptt_admin.admin import DjangoMpttAdmin

from .models import Category

@admin.register(Category)
class CategoryAdmin(DjangoMpttAdmin):
    list_display = ["title", "created", "modified"]
    list_filter = ["created"]
```

How it works...

The administration interface for the categories will have two modes: **tree view** and **grid view**. Your tree view will look similar to the following screenshot:

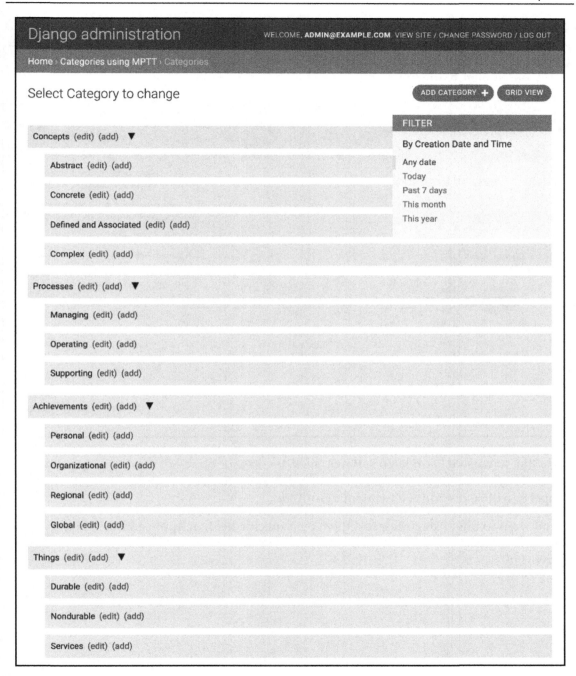

The tree view uses the **jqTree** jQuery library for node manipulation. You can expand and collapse categories for a better overview. To reorder them or change the dependencies, you can drag and drop the titles in this list view. During reordering, the **User Interface (UI)** looks similar to the following screenshot:

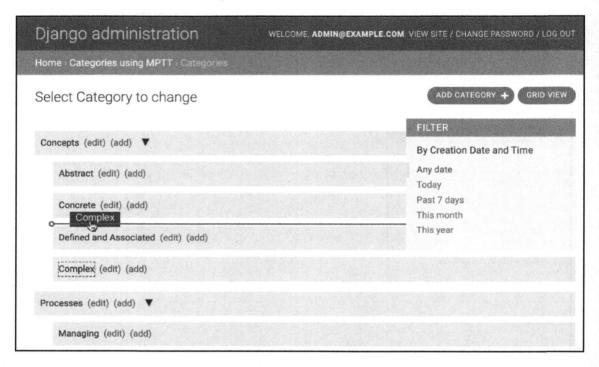

Note that any usual list-related settings, such as `list_display` or `list_filter`, will be ignored in the tree view. Also, any ordering driven by the `order_insertion_by` meta property will be overridden by manual sorting.

If you want to filter categories, sort them by a specific field, or apply admin actions, you can switch to the grid view, which shows the default category change list, as in the following screenshot:

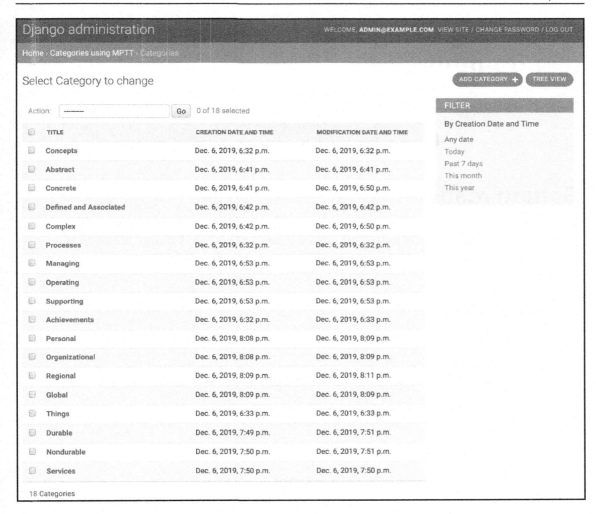

See also

- The *Creating hierarchical categories with django-mptt* recipe
- The *Creating a category administration interface with django-treebeard* recipe

Rendering categories in a template with django-mptt

Once you have created categories in your app, you need to display them hierarchically in a template. The easiest way to do this with MPTT trees, as described in the *Creating hierarchical categories with django-mptt* recipe, is to use the {% recursetree %} template tag from the django-mptt app. We will show you how to do that in this recipe.

Getting ready

Make sure you have the categories and ideas apps. There, your Idea model should have many-to-many relation to the Category model, as per the *Creating hierarchical categories with django-mptt* recipe. Enter some categories in the database.

How to do it...

Pass QuerySet of your hierarchical categories to the template and then use the {% recursetree %} template tag as follows:

1. Create a view that loads all of the categories and passes them to a template:

```python
# myproject/apps/categories/views.py
from django.views.generic import ListView

from .models import Category

class IdeaCategoryList(ListView):
    model = Category
    template_name = "categories/category_list.html"
    context_object_name = "categories"
```

2. Create a template with the following content to output the hierarchy of categories:

```
{# categories/category_list.html #}
{% extends "base.html" %}
{% load mptt_tags %}

{% block content %}
    <ul class="root">
        {% recursetree categories %}
            <li>
                {{ node.title }}
                {% if not node.is_leaf_node %}
                    <ul class="children">
                        {{ children }}
                    </ul>
                {% endif %}
            </li>
        {% endrecursetree %}
    </ul>
{% endblock %}
```

3. Create a URL rule to show the view:

```
# myproject/urls.py
from django.conf.urls.i18n import i18n_patterns
from django.urls import path

from myproject.apps.categories import views as categories_views

urlpatterns = i18n_patterns(
    # ...
    path(
        "idea-categories/",
        categories_views.IdeaCategoryList.as_view(),
        name="idea_categories",
    ),
)
```

How it works...

The template will be rendered as nested lists, as shown in the following screenshot:

- Concepts
  - Abstract
  - Concrete
  - Defined and Associated
  - Complex
- Processes
  - Managing
  - Operating
  - Supporting
- Achievements
  - Personal
  - Organizational
  - Regional
  - Global
- Things
  - Durable
  - Nondurable
  - Services

The `{% recursetree %}` block template tag takes `QuerySet` of the categories and renders the list using the template content nested within the tag. There are two special variables used here:

- The `node` variable is an instance of the `Category` model whose fields or methods can be used to add specific CSS classes or HTML5 `data-*` attributes for JavaScript, such as `{{ node.get_descendent_count }}`, `{{ node.level }}`, or `{{ node.is_root }}`.
- Secondly, we have a `children` variable that defines where the rendered child nodes of the current category will be placed.

There's more...

If your hierarchical structure is very complex, with more than 20 levels, it is recommended to use the `{% full_tree_for_model %}` and `{% drilldown_tree_for_node %}` iterative tags or the non-recursive `tree_info` template filter.

 For more information on how to do this, refer to the official documentation at `https://django-mptt.readthedocs.io/en/latest/templates.html#iterative-tags`.

See also

- The *Using HTML5 data attributes* recipe in `Chapter 4`, *Templates and JavaScript*
- The *Creating hierarchical categories with django-mptt* recipe
- The *Creating hierarchical categories with django-treebeard* recipe
- The *Using a single selection field to choose a category in forms with django-mptt* recipe

Using a single selection field to choose a category in forms with django-mptt

What happens if you want to show category selection in a form? How will the hierarchy be presented? In `django-mptt`, there is a special `TreeNodeChoiceField` form field that you can use to show the hierarchical structures in a selected field. Let's take a look at how to do this.

Getting ready

We will start with the `categories` and `ideas` apps that we defined in the previous recipes. For this recipe, we will also need `django-crispy-forms`. Have a look at how to install it in the *Creating a form layout with django-crispy-forms* recipe in `Chapter 3`, *Forms and Views*.

How to do it...

Let's enhance the filter form for `ideas` that we created in the *Filtering object lists* recipe in `Chapter 3`, *Forms and Views*, by adding a field for filtering by category:

1. In the `forms.py` file of the `ideas` app, create a form with a category field as follows:

```python
# myproject/apps/ideas/forms.py
from django import forms
from django.utils.safestring import mark_safe
from django.utils.translation import ugettext_lazy as _
from django.contrib.auth import get_user_model

from crispy_forms import bootstrap, helper, layout
from mptt.forms import TreeNodeChoiceField

from myproject.apps.categories.models import Category

from .models import Idea, RATING_CHOICES

User = get_user_model()


class IdeaFilterForm(forms.Form):
    author = forms.ModelChoiceField(
        label=_("Author"),
        required=False,
        queryset=User.objects.all(),
    )
    category = TreeNodeChoiceField(
        label=_("Category"),
        required=False,
        queryset=Category.objects.all(),
        level_indicator=mark_safe("        ")
    )
    rating = forms.ChoiceField(
        label=_("Rating"), required=False, choices=RATING_CHOICES
```

```
    )
    def __init__(self, *args, **kwargs):
        super().__init__(*args, **kwargs)

        author_field = layout.Field("author")
        category_field = layout.Field("category")
        rating_field = layout.Field("rating")
        submit_button = layout.Submit("filter", _("Filter"))
        actions = bootstrap.FormActions(submit_button)

        main_fieldset = layout.Fieldset(
            _("Filter"),
            author_field,
            category_field,
            rating_field,
            actions,
        )

        self.helper = helper.FormHelper()
        self.helper.form_method = "GET"
        self.helper.layout = layout.Layout(main_fieldset)
```

2. We should already have created `IdeaListView`, an associated URL rule, and the
   `idea_list.html` template to show this form. Make sure to render the filter form
   in the template using the `{% crispy %}` template tag, as follows:

```
{# ideas/idea_list.html #}
{% extends "base.html" %}
{% load i18n utility_tags crispy_forms_tags %}

{% block sidebar %}
    {% crispy form %}
{% endblock %}

{% block main %}
    {# ... #}
{% endblock %}
```

How it works...

The category selection drop-down menu will look similar to the following:

`TreeNodeChoiceField` acts like `ModelChoiceField`; however, it shows hierarchical choices as indented. By default, `TreeNodeChoiceField` represents each deeper level prefixed by three dashes, `---`. In our example, we have changed the level indicator to be four non-breaking spaces (the ` ` HTML entities) by passing the `level_indicator` parameter to the field. To ensure that the non-breaking spaces aren't escaped, we use the `mark_safe()` function.

See also

- The *Rendering categories in a template with django-mptt* recipe
- The *Using a checkbox list to choose multiple categories in forms with django-mptt* recipe

Using a checkbox list to choose multiple categories in forms with django-mptt

When one or more categories need to be selected at once in a form, you can use the `TreeNodeMultipleChoiceField` multiple selection field that is provided by django-mptt. However, multiple selection fields (for example, `<select multiple>`) are not very user-friendly from an interface point of view, as the user needs to scroll and hold control or command keys while clicking to make multiple choices. Especially when there is a fairly large number of items to choose from, and the user wants to select several at once, or the user has accessibility handicaps, such as poor motor control, this can lead to a really awful user experience. A much better approach is to provide a checkbox list from which the user can choose categories. In this recipe, we will create a field that allows you to show the hierarchical tree structure as indented checkboxes in the form.

Getting ready

We will start with the `categories` and `ideas` apps that we defined in the previous recipes and the `core` app, which you should have in your project.

How to do it...

To render an indented list of categories with checkboxes, we will create and use a new `MultipleChoiceTreeField` form field and create an HTML template for this field.

The specific template will be passed to the `crispy_forms` layout in the form. To do this, perform the following steps:

1. In the `core` app, add a `form_fields.py` file and create a `MultipleChoiceTreeField` form field that extends `ModelMultipleChoiceField`, as follows:

    ```python
    # myproject/apps/core/form_fields.py
    from django import forms

    class MultipleChoiceTreeField(forms.ModelMultipleChoiceField):
        widget = forms.CheckboxSelectMultiple

        def label_from_instance(self, obj):
            return obj
    ```

2. Use the new field with the categories to choose from in a new form for idea creation. Also, in the form layout, pass a custom template to the `categories` field, as shown in the following:

    ```python
    # myproject/apps/ideas/forms.py
    from django import forms
    from django.utils.translation import ugettext_lazy as _
    from django.contrib.auth import get_user_model

    from crispy_forms import bootstrap, helper, layout

    from myproject.apps.categories.models import Category
    from myproject.apps.core.form_fields import MultipleChoiceTreeField

    from .models import Idea, RATING_CHOICES

    User = get_user_model()


    class IdeaForm(forms.ModelForm):
        categories = MultipleChoiceTreeField(
            label=_("Categories"),
            required=False,
            queryset=Category.objects.all(),
        )

        class Meta:
            model = Idea
            exclude = ["author"]

        def __init__(self, request, *args, **kwargs):
    ```

```
        self.request = request
        super().__init__(*args, **kwargs)

        title_field = layout.Field("title")
        content_field = layout.Field("content", rows="3")
        main_fieldset = layout.Fieldset(_("Main data"),
         title_field, content_field)

        picture_field = layout.Field("picture")
        format_html = layout.HTML(
            """{% include "ideas/includes/picture_guidelines.html"
              %}"""
        )

        picture_fieldset = layout.Fieldset(
            _("Picture"),
            picture_field,
            format_html,
            title=_("Image upload"),
            css_id="picture_fieldset",
        )

        categories_field = layout.Field(
            "categories",
            template="core/includes
            /checkboxselectmultiple_tree.html"
        )
        categories_fieldset = layout.Fieldset(
            _("Categories"), categories_field,
             css_id="categories_fieldset"
        )

        submit_button = layout.Submit("save", _("Save"))
        actions = bootstrap.FormActions(submit_button,
         css_class="my-4")

        self.helper = helper.FormHelper()
        self.helper.form_action = self.request.path
        self.helper.form_method = "POST"
        self.helper.layout = layout.Layout(
            main_fieldset,
            picture_fieldset,
            categories_fieldset,
            actions,
        )

    def save(self, commit=True):
        instance = super().save(commit=False)
```

```
            instance.author = self.request.user
            if commit:
                instance.save()
                self.save_m2m()
            return instance
```

3. Create a template for a Bootstrap-style checkbox list based on the `crispy` forms template, `bootstrap4/layout/checkboxselectmultiple.html`, as shown in the following:

```
{# core/include/checkboxselectmultiple_tree.html #}
{% load crispy_forms_filters l10n %}

<div class="{% if field_class %} {{ field_class }}{% endif %}"{% if
flat_attrs %} {{ flat_attrs|safe }}{% endif %}>

    {% for choice_value, choice_instance in field.field.choices %}
    <div class="{%if use_custom_control%}custom-control custom-
    checkbox{% if inline_class %} custom-control-inline{% endif
    %}{% else %}form-check{% if inline_class %} form-check-
    inline{% endif %}{% endif %}">
        <input type="checkbox" class="{%if use_custom_control%}
        custom-control-input{% else %}form-check-input
        {% endif %}{% if field.errors %} is-invalid{% endif %}"
        {% if choice_value in field.value or choice_
        value|stringformat:"s" in field.value or
        choice_value|stringformat:"s" == field.value
        |default_if_none:""|stringformat:"s" %} checked=
        "checked"{% endif %} name="{{ field.html_name }}"
         id="id_{{ field.html_name }}_{{ forloop.counter }}"
         value="{{ choice_value|unlocalize }}" {{ field.field
         .widget.attrs|flatatt }}>
        <label class="{%if use_custom_control%}custom-control-
        label{% else %}form-check-label{% endif %} level-{{
        choice_instance.level }}" for="id_{{ field.html_name
        }}_{{ forloop.counter }}">
            {{ choice_instance|unlocalize }}
        </label>
        {% if field.errors and forloop.last and not inline_class %}
            {% include 'bootstrap4/layout/field_errors_block.html'
             %}
        {% endif %}
    </div>
    {% endfor %}
    {% if field.errors and inline_class %}
    <div class="w-100 {%if use_custom_control%}custom-control
     custom-checkbox{% if inline_class %} custom-control-inline
     {% endif %}{% else %}form-check{% if inline_class %} form-
```

```
      check-inline{% endif %}{% endif %}">
        <input type="checkbox" class="custom-control-input {% if
         field.errors %}is-invalid{%endif%}">
        {% include 'bootstrap4/layout/field_errors_block.html' %}
      </div>
      {% endif %}

      {% include 'bootstrap4/layout/help_text.html' %}
    </div>
```

4. Create a new view for adding an idea, using the form we just created:

```python
# myproject/apps/ideas/views.py
from django.contrib.auth.decorators import login_required
from django.shortcuts import render, redirect, get_object_or_404

from .forms import IdeaForm
from .models import Idea

@login_required
def add_or_change_idea(request, pk=None):
    idea = None
    if pk:
        idea = get_object_or_404(Idea, pk=pk)
    if request.method == "POST":
        form = IdeaForm(request, data=request.POST,
         files=request.FILES, instance=idea)
        if form.is_valid():
            idea = form.save()
            return redirect("ideas:idea_detail", pk=idea.pk)
    else:
        form = IdeaForm(request, instance=idea)

    context = {"idea": idea, "form": form}
    return render(request, "ideas/idea_form.html", context)
```

5. Add the associated template to show the form with the `{% crispy %}` template tag, whose usage you can learn more about in the *Creating a form layout with django-crispy-forms* recipe in `Chapter 3`, *Forms and Views*:

```
{# ideas/idea_form.html #}
{% extends "base.html" %}
{% load i18n crispy_forms_tags static %}

{% block content %}
    <a href="{% url "ideas:idea_list" %}">{% trans "List of ideas"
%}</a>
```

```
        <h1>
            {% if idea %}
                {% blocktrans trimmed with title=idea.translated_title
                  %}
                    Change Idea "{{ title }}"
                {% endblocktrans %}
            {% else %}
                {% trans "Add Idea" %}
            {% endif %}
        </h1>
    {% crispy form %}
{% endblock %}
```

6. We also need a URL rule pointing to the new view, as follows:

```
# myproject/apps/ideas/urls.py
from django.urls import path

from .views import add_or_change_idea

urlpatterns = [
    # ...
    path("add/", add_or_change_idea, name="add_idea"),
    path("<uuid:pk>/change/", add_or_change_idea,
      name="change_idea"),
]
```

7. Add rules to your CSS file to indent the labels using the classes generated in the checkbox tree field template, such as .level-0, .level-1, and .level-2, by setting the margin-left parameter. Make sure that you have a reasonable amount of these CSS classes for the expected maximum depth of trees in your context, as follows:

```
/* myproject/site_static/site/css/style.css */
.level-0 {margin-left: 0;}
.level-1 {margin-left: 20px;}
.level-2 {margin-left: 40px;}
```

How it works...

As a result, we get the following form:

List of ideas

Add Idea

Main data

Title*

Content*

Picture

Picture*

Choose file   No file chosen

Available formats are JPG, GIF, and PNG. Minimal size is 800 × 800 px.

Categories

- [ ] Concepts
  - [ ] Abstract
  - [ ] Concrete
  - [ ] Defined and Associated
  - [ ] Complex
- [ ] Processes
  - [ ] Managing
  - [ ] Operating
  - [ ] Supporting
- [ ] Achievements
  - [ ] Personal
  - [ ] Organizational
  - [ ] Regional
  - [ ] Global
- [ ] Things
  - [ ] Durable
  - [ ] Nondurable
  - [ ] Services

Save

Contrary to the default behavior of Django, which hardcodes field generation in Python code, the `django-crispy-forms` app uses templates to render the fields. You can browse them under `crispy_forms/templates/bootstrap4` and copy some of them to an analogous path in your project's template directory to overwrite them when necessary.

In our idea creation and editing form, we pass a custom template for the `categories` field that will add the `.level-*` CSS classes to the `<label>` tag, wrapping the checkboxes. One problem with the normal `CheckboxSelectMultiple` widget is that when rendered, it only uses choice values and choice texts, whereas we need other properties of the category, such as the depth level. To solve this, we also created a custom `MultipleChoiceTreeField` form field, which extends `ModelMultipleChoiceField` and overrides the `label_from_instance()` method to return the category instance itself, instead of its Unicode representation. The template for the field looks complicated; however, it is mostly a refactored multiple checkbox field template (`crispy_forms/templates/bootstrap4/layout/checkboxselectmultiple.html`), with all of the necessary Bootstrap markup. We mainly just made a slight modification to add the `.level-*` CSS classes.

See also

- The *Creating a form layout with django-crispy-forms* recipe in `Chapter 3`, *Forms and Views*
- The *Rendering categories in a template with django-mptt* recipe
- The *Using a single selection field to choose a category in forms* recipe

Creating hierarchical categories with django-treebeard

There are several algorithms for tree structures, each with its own benefits. An app called `django-treebeard`, an alternative to `django-mptt` that is used by django CMS, provides support for three tree forms:

- **Adjacency List** trees are simple structures, where each node has a parent attribute. Although read operations are fast, this comes at the cost of slow writes.

- **Nested Sets** trees and MPTT trees are the same; they structure nodes as sets nested beneath the parent. This structure also provides very fast read access at the cost of more expensive writing and deletion, particularly when writes require some particular ordering.
- **Materialized Path** trees are built with each node in the tree having an associated path attribute, which is a string indicating the full path from the root to the node—much like a URL path indicates where to find a particular page on a website. This is the most efficient approach supported.

As a demonstration of the support it has for all of these algorithms, we will use django-treebeard and its consistent API. We will extend the categories app from Chapter 3, *Forms and Views*. In our changes, we will enhance the Category model with support for hierarchy via one of the supported tree algorithms.

Getting ready

To get started, perform the following steps:

1. Install django-treebeard in your virtual environment using the following command:

   ```
   (env)$ pip install django-treebeard==4.3
   ```

2. Create the categories and ideas apps if you have not done so already. Add the categories app as well as treebeard to INSTALLED_APPS in the settings, as follows:

   ```python
   # myproject/settings/_base.py
   INSTALLED_APPS = [
       # ...
       "treebeard",
       # ...
       "myproject.apps.categories",
       "myproject.apps.ideas",
   ]
   ```

How to do it...

We will enhance the `Category` model using the **Materialized Path** algorithm, as follows:

1. Open the `models.py` file and update the `Category` model to extend `treebeard.mp_tree.MP_Node` instead of the standard Django model. It should also inherit from `CreationModificationDateMixin`, which we defined in Chapter 2, *Models and Database Structure*. In addition to the fields coming from the mixins, the `Category` model will need to have a `title` field:

   ```python
   # myproject/apps/categories/models.py
   from django.db import models
   from django.utils.translation import ugettext_lazy as _
   from treebeard.mp_tree import MP_Node

   from myproject.apps.core.models import CreationModificationDateBase


   class Category(MP_Node, CreationModificationDateBase):
       title = models.CharField(_("Title"), max_length=200)

       class Meta:
           verbose_name = _("Category")
           verbose_name_plural = _("Categories")

       def __str__(self):
           return self.title
   ```

2. This will require an update to the database, so next, we'll need to migrate the `categories` app:

   ```
   (env)$ python manage.py makemigrations
   (env)$ python manage.py migrate
   ```

3. With the use of abstract model inheritance, treebeard tree nodes can be related to other models using standard relationships. As such, the `Idea` model can continue to have a simple `ManyToManyField` relation to `Category`:

   ```python
   # myproject/apps/ideas/models.py
   from django.db import models
   from django.utils.translation import gettext_lazy as _

   from myproject.apps.core.models import
   CreationModificationDateBase, UrlBase
   ```

```
class Idea(CreationModificationDateBase, UrlBase):
    # ...
    categories = models.ManyToManyField(
        "categories.Category",
        verbose_name=_("Categories"),
        related_name="category_ideas",
    )
```

How it works...

The MP_Node abstract model provides the path, depth, and numchild fields, as well as the steplen, alphabet, and node_order_by attributes, to the Category model as necessary for constructing the tree:

- The depth and numchild fields provide metadata about a node's location and descendants.
- The path field is indexed, enabling database queries against it using LIKE to be very fast.
- The path field is made up of fixed-length encoded segments, where the size of each segment is determined by the steplen attribute value (which defaults to 4), and the encoding uses characters found in the given alphabet attribute value (defaults to Latin alphanumeric characters).

The path, depth, and numchild fields should be treated as read-only. Also, steplen, alphabet, and node_order_by values should never be changed after saving the first object to a tree; otherwise, the data will be corrupted.

Besides new fields and attributes, the MP_Node abstract class adds methods for navigation through the tree structure. Some important examples of these methods are listed here:

- If you want to get the **ancestors** of a category, which are returned as QuerySet of ancestors from the root to the parent of the current node, use the following code:

```
ancestor_categories = category.get_ancestors()
```

- To just get the root category, which is identified by having a depth of 1, use the following code:

```
root = category.get_root()
```

- If you want to get the direct `children` of a category, use the following code:

```
children = category.get_children()
```

- To get all `descendants` of a category, returned as `QuerySet` of all children and their children, and so on, but not including the current node itself, use the following code:

```
descendants = category.get_descendants()
```

- If you want to get just the `descendant` count, use the following code:

```
descendants_count = category.get_descendant_count()
```

- To get all `siblings`, including the reference node, call the following method:

```
siblings = category.get_siblings()
```

 Root categories are considered to be siblings of other root categories.

- To just get the previous and next `siblings`, call the following methods, where `get_prev_sibling()` will return `None` for the leftmost sibling, as will `get_next_sibling()` for the rightmost one:

```
previous_sibling = category.get_prev_sibling()
next_sibling = category.get_next_sibling()
```

- Also, there are methods to check whether the category is `root`, `leaf`, or related to another node:

```
category.is_root()
category.is_leaf()
category.is_child_of(another_category)
category.is_descendant_of(another_category)
category.is_sibling_of(another_category)
```

There's more...

This recipe only scratched the surface of the power of `django-treebeard` and its Materialized Path trees. There are many other methods available for the navigation as well as the construction of trees. In addition, the API for Materialized Path trees is largely identical to those for Nested Sets trees and Adjacency List trees, which are available simply by implementing your model with the `NS_Node` or `AL_Node` abstract classes, respectively, instead of using `MP_Node`.

 Read the `django-treebeard` API documentation for a complete listing of the available properties and methods for each of the tree implementations at `https://django-treebeard.readthedocs.io/en/latest/api.html`.

See also

- Chapter 3, *Forms and Views*
- The *Creating hierarchical categories with django-mptt* recipe
- The *Creating a category administration interface with django-treebeard* recipe

Creating a basic category administration interface with django-treebeard

The `django-treebeard` app provides its own `TreeAdmin`, extending from the standard `ModelAdmin`. This allows you to view tree nodes hierarchically in the administration interface, with interface features dependent upon the tree algorithm used. Let's take a look at this in this recipe.

Getting ready

First, set up the categories app and django-treebeard as described in the *Creating hierarchical categories with django-treebeard* recipe earlier in this chapter. Also, make sure that the static files for django-treebeard are available to your project:

```
(env)$ python manage.py collectstatic
```

How to do it...

Create an administration interface for the Category model from the categories app that extends treebeard.admin.TreeAdmin instead of admin.ModelAdmin and uses a custom form factory, as follows:

```python
# myproject/apps/categories/admin.py
from django.contrib import admin
from treebeard.admin import TreeAdmin
from treebeard.forms import movenodeform_factory

from .models import Category

@admin.register(Category)
class CategoryAdmin(TreeAdmin):
    form = movenodeform_factory(Category)
    list_display = ["title", "created", "modified"]
    list_filter = ["created"]
```

How it works...

The administration interface for the categories will have one of two modes, dependent upon the tree implementation used. For Materialized Path and Nested Sets trees, an advanced UI is provided, as seen here:

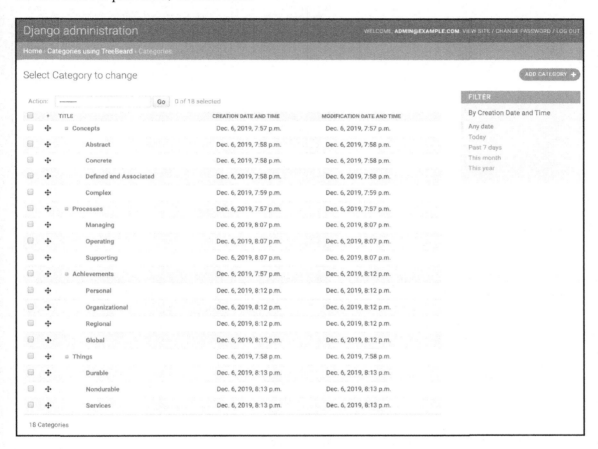

This advanced view allows you to expand and collapse categories for a better overview. To reorder them or change the dependencies, you can drag and drop the titles. During reordering, the user interface looks similar to the following screenshot:

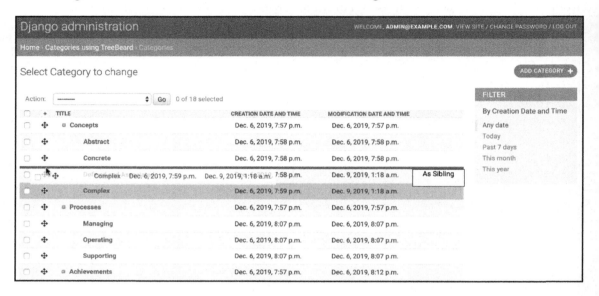

If you apply filtering or sorting of categories by a specific field, the advanced functionality is disabled, but the more attractive look and feel of the advanced interface remains. We can see this intermediate view here, where only categories created in the **Past 7 days** are shown:

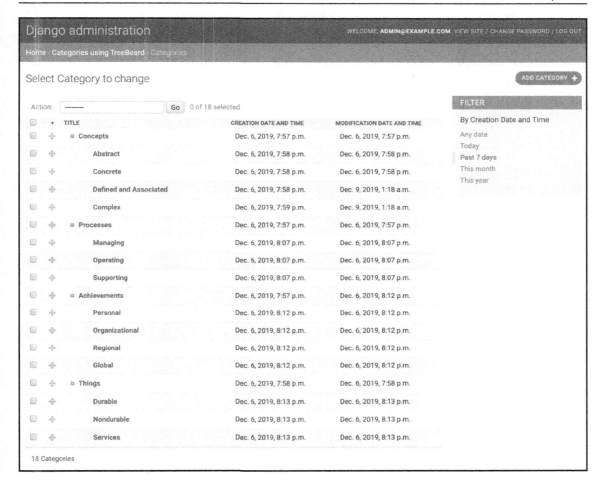

However, if your tree uses the Adjacency List algorithm, a basic UI is provided with less aesthetic presentation and none of the toggling or reordering functionality given in the advanced UI.

 More details about `django-treebeard` administration, including a screenshot of the basic interface, can be found in the documentation at: `https://django-treebeard.readthedocs.io/en/latest/admin.html`.

See also

- The *Creating hierarchical categories with django-mptt* recipe
- The *Creating hierarchical categories with django-treebeard* recipe
- The *Creating a category administration interface with django-mptt-admin* recipe

Importing and Exporting Data

9

In this chapter, we will cover the following topics:

- Importing data from a local CSV file
- Importing data from a local Excel file
- Importing data from an external JSON file
- Importing data from an external XML file
- Preparing paginated sitemaps for search engines
- Creating filterable RSS feeds
- Using the Django REST framework to create an API

Introduction

Once in a while, your data needs to be transported from a local format to the database, imported from external resources, or provided to third parties. In this chapter, we will take a look at some practical examples of how to write management commands and APIs to do this.

Technical requirements

For working with the code of this chapter, you will need the latest stable version of Python, MySQL, or PostgreSQL database and a Django project with a virtual environment. Also, make sure to install Django, Pillow, and database bindings into your virtual environment.

You can find all of the code for this chapter in the `ch09` directory of the GitHub repository: https://github.com/PacktPublishing/Django-3-Web-Development-Cookbook-Fourth-Edition.

Importing data from a local CSV file

The **Comma-Separated Values (CSV)** format is probably the simplest way to store tabular data in a text file. In this recipe, we will create a management command that imports data from a CSV file to a Django database. We will need a CSV list of songs. You can easily create such a file with Excel, Calc, or another spreadsheet application.

Getting ready

Let's create a `music` app that we'll be using throughout this chapter:

1. Create the `music` app itself and put it under `INSTALLED_APPS` in the settings:

```python
# myproject/settings/_base.py
INSTALLED_APPS = [
    # ...
    "myproject.apps.core",
    "myproject.apps.music",
]
```

2. The `Song` model there should contain the `uuid`, `artist`, `title`, `url`, and `image` fields. We'll also extend `CreationModificationDateBase` to add creation and modification timestamps, as well as `UrlBase` to add methods to work with the model's detail URLs:

```python
# myproject/apps/music/models.py
import os
import uuid
from django.urls import reverse
from django.utils.translation import ugettext_lazy as _
from django.db import models
from django.utils.text import slugify
from myproject.apps.core.models import
CreationModificationDateBase, UrlBase

def upload_to(instance, filename):
    filename_base, filename_ext = os.path.splitext(filename)
    artist = slugify(instance.artist)
    title = slugify(instance.title)
    return f"music/{artist}--{title}{filename_ext.lower()}"

class Song(CreationModificationDateBase, UrlBase):
    uuid = models.UUIDField(primary_key=True, default=None,
      editable=False)
    artist = models.CharField(_("Artist"), max_length=250)
```

```
title = models.CharField(_("Title"), max_length=250)
url = models.URLField(_("URL"), blank=True)
image = models.ImageField(_("Image"), upload_to=upload_to,
 blank=True, null=True)

class Meta:
    verbose_name = _("Song")
    verbose_name_plural = _("Songs")
    unique_together = ["artist", "title"]

def __str__(self):
    return f"{self.artist} - {self.title}"

def get_url_path(self):
    return reverse("music:song_detail", kwargs={"pk": self.pk})

def save(self, *args, **kwargs):
    if self.pk is None:
        self.pk = uuid.uuid4()
    super().save(*args, **kwargs)
```

3. Make and run migrations with the following commands:

```
(env)$ python manage.py makemigrations
(env)$ python manage.py migrate
```

4. Then, let's add a simple administration for the Song model:

```
# myproject/apps/music/admin.py
from django.contrib import admin
from .models import Song

@admin.register(Song)
class SongAdmin(admin.ModelAdmin):
    list_display = ["title", "artist", "url"]
    list_filter = ["artist"]
    search_fields = ["title", "artist"]
```

5. Also, we need a form for validating and creating `Song` models in the import scripts. It's the most straightforward model form, as follows:

```python
# myproject/apps/music/forms.py
from django import forms
from django.utils.translation import ugettext_lazy as _
from .models import Song


class SongForm(forms.ModelForm):
    class Meta:
        model = Song
        fields = "__all__"
```

How to do it...

Follow these steps to create and use a management command that imports songs from a local CSV file:

1. Create a CSV file with the column names, `artist`, `title`, and `url`, in the first row. Add some song data to it in the next rows matching the columns. For example, it could be a `data/music.csv` file with content like this:

```
artist,title,url
Capital Cities,Safe And
Sound,https://open.spotify.com/track/40Fs0YrUGuwLNQSaHGVfqT?si=2OUa
wusIT-evyZKonT5GgQ
Milky Chance,Stolen
Dance,https://open.spotify.com/track/3miMZ2IlJiaeSWo1DohXlN?si=g-xM
M4m9S_yScOm02C2MLQ
Lana Del Rey,Video Games –
Remastered,https://open.spotify.com/track/5UOo694cVvjcPFqLFiNWGU?si
=maZ7JCJ7Rb6WzESLXg1Gdw
Men I
Trust,Tailwhip,https://open.spotify.com/track/2DoO0sn4SbUrz7Uay9ACT
M?si=SC_MixNKSnuxNvQMf3yBBg
```

2. In the `music` app, create a `management` directory and then a `commands` directory in the new `management` directory. Put empty `__init__.py` files in both new directories to make them Python packages.

3. Add an `import_music_from_csv.py` file there with the following content:

```python
# myproject/apps/music/management/commands/import_music_from_csv.py
from django.core.management.base import BaseCommand

class Command(BaseCommand):
    help = (
        "Imports music from a local CSV file. "
        "Expects columns: artist, title, url"
    )
    SILENT, NORMAL, VERBOSE, VERY_VERBOSE = 0, 1, 2, 3

    def add_arguments(self, parser):
        # Positional arguments
        parser.add_argument("file_path", nargs=1, type=str)

    def handle(self, *args, **options):
        self.verbosity = options.get("verbosity", self.NORMAL)
        self.file_path = options["file_path"][0]
        self.prepare()
        self.main()
        self.finalize()
```

4. Then, in the same file for the `Command` class, create a `prepare()` method:

```python
    def prepare(self):
        self.imported_counter = 0
        self.skipped_counter = 0
```

5. Then, we should create the `main()` method:

```python
    def main(self):
        import csv
        from ...forms import SongForm

        if self.verbosity >= self.NORMAL:
            self.stdout.write("=== Importing music ===")

        with open(self.file_path, mode="r") as f:
            reader = csv.DictReader(f)
            for index, row_dict in enumerate(reader):
                form = SongForm(data=row_dict)
                if form.is_valid():
                    song = form.save()
                    if self.verbosity >= self.NORMAL:
                        self.stdout.write(f" - {song}\n")
                    self.imported_counter += 1
                else:
```

```
                    if self.verbosity >= self.NORMAL:
                        self.stderr.write(
                            f"Errors importing song "
                            f"{row_dict['artist']} -
                            {row_dict['title']}:\n"
                        )
                        self.stderr.write(f"{form.errors.as_json()}\n")
                    self.skipped_counter += 1
```

6. We'll finish the class with the `finalize()` method:

```
def finalize(self)
    if self.verbosity >= self.NORMAL:
        self.stdout.write(f"------------------------\n")
        self.stdout.write(f"Songs imported:
        {self.imported_counter}\n")
        self.stdout.write(f"Songs skipped:
        {self.skipped_counter}\n\n")
```

7. To run the import, call the following in the command line:

```
(env)$ python manage.py import_music_from_csv data/music.csv
```

How it works...

Django management commands are scripts with `Command` classes deriving from `BaseCommand` and overwriting the `add_arguments()` and `handle()` methods. The `help` attribute defines the help text for the management command. It can be seen when you type the following in the command line:

```
(env)$ python manage.py help import_music_from_csv
```

Django management commands use the built-in `argparse` module to parse the passed arguments. The `add_arguments()` method defines what positional or named arguments should be passed to the management command. In our case, we will add a positional `file_path` argument of the Unicode type. By having the `nargs` variable set to the `1` attribute, we allow only one value.

 To learn about the other arguments that you can define and how to do this, refer to the official `argparse` documentation at `https://docs.python.org/3/library/argparse.html#adding-arguments`.

At the beginning of the `handle()` method, the `verbosity` argument is checked. Verbosity defines how much Terminal output the command should provide from 0, not giving any logging, to 3, providing extensive logging. You can pass this named argument to the command as follows:

```
(env)$ python manage.py import_music_from_csv data/music.csv --verbosity=0
```

We also expect the filename as the first positional argument. `options["file_path"]` returns a list of the values with the length defined in `nargs`. In our case, `nargs` equals one; therefore, `options["file_path"]` will be equal to a list of one element.

It's a good practice to split the logics of your management command into multiple smaller methods, for example, like we use in this script with `prepare()`, `main()`, and `finalize()`:

- The `prepare()` method sets import counters to zero. It could also be used for any other setup that is necessary for the script.
- In the `main()` method, we execute the main logic of the management command. At first, we open the given file for reading and pass its pointer to `csv.DictReader`. The first line in the file is assumed to contain headings for each of the columns. `DictReader` uses them as keys for the dictionaries for each row. When we iterate through the rows, we pass the dictionaries to the model form and try to validate it. If validation passes, a song is saved and `imported_counter` is incremented. If validation fails, because of too long values, missing required values, wrong types, or other validation errors, `skipped_counter` is incremented. If verbosity is equal or greater than NORMAL (which is number 1), each imported or skipped song is also printed out together with possible validation errors.

- The `finalize()` method prints out how many songs were imported and how many were skipped because of validation errors.

If you want to debug the errors of a management command while developing it, pass the --traceback parameter to it. When an error occurs, you will see the full stack trace of the problem.

Assuming we invoked the command twice with `--verbosity=1` or higher, the output we could expect might be as follows:

```
django-myproject — -bash — 120×31
[(venv) Aidass-MacBook-Pro:django-myproject archatas$ python manage.py import_music_from_csv data/music.csv
=== Importing music ===
 - Capital Cities - Safe And Sound
 - Milky Chance - Stolen Dance
 - Lana Del Rey - Video Games - Remastered
 - Men I Trust - Tailwhip
-------------------------
Songs imported: 4
Songs skipped: 0

[(venv) Aidass-MacBook-Pro:django-myproject archatas$ python manage.py import_music_from_csv data/music.csv
=== Importing music ===
Errors importing song Capital Cities - Safe And Sound:
{"__all__": [{"message": "Song with this Artist and Title already exists.", "code": "unique_together"}]}
Errors importing song Milky Chance - Stolen Dance:
{"__all__": [{"message": "Song with this Artist and Title already exists.", "code": "unique_together"}]}
Errors importing song Lana Del Rey - Video Games - Remastered:
{"__all__": [{"message": "Song with this Artist and Title already exists.", "code": "unique_together"}]}
Errors importing song Men I Trust - Tailwhip:
{"__all__": [{"message": "Song with this Artist and Title already exists.", "code": "unique_together"}]}
-------------------------
Songs imported: 0
Songs skipped: 4

(venv) Aidass-MacBook-Pro:django-myproject archatas$
```

As you can see, when a song is being imported a second time, it doesn't pass the `unique_together` constraint and therefore is skipped.

See also

- The *Importing data from a local Excel file* recipe
- The *Importing data from an external JSON file* recipe
- The *Importing data from an external XML file* recipe

Importing data from a local Excel file

Another popular format for storing tabular data is an Excel spreadsheet. In this recipe, we will import songs from a file of this format.

Getting ready

Let's start with the `music` app that we created in the previous recipe. To read Excel files, you will need to install the `openpyxl` package, as follows:

```
(env)$ pip install openpyxl==3.0.2
```

How to do it...

Follow these steps to create and use a management command that imports songs from a local XLSX file:

1. Create an XLSX file with the column names **Artist**, **Title**, and **URL** in the first row. Add some song data to it in the next rows matching the columns. You can do this in a spreadsheet application, by saving the CSV file from the previous recipe as an XLSX file, `data/music.xlsx`. Here is an example:

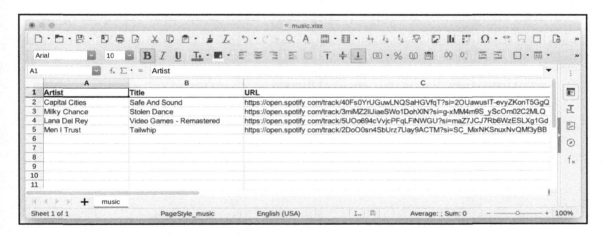

2. If you haven't done so, in the `music` app, create a `management` directory and then a `commands` subdirectory beneath it. Add empty `__init__.py` files in both of the new directories to make them Python packages.

3. Add an `import_music_from_xlsx.py` file with the following content:

```
# myproject/apps/music/management/commands
# /import_music_from_xlsx.py
from django.core.management.base import BaseCommand

class Command(BaseCommand):
```

```
        help = (
            "Imports music from a local XLSX file. "
            "Expects columns: Artist, Title, URL"
        )
        SILENT, NORMAL, VERBOSE, VERY_VERBOSE = 0, 1, 2, 3

        def add_arguments(self, parser):
            # Positional arguments
            parser.add_argument("file_path",
                                nargs=1,
                                type=str)

        def handle(self, *args, **options):
            self.verbosity = options.get("verbosity", self.NORMAL)
            self.file_path = options["file_path"][0]
            self.prepare()
            self.main()
            self.finalize()
```

4. Then, in the same file for the Command class, create a prepare() method:

```
def prepare(self):
    self.imported_counter = 0
    self.skipped_counter = 0
```

5. Then, create the main() method there:

```
def main(self):
    from openpyxl import load_workbook
    from ...forms import SongForm

    wb = load_workbook(filename=self.file_path)
    ws = wb.worksheets[0]

    if self.verbosity >= self.NORMAL:
        self.stdout.write("=== Importing music ===")

    columns = ["artist", "title", "url"]
    rows = ws.iter_rows(min_row=2)  # skip the column captions
    for index, row in enumerate(rows, start=1):
        row_values = [cell.value for cell in row]
        row_dict = dict(zip(columns, row_values))
        form = SongForm(data=row_dict)
        if form.is_valid():
            song = form.save()
            if self.verbosity >= self.NORMAL:
                self.stdout.write(f" - {song}\n")
            self.imported_counter += 1
```

```
        else:
            if self.verbosity >= self.NORMAL:
                self.stderr.write(
                    f"Errors importing song "
                    f"{row_dict['artist']} -
                    {row_dict['title']}:\n"
                )
                self.stderr.write(f"{form.errors.as_json()}\n")
            self.skipped_counter += 1
```

6. And we'll finish the class with the `finalize()` method:

```
def finalize(self):
    if self.verbosity >= self.NORMAL:
        self.stdout.write(f"------------------------\n")
        self.stdout.write(f"Songs imported:
          {self.imported_counter}\n")
        self.stdout.write(f"Songs skipped:
          {self.skipped_counter}\n\n")
```

7. To run the import, call the following in the command line:

```
(env) $ python manage.py import_music_from_xlsx data/music.xlsx
```

How it works...

The principle of importing from an XLSX file is the same as with CSV. We open the file, read it row by row, form data dictionaries, validate them via a model form, and create the `Song` objects from the provided data.

Again, we are using the `prepare()`, `main()`, and `finalize()` methods to split the logic into more atomic parts.

Here is a detailed explanation of the `main()` method as it is probably the only different part of the management command:

- Excel files are workbooks containing sheets as different tabs.
- We are using the `openpyxl` library to open a file passed as a positional argument to the command. Then, we read the first sheet from the workbook.
- The first row contains the column captions. We skip it.
- Afterward, we will read the rows one by one as lists of values, use the `zip()` function to create dictionaries, pass them to a model form, validate, and create the `Song` objects from them.

- If there are any validation errors and verbosity is greater than or equal to NORMAL, then we output the validation errors.
- Once again, the management command will print out the imported songs to the console, unless you set --verbosity=0.

If we run the command twice with --verbosity=1 or higher, the output would be as follows:

```
● ● ●                        django-myproject — -bash — 120×31
[(venv) Aidass-MacBook-Pro:django-myproject archatas$ python manage.py import_music_from_xlsx data/music.xlsx
=== Importing music ===
 - Capital Cities - Safe And Sound
 - Milky Chance - Stolen Dance
 - Lana Del Rey - Video Games - Remastered
 - Men I Trust - Tailwhip
-------------------------
Songs imported: 4
Songs skipped: 0

[(venv) Aidass-MacBook-Pro:django-myproject archatas$ python manage.py import_music_from_xlsx data/music.xlsx
=== Importing music ===
Errors importing song Capital Cities - Safe And Sound:
{"__all__": [{"message": "Song with this Artist and Title already exists.", "code": "unique_together"}]}
Errors importing song Milky Chance - Stolen Dance:
{"__all__": [{"message": "Song with this Artist and Title already exists.", "code": "unique_together"}]}
Errors importing song Lana Del Rey - Video Games - Remastered:
{"__all__": [{"message": "Song with this Artist and Title already exists.", "code": "unique_together"}]}
Errors importing song Men I Trust - Tailwhip:
{"__all__": [{"message": "Song with this Artist and Title already exists.", "code": "unique_together"}]}
-------------------------
Songs imported: 0
Songs skipped: 4

(venv) Aidass-MacBook-Pro:django-myproject archatas$ ▮
```

 You can learn more about how to work with Excel files at http://www. python-excel.org/.

See also

- The *Importing data from a local CSV file* recipe
- The *Importing data from an external JSON file* recipe
- The *Importing data from an external XML file* recipe

Importing data from an external JSON file

The `Last.fm` music website has an API under the `https://ws.audioscrobbler.com/` domain that you can use to read the albums, artists, tracks, events, and more. The API allows you to either use the JSON or XML format. In this recipe, we will import the top tracks tagged `indie` using the JSON format.

Getting ready

Follow these steps to import data in the JSON format from `Last.fm`:

1. Let's start with the `music` app that we created in the *Importing data from a local CSV file* recipe.

2. To use `Last.fm`, you need to register and get an API key. The API key can be created at `https://www.last.fm/api/account/create`.

3. The API key has to be set in the settings as `LAST_FM_API_KEY`. We recommend providing it from the secrets file or an environment variable and drawing that into your settings, as shown here:

   ```python
   # myproject/settings/_base.py
   LAST_FM_API_KEY = get_secret("LAST_FM_API_KEY")
   ```

4. Also, install the `requests` library in your virtual environment using the following command:

   ```
   (env)$ pip install requests==2.22.0
   ```

5. Let's check the structure of the JSON endpoint for the top indie tracks (`https://ws.audioscrobbler.com/2.0/?method=tag.gettoptracks&tag=indie&api_key=YOUR_API_KEY&format=json`), which should look something like this:

   ```json
   {
     "tracks": {
       "track": [
         {
           "name": "Mr. Brightside",
           "duration": "224",
           "mbid": "37d516ab-d61f-4bcb-9316-7a0b3eb845a8",
           "url": "https://www.last.fm/music
            /The+Killers/_/Mr.+Brightside",
           "streamable": {
             "#text": "0",
   ```

```
                        "fulltrack": "0"
                },
                "artist": {
                    "name": "The Killers",
                    "mbid": "95e1ead9-4d31-4808-a7ac-32c3614c116b",
                    "url": "https://www.last.fm/music/The+Killers"
                },
                "image": [
                    {
                        "#text":
                        "https://lastfm.freetls.fastly.net/i/u/34s
                            /2a96cbd8b46e442fc41c2b86b821562f.png",
                        "size": "small"
                    },
                    {
                        "#text":
                        "https://lastfm.freetls.fastly.net/i/u/64s
                            /2a96cbd8b46e442fc41c2b86b821562f.png",
                        "size": "medium"
                    },
                    {
                        "#text":
                        "https://lastfm.freetls.fastly.net/i/u/174s
                            /2a96cbd8b46e442fc41c2b86b821562f.png",
                        "size": "large"
                    },
                    {
                        "#text":
                        "https://lastfm.freetls.fastly.net/i/u/300x300
                            /2a96cbd8b46e442fc41c2b86b821562f.png",
                        "size": "extralarge"
                    }
                ],
                "@attr": {
                    "rank": "1"
                }
            },
            ...
        ],
        "@attr": {
            "tag": "indie",
            "page": "1",
            "perPage": "50",
            "totalPages": "4475",
            "total": "223728"
        }
    }
}
```

We want to read the track `name`, `artist`, `URL`, and medium-sized images. In addition, we are interested in how many pages there exist in total, which is provided as meta information at the end of the JSON file.

How to do it...

Follow these steps to create a `Song` model and a management command, which imports the top tracks from `Last.fm` to the database in JSON format:

1. If you haven't done so, in the `music` app, create a `management` directory, and then a `commands` subdirectory beneath it. Add empty __init__.py files in both of the new directories to make them Python packages.

2. Add an `import_music_from_lastfm_json.py` file with the following content:

```
# myproject/apps/music/management/commands
# /import_music_from_lastfm_json.py
from django.core.management.base import BaseCommand

class Command(BaseCommand):
    help = "Imports top songs from last.fm as JSON."
    SILENT, NORMAL, VERBOSE, VERY_VERBOSE = 0, 1, 2, 3
    API_URL = "https://ws.audioscrobbler.com/2.0/"

    def add_arguments(self, parser):
        # Named (optional) arguments
        parser.add_argument("--max_pages", type=int, default=0)

    def handle(self, *args, **options):
        self.verbosity = options.get("verbosity", self.NORMAL)
        self.max_pages = options["max_pages"]
        self.prepare()
        self.main()
        self.finalize()
```

3. Then, in the same file for the `Command` class, create a `prepare()` method:

```
    def prepare(self):
        from django.conf import settings

        self.imported_counter = 0
        self.skipped_counter = 0
        self.params = {
            "method": "tag.gettoptracks",
            "tag": "indie",
            "api_key": settings.LAST_FM_API_KEY,
```

```
        "format": "json",
        "page": 1,
    }
```

4. Then, create the `main()` method there:

```python
def main(self):
    import requests

    response = requests.get(self.API_URL, params=self.params)
    if response.status_code != requests.codes.ok:
        self.stderr.write(f"Error connecting to
         {response.url}")
        return
    response_dict = response.json()
    pages = int(
        response_dict.get("tracks", {})
        .get("@attr", {}).get("totalPages", 1)
    )

    if self.max_pages > 0:
        pages = min(pages, self.max_pages)

    if self.verbosity >= self.NORMAL:
        self.stdout.write(f"=== Importing {pages} page(s)
         of tracks ===")

    self.save_page(response_dict)

    for page_number in range(2, pages + 1):
        self.params["page"] = page_number
        response = requests.get(self.API_URL,
        params=self.params)
        if response.status_code != requests.codes.ok:
            self.stderr.write(f"Error connecting to
             {response.url}")
            return
        response_dict = response.json()
        self.save_page(response_dict)
```

5. Each page from the paginated feed will be saved by the `save_page()` method that we should create, as follows:

```python
def save_page(self, data):
    import os
    import requests
    from io import BytesIO
    from django.core.files import File
```

```python
from ...forms import SongForm

for track_dict in data.get("tracks", {}).get("track"):
    if not track_dict:
        continue

    song_dict = {
        "artist": track_dict.get("artist", {}).get("name", ""),
        "title": track_dict.get("name", ""),
        "url": track_dict.get("url", ""),
    }
    form = SongForm(data=song_dict)
    if form.is_valid():
        song = form.save()

        image_dict = track_dict.get("image", None)
        if image_dict:
            image_url = image_dict[1]["#text"]
            image_response = requests.get(image_url)
            song.image.save(
                os.path.basename(image_url),
                File(BytesIO(image_response.content)),
            )

        if self.verbosity >= self.NORMAL:
            self.stdout.write(f" - {song}\n")
        self.imported_counter += 1
    else:
        if self.verbosity >= self.NORMAL:
            self.stderr.write(
                f"Errors importing song "
                f"{song_dict['artist']} - "
                  f"{song_dict['title']}:\n"
            )
            self.stderr.write(f"{form.errors.as_json()}\n")
        self.skipped_counter += 1
```

6. And we'll finish the class with the `finalize()` method:

```python
def finalize(self):
    if self.verbosity >= self.NORMAL:
        self.stdout.write(f"-------------------------\n")
        self.stdout.write(f"Songs imported: "
          f"{self.imported_counter}\n")
        self.stdout.write(f"Songs skipped: "
          f"{self.skipped_counter}\n\n")
```

7. To run the import, call the following in the command line:

```
(env)$ python manage.py import_music_from_lastfm_json --max_pages=3
```

How it works...

As mentioned before, the arguments for scripts can be **positional** if they just list a sequence of strings, or **named** if they start with a -- and a variable name. The named --max_pages argument limits the imported data to three pages. Just skip it, or explicitly pass 0 (zero) if you want to download all of the available top tracks.

Beware that there are around 4,500 pages as detailed in the totalPages value, and this will take a long time and a lot of processing.

The structure of our script is similar to the previous import scripts:

- The prepare() method is for the setup
- The main() method handles the requests and processes the responses
- The save_page() method saves songs from a single pagination page
- The finalize() method prints out the import statistics

In the main() method, we use requests.get() to read the data from Last.fm, passing the params query parameters. The response object has a built-in method called json(), which converts a JSON string into a parsed dictionary object. From the first request, we learn about the total number of pages and then read each of them and call the save_page() method to parse information and save the songs.

In the save_page() method, we read the values from the tracks and build a dictionary necessary for the model form. We validate the form. If the data is valid, the Song object is created.

One interesting part of the import is downloading and saving the image. Here, we also use requests.get() to retrieve the image data and then we pass it to File through BytesIO, which is accordingly used in the image.save() method. The first parameter of image.save() is a filename that will be overwritten anyway by the value from the upload_to function and is necessary only for the file extension.

If the command is invoked with a --verbosity=1 or higher, we will see detailed information about the import just like in the previous recipes.

You can learn more about how to work with `Last.fm` at `https://www.last.fm/api/`.

See also

- The *Importing data from a local CSV file* recipe
- The *Importing data from a local Excel file* recipe
- The *Importing data from an external XML file* recipe

Importing data from an external XML file

Just as we showed what could be done with JSON in the preceding recipe, the `Last.fm` file also allows you to take data from its services in XML format. In this recipe, we will show you how to do this.

Getting ready

Follow these steps to import data in the XML format from `Last.fm`:

1. Let's start with the `music` app that we created in the *Importing data from a local CSV file* recipe.
2. To use `Last.fm`, you need to register and get an API key. The API key can be created at `https://www.last.fm/api/account/create`.
3. The API key has to be set in the settings as `LAST_FM_API_KEY`. We recommend providing it from the secrets file or an environment variable and drawing that into your settings, as shown here:

```
# myproject/settings/_base.py
LAST_FM_API_KEY = get_secret("LAST_FM_API_KEY")
```

4. Also, install the `requests` and `defusedxml` libraries in your virtual environment using the following commands:

```
(env)$ pip install requests==2.22.0
(env)$ pip install defusedxml==0.6.0
```

5. Let's check the structure of the JSON endpoint for the top indie tracks (`https://ws.audioscrobbler.com/2.0/?method=tag.gettoptracks&tag =indie&api_key=YOUR_API_KEY&format=xml`), which should look something like this:

```xml
<?xml version="1.0" encoding="UTF-8" ?>
<lfm status="ok">
    <tracks tag="indie" page="1" perPage="50"
     totalPages="4475" total="223728">
        <track rank="1">
            <name>Mr. Brightside</name>
            <duration>224</duration>
            <mbid>37d516ab-d61f-4bcb-9316-7a0b3eb845a8</mbid>
            <url>https://www.last.fm/music
            /The+Killers/_/Mr.+Brightside</url>
            <streamable fulltrack="0">0</streamable>
            <artist>
                <name>The Killers</name>
                <mbid>95e1ead9-4d31-4808-a7ac-32c3614c116b</mbid>
                <url>https://www.last.fm/music/The+Killers</url>
            </artist>
            <image size="small">https://lastfm.freetls.fastly.net/i
            /u/34s/2a96cbd8b46e442fc41c2b86b821562f.png</image>
            <image size="medium">
            https://lastfm.freetls.fastly.net/i
            /u/64s/2a96cbd8b46e442fc41c2b86b821562f.png</image>
            <image size="large">https://lastfm.freetls.fastly.net/i
            /u/174s/2a96cbd8b46e442fc41c2b86b821562f.png</image>
            <image size="extralarge">
                https://lastfm.freetls.fastly.net/i/u/300x300
                /2a96cbd8b46e442fc41c2b86b821562f.png
            </image>
        </track>
        ...
    </tracks>
</lfm>
```

How to do it...

Follow these steps to create a Song model and a management command, which imports the top tracks from Last.fm to the database in XML format:

1. If you haven't done so, in the music app, create a management directory and then a commands subdirectory beneath it. Add empty __init__.py files in both of the new directories to make them Python packages.

2. Add an import_music_from_lastfm_xml.py file with the following content:

```
# myproject/apps/music/management/commands
# /import_music_from_lastfm_xml.py
from django.core.management.base import BaseCommand


class Command(BaseCommand):
    help = "Imports top songs from last.fm as XML."
    SILENT, NORMAL, VERBOSE, VERY_VERBOSE = 0, 1, 2, 3
    API_URL = "https://ws.audioscrobbler.com/2.0/"

    def add_arguments(self, parser):
        # Named (optional) arguments
        parser.add_argument("--max_pages", type=int, default=0)

    def handle(self, *args, **options):
        self.verbosity = options.get("verbosity", self.NORMAL)
        self.max_pages = options["max_pages"]
        self.prepare()
        self.main()
        self.finalize()
```

3. Then, in the same file for the Command class, create a prepare() method:

```
def prepare(self):
    from django.conf import settings

    self.imported_counter = 0
    self.skipped_counter = 0
    self.params = {
        "method": "tag.gettoptracks",
        "tag": "indie",
        "api_key": settings.LAST_FM_API_KEY,
        "format": "xml",
        "page": 1,
    }
```

4. Then, create the `main()` method there:

```python
def main(self):
    import requests
    from defusedxml import ElementTree

    response = requests.get(self.API_URL, params=self.params)
    if response.status_code != requests.codes.ok:
        self.stderr.write(f"Error connecting to {response.url}")
        return
    root = ElementTree.fromstring(response.content)

    pages = int(root.find("tracks").attrib.get("totalPages", 1))
    if self.max_pages > 0:
        pages = min(pages, self.max_pages)

    if self.verbosity >= self.NORMAL:
        self.stdout.write(f"=== Importing {pages} page(s)
         of songs ===")

    self.save_page(root)

    for page_number in range(2, pages + 1):
        self.params["page"] = page_number
        response = requests.get(self.API_URL, params=self.params)
        if response.status_code != requests.codes.ok:
            self.stderr.write(f"Error connecting to {response.url}")
            return
        root = ElementTree.fromstring(response.content)
        self.save_page(root)
```

5. Each page from the paginated feed will be saved by the `save_page()` method that we should create, as follows:

```python
def save_page(self, root):
    import os
    import requests
    from io import BytesIO
    from django.core.files import File
    from ...forms import SongForm

    for track_node in root.findall("tracks/track"):
        if not track_node:
            continue

        song_dict = {
            "artist": track_node.find("artist/name").text,
            "title": track_node.find("name").text,
```

```
                "url": track_node.find("url").text,
        }
        form = SongForm(data=song_dict)
        if form.is_valid():
            song = form.save()

            image_node = track_node.find("image[@size='medium']")
            if image_node is not None:
                image_url = image_node.text
                image_response = requests.get(image_url)
                song.image.save(
                    os.path.basename(image_url),
                    File(BytesIO(image_response.content)),
                )

            if self.verbosity >= self.NORMAL:
                self.stdout.write(f" - {song}\n")
            self.imported_counter += 1
        else:
            if self.verbosity >= self.NORMAL:
                self.stderr.write(
                    f"Errors importing song "
                    f"{song_dict['artist']} - {song_dict['title']}:\n"
                )
                self.stderr.write(f"{form.errors.as_json()}\n")
            self.skipped_counter += 1
```

6. We'll finish the class with the `finalize()` method:

```
def finalize(self):
    if self.verbosity >= self.NORMAL:
        self.stdout.write(f"------------------------\n")
        self.stdout.write(f"Songs imported: {self.imported_counter}\n")
        self.stdout.write(f"Songs skipped: {self.skipped_counter}\n\n")
```

7. To run the import, call the following in the command line:

```
(env)$ python manage.py import_music_from_lastfm_xml --max_pages=3
```

How it works...

The process is analogous to the JSON approach. Using the `requests.get()` method, we read the data from `Last.fm`, passing the query parameters as `params`. The XML content of the response is passed to the `ElementTree` parser from the `defusedxml` module, and the `root` node is returned.

The `defusedxml` module is a safer replacement for the `xml` module. It prevents XML bombs—a vulnerability allowing the attacker to use a few hundred bytes of XML data to occupy Gigabytes of memory.

The `ElementTree` nodes have the `find()` and `findall()` methods, where you can pass `XPath` queries to filter out specific subnodes.

The following is a table of the available XPath syntax supported by `ElementTree`:

XPath syntax component	Meaning
`tag`	This selects all of the child elements with the given tag.
`*`	This selects all of the child elements.
`.`	This selects the current node.
`//`	This selects all of the subelements on all of the levels beneath the current element.
`..`	This selects the parent element.
`[@attrib]`	This selects all of the elements that have the given attribute.
`[@attrib='value']`	This selects all of the elements for which the given attribute has the given value.
`[tag]`	This selects all of the elements that have a child named tag. Only immediate children are supported.
`[position]`	This selects all of the elements that are located at the given position. The position can either be an integer (1 is the first position), the `last()` expression (for the last position), or a position relative to the last position (for example, `last()-1`).

Therefore, in the `main()` method, using `root.find("tracks").attrib.get("totalPages", 1)`, we read the total amount of pages, defaulting to one if the data is missing somehow. We will save the first page and then go through the other pages one by one and save them too.

In the `save_page()` method, `root.findall("tracks/track")` returns an iterator through the `<track>` nodes under the `<tracks>` node. With `track_node.find("image[@size='medium']")`, we get the medium-sized image. Again, `Song` creation happens through the model form which is used to validate the incoming data.

If we call the command with `--verbosity=1` or higher, we will see detailed information about the imported songs just like in the previous recipes.

There's more...

You can learn more from the following links:

- Read about how to work with Last.fm at https://www.last.fm/api/.
- Read about XPath at https://en.wikipedia.org/wiki/XPath.
- The full documentation of ElementTree can be found at https://docs.python.org/3/library/xml.etree.elementtree.html.

See also

- The *Importing data from a local CSV file* recipe
- The *Importing data from a local Excel file* recipe
- The *Importing data from an external JSON file* recipe

Preparing paginated sitemaps for search engines

Sitemaps protocol tells search engines about all different pages on your website. Usually, it's a single sitemap.xml file that informs what can be indexed and how often. If you have lots of different pages on your website, you can also split and paginate the XML file to render each list of resources faster.

In this recipe, we will show you how to create a paginated sitemap to use in your Django website.

Getting ready

For this and further recipes, we need to extend the music app and add list and detail views there:

1. Create the views.py file with the following content:

```python
# myproject/apps/music/views.py
from django.views.generic import ListView, DetailView
from django.utils.translation import ugettext_lazy as _
from .models import Song
```

```
class SongList(ListView):
    model = Song

class SongDetail(DetailView):
    model = Song
```

2. Create the `urls.py` file with the following content:

```
# myproject/apps/music/urls.py
from django.urls import path
from .views import SongList, SongDetail

app_name = "music"

urlpatterns = [
    path("", SongList.as_view(), name="song_list"),
    path("<uuid:pk>/", SongDetail.as_view(), name="song_detail"),
]
```

3. Include that URL configuration into the project's URL configuration:

```
# myproject/urls.py
from django.conf.urls.i18n import i18n_patterns
from django.urls import include, path

urlpatterns = i18n_patterns(
    # ...
    path("songs/", include("myproject.apps.music.urls",
      namespace="music")),
)
```

4. Create a template for the song list view:

```
{# music/song_list.html #}
{% extends "base.html" %}
{% load i18n %}

{% block main %}
    <ul>
        {% for song in object_list %}
            <li><a href="{{ song.get_url_path }}">
            {{ song }}</a></li>
        {% endfor %}
    </ul>
{% endblock %}
```

5. Then, create one for the song detail view:

```
{# music/song_detail.html #}
{% extends "base.html" %}
{% load i18n %}

{% block content %}
    {% with song=object %}
        <h1>{{ song }}</h1>
        {% if song.image %}
            <img src="{{ song.image.url }}" alt="{{ song }}" />
        {% endif %}
        {% if song.url %}
            <a href="{{ song.url }}" target="_blank"
             rel="noreferrer noopener">
                {% trans "Check this song" %}
            </a>
        {% endif %}
    {% endwith %}
{% endblock %}
```

How to do it...

To add the paginated sitemap, follow these steps:

1. Include django.contrib.sitemaps in INSTALLED_APPS in the settings:

```
# myproject/settings/_base.py
INSTALLED_APPS = [
    # ...
    "django.contrib.sitemaps",
    # ...
]
```

2. Modify urls.py of your project as follows:

```
# myproject/urls.py
from django.conf.urls.i18n import i18n_patterns
from django.urls import include, path
from django.contrib.sitemaps import views as sitemaps_views
from django.contrib.sitemaps import GenericSitemap
from myproject.apps.music.models import Song

class MySitemap(GenericSitemap):
    limit = 50
```

```python
        def location(self, obj):
            return obj.get_url_path()


    song_info_dict = {
        "queryset": Song.objects.all(),
        "date_field": "modified",
    }
    sitemaps = {"music": MySitemap(song_info_dict, priority=1.0)}


    urlpatterns = [
        path("sitemap.xml", sitemaps_views.index,
          {"sitemaps": sitemaps}),
        path("sitemap-<str:section>.xml", sitemaps_views.sitemap,
          {"sitemaps": sitemaps},
            name="django.contrib.sitemaps.views.sitemap"
        ),
    ]

    urlpatterns += i18n_patterns(
        # ...
        path("songs/", include("myproject.apps.music.urls",
          namespace="music")),
    )
```

How it works...

If you look at http://127.0.0.1:8000/sitemap.xml, you will see the index with paginated sitemaps:

```xml
<?xml version="1.0" encoding="UTF-8"?>
<sitemapindex xmlns="http://www.sitemaps.org/schemas/sitemap/0.9">
    <sitemap>
        <loc>http://127.0.0.1:8000/sitemap-music.xml</loc>
    </sitemap>
    <sitemap>
        <loc>http://127.0.0.1:8000/sitemap-music.xml?p=2</loc>
    </sitemap>
    <sitemap>
        <loc>http://127.0.0.1:8000/sitemap-music.xml?p=3</loc>
    </sitemap>
</sitemapindex>
```

Here each page will display up to 50 entries with a URL, its last modification, and priority:

```xml
<?xml version="1.0" encoding="UTF-8"?>
<urlset xmlns="http://www.sitemaps.org/schemas/sitemap/0.9">
    <url>
        <loc>http://127.0.0.1:8000/en/songs/b2d3627b-dbc7
        -4c11-a13e-03d86f32a719/</loc>
        <lastmod>2019-12-15</lastmod>
        <priority>1.0</priority>
    </url>
    <url>
        <loc>http://127.0.0.1:8000/en/songs/f5c386fd-1952
        -4ace-9848-717d27186fa9/</loc>
        <lastmod>2019-12-15</lastmod>
        <priority>1.0</priority>
    </url>
    <url>
        <loc>http://127.0.0.1:8000/en/songs/a59cbb5a-16e8
        -46dd-9498-d86e24e277a5/</loc>
        <lastmod>2019-12-15</lastmod>
        <priority>1.0</priority>
    </url>
    ...
</urlset>
```

When your site is ready and published to production, you can inform **Google Search Engine** about your pages with the `ping_google` management command provided by the sitemap framework. Execute this command at the production server as follows:

```
(env)$ python manage.py ping_google --
settings=myproject.settings.production
```

There's more...

You can learn more from the following links:

- Read about the sitemaps protocol at https://www.sitemaps.org/
- Read more about Django sitemap framework at
  https://docs.djangoproject.com/en/3.0/ref/contrib/sitemaps/

See also

- The *Creating filterable RSS feeds* recipe

Creating filterable RSS feeds

Django comes with a **syndication feed framework** that allows you to create **Really Simple Syndication** (**RSS**) and **Atom** feeds. RSS and Atom feeds are XML documents with specific semantics. They can be subscribed to an RSS reader, such as Feedly, or they can be aggregated in other websites, mobile applications, or desktop applications. In this recipe, we will create an RSS feed that provides information about songs. Moreover, the results will be filterable by URL query parameters.

Getting ready

Start by creating the `music` app from the *Importing data from a local CSV file* and *Preparing paginated sitemaps for search engines* recipes. Specifically, follow the steps in the *Getting ready* section to set up the models, forms, views, URL configurations, and templates.

To the view listing songs, we will add filtering by artist that later will be used by the RSS feed too:

1. Add a filter form to `forms.py`. It will have the `artist` choice field with all artist names sorted alphabetically with letter case ignored:

```
# myproject/apps/music/forms.py
from django import forms
from django.utils.translation import ugettext_lazy as _
from .models import Song

# ...

class SongFilterForm(forms.Form):
    def __init__(self, *args, **kwargs):
        super().__init__(*args, **kwargs)
        artist_choices = [
            (artist, artist)
            for artist in sorted(
                Song.objects.values_list("artist",
                    flat=True).distinct(),
                key=str.casefold
            )
```

```
    ]
    self.fields["artist"] = forms.ChoiceField(
        label=_("Artist"),
        choices=artist_choices,
        required=False,
    )
```

2. Enhance the `SongList` view with the methods to manage the filtering: the `get()` method will handle the filtering and display results, the `get_form_kwargs()` method will prepare the keyword arguments for the filter form, and the `get_queryset()` method will filter songs by artist:

```python
# myproject/apps/music/views.py
from django.http import Http404
from django.views.generic import ListView, DetailView, FormView
from django.utils.translation import ugettext_lazy as _
from .models import Song
from .forms import SongFilterForm

class SongList(ListView, FormView):
    form_class = SongFilterForm
    model = Song

    def get(self, request, *args, **kwargs):
        form_class = self.get_form_class()
        self.form = self.get_form(form_class)

        self.object_list = self.get_queryset()
        allow_empty = self.get_allow_empty()
        if not allow_empty and len(self.object_list) == 0:
            raise Http404(_(u"Empty list and '%(class_name)s
             .allow_empty' is False.")
                            % {'class_name':
                               self.__class__.__name__})

        context = self.get_context_data(object_list=
         self.object_list, form=self.form)
        return self.render_to_response(context)

    def get_form_kwargs(self):
        kwargs = {
            'initial': self.get_initial(),
            'prefix': self.get_prefix(),
        }
        if self.request.method == 'GET':
            kwargs.update({
                'data': self.request.GET,
```

```
        })
    return kwargs

def get_queryset(self):
    queryset = super().get_queryset()
    if self.form.is_valid():
        artist = self.form.cleaned_data.get("artist")
        if artist:
            queryset = queryset.filter(artist=artist)
    return queryset
```

3. Modify the song list template to add the form for filtering:

```
{# music/song_list.html #}
{% extends "base.html" %}
{% load i18n %}

{% block sidebar %}
  <form action="" method="get">
      {{ form.errors }}
      {{ form.as_p }}
      <button type="submit" class="btn btn-primary">
       {% trans "Filter" %}</button>
  </form>
{% endblock %}

{% block main %}
  <ul>
      {% for song in object_list %}
          <li><a href="{{ song.get_url_path }}">
             {{ song }}</a></li>
      {% endfor %}
  </ul>
{% endblock %}
```

If you now check the song list view in the browser and filter songs by, let's say, **Lana Del Rey**, you would see results like this:

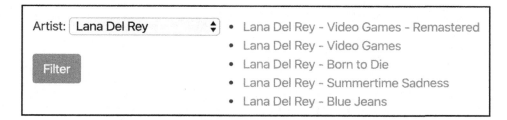

The URL of the filtered song list will
be `http://127.0.0.1:8000/en/songs/?artist=Lana+Del+Rey`.

How to do it...

Now, we will add the RSS feed to the music app:

1. In the `music` app, create the `feeds.py` file and add the following content:

    ```python
    # myproject/apps/music/feeds.py
    from django.contrib.syndication.views import Feed
    from django.urls import reverse

    from .models import Song
    from .forms import SongFilterForm


    class SongFeed(Feed):
        description_template = "music/feeds/song_description.html"

        def get_object(self, request, *args, **kwargs):
            form = SongFilterForm(data=request.GET)
            obj = {}
            if form.is_valid():
                obj = {"query_string": request.META["QUERY_STRING"]}
                for field in ["artist"]:
                    value = form.cleaned_data[field]
                    obj[field] = value
            return obj

        def title(self, obj):
            the_title = "Music"
            artist = obj.get("artist")
            if artist:
                the_title = f"Music by {artist}"
            return the_title
    ```

```python
    def link(self, obj):
        return self.get_named_url("music:song_list", obj)

    def feed_url(self, obj):
        return self.get_named_url("music:song_rss", obj)

    @staticmethod
    def get_named_url(name, obj):
        url = reverse(name)
        qs = obj.get("query_string", False)
        if qs:
            url = f"{url}?{qs}"
        return url

    def items(self, obj):
        queryset = Song.objects.order_by("-created")

        artist = obj.get("artist")
        if artist:
            queryset = queryset.filter(artist=artist)

        return queryset[:30]

    def item_pubdate(self, item):
        return item.created
```

2. Create a template for the song descriptions in the RSS feed:

```html
{# music/feeds/song_description.html #}
{% load i18n %}
{% with song=obj %}
    {% if song.image %}
        <img src="{{ song.image.url }}" alt="{{ song }}" />
    {% endif %}
    {% if song.url %}
        <a href="{{ song.url }}" target="_blank"
         rel="noreferrer noopener">
            {% trans "Check this song" %}
        </a>
    {% endif %}
{% endwith %}
```

3. Plug in the RSS feed in the URL configuration of the app:

```
# myproject/apps/music/urls.py
from django.urls import path

from .feeds import SongFeed
from .views import SongList, SongDetail

app_name = "music"

urlpatterns = [
    path("", SongList.as_view(), name="song_list"),
    path("<uuid:pk>/", SongDetail.as_view(), name="song_detail"),
    path("rss/", SongFeed(), name="song_rss"),
]
```

4. In the template of the song list view, add a link to the RSS feed:

```
{# music/song_list.html #}

{% url "music:songs_rss" as songs_rss_url %}
<p>
    <a href="{{ songs_rss_url }}?{{ request.META.QUERY_STRING }}">
        {% trans "Subscribe to RSS feed" %}
    </a>
</p>
```

How it works...

If you refresh the filtered list view
at http://127.0.0.1:8000/en/songs/?artist=Lana+Del+Rey, you will see
the **Subscribe to RSS feed** link that leads
to http://127.0.0.1:8000/en/songs/rss/?artist=Lana+Del+Rey. This will be the
RSS feed of up to 30 songs filtered by the artist.

The `SongFeed` class takes care of automatically generating the XML markup for the RSS feed. We specified the following methods there:

- The `get_object()` method defines the context dictionary for the `Feed` class that will be used by other methods.
- The `title()` method defines the title of the feed depending on whether the results are filtered or not.
- The `link()` method returns the URL of the list view, whereas `feed_url()` returns the URL of the feed. Both of them are using a helper method, `get_named_url()`, which forms a URL by pathname and query parameters.
- The `items()` method returns the `queryset` of songs, optionally filtered by artist.
- The `item_pubdate()` method returns the creation date of the song.

 To see all of the available methods and properties of the `Feed` class that we are extending, refer to the following documentation at `https://docs.djangoproject.com/en/3.0/ref/contrib/syndication/#feed-class-reference`.

See also

- The *Importing data from a local CSV file* recipe
- The *Preparing paginated sitemaps for search engines* recipe

Using Django REST framework to create an API

When you need to create a RESTful API for your models to transfer data to and from third parties, the **Django REST framework** is probably the best tool you can use. This framework has extensive documentation and a Django-centric implementation, helping to make it more maintainable. In this recipe, you will learn how to use the Django REST framework to allow your project partners, mobile clients, or Ajax-based website to access data on your site to create, read, update, and delete content as appropriate.

Getting ready

First of all, install the Django REST Framework in your virtual environment using the following command:

```
(env)$ pip install djangorestframework==3.11.0
```

Add "rest_framework" to INSTALLED_APPS in the settings.

Then, enhance the music app that we defined in the *Importing data from a local CSV file* recipe. You will also want to collect the static files provided by the Django REST framework for the pages it provides to be as nicely styled as possible:

```
(env)$ python manage.py collectstatic
```

How to do it...

To integrate a new RESTful API in our music app, execute the following steps:

1. Add configurations for the Django REST framework to the settings, as shown here:

```python
# myproject/settings/_base.py
REST_FRAMEWORK = {
    "DEFAULT_PERMISSION_CLASSES": [ "rest_framework.permissions
        .DjangoModelPermissionsOrAnonReadOnly"
    ],
    "DEFAULT_PAGINATION_CLASS":
    "rest_framework.pagination.LimitOffsetPagination",
    "PAGE_SIZE": 50,
}
```

2. In the music app, create the serializers.py file with the following content:

```python
from rest_framework import serializers
from .models import Song

class SongSerializer(serializers.ModelSerializer):
    class Meta:
        model = Song
        fields = ["uuid", "artist", "title", "url", "image"]
```

3. Add two new class-based views to the `views.py` file in the `music` app:

```python
from rest_framework import generics

from .serializers import SongSerializer
from .models import Song

# ...

class RESTSongList(generics.ListCreateAPIView):
    queryset = Song.objects.all()
    serializer_class = SongSerializer

    def get_view_name(self):
        return "Song List"


class RESTSongDetail(generics.RetrieveUpdateDestroyAPIView):
    queryset = Song.objects.all()
    serializer_class = SongSerializer

    def get_view_name(self):
        return "Song Detail"
```

4. Finally, plug in the new views to the project URL configuration:

```python
# myproject/urls.py
from django.urls import include, path
from myproject.apps.music.views import RESTSongList, RESTSongDetail


urlpatterns = [
    path("api-auth/", include("rest_framework.urls",
      namespace="rest_framework")),
    path("rest-api/songs/", RESTSongList.as_view(),
      name="rest_song_list"),
    path(
        "rest-api/songs/<uuid:pk>/", RESTSongDetail.as_view(),
            name="rest_song_detail"
    ),
    # ...
]
```

How it works...

What we created here is an API for the music, where you can read a paginated song list, create a new song, and read, change, or delete a single song by ID. Reading is allowed without authentication, but you have to have a user account with the appropriate permissions to add, change, or delete a song. The Django REST framework provides you with web-based API documentation that is shown when you access the API endpoints in a browser via GET. Without logging in, the framework would display something like this:

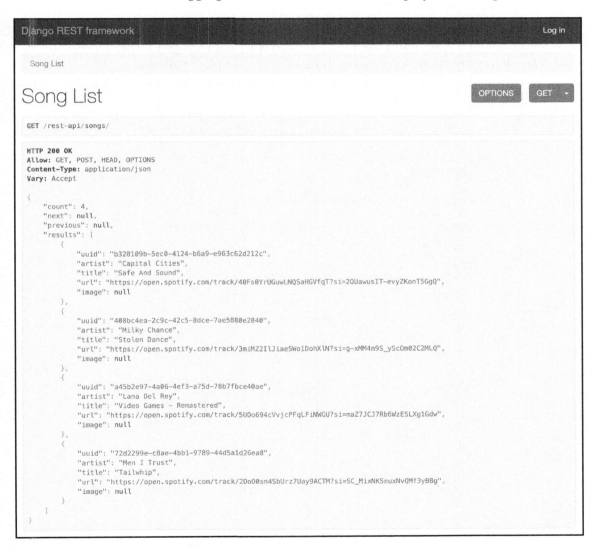

Here's how you can approach the created API:

URL	HTTP Method	Description
/rest-api/songs/	GET	List songs paginated by 50.
/rest-api/songs/	POST	Create a new song if the requesting user is authenticated and authorized to create songs.
/rest-api/songs/b328109b-5ec0-4124-b6a9-e963c62d212c/	GET	Get a song with the ID b328109b-5ec0-4124-b6a9-e963c62d212c.
/rest-api/songs/b328109b-5ec0-4124-b6a9-e963c62d212c/	PUT	Update a song with the ID b328109b-5ec0-4124-b6a9-e963c62d212c if the user is authenticated and authorized to change songs.
/rest-api/songs/b328109b-5ec0-4124-b6a9-e963c62d212c/	DELETE	Delete the song with the ID b328109b-5ec0-4124-b6a9-e963c62d212c if the user is authenticated and authorized to delete songs.

You might ask how you would use the API practically. For example, we might use the `requests` library to create a new song from a Python script, as follows:

```
import requests

response = requests.post(
    url="http://127.0.0.1:8000/rest-api/songs/",
    data={
        "artist": "Luwten",
        "title": "Go Honey",
    },
    auth=("admin", "<YOUR_ADMIN_PASSWORD>"),
)
assert(response.status_code == requests.codes.CREATED)
```

The same could be done via **Postman** app, which provides a user-friendly interface for submitting requests, as seen here:

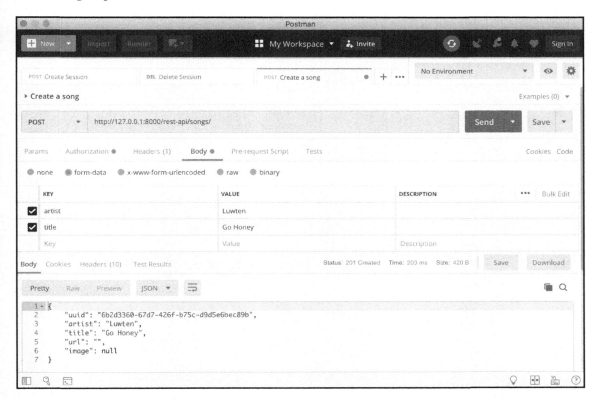

You can also try out the APIs via integrated forms under the framework-generated API documentation when logged in, as shown in the following screenshot:

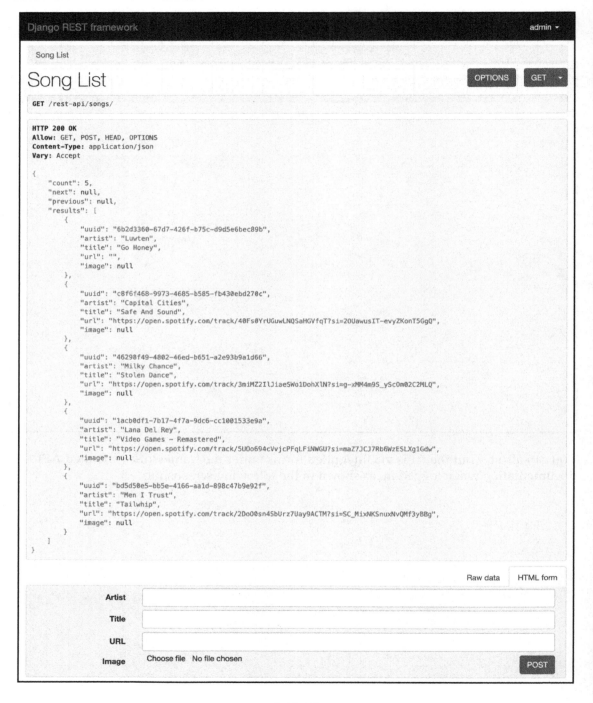

Let's take a quick look at how the code that we wrote works. In the settings, we have set the access to be dependent on the permissions of the Django system. For anonymous requests, only reading is allowed. Other access options include allowing any permission to everyone, any permission only to authenticated users, any permission to staff users, and so on. The full list can be found at `https://www.django-rest-framework.org/api-guide/permissions/`.

Then, in the settings, pagination is set. The current option is to have the limit and offset parameters as in an SQL query. Other options are to have either the pagination by page numbers for rather static content or cursor pagination for real-time data. We set the default pagination to 50 items per page.

Later, we define a serializer for the songs. It controls the data that will be shown in the output and validates the input. There are various ways to serialize relations in the Django REST framework, and we chose the most verbose one in our example.

> To read more about how to serialize relations, refer to the documentation at `https://www.django-rest-framework.org/api-guide/relations/`.

After defining the serializers, we created two class-based views to handle the API endpoints and plugged them into the URL configuration. In the URL configuration, we also have a rule (`/api-auth/`) for browsable API pages, login, and logout.

See also

- The *Preparing paginated sitemaps for search engines* recipe
- The *Creating filterable RSS feeds* recipe
- The *Testing an API created using Django REST framework* recipe in `Chapter 11, Testing`

10
Bells and Whistles

In this chapter, we will cover the following topics:

- Using the Django shell
- Using database query expressions
- Monkey patching the `slugify()` function for better internationalization support
- Toggling the Debug toolbar
- Using ThreadLocalMiddleware
- Using signals to notify administrators about new entries
- Checking for missing settings

Introduction

In this chapter, we will go over several important bits and pieces that will help you to better understand and utilize Django. We will provide an overview of how to use the Django shell to experiment with the code before writing it in the files. You will be introduced to monkey patching, also known as guerrilla patching, which is a powerful feature of dynamic languages, such as Python and Ruby. We will also talk about full-text search capabilities, and you will learn how to debug your code and check its performance. Then, you will learn how to access the currently logged-in user (and other request parameters) from any module. You will also learn how to handle signals and create system checks. Get ready for an interesting programming experience!

Technical requirements

To work with the code of this chapter, you will need the latest stable version of a Python, MySQL, or PostgreSQL database and a Django project with a virtual environment.

You can find all the code for this chapter in the `ch10` directory of the GitHub repository at `https://github.com/PacktPublishing/Django-3-Web-Development-Cookbook-Fourth-Edition`.

Using the Django shell

With the virtual environment activated and your project directory selected as the current directory, enter the following command in your command-line tool:

```
(env)$ python manage.py shell
```

By executing the preceding command, you will enter an interactive Python shell, configured for your Django project, where you can play around with the code, inspect the classes, try out methods, or execute scripts on the fly. In this recipe, we will go over the most important functions that you need to know in order to work with the Django shell.

Getting ready

You can install either **IPython** or **bpython** to provide additional interface options for Python shells or you can install both if you want a choice. These will highlight the syntax for the output of your Django shell and will add some other helpers. Install them both by using the following commands for a virtual environment:

```
(env)$ pip install ipython
(env)$ pip install bpython
```

How to do it...

Learn the basics of using the Django shell by following these instructions:

- Run the Django shell by typing the following command:

```
(env)$ python manage.py shell
```

If you have installed IPython or bpython, then whichever one you have installed will automatically become the default interface when you are entering the shell. You can also use a particular interface by adding the -i <interface> option to the preceding command. The prompt will change according to which interface you use. The following screenshot shows what an IPython shell might look like, starting with In [1]: as the prompt:

```
django-myproject — IPython: src/django-myproject — python manage.py shell -i ipython — 123×20
[(venv) archatas@Aidass-MacBook-Pro django-myproject % python manage.py shell -i ipython
Python 3.7.4 (default, Jul  9 2019, 18:13:23)
Type 'copyright', 'credits' or 'license' for more information
IPython 7.10.2 -- An enhanced Interactive Python. Type '?' for help.

In [1]:
```

If you use bpython, the shell will be shown with the >>> prompt, along with code highlighting and text autocompletion when you type, as follows:

```
django-myproject — IPython: src/django-myproject — python manage.py shell -i bpython — 123×20
[(venv) archatas@Aidass-MacBook-Pro django-myproject % python manage.py shell -i bpython
>>>
Welcome to bpython! Press <F1> for help.
```

The **default Python interface** shell looks as follows, also using the >>> prompt, but with a preamble that provides information about the system:

```
django-myproject — IPython: src/django-myproject — python manage.py shell -i python — 123×20
[(venv) archatas@Aidass-MacBook-Pro django-myproject % python manage.py shell -i python
Python 3.7.4 (default, Jul  9 2019, 18:13:23)
[Clang 10.0.1 (clang-1001.0.46.4)] on darwin
Type "help", "copyright", "credits" or "license" for more information.
(InteractiveConsole)
>>>
```

Now you can import classes, functions, or variables, and play around with them. For example, to see the version of an installed module, you can import the module and then try to read its __version__, VERSION, or version attribute (shown using bpython, which will also demonstrate both its highlighting and autocompletion features), as follows:

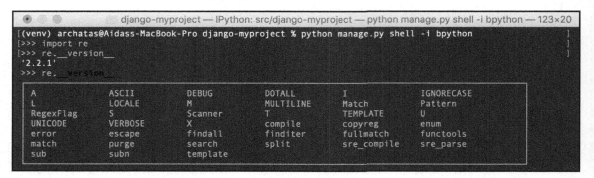

```
(venv) archatas@Aidass-MacBook-Pro django-myproject % python manage.py shell -i bpython
>>> import re
>>> re.__version__
'2.2.1'
>>> re.__version__

A              ASCII          DEBUG          DOTALL         I              IGNORECASE
L              LOCALE         M              MULTILINE      Match          Pattern
RegexFlag      S              Scanner        T              TEMPLATE       U
UNICODE        VERBOSE        X              compile        copyreg        enum
error          escape         findall        finditer       fullmatch      functools
match          purge          search         split          sre_compile    sre_parse
sub            subn           template
```

- To get a comprehensive description of a module, class, function, method, keyword, or documentation topic, use the help() function. You can either pass a string with the path to a specific entity or the entity itself, as follows:

```
>>> help("django.forms")
```

This will open the help page for the django.forms module. Use the arrow keys to scroll the page up and down. Press Q to get back to the shell. If you run help() without the parameters, it opens an interactive help page. There, you can enter any path of a module, class, function, and so on, and get information on what it does and how to use it. To quit the interactive help, press Ctrl + D.

- The following is an example of how to pass an entity to the help() function with IPython:

```
(venv) archatas@Aidass-MacBook-Pro django-myproject % python manage.py shell -i ipython
Python 3.7.4 (default, Jul  9 2019, 18:13:23)
Type 'copyright', 'credits' or 'license' for more information
IPython 7.10.2 -- An enhanced Interactive Python. Type '?' for help.

In [1]: from django.forms import ModelForm

In [2]: help(ModelForm)
```

Doing this will open a help page for the `ModelForm` class, as follows:

```
django-myproject — IPython: src/django-myproject — less < python manage.py shell -i ipython — 123×35
Help on class ModelForm in module django.forms.models:

class ModelForm(BaseModelForm)
 |  ModelForm(data=None, files=None, auto_id='id_%s', prefix=None, initial=None, error_class=<class 'django.forms.utils.Err
orList'>, label_suffix=None, empty_permitted=False, instance=None, use_required_attribute=None, renderer=None)
 |
 |  The main implementation of all the Form logic. Note that this class is
 |  different than Form. See the comments by the Form class for more info. Any
 |  improvements to the form API should be made to this class, not to the Form
 |  class.
 |
 |  Method resolution order:
 |      ModelForm
 |      BaseModelForm
 |      django.forms.forms.BaseForm
 |      builtins.object
 |
 |  Data descriptors defined here:
 |
 |  media
 |
 |  ----------------------------------------------------------------------
 |  Data and other attributes defined here:
 |
 |  base_fields = {}
 |
 |  declared_fields = {}
 |
 |  ----------------------------------------------------------------------
 |  Methods inherited from BaseModelForm:
 |
 |  __init__(self, data=None, files=None, auto_id='id_%s', prefix=None, initial=None, error_class=<class 'django.forms.util
s.ErrorList'>, label_suffix=None, empty_permitted=False, instance=None, use_required_attribute=None, renderer=None)
 |      Initialize self.  See help(type(self)) for accurate signature.
:
```

To quickly see what fields and values are available for a model instance, use the `__dict__` attribute. You can use the `pprint()` function to print the dictionaries in a more readable format (not just one long line), as shown in the following screenshot. Note that when we use `__dict__`, we don't get many-to-many relationships; however, this might be enough for a quick overview of the fields and values:

```
django-myproject — IPython: src/django-myproject — python manage.py shell -i bpython — 123×20
(venv) archatas@Aidass-MacBook-Pro django-myproject % python manage.py shell -i bpython
>>> from django.contrib.contenttypes.models import ContentType
>>> content_type = ContentType.objects.first()
>>> content_type.__dict__
{'_state': <django.db.models.base.ModelState object at 0x10aee8490>, 'id': 1, 'app_label': 'admin', 'model': 'logentry'}
>>> from pprint import pprint
>>> pprint(content_type.__dict__)
{'_state': <django.db.models.base.ModelState object at 0x10aee8490>,
 'app_label': 'admin',
 'id': 1,
 'model': 'logentry'}
>>>
```

- To get all of the available properties and methods of an object, you can use the `dir()` function, as follows:

```
django-myproject — IPython: src/django-myproject — python manage.py shell -i bpython — 123×20
>>> pprint(content_type.__dict__)
{'_state': <django.db.models.base.ModelState object at 0x10aee8490>,
 'app_label': 'admin',
 'id': 1,
 'model': 'logentry'}
>>> dir(ContentType)
['DoesNotExist', 'MultipleObjectsReturned', '__class__', '__delattr__', '__dict__', '__dir__', '__doc__', '__eq__', '__form
at__', '__ge__', '__getattribute__', '__getstate__', '__gt__', '__hash__', '__init__', '__init_subclass__', '__le__', '__lt
__', '__module__', '__ne__', '__new__', '__reduce__', '__reduce_ex__', '__repr__', '__setattr__', '__setstate__', '__sizeof
__', '__str__', '__subclasshook__', '__weakref__', '_check_column_name_clashes', '_check_constraints', '_check_field_name_c
lashes', '_check_fields', '_check_id_field', '_check_index_together', '_check_indexes', '_check_local_fields', '_check_long
_column_names', '_check_m2m_through_same_relationship', '_check_managers', '_check_model', '_check_model_name_db_lookup_cla
shes', '_check_ordering', '_check_property_name_related_field_accessor_clashes', '_check_single_primary_key', '_check_swapp
able', '_check_unique_together', '_do_insert', '_do_update', '_get_FIELD_display', '_get_next_or_previous_by_FIELD', '_get_
next_or_previous_in_order', '_get_pk_val', '_get_unique_checks', '_meta', '_perform_date_checks', '_perform_unique_checks',
 '_save_parents', '_save_table', '_set_pk_val', 'app_label', 'app_labeled_name', 'check', 'clean', 'clean_fields', 'date_er
ror_message', 'delete', 'from_db', 'full_clean', 'get_all_objects_for_this_type', 'get_deferred_fields', 'get_object_for_th
is_type', 'id', 'logentry_set', 'model', 'model_class', 'name', 'natural_key', 'objects', 'permission_set', 'pk', 'prepare_
database_save', 'refresh_from_db', 'save', 'save_base', 'serializable_value', 'unique_error_message', 'validate_unique']
>>>
```

- To print one attribute per line, you can use the code shown in the following screenshot:

```
django-myproject — IPython: src/django-myproject — python manage.py shell -i bpython — 123×20
>>> pprint(dir(ContentType))
['DoesNotExist',
 'MultipleObjectsReturned',
 '__class__',
 '__delattr__',
 '__dict__',
 '__dir__',
 '__doc__',
 '__eq__',
 '__format__',
 '__ge__',
 '__getattribute__',
 '__getstate__',
 '__gt__',
 '__hash__',
 '__init__',
 '__init_subclass__',
 '__le__',
 '__lt__',
 '__module__',
```

- The Django shell is useful for experimenting with `QuerySets` or regular expressions before putting them into your model methods, views, or management commands. For example, to check the email validation regular expression, you can type the following into the Django shell:

```
>>> import re
>>> email_pattern = re.compile(r"[^@]+@[^@]+\.[^@]+")
>>> email_pattern.match("aidas@bendoraitis.lt")
<_sre.SRE_Match object at 0x1075681d0>
```

- If you want to try out different `QuerySets`, use the following code:

```
>>> from django.contrib.auth.models import User
>>> User.objects.filter(groups__name="Editors")
[<User: admin>]
```

- To exit the Django shell, press *Ctrl + D* or type the following command:

```
>>> exit()
```

How it works...

The difference between a normal Python shell and the Django shell is that when you run the Django shell, `manage.py` sets the `DJANGO_SETTINGS_MODULE` environment variable so that it points to the project's `settings.py` path, and then all of the code in the Django shell is handled in the context of your project. With the use of the third-party IPython or bpython interfaces, we can enhance the default Python shell further, with syntax highlighting, autocompletion, and more.

See also

The *Using database query expressions* recipe

The *Monkey patching the slugify() function for better internationalization support* recipe

Using database query expressions

Django Object-Relational Mapping (ORM) comes with special abstraction constructs that can be used to build complex database queries. They are called **query expressions**, and they allow you to filter data, order it, annotate new columns, and aggregate relations. In this recipe, you will see how these can be used in practice. We will create an app that shows viral videos and counts how many times each video has been seen by anonymous or logged-in users.

Getting ready

To start with, create a `viral_videos` app with a `ViralVideo` model and set up the system so that it logs to a log file by default:

Create the `viral_videos` app and add it under `INSTALLED_APPS` in the settings:

```python
# myproject/settings/_base.py
INSTALLED_APPS = [
    # ...
    "myproject.apps.core",
    "myproject.apps.viral_videos",
]
```

Next, create a model for viral videos with a **Universally Unique Identifier (UUID)** as a primary key, along with creation and modification timestamps, a title, embedded code, impressions by anonymous users, and impressions by authenticated users, as follows:

```python
# myproject/apps/viral_videos/models.py
import uuid
from django.db import models
from django.utils.translation import ugettext_lazy as _

from myproject.apps.core.models import (
    CreationModificationDateBase,
    UrlBase,
)


class ViralVideo(CreationModificationDateBase, UrlBase):
    uuid = models.UUIDField(primary_key=True, default=None,
      editable=False)
    title = models.CharField(_("Title"), max_length=200, blank=True)
    embed_code = models.TextField(_("YouTube embed code"), blank=True)
    anonymous_views = models.PositiveIntegerField(_("Anonymous
      impressions"), default=0)
```

```
    authenticated_views = models.PositiveIntegerField(
        _("Authenticated impressions"), default=0
    )

    class Meta:
        verbose_name = _("Viral video")
        verbose_name_plural = _("Viral videos")

    def __str__(self):
        return self.title

    def get_url_path(self):
        from django.urls import reverse

        return reverse("viral_videos:viral_video_detail",
         kwargs={"pk": self.pk})

    def save(self, *args, **kwargs):
        if self.pk is None:
            self.pk = uuid.uuid4()
        super().save(*args, **kwargs)
```

Make and run migrations for the new app so that your database will be ready to go:

```
(env)$ python manage.py makemigrations
(env)$ python manage.py migrate
```

Add logging configuration to the settings:

```
LOGGING = {
    "version": 1,
    "disable_existing_loggers": False,
    "handlers": {
        "file": {
            "level": "DEBUG",
            "class": "logging.FileHandler",
            "filename": os.path.join(BASE_DIR, "tmp", "debug.log"),
        }
    },
    "loggers": {"django": {"handlers": ["file"], "level": "DEBUG",
     "propagate": True}},
}
```

This will log debugging information into a temporary file named `tmp/debug.log`.

How to do it...

To illustrate the query expressions, let's create the viral video detail view and plug it into the URL configuration, as follows:

1. Create the viral video list and detail views in `views.py` as follows:

```python
# myproject/apps/viral_videos/views.py
import logging

from django.conf import settings
from django.db import models
from django.utils.timezone import now, timedelta
from django.shortcuts import render, get_object_or_404
from django.views.generic import ListView

from .models import ViralVideo

POPULAR_FROM = getattr(settings, "VIRAL_VIDEOS_POPULAR_FROM", 500)

logger = logging.getLogger(__name__)


class ViralVideoList(ListView):
    template_name = "viral_videos/viral_video_list.html"
    model = ViralVideo


def viral_video_detail(request, pk):
    yesterday = now() - timedelta(days=1)

    qs = ViralVideo.objects.annotate(
        total_views=models.F("authenticated_views") +
         models.F("anonymous_views"),
        label=models.Case(
            models.When(total_views__gt=POPULAR_FROM,
             then=models.Value("popular")),
            models.When(created__gt=yesterday,
             then=models.Value("new")),
            default=models.Value("cool"),
            output_field=models.CharField(),
        ),
    )
```

```
# DEBUG: check the SQL query that Django ORM generates
logger.debug(f"Query: {qs.query}")

qs = qs.filter(pk=pk)
if request.user.is_authenticated:
    qs.update(authenticated_views=models
     .F("authenticated_views") + 1)
else:
    qs.update(anonymous_views=models.F("anonymous_views") + 1)

video = get_object_or_404(qs)

return render(request, "viral_videos/viral_video_detail.html",
 {"video": video})
```

2. Define the URL configuration for the app as follows:

```
# myproject/apps/viral_videos/urls.py
from django.urls import path

from .views import ViralVideoList, viral_video_detail

app_name = "viral_videos"


urlpatterns = [
    path("", ViralVideoList.as_view(), name="viral_video_list"),
    path("<uuid:pk>/", viral_video_detail,
     name="viral_video_detail"),
]
```

3. Include the URL configuration of the app in the project's root URL configuration as follows:

```
# myproject/urls.py
from django.conf.urls.i18n import i18n_patterns
from django.urls import include, path

urlpatterns = i18n_patterns(
path("viral-videos/", include("myproject.apps.viral_videos.urls",
namespace="viral_videos")),
)
```

4. Create a template for the viral video list view as follows:

```
{# viral_videos/viral_video_list.html #}
{% extends "base.html" %}
{% load i18n %}

{% block content %}
    <h1>{% trans "Viral Videos" %}</h1>
    <ul>
        {% for video in object_list %}
            <li><a href="{{ video.get_url_path }}">
                {{ video.title }}</a></li>
        {% endfor %}
    </ul>
{% endblock %}
```

5. Create a template for the viral video detail view as follows:

```
{# viral_videos/viral_video_detail.html #}
{% extends "base.html" %}
{% load i18n %}

{% block content %}
    <h1>{{ video.title }}
        <span class="badge">{{ video.label }}</span>
    </h1>
    <div>{{ video.embed_code|safe }}</div>
    <div>
        <h2>{% trans "Impressions" %}</h2>
        <ul>
            <li>{% trans "Authenticated views" %}:
                {{ video.authenticated_views }}
            </li>
            <li>{% trans "Anonymous views" %}:
                {{ video.anonymous_views }}
            </li>
            <li>{% trans "Total views" %}:
                {{ video.total_views }}
            </li>
        </ul>
    </div>
{% endblock %}
```

6. Set up the administration for the `viral_videos` app as follows, and add some videos to the database when you are finished:

```
# myproject/apps/viral_videos/admin.py
from django.contrib import admin
```

```
from .models import ViralVideo

@admin.register(ViralVideo)
class ViralVideoAdmin(admin.ModelAdmin):
    list_display = ["title", "created", "modified"]
```

How it works...

You might have noticed the `logger.debug()` statement in the view. If you run the server in DEBUG mode and access a video in the browser (for example, `http://127.0.0.1:8000/en/viral-videos/2b14ffd3-d1f1-4699-a07b-1328421d8 312/`, in local development), you will see an SQL query like the following printed in the logs (`tmp/debug.log`):

```
SELECT "viral_videos_viralvideo"."created",
"viral_videos_viralvideo"."modified", "viral_videos_viralvideo"."uuid",
"viral_videos_viralvideo"."title", "viral_videos_viralvideo"."embed_code",
"viral_videos_viralvideo"."anonymous_views",
"viral_videos_viralvideo"."authenticated_views",
("viral_videos_viralvideo"."authenticated_views" +
"viral_videos_viralvideo"."anonymous_views") AS "total_views", CASE WHEN
("viral_videos_viralvideo"."authenticated_views" +
"viral_videos_viralvideo"."anonymous_views") > 500 THEN 'popular' WHEN
"viral_videos_viralvideo"."created" >
'2019-12-21T05:01:58.775441+00:00'::timestamptz THEN 'new' ELSE 'cool' END
 AS "label" FROM "viral_videos_viralvideo" WHERE
"viral_videos_viralvideo"."uuid" = '2b14ffd3-d1f1-4699-
a07b-1328421d8312'::uuid LIMIT 21; args=(500, 'popular',
datetime.datetime(2019, 12, 21, 5, 1, 58, 775441, tzinfo=<UTC>), 'new',
'cool', UUID('2b14ffd3-d1f1-4699-a07b-1328421d8312'))
```

Then, in the browser, you will see a simple page showing the following:

- The title of the video
- The label of the video
- The embedded video
- The number of views from authenticated and anonymous users, and the number of views in total

It will be similar to the following image:

The `annotate()` method in Django `QuerySets` allows you to add extra columns to the `SELECT` SQL statement, as well as properties that were created on the fly for the objects retrieved from `QuerySets`. With `models.F()`, we can reference different field values from the selected database table. In this example, we will create the `total_views` attribute, which is the sum of the views from authenticated and anonymous users.

With `models.Case()` and `models.When()`, we can return the values according to different conditions. To mark the values, we are using `models.Value()`. In our example, we will create the `label` column for the SQL query and the property for the objects returned by `QuerySet`. It will be set to **popular** if it has more than 500 impressions, **new** if it was created in the last 24 hours, and **cool** otherwise.

At the end of the view, we called the `qs.update()` methods. They increment the `authenticated_views` or `anonymous_views` of the current video, depending on whether the user looking at the video was logged in. The incrementation happens not at the Python level, but at the SQL level. This solves issues with so-called race conditions where two or more visitors are accessing the view at the same time, trying to increase the view count simultaneously.

See also

- The *Using the Django shell* recipe
- The *Creating a model mixin with URL-related methods* recipe in `Chapter 2`, *Models and Database Structure*
- The *Creating a model mixin to handle creation and modification dates* recipe in `Chapter 2`, *Models and Database Structure*

Monkey patching the slugify() function for better internationalization support

A monkey patch (or guerrilla patch) is a piece of code that extends or modifies another piece of code at runtime. It is not recommended that you use monkey patches often; however, sometimes, they are the only possible way to fix a bug in complex third-party modules without creating a separate branch of the module. Also, monkey patching can be used to prepare functional or unit tests without using complicated and time-consuming database or file manipulations.

In this recipe, you will learn how to exchange the default slugify() function with the one from the third-party transliterate package, which handles the conversion of Unicode characters to ASCII equivalents more intelligently and includes a number of language packs that provide even more specific transformations as needed. As a quick reminder, we use the slugify() utility to create a URL-friendly version of an object's title or uploaded filename. When processed, the function strips any leading and trailing whitespace, converts the text to lowercase, removes non-alphanumeric characters, and converts spaces to hyphens.

Getting ready

Let's start with these small steps:

1. Install transliterate in your virtual environment as follows:

   ```
   (env)$ pip install transliterate==1.10.2
   ```

2. Then, create a guerrilla_patches app in your project and put it under INSTALLED_APPS in the settings.

How to do it...

In the models.py file of the guerrilla_patches app, overwrite the slugify function from django.utils.text with the one from the transliterate package:

```python
# myproject/apps/guerrilla_patches/models.py
from django.utils import text
from transliterate import slugify

text.slugify = slugify
```

How it works...

The default Django `slugify()` function handles German diacritical symbols incorrectly. To see this for yourself, try to slugify a very long German word with all the German diacritical symbols. First, run the following code in the Django shell, without the monkey patch:

```
(env)$ python manage.py shell
>>> from django.utils.text import slugify
>>> slugify("Heizölrückstoßabdämpfung")
'heizolruckstoabdampfung'
```

This is incorrect in German, as the letter ß is totally stripped out instead of being substituted for `ss` and the letters ä, ö, and ü are changed to `a`, `o`, and `u`, where they should have been substituted with `ae`, `oe`, and `ue`.

The monkey patch that we created loads the `django.utils.text` module at initialization and reassigns `transliteration.slugify` in place of the core `slugify()` function. Now, if you run the same code in the Django shell, you will get the correct results, as follows:

```
(env)$ python manage.py shell
>>> from django.utils.text import slugify
>>> slugify("Heizölrückstoßabdämpfung")
'heizoelrueckstossabdaempfung'
```

To read more about how to utilize the `transliterate` module, refer to `https://pypi.org/project/transliterate`.

There's more...

Before creating a monkey patch, we need to completely understand how the code that we want to modify works. This can be done by analyzing the existing code and inspecting the values of different variables. To do this, there is a useful built-in Python debugger module, **pdb,** that can be temporarily added to the Django code (or any third-party module) to stop the execution of a development server at any breakpoint. Use the following code to debug an unclear part of a Python module:

```
breakpoint()
```

This launches the interactive shell, where you can type in the variables in order to see their values. If you type c or continue, the code execution will continue until the next breakpoint. If you type q or quit, the management command will be aborted.

 You can learn more Python debugger commands and how to inspect the traceback of the code at https://docs.python.org/3/library/pdb.html.

Another quick way to see the value of a variable in the development server is to raise a warning with the variable as a message, as follows:

```
raise Warning, some_variable
```

When you are in DEBUG mode, the Django logger will provide you with the traceback and other local variables.

 Don't forget to remove debugging code before committing your work to a repository.

If you are using the PyCharm interactive development environment, you can set breakpoints and debug variables there visually without modifying the source code.

See also

- The *Using the Django shell* recipe

Toggling the Debug toolbar

While developing with Django, you may want to inspect request headers and parameters, check the current template context, or measure the performance of SQL queries. All of this and more is possible with the **Django Debug Toolbar**. It is a configurable set of panels that display various debugging information about the current request and response. In this recipe, we will guide you through how to toggle the visibility of the Debug toolbar, depending on a cookie whose value can be set by a bookmarklet. A bookmarklet is a bookmark with a small piece of JavaScript code that you can run on any page in a browser.

Getting ready

To get started with toggling the visibility of the Debug toolbar, go through the following steps:

1. Install the Django Debug Toolbar in your virtual environment:

   ```
   (env)$ pip install django-debug-toolbar==2.1
   ```

2. Add `"debug_toolbar"` under `INSTALLED_APPS` in the settings:

   ```python
   # myproject/settings/_base.py
   INSTALLED_APPS = [
       # ...
       "debug_toolbar",
   ]
   ```

How to do it...

Follow these steps to set up the Django Debug Toolbar, which can be switched on or off using a bookmarklet in the browser:

1. Add the following project settings:

   ```python
   # myproject/settings/_base.py
   DEBUG_TOOLBAR_CONFIG = {
       "DISABLE_PANELS": [],
       "SHOW_TOOLBAR_CALLBACK":
       "myproject.apps.core.misc.custom_show_toolbar",
       "SHOW_TEMPLATE_CONTEXT": True,
   }

   DEBUG_TOOLBAR_PANELS = [
       "debug_toolbar.panels.versions.VersionsPanel",
       "debug_toolbar.panels.timer.TimerPanel",
       "debug_toolbar.panels.settings.SettingsPanel",
       "debug_toolbar.panels.headers.HeadersPanel",
       "debug_toolbar.panels.request.RequestPanel",
       "debug_toolbar.panels.sql.SQLPanel",
       "debug_toolbar.panels.templates.TemplatesPanel",
       "debug_toolbar.panels.staticfiles.StaticFilesPanel",
       "debug_toolbar.panels.cache.CachePanel",
       "debug_toolbar.panels.signals.SignalsPanel",
       "debug_toolbar.panels.logging.LoggingPanel",
       "debug_toolbar.panels.redirects.RedirectsPanel",
   ]
   ```

2. In the `core` app, create a `misc.py` file with the `custom_show_toolbar()` function, as follows:

```
# myproject/apps/core/misc.py
def custom_show_toolbar(request):
    return "1" == request.COOKIES.get("DebugToolbar", False)
```

3. In the `urls.py` of the project, add these configuration rules:

```
# myproject/urls.py
from django.conf.urls.i18n import i18n_patterns
from django.urls import include, path
from django.conf import settings
import debug_toolbar


urlpatterns = i18n_patterns(
    # ...
)

urlpatterns = [
    path('__debug__/', include(debug_toolbar.urls)),
] + urlpatterns
```

4. Open the Chrome or Firefox browser and go to the bookmark manager. Then, create two new bookmarks that contain JavaScript. The first link will show the toolbar, and will look similar to the following:

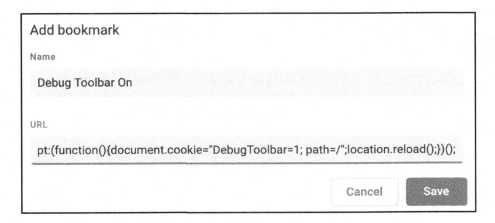

The JavaScript code is as follows:

```
javascript:(function(){document.cookie="DebugToolbar=1;
path=/";location.reload();})();
```

5. The second JavaScript link will hide the toolbar, and will look similar to the following:

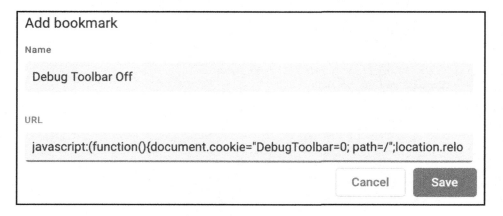

This is the full JavaScript code:

```
javascript:(function(){document.cookie="DebugToolbar=0;
path=/";location.reload();})();
```

How it works...

The DEBUG_TOOLBAR_PANELS setting defines the panels to show in the toolbar. The DEBUG_TOOLBAR_CONFIG dictionary defines the configuration for the toolbar, including a path to the function that is used to check whether or not to show the toolbar.

By default, when you browse through your project, the Django Debug Toolbar will not be shown; however, as you click on your bookmarklet, **Debug Toolbar On**, the `DebugToolbar` cookie will be set to `1`, the page will be refreshed, and you will see the toolbar with debugging panels—for example, you will be able to inspect the performance of SQL statements for optimization, as shown in the following screenshot:

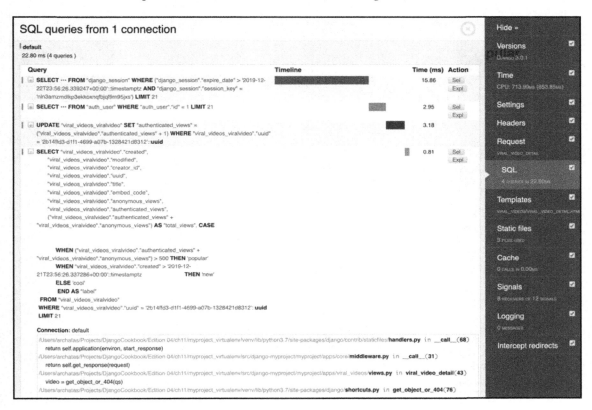

You will also be able to check the template context variables for the current view, as shown in the following screenshot:

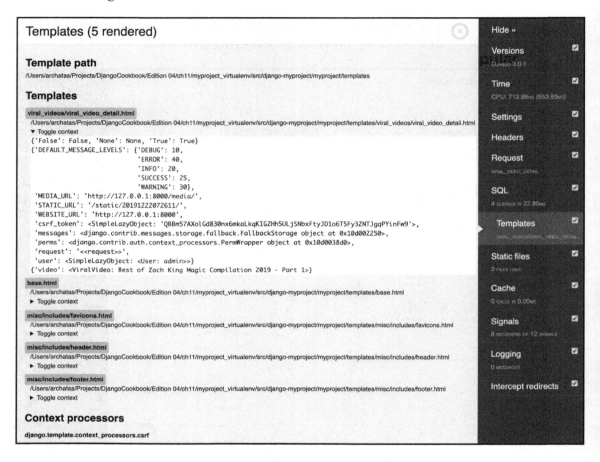

Clicking on the second bookmarklet, **Debug Toolbar Off**, will similarly set the `DebugToolbar` cookie to `0` and refresh the page, hiding the toolbar again.

See also

- The *Getting detailed error reporting via email* recipe in `Chapter 13`, *Maintenance*

Using ThreadLocalMiddleware

The `HttpRequest` object contains useful information about the current user, language, server variables, cookies, session, and so on. As a matter of fact, `HttpRequest` is provided in the views and middleware, and you can pass it (or its attribute values) to forms, model methods, model managers, templates, and so on. To make life easier, you can use a so-called `ThreadLocalMiddleware` that stores the current `HttpRequest` object in the globally accessible Python thread. Therefore, you can access it from model methods, forms, signal handlers, and other places that didn't have direct access to the `HttpRequest` object previously. In this recipe, we will define this middleware.

Getting ready

Create the `core` app and put it under `INSTALLED_APPS` in the settings, if you have not done so already.

How to do it...

Execute the following two steps to set up `ThreadLocalMiddleware`, which can be used to get the current `HttpRequest` or user in any function or method of the project's code:

1. Add a `middleware.py` file to the `core` app with the following content:

```python
# myproject/apps/core/middleware.py
from threading import local

_thread_locals = local()


def get_current_request():
    """
    :returns the HttpRequest object for this thread
    """
    return getattr(_thread_locals, "request", None)


def get_current_user():
    """
    :returns the current user if it exists or None otherwise """
    request = get_current_request()
    if request:
        return getattr(request, "user", None)
```

```
class ThreadLocalMiddleware(object):
    """
    Middleware to add the HttpRequest to thread local storage
    """

    def __init__(self, get_response):
        self.get_response = get_response

    def __call__(self, request):
        _thread_locals.request = request
        return self.get_response(request)
```

2. Add this middleware to MIDDLEWARE in the settings:

```
# myproject/settings/_base.py
MIDDLEWARE = [
    "django.middleware.security.SecurityMiddleware",
    "django.contrib.sessions.middleware.SessionMiddleware",
    "django.middleware.common.CommonMiddleware",
    "django.middleware.csrf.CsrfViewMiddleware",
    "django.contrib.auth.middleware.AuthenticationMiddleware",
    "django.contrib.messages.middleware.MessageMiddleware",
    "django.middleware.clickjacking.XFrameOptionsMiddleware",
    "django.middleware.locale.LocaleMiddleware",
    "debug_toolbar.middleware.DebugToolbarMiddleware",
    "myproject.apps.core.middleware.ThreadLocalMiddleware",
]
```

How it works...

The ThreadLocalMiddleware processes each request and stores the current HttpRequest object in the current thread. Each request–response cycle in Django is single threaded. We have created two functions: get_current_request() and get_current_user(). These functions can be used from anywhere to grab the current HttpRequest object or the current user, respectively.

For example, you can use this middleware to develop and use CreatorMixin, which will save the current user as the creator of a new model object, as follows:

```
# myproject/apps/core/models.py
from django.conf import settings
from django.db import models
from django.utils.translation import gettext_lazy as _
```

```
class CreatorBase(models.Model):
    """
    Abstract base class with a creator
    """

    creator = models.ForeignKey(
        settings.AUTH_USER_MODEL,
        verbose_name=_("creator"),
        editable=False,
        blank=True,
        null=True,
        on_delete=models.SET_NULL,
    )

    class Meta:
        abstract = True

    def save(self, *args, **kwargs):
        from .middleware import get_current_user

        if not self.creator:
            self.creator = get_current_user()
        super().save(*args, **kwargs)

    save.alters_data = True
```

See also

- The *Creating a model mixin with URL-related methods* recipe in Chapter 2, *Models and Database Structure*
- The *Creating a model mixin to handle creation and modification dates* recipe in Chapter 2, *Models and Database Structure*
- The *Creating a model mixin to take care of meta tags* recipe in Chapter 2, *Models and Database Structure*
- The *Creating a model mixin to handle generic relations* recipe in Chapter 2, *Models and Database Structure*

Using signals to notify administrators about new entries

The Django framework includes the concept of **signals**, which are similar to events in JavaScript. There are a handful of built-in signals. You can use them to trigger actions before and after the initialization of a model, saving or deleting an instance, migrating the database schema, handling a request, and so on. Moreover, you can create your own signals in your reusable apps and handle them in other apps. In this recipe, you will learn how to use signals to send emails to administrators whenever a specific model is saved.

Getting ready

Let's start with the `viral_videos` app that we created in the *Using database query expressions* recipe.

How to do it...

Follow these steps to create notifications for administrators:

1. Create a `signals.py` file with the following content:

```python
# myproject/apps/viral_videos/signals.py
from django.db.models.signals import post_save
from django.dispatch import receiver
from django.template.loader import render_to_string

from .models import ViralVideo


@receiver(post_save, sender=ViralVideo)
def inform_administrators(sender, **kwargs):
    from django.core.mail import mail_admins

    instance = kwargs["instance"]
    created = kwargs["created"]

    if created:
        context = {"title": instance.title, "link":
          instance.get_url()}
        subject = render_to_string(
            "viral_videos/email/administrator/subject.txt", context
        )
```

```
plain_text_message = render_to_string(
    "viral_videos/email/administrator/message.txt", context
)
html_message = render_to_string(
    "viral_videos/email/administrator/message.html",
        context
)

mail_admins(
    subject=subject.strip(),
    message=plain_text_message,
    html_message=html_message,
    fail_silently=True,
)
```

2. Then we need to create some templates. Start with the template for the email subject:

```
{# viral_videos/email/administrator/subject.txt #}
New Viral Video Added
```

3. Then create a template for a plain text message—something like the following:

```
{# viral_videos/email/administrator/message.txt #}
A new viral video called "{{ title }}" has been created.
You can preview it at {{ link }}.
```

4. Then create a template for the HTML message as follows:

```
{# viral_videos/email/administrator/message.html #}
<p>A new viral video called "{{ title }}" has been created.</p>
<p>You can <a href="{{ link }}">preview it here</a>.</p>
```

5. Create the apps.py file with the following content:

```
# myproject/apps/viral_videos/apps.py
from django.apps import AppConfig
from django.utils.translation import ugettext_lazy as _


class ViralVideosAppConfig(AppConfig):
    name = "myproject.apps.viral_videos"
    verbose_name = _("Viral Videos")

    def ready(self):
        from .signals import inform_administrators
```

6. Update the `__init__.py` file with the following content:

```
# myproject/apps/viral_videos/__init__.py
default_app_config = 
"myproject.apps.viral_videos.apps.ViralVideosAppConfig"
```

Make sure that you have `ADMINS` set in the project settings similar to the following:

```
# myproject/settings/_base.py
ADMINS = [("Administrator", "admin@example.com")]
```

How it works...

The `ViralVideosAppConfig` app configuration class has the `ready()` method, which will be called when all of the models of the project are loaded into the memory. According to the Django documentation, signals allow for certain senders to notify a set of receivers that an action has taken place. In the `ready()` method, therefore, we import the `inform_administrators()` function.

Through the `@receiver` decorator, `inform_administrators()` is registered for the `post_save` signal, and we have limited it to handle only the signals where the `ViralVideo` model is `sender`. Therefore, whenever we save a `ViralVideo` object, the `receiver` function will be called. The `inform_administrators()` function checks whether a video is newly created. If it is, it sends an email to the system administrators that are listed in `ADMINS` in the settings.

We use templates to generate the content of the `subject`, `plain_text_message`, and the `html_message` so that we can define default templates for each of these within our app. If we make our `viral_videos` app publicly available, those who pull it into their own projects can then customize the templates as desired, perhaps to wrap them in a company email template wrapper.

 You can learn more about the Django signals in the official documentation at https://docs.djangoproject.com/en/3.0/topics/signals/.

See also

- The *Creating app configuration* recipe in `Chapter 1`, *Getting Started with Django 3.0*
- The *Using database query expressions* recipe
- The *Checking for missing settings* recipe

Checking for missing settings

From Django 1.7 onward, you can use an extensible **system-check framework**, which replaces the old `validate` management command. In this recipe, you will learn how to create a check if the ADMINS setting is set. Similarly, you will be able to check whether different secret keys or access tokens are set for the APIs that you are using.

Getting ready

Let's start with the `viral_videos` app that was created in the *Using database query expressions* recipe and was extended in the previous recipe.

How to do it...

To use the system-check framework, go through these steps:

1. Create the `checks.py` file with the following content:

```python
# myproject/apps/viral_videos/checks.py
from textwrap import dedent

from django.core.checks import Warning, register, Tags


@register(Tags.compatibility)
def settings_check(app_configs, **kwargs):
    from django.conf import settings

    errors = []

    if not settings.ADMINS:
        errors.append(
            Warning(
                dedent("""
```

```
                            The system admins are not set in the project
                            settings
                """),
                obj=settings,
                hint=dedent("""
                    In order to receive notifications when new
                     videos are created, define system admins
                     in your settings, like:
                    ADMINS = (
                        ("Admin", "administrator@example.com"),
                    )
                """),
                id="viral_videos.W001",
            )
        )

    return errors
```

2. Import the checks in the `ready()` method of the app configuration as follows:

```
# myproject/apps/viral_videos/apps.py
from django.apps import AppConfig
from django.utils.translation import ugettext_lazy as _


class ViralVideosAppConfig(AppConfig):
    name = "myproject.apps.viral_videos"
    verbose_name = _("Viral Videos")

    def ready(self):
        from .signals import inform_administrators
        from .checks import settings_check
```

3. To try the check that you just created, remove or comment out the ADMINS setting and then run the check management command in your virtual environment:

```
(env)$ python manage.py check
System check identified some issues:

WARNINGS:
<Settings "myproject.settings.dev">: (viral_videos.W001)
The system admins are not set in the project settings

HINT:
In order to receive notifications when new videos are
created, define system admins in your settings, like:
```

```
ADMINS = (
    ("Admin", "administrator@example.com"),
)


System check identified 1 issue (0 silenced).
```

How it works...

The system-check framework has a bunch of checks in the models, fields, databases, administration authentication configuration, content types, and security settings, where it raises errors or warnings if something in the project is not set correctly. Additionally, you can create your own checks, similar to what we did in this recipe.

We have registered the `settings_check()` function, which returns a list with `Warning` if there is no `ADMINS` setting defined for the project.

Aside from the `Warning` instances from the `django.core.checks` module, the returned list can also contain instances of the `Debug`, `Info`, `Error`, and `Critical` built-in classes or any other class inheriting from `django.core.checks.CheckMessage`. Logging at the debug, info, and warning levels would fail silently, whereas logging at the error and critical levels would prevent the project from running.

In this example, the check is tagged as a compatibility check via the `Tags.compatibility` argument passed to the `@register` decorator. Other options provided in `Tags` include the following:

- `admin` for checks related to the admin site
- `caches` for checks related to server caching
- `database` for checks related to the database configuration
- `models` for checks related to models, model fields, and managers
- `security` for security-related checks
- `signals` for checks related to signal declarations and handlers
- `staticfiles` for static-file checks
- `templates` for template-related checks
- `translation` for checks related to string translations
- `url` for checks related to URL configuration

Learn more about the system-check framework in the official documentation at `https://docs.djangoproject.com/en/3.0/topics/checks/`.

See also

- The *Creating app configurations* recipe in `Chapter 1`, *Getting Started with Django 3.0*
- The *Using database query expressions* recipe
- The *Using signals to notify administrators about new entries* recipe

11
Testing

In this chapter, we will cover the following topics:

- Testing views with mock
- Testing the user interface with Selenium
- Testing APIs created using Django REST framework
- Ensuring test coverage

Introduction

To ensure the quality and correctness of your code, you should have automated software tests. Django provides tools for you to write test suites for your website. Test suites automatically check your website and its components to ensure that everything is working correctly. When you modify your code, you can run the tests to check whether your changes affected the application's behavior negatively.

The world of automated software testing has a wide range of divisions and terminologies. For the sake of this book, we will divide testing into the following categories:

- **Unit testing** refers to tests that are strictly targeted at individual pieces, or units, of code. Most commonly, a unit corresponds to a single file or module, and unit tests do their best to validate that the logic and behaviors are as expected.
- **Integration testing** goes one step further, dealing with the way that two or more units work with one another. Such tests do not get as granular as unit tests, and they are generally written under the assumption that all unit tests have passed by the time an integration is validated. Hence, integration tests only cover the set of behaviors that must be true for the units to work properly with one another.

- **Component interface testing** is a higher-order form of integration testing, in which a single component is verified from end to end. Such tests are written in a way that is ignorant of the underlying logic used to provide the behaviors of the component, so that logic can change without modifying the behavior, and the tests will still pass.
- **System testing** verifies the end-to-end integration of all components that make up a system, often corresponding to complete user flows.
- **Operational acceptance testing** checks that all of the non-functional aspects of a system operate correctly. Acceptance tests check the business logic to find out whether the project works the way it is supposed to, from an end user's point of view.

Technical requirements

For working with the code in this chapter, you will need the latest stable version of Python, a MySQL or PostgreSQL database, and a Django project with a virtual environment.

You can find all of the code for this chapter at the `ch11` directory of the GitHub repository at: `https://github.com/PacktPublishing/Django-3-Web-Development-Cookbook-Fourth-Edition`.

Testing views with mock

In this recipe, we will take a look at how to write unit tests. Unit tests are those that check whether individual functions or methods return the correct results. We will look at the `likes` app and write tests that check whether posting to the `json_set_like()` view returns a failure response for unauthenticated users and a successful result for authenticated users. We will use `Mock` objects to simulate the `HttpRequest` and `AnonymousUser` objects.

Getting ready

Let's start with the `locations` and `likes` apps from the *Implementing the Like widget* recipe in `Chapter 4`, *Templates and JavaScript*.

We are going to use the `mock` library, which has been available as a built-in at `unittest.mock` since Python 3.3.

How to do it...

We will test the liking action with `mock` by performing the following steps:

1. Create the `tests` module in your `likes` app
2. In this module, create a `test_views.py` file with the following content:

```python
# myproject/apps/likes/tests/test_views.py
import json
from unittest import mock
from django.contrib.auth.models import User
from django.contrib.contenttypes.models import ContentType
from django.test import TestCase
from myproject.apps.locations.models import Location


class JSSetLikeViewTest(TestCase):
    @classmethod
    def setUpClass(cls):
        super(JSSetLikeViewTest, cls).setUpClass()

        cls.location = Location.objects.create(
            name="Park Güell",
            description="If you want to see something spectacular, "
            "come to Barcelona, Catalonia, Spain and visit Park "
            "Güell. Located on a hill, Park Güell is a public "
            "park with beautiful gardens and organic "
            "architectural elements.",
            picture="locations/2020/01/20200101012345.jpg",
            # dummy path
        )
        cls.content_type = \
         ContentType.objects.get_for_model(Location)
        cls.superuser = User.objects.create_superuser(
            username="admin", password="admin",
             email="admin@example.com"
        )

    @classmethod
    def tearDownClass(cls):
        super(JSSetLikeViewTest, cls).tearDownClass()
        cls.location.delete()
        cls.superuser.delete()

    def test_authenticated_json_set_like(self):
        from ..views import json_set_like

        mock_request = mock.Mock()
```

```
        mock_request.user = self.superuser
        mock_request.method = "POST"

        response = json_set_like(mock_request,
          self.content_type.pk, self.location.pk)
        expected_result = json.dumps(
            {"success": True, "action": "add", "count":
            Location.objects.count()}
        )
        self.assertJSONEqual(response.content, expected_result)

    @mock.patch("django.contrib.auth.models.User")
    def test_anonymous_json_set_like(self, MockUser):
        from ..views import json_set_like

        anonymous_user = MockUser()
        anonymous_user.is_authenticated = False

        mock_request = mock.Mock()
        mock_request.user = anonymous_user
        mock_request.method = "POST"

        response = json_set_like(mock_request,
        self.content_type.pk, self.location.pk)
        expected_result = json.dumps({"success": False})
        self.assertJSONEqual(response.content, expected_result)
```

3. Run the tests for the `likes` app, as follows:

```
(env)$ python manage.py test myproject.apps.likes --
settings=myproject.settings.test
Creating test database for alias 'default'...
System check identified no issues (0 silenced).
..
----------------------------------------------------------------
---
Ran 2 tests in 0.268s
OK
Destroying test database for alias 'default'...
```

How it works...

When you run tests for the `likes` app, at first, a temporary test database is created. Then, the `setUpClass()` method is called. Later, the methods whose names start with `test` are executed, and, finally, the `tearDownClass()` method is called. For each passed test, you will see a dot (.) in the command-line tool, for each failed test there will be the letter **F**, and for each error in the tests, you will see the letter **E**. At the end, you will see hints about the failed and erroneous tests. As we currently have only two tests in the suite for the `likes` app, you will see two dots in the results.

In `setUpClass()`, we create a location and a superuser. Also, we find out the `ContentType` object for the `Location` model. We will need it for the `json_set_like()` view that sets or removes likes for different objects. As a reminder, the view looks similar to the following, and returns a JSON string as a result:

```
def json_set_like(request, content_type_id, object_id):
    # all the view logic goes here...
    return JsonResponse(result)
```

In the `test_authenticated_json_set_like()` and `test_anonymous_json_set_like()` methods, we use the `Mock` objects. These are objects that can have any attributes or methods. Each undefined attribute or method of a `Mock` object is another `Mock` object. Therefore, in the shell, you can try to chain attributes, as follows:

```
>>> from unittest import mock
>>> m = mock.Mock()
>>> m.whatever.anything().whatsoever
<Mock name='mock.whatever.anything().whatsoever' id='4320988368'>
```

In our tests, we use `Mock` objects to simulate the `HttpRequest` object. For the anonymous user, `MockUser` is generated as a patch of the standard Django `User` object, via the `@mock.patch()` decorator. For the authenticated user, we still need the real `User` object because the view uses the user's ID for the `Like` object.

Therefore, we call the `json_set_like()` function, and check that the returned JSON response is correct:

- It returns `{"success": false}` in the response if the visitor is unauthenticated
- It returns something like `{"action": "add", "count": 1, "success": true}` for authenticated users

In the end, the `tearDownClass()` class method is called, deleting the location and superuser from the test database.

There's more...

To test something that uses the `HttpRequest` object, you can also use Django Request Factory. You can read how to use it at `https://docs.djangoproject.com/en/3.0/topics/testing/advanced/#the-request-factory`.

See also

- The *Implementing the Like widget* recipe in `Chapter 4`, *Templates and JavaScript*
- The *Testing the user interface with Selenium* recipe
- The *Testing APIs created using Django REST framework* recipe
- The *Ensuring test coverage* recipe

Testing the user interface with Selenium

Operational acceptance tests check the business logic to know whether the project works the way it is supposed to. In this recipe, you will learn how to write acceptance tests with **Selenium**, which allows you to simulate activities at the frontend such as filling in forms or clicking on specific DOM elements in a browser.

Getting ready

Let's start with the `locations` and `likes` apps from the *Implementing the Like widget* recipe in `Chapter 4`, *Templates and JavaScript*.

For this recipe, we'll be using the Selenium library with the **Chrome** browser and **ChromeDriver** to control it. Let's prepare that:

1. Download and install the Chrome browser from `https://www.google.com/chrome/`.

2. Create a `drivers` directory in your Django project. Download the latest stable version of ChromeDriver from `https://sites.google.com/a/chromium.org/chromedriver/`, unzip it, and place it into the newly created `drivers` directory.

3. Install Selenium in your virtual environment, as follows:

```
(env)$ pip install selenium
```

How to do it...

We will test the Ajax-based liking functionality with Selenium by performing the following steps:

1. In your project settings, add a `TESTS_SHOW_BROWSER` setting:

```
# myproject/settings/_base.py
TESTS_SHOW_BROWSER = True
```

2. Create the `tests` module in your `locations` app and add a `test_frontend.py` file in it with the following content:

```
# myproject/apps/locations/tests/test_frontend.py
import os
from io import BytesIO
from time import sleep

from django.core.files.storage import default_storage
from django.test import LiveServerTestCase
from django.contrib.contenttypes.models import ContentType
from django.contrib.auth.models import User
from django.conf import settings
from django.test import override_settings
from django.urls import reverse
from selenium import webdriver
from selenium.webdriver.chrome.options import Options
from selenium.webdriver.support.ui import WebDriverWait
from myproject.apps.likes.models import Like
from ..models import Location

SHOW_BROWSER = getattr(settings, "TESTS_SHOW_BROWSER", False)
```

```python
@override_settings(DEBUG=True)
class LiveLocationTest(LiveServerTestCase):
    @classmethod
    def setUpClass(cls):
        super(LiveLocationTest, cls).setUpClass()
        driver_path = os.path.join(settings.BASE_DIR, "drivers",
        "chromedriver")
        chrome_options = Options()
        if not SHOW_BROWSER:
            chrome_options.add_argument("--headless")
        chrome_options.add_argument("--window-size=1200,800")

        cls.browser = webdriver.Chrome(
            executable_path=driver_path, options=chrome_options
        )
        cls.browser.delete_all_cookies()

        image_path = cls.save_test_image("test.jpg")
        cls.location = Location.objects.create(
            name="Park Güell",
            description="If you want to see something spectacular,
             come to Barcelona, Catalonia, Spain and visit Park
             Güell. Located on a hill, Park Güell is a public
             park with beautiful gardens and organic
             architectural elements.",
            picture=image_path,  # dummy path
        )
        cls.username = "admin"
        cls.password = "admin"
        cls.superuser = User.objects.create_superuser(
            username=cls.username, password=cls.password,
            email="admin@example.com"
        )

    @classmethod
    def tearDownClass(cls):
        super(LiveLocationTest, cls).tearDownClass()
        cls.browser.quit()
        cls.location.delete()
        cls.superuser.delete()

    @classmethod
    def save_test_image(cls, filename):
        from PIL import Image

        image = Image.new("RGB", (1, 1), 0)
        image_buffer = BytesIO()
        image.save(image_buffer, format="JPEG")
```

```
        path = f"tests/{filename}"
        default_storage.save(path, image_buffer)
        return path

    def wait_a_little(self):
        if SHOW_BROWSER:
            sleep(2)

    def test_login_and_like(self):
        # login
        login_path = reverse("admin:login")
        self.browser.get(
            f"{self.live_server_url}{login_path}?next=
          {self.location.get_url_path()}"
        )
        username_field =
        self.browser.find_element_by_id("id_username")
        username_field.send_keys(self.username)
        password_field =
        self.browser.find_element_by_id("id_password")
        password_field.send_keys(self.password)
        self.browser.find_element_by_css_selector
        ('input[type="submit"]').click()
        WebDriverWait(self.browser, timeout=10).until(
            lambda x:
        self.browser.find_element_by_css_selector(".like-button")
        )
        # click on the "like" button
        like_button =
        self.browser.find_element_by_css_selector(".like-button")
        is_initially_active = "active" in
          like_button.get_attribute("class")
        initial_likes = int(
            self.browser.find_element_by_css_selector
              (".like-badge").text
        )

        self.assertFalse(is_initially_active)
        self.assertEqual(initial_likes, 0)

        self.wait_a_little()

        like_button.click()
        WebDriverWait(self.browser, timeout=10).until(
            lambda x:
            int(self.browser.find_element_by_css_selector
              (".like-badge").text) != initial_likes
        )
```

```
likes_in_html = int(
    self.browser.find_element_by_css_selector
    (".like-badge").text
)
likes_in_db = Like.objects.filter(
content_type=ContentType.objects.get_for_model(Location),
    object_id=self.location.pk,
).count()
self.assertEqual(likes_in_html, 1)
self.assertEqual(likes_in_html, likes_in_db)

self.wait_a_little()

self.assertGreater(likes_in_html, initial_likes)

# click on the "like" button again to switch back to the
# previous state
like_button.click()
WebDriverWait(self.browser, timeout=10).until(
    lambda x: int(self.browser.find_element_by_css_selector
    (".like-badge").text) == initial_likes
)

self.wait_a_little()
```

3. Run the tests for the `locations` app, as shown in the following:

```
(env)$ python manage.py test myproject.apps.locations --
settings=myproject.settings.test
Creating test database for alias 'default'...
System check identified no issues (0 silenced).
.
----------------------------------------------------------------
---
Ran 1 test in 4.284s

OK
Destroying test database for alias 'default'...
```

How it works...

When we run these tests, we will see a Chrome window opened with the administration login screen under the URL, for example,
http://localhost:63807/en/admin/login/?next=/en/locations/176255a9-9c07
-4542-8324-83ac0d21b7c3/.

The username and password fields will get filled in with **admin** and you will get redirected to the detail page of the Park Güell location, under such a URL as `http://localhost:63807/en/locations/176255a9-9c07-4542-8324-83ac0d21b7c 3/`. There you will see the **Like** button clicked twice, causing liking and unliking actions.

If we change the `TESTS_SHOW_BROWSER` setting to `False` (or remove it all) and run the tests again, the testing will happen with minimal waiting time and in the background without opening a browser's window.

Let's see how this works in the test suite. We define a class extending `LiveServerTestCase`. This creates a test suite that will run a local server under a random unused port such as `63807`. By default, `LiveServerTestCase` runs a server in non-DEBUG mode. But we switch it to the DEBUG mode using the `override_settings()` decorator to make the static files accessible without collecting them and to show error traceback if any errors happen on any page. The `setUpClass()` class method will be executed at the beginning of all of the tests and the `tearDownClass()` class method will be executed after the tests have been run. In the middle, the testing will execute all the methods of the suite whose names start with `test`.

When we start testing, a new test database is created. In `setUpClass()`, we create a browser object, one location, and one superuser. Then, the `test_login_and_like()` method is executed, which opens the administration login page, finds the username field, types in the administrator's username, finds the password field, types in the administrator's password, finds the submit button, and clicks on it. Then, it waits a maximum of 10 seconds until a DOM element with the `.like-button` CSS class can be found on the page.

As you might remember from the *Implementing the Like widget* recipe in `Chapter 4`, *Templates and JavaScript*, our widget consists of two elements:

- A **Like** button
- A badge showing the total number of likes

If a button is clicked, your `Like` instance is either added or removed from the database by an Ajax call. Moreover, the badge count is updated to reflect the number of likes in the database.

Further in the test, we check what is the initial state of the button (whether it has an `.active` CSS class or not), check the initial number of likes, and simulate a click on the button. We wait a maximum of 10 seconds until the count in the badge changes. Then, we check whether the count in the badge matches the total likes for the location in the database. We will also check how the count in the badge has changed (increased). Lastly, we will simulate the click on the button again to switch back to the previous state.

Finally, the `tearDownClass()` method is called, which closes the browser and removes the location and the superuser from the test database.

See also

- The *Implementing the Like widget* recipe in `Chapter 4`, *Templates and JavaScript*
- The *Testing views with mock* recipe
- The *Testing API created using Django REST framework* recipe
- The *Ensuring test coverage* recipe

Testing APIs created using Django REST framework

You should already have an understanding of how to write unit and operational acceptance tests. In this recipe, we will go through **component interface testing** for the RESTful API that we created earlier in this book.

If you are not familiar with what a RESTful API is and how APIs are used, you can learn more at `http://www.restapitutorial.com/`.

Getting ready

Let's start with the `music` app from the *Using Django REST framework to create APIs* recipe in `Chapter 9`, *Importing and Exporting Data*.

How to do it...

To test RESTful APIs, perform the following steps:

1. Create a `tests` module in your `music` app. In the `tests` module, create a `test_api.py` file with the `SongTests` class. The class will have `setUpClass()` and `tearDownClass()` methods, as follows:

   ```
   # myproject/apps/music/tests/test_api.py
   from django.contrib.auth.models import User
   from django.urls import reverse
   ```

```python
from rest_framework import status
from rest_framework.test import APITestCase
from ..models import Song

class SongTests(APITestCase):
    @classmethod
    def setUpClass(cls):
        super().setUpClass()

        cls.superuser = User.objects.create_superuser(
            username="admin", password="admin",
             email="admin@example.com"
        )

        cls.song = Song.objects.create(
            artist="Lana Del Rey",
            title="Video Games - Remastered",
            url="https://open.spotify.com/track/5UOo694cVvj
              cPFqLFiNWGU?si=maZ7JCJ7Rb6WzESLXg1Gdw",
        )

        cls.song_to_delete = Song.objects.create(
            artist="Milky Chance",
            title="Stolen Dance",
            url="https://open.spotify.com/track/3miMZ2IlJ
              iaeSWo1DohXlN?si=g-xMM4m9S_yScOm02C2MLQ",
        )

    @classmethod
    def tearDownClass(cls):
        super().tearDownClass()

        cls.song.delete()
        cls.superuser.delete()
```

2. Add an API test checking the listing songs:

```python
def test_list_songs(self):
    url = reverse("rest_song_list")
    data = {}
    response = self.client.get(url, data, format="json")

    self.assertEqual(response.status_code, status.HTTP_200_OK)
    self.assertEqual(response.data["count"], Song.objects.count())
```

3. Add an API test checking the details of a single song:

```
def test_get_song(self):
    url = reverse("rest_song_detail", kwargs={"pk": self.song.pk})
    data = {}
    response = self.client.get(url, data, format="json")

    self.assertEqual(response.status_code, status.HTTP_200_OK)
    self.assertEqual(response.data["uuid"], str(self.song.pk))
    self.assertEqual(response.data["artist"], self.song.artist)
    self.assertEqual(response.data["title"], self.song.title)
    self.assertEqual(response.data["url"], self.song.url)
```

4. Add an API test checking for the successful creation of a new song:

```
def test_create_song_allowed(self):
    # login
    self.client.force_authenticate(user=self.superuser)

    url = reverse("rest_song_list")
    data = {
        "artist": "Capital Cities",
        "title": "Safe And Sound",
        "url": "https://open.spotify.com/track/40Fs0YrUGu
            wLNQSaHGVfqT?si=2OUawusIT-evyZKonT5GgQ",
    }
    response = self.client.post(url, data, format="json")

    self.assertEqual(response.status_code,
     status.HTTP_201_CREATED)

    song = Song.objects.filter(pk=response.data["uuid"])
    self.assertEqual(song.count(), 1)

    # logout
    self.client.force_authenticate(user=None)
```

5. Add a test that tries to create a song without authentication and failing, therefore:

```
def test_create_song_restricted(self):
    # make sure the user is logged out
    self.client.force_authenticate(user=None)

    url = reverse("rest_song_list")
    data = {
        "artist": "Men I Trust",
        "title": "Tailwhip",
        "url": "https://open.spotify.com/track/2Do0Osn4S
```

```
                       bUrz7Uay9ACTM?si=SC_MixNKSnuxNvQMf3yBBg",
       }
       response = self.client.post(url, data, format="json")

       self.assertEqual(response.status_code,
         status.HTTP_403_FORBIDDEN)
```

6. Add a test for checking the successful changing of a song:

```
def test_change_song_allowed(self):
       # login
       self.client.force_authenticate(user=self.superuser)

       url = reverse("rest_song_detail", kwargs=
        {"pk": self.song.pk})

       # change only title
       data = {
           "artist": "Men I Trust",
           "title": "Tailwhip",
           "url": "https://open.spotify.com/track/2DoO0sn4S
              bUrz7Uay9ACTM?si=SC_MixNKSnuxNvQMf3yBBg",
       }
       response = self.client.put(url, data, format="json")

       self.assertEqual(response.status_code, status.HTTP_200_OK)
       self.assertEqual(response.data["uuid"], str(self.song.pk))
       self.assertEqual(response.data["artist"], data["artist"])
       self.assertEqual(response.data["title"], data["title"])
       self.assertEqual(response.data["url"], data["url"])

       # logout
       self.client.force_authenticate(user=None)
```

7. Add a test checking for failed changes because of missing authentication:

```
def test_change_song_restricted(self):
       # make sure the user is logged out
       self.client.force_authenticate(user=None)

       url = reverse("rest_song_detail", kwargs=
        {"pk": self.song.pk})

       # change only title
       data = {
           "artist": "Capital Cities",
           "title": "Safe And Sound",
           "url": "https://open.spotify.com/track/40Fs0YrU
```

```
                    GuwLNQSaHGVfqT?si=2OUawusIT-evyZKonT5GgQ",
    }
    response = self.client.put(url, data, format="json")

    self.assertEqual(response.status_code,
      status.HTTP_403_FORBIDDEN)
```

8. Add a test checking for the failed deletion of a song:

```
def test_delete_song_restricted(self):
    # make sure the user is logged out
    self.client.force_authenticate(user=None)

    url = reverse("rest_song_detail", kwargs=
      {"pk": self.song_to_delete.pk})

    data = {}
    response = self.client.delete(url, data, format="json")

    self.assertEqual(response.status_code,
      status.HTTP_403_FORBIDDEN)
```

9. Add a test checking for the successful deletion of a song:

```
def test_delete_song_allowed(self):
    # login
    self.client.force_authenticate(user=self.superuser)

    url = reverse("rest_song_detail", kwargs=
      {"pk": self.song_to_delete.pk})

    data = {}
    response = self.client.delete(url, data, format="json")

    self.assertEqual(response.status_code,
      status.HTTP_204_NO_CONTENT)

    # logout
    self.client.force_authenticate(user=None)
```

10. Run the tests for the music app, as shown in the following:

```
(env)$ python manage.py test myproject.apps.music --
settings=myproject.settings.test
Creating test database for alias 'default'...
System check identified no issues (0 silenced).
........
----------------------------------------------------------------
```

```
---
Ran 8 tests in 0.370s

OK
Destroying test database for alias 'default'...
```

How it works...

This RESTful API test suite extends the `APITestCase` class. Once again, we have the `setUpClass()` and `tearDownClass()` class methods that will be executed before and after the different tests. Also, the test suite has a client attribute of the `APIClient` type, which can be used to simulate API calls. The client provides methods for all standard HTTP calls: `get()`, `post()`, `put()`, `patch()`, `delete()`, `head()`, and `options()`.

In our tests, we are using the `GET`, `POST`, and `DELETE` requests. Also, the client has methods to force the authentication of a user based on login credentials, a token, or a `User` object. In our tests, we are authenticating the third way: passing a user directly to the `force_authenticate()` method.

The rest of the code is self-explanatory.

See also

- The *Using Django REST framework to create APIs* recipe in `Chapter 9`, *Importing and Exporting Data*
- The *Testing views with mock* recipe
- The *Testing the user interface with Selenium* recipe
- The *Ensuring test coverage* recipe

Ensuring test coverage

Django allows the rapid prototyping and building of a project from idea to realization in a timely manner. But to make sure that your project is stable and production-ready, you should have tests for as many functionalities as possible. With test coverage, you can check how much of your project code is tested. Let's have a look at how you can do that.

Getting ready

Have some tests ready for your project.

Install the `coverage` utility in your virtual environment:

```
(env)$ pip install coverage~=5.0.1
```

How to do it...

This is how to check the test coverage of your project:

1. Create a `setup.cfg` configuration file for the coverage utility with the following content:

```
# setup.cfg
[coverage:run]
source = .
omit =
    media/*
    static/*
    tmp/*
    drivers/*
    locale/*
    myproject/site_static/*
    myprojext/templates/*
```

2. Make sure to have these lines in the `.gitignore` file if you are using Git version control:

```
# .gitignore
htmlcov/
.coverage
.coverage.*
coverage.xml
*.cover
```

3. Create a shell script, `run_tests_with_coverage.sh`, with the commands to run tests with coverage and report the results:

```
# run_tests_with_coverage.sh
#!/usr/bin/env bash
coverage erase
coverage run manage.py test --settings=myproject.settings.test
coverage report
```

4. Add execution permissions for that script:

```
(env)$ chmod +x run_tests_with_coverage.sh
```

5. Run the script:

```
(env)$ ./run_tests_with_coverage.sh
Creating test database for alias 'default'...
System check identified no issues (0 silenced).
...........
----------------------------------------------------------------
---
Ran 11 tests in 12.940s

OK
Destroying test database for alias 'default'...
Name Stmts Miss Cover
----------------------------------------------------------------
------------------------------
manage.py 12 2 83%
myproject/__init__.py 0 0 100%
myproject/apps/__init__.py 0 0 100%
myproject/apps/core/__init__.py 0 0 100%
myproject/apps/core/admin.py 16 10 38%
myproject/apps/core/context_processors.py 3 0 100%
myproject/apps/core/model_fields.py 48 48 0%
myproject/apps/core/models.py 87 29 67%
myproject/apps/core/templatetags/__init__.py 0 0 100%
myproject/apps/core/templatetags/utility_tags.py 171 135 21%

the statistics go on...

myproject/settings/test.py 5 0 100%
myproject/urls.py 10 0 100%
myproject/wsgi.py 4 4 0%
----------------------------------------------------------------
------------------------------
TOTAL 1363 712 48%
```

How it works...

The coverage utility runs the tests and checks how many lines of code are covered by tests. In our example, the tests we wrote covered 48% of the code. If project stability is important to you, when you have time, seek to get closer to 100%.

In the coverage configuration, we skipped the static assets, templates, and other non-Python files.

See also

- The *Testing views with mock* recipe
- The *Testing the user interface with Selenium* recipe
- The *Testing APIs created using Django REST framework* recipe

12
Deployment

In this chapter, we will cover the following recipes:

- Releasing a reusable Django app
- Deploying on Apache with mod_wsgi for the staging environment
- Deploying on Apache with mod_wsgi for the production environment
- Deploying on Nginx and Gunicorn for the staging environment
- Deploying on Nginx and Gunicorn for the production environment

Introduction

Once you have a working website or reusable app, you will want to make it public. Deploying websites is one of the most difficult activities of development with Django, because there are lots of moving parts that you have to tackle:

- Managing the web server
- Configuring the database
- Serving static and media files
- Processing the Django project
- Configuring caching
- Setting up email sending
- Managing domains
- Arranging background tasks and cron jobs
- Setting up continuous integration
- Other tasks, depending on your project's scale and complexity

In bigger teams, all those tasks are done by DevOps engineers and they require skills like deeply understanding networking and computer architecture, administering Linux servers, bash scripting, using vim, and so on.

Professional websites usually have **development**, **staging**, and **production** environments. Each of them has a specific purpose. Development environments are used for creating the project. The production environment is the server (or servers) on which your public website is hosted. The staging environment is a system technically analogous to production, but is used to check the new features and optimizations before publishing them.

Technical requirements

For working with the code of this chapter, you will need the latest stable version of Python, MySQL, or PostgreSQL, and a Django project with a virtual environment.

You can find all the code for this chapter at the `ch12` directory of the GitHub repository, at `https://github.com/PacktPublishing/Django-3-Web-Development-Cookbook-Fourth-Edition`.

Releasing a reusable Django app

The Django documentation has a tutorial on how to package your reusable apps so that they can be installed later, with pip, in any virtual environment. This can be viewed at `https://docs.djangoproject.com/en/3.0/intro/reusable-apps/`.

However, there is another (and arguably better) way to package and release a reusable Django app, using the tool, which creates templates for different coding projects, such as the new Django CMS website, the Flask website, or the jQuery plugin. One of the available project templates is `cookiecutter-djangopackage`. In this recipe, you will learn how to use it to distribute the reusable `likes` app.

Getting ready

Create a new project with a virtual environment and install `cookiecutter` there, as follows:

```
(env)$ pip install cookiecutter~=1.7.0
```

How to do it...

To release your `likes` app, follow these steps:

1. Start a new Django app project, as follows:

    (env)\$ cookiecutter
    https://github.com/pydanny/cookiecutter-djangopackage.git

    Or, since this is a GitHub-hosted `cookiecutter` template, we can use a shorthand syntax, as follows:

    (env)\$ cookiecutter gh:pydanny/cookiecutter-djangopackage

2. Answer the questions to create the app template, as follows:

    ```
    full_name [Your full name here]: Aidas Bendoraitis
    email [you@example.com]: aidas@bendoraitis.lt
    github_username [yourname]: archatas
    project_name [Django Package]: django-likes
    repo_name [dj-package]: django-likes
    app_name [django_likes]: likes
    app_config_name [LikesConfig]:
    project_short_description [Your project description goes here]:
    Django app for liking anything on your website.
    models [Comma-separated list of models]: Like
    django_versions [1.11,2.1]: master
    version [0.1.0]:
    create_example_project [N]:
    Select open_source_license:
    1 - MIT
    2 - BSD
    3 - ISCL
    4 - Apache Software License 2.0
    5 - Not open source
    Choose from 1, 2, 3, 4, 5 [1]:
    ```

    This will create a basic file structure for the releasable Django package, similar to the following:

    ```
    django-likes/
    ├── docs/
    │   ├── Makefile
    │   ├── authors.rst
    │   ├── conf.py
    │   ├── contributing.rst
    │   ├── history.rst
    │   ├── index.rst
    ```

```
│    ├── installation.rst
│    ├── make.bat
│    ├── readme.rst
│    └── usage.rst
├── likes/
│    ├── static/
│    │    ├── css/
│    │    │    └── likes.css
│    │    ├── img/
│    │    └── js/
│    │         └── likes.js
│    ├── templates/
│    │    └── likes/
│    │         └── base.html
│    └── test_utils/
│         ├── test_app/
│         │    ├── migrations/
│         │    │    └── __init__.py
│         │    ├── __init__.py
│         │    ├── admin.py
│         │    ├── apps.py
│         │    └── models.html
│         ├── __init__.py
│         ├── admin.py
│         ├── apps.py
│         ├── models.py
│         ├── urls.py
│         └── views.py
├── tests/
│    ├── __init__.py
│    ├── README.md
│    ├── requirements.txt
│    ├── settings.py
│    ├── test_models.py
│    └── urls.py
├── .coveragerc
├── .editorconfig
├── .gitignore
├── .travis.yml
├── AUTHORS.rst
├── CONTRIBUTING.rst
├── HISTORY.rst
├── LICENSE
├── MANIFEST.in
├── Makefile
├── README.rst
├── manage.py
├── requirements.txt
```

```
├──── requirements_dev.txt
├──── requirements_test.txt
├──── runtests.py
├──── setup.cfg
├──── setup.py*
└──── tox.ini
```

3. Copy the files of the `likes` app from the Django project where you are using it to the `django-likes/likes` directory. In cases where `cookiecutter` created the same files, the content will need to be merged, rather than overwritten. For instance, the `likes/__init__.py` file will need to contain a version string to work properly with `setup.py` in later steps, as follows:

```
# django-likes/likes/__init__.py
__version__ = '0.1.0'
```

4. Rework dependencies so that there are no imports from the Django project and all the used functions and classes are inside of this app. For example, in the `likes` app, we have a dependency upon some mixins in the `core` app. We'll need to copy the related code directly into the files in the `django-likes` app.

> Alternatively, if there is a lot of dependent code, we can release the `core` app as an uncoupled package, but then we have to maintain it separately.

5. Add the reusable app project to the Git repository in GitHub, using the `repo_name` that was entered previously.

6. Explore the different files and complete the license, README, documentation, configuration, and other files.

7. Make sure that the app passes the `cookiecutter` template tests:

```
(env)$ pip install -r requirements_test.txt
(env)$ python runtests.py
Creating test database for alias 'default'...
System check identified no issues (0 silenced).
.
-------------------------------------------------------------------
---
Ran 1 test in 0.001s

OK
Destroying test database for alias 'default'...
```

8. If your package is closed source, create a shareable release as a ZIP archive, as follows:

```
(env)$ python setup.py sdist
```

This will create a `django-likes/dist/django-likes-0.1.0.tar.gz` file that can then be installed or uninstalled into a virtual environment of any project with `pip`, as follows:

```
(env)$ pip install django-likes-0.1.0.tar.gz
(env)$ pip uninstall django-likes
```

9. If your package is open source, you can register and publish your app to the Python Package Index (PyPI):

```
(env)$ python setup.py register
(env)$ python setup.py publish
```

10. Also, to spread the word, add your app to the Django packages by submitting a form at `https://www.djangopackages.com/packages/add/`.

How it works...

Cookiecutter fills in the requested data in different parts of the Django app project template, using the defaults given in **[square brackets]** if you simply press *Enter* without entering anything. As a result, you get the `setup.py` file ready for distribution to the Python Package Index, Sphinx documentation, MIT as the default license, the universal text editor configuration for the project, static files and templates included in your app, and other goodies.

See also

- The *Creating a project file structure* recipe in `Chapter 1`, *Getting Started with Django 3.0*
- The *Working with Docker containers for Django, Gunicorn, Nginx, and PostgreSQL* recipe in `Chapter 1`, *Getting Started with Django 3.0*
- The *Handling project dependencies with pip* recipe in `Chapter 1`, *Getting Started with Django 3.0*
- The *Implementing the Like widget* recipe in `Chapter 4`, *Templates and JavaScript*
- The *Testing views with mock* recipe in `Chapter 11`, *Testing*

Deploying on Apache with mod_wsgi for the staging environment

In this recipe, I will show you how to create a script for deploying your project to a staging environment on a virtual machine on your computer. The project will be using the **Apache** web server with the **mod_wsgi** module. For the installation, we are going to use **Ansible**, **Vagrant**, and **VirtualBox**. As mentioned before, there are lots of details to take care of and usually, several days are necessary to develop an optimal deployment script similar to this.

Getting ready

Go through the deployment checklist and make sure that your configuration passes all security recommendations, as listed at `https://docs.djangoproject.com/en/3.0/howto/deployment/checklist/`. At least make sure that your project configuration doesn't raise warnings when you run the following:

```
(env)$ python manage.py check --deploy --
settings=myproject.settings.staging
```

Install the latest stable versions of Ansible, Vagrant, and VirtualBox. You can get them from the following official websites:

- **Ansible**: `https://docs.ansible.com/ansible/latest/installation_guide/intro_installation.html`
- **VirtualBox**: `https://www.virtualbox.org/wiki/Downloads`
- **Vagrant**: `https://www.vagrantup.com/downloads.html`

On macOS X, you can install all of them with **HomeBrew**:

```
$ brew install ansible
$ brew cask install virtualbox
$ brew cask install vagrant
```

How to do it...

First of all, we'll need to create some configuration templates for different services used on the server. Both staging and production deployment procedures will be using them:

1. In your Django project, create a `deployment` directory and, inside of it, create an `ansible_templates` directory.

2. Create a Jinja template file for time zone configuration:

   ```
   {# deployment/ansible_templates/timezone.j2 #}
   {{ timezone }}
   ```

3. Create a Jinja template file for Apache domain configuration before setting up the SSL certificates:

   ```
   {# deployment/ansible_templates/apache_site-pre.conf.j2 #}
   <VirtualHost *:80>
       ServerName {{ domain_name }}
       ServerAlias {{ domain_name }} www.{{ domain_name }}

       DocumentRoot {{ project_root }}/public_html
       DirectoryIndex index.html

       ErrorLog ${APACHE_LOG_DIR}/error.log
       CustomLog ${APACHE_LOG_DIR}/access.log combined

       AliasMatch ^/.well-known/(.*) "/var/www/letsencrypt/$1"

       <Directory "/var/www/letsencrypt">
           Require all granted
       </Directory>

       <Directory "/">
           Require all granted
       </Directory>

   </VirtualHost>
   ```

4. Create a Jinja template file

   `deployment/ansible_templates/apache_site.conf.j2` for Apache domain configuration also including SSL certificates. For this file, copy the content from `https://raw.githubusercontent.com/PacktPublishing/Django-3-Web-Development-Cookbook-Fourth-Edition/master/ch12/myproject_virtualenv/src/django-myproject/deployment-apache/ansible_templates/apache_site.conf.j2`

5. Create a template for the PostgreSQL configuration file

   `deployment/ansible_templates/postgresql.j2` with content from `https://github.com/postgres/postgres/blob/REL_10_STABLE/src/backend/utils/misc/postgresql.conf.sample`. Later you can tweak the configuration there to match your server needs.

6. Create a template for the PostgreSQL permissions configuration file (currently, it is very permissive, but you can tweak it later according to your needs):

```
{# deployment/ansible_templates/pg_hba.j2 #}
# TYPE  DATABASE        USER            CIDR-ADDRESS        METHOD
local   all             all                                 ident
host    all             all             ::0/0               md5
host    all             all             0.0.0.0/32          md5
host    {{ db_name }}   {{ db_user }}   127.0.0.1/32        md5
```

7. Create a template for the Postfix email server configuration:

```
{# deployment/ansible_templates/postfix.j2 #}
# See /usr/share/postfix/main.cf.dist for a commented, more
# complete version


# Debian specific:  Specifying a file name will cause the first
# line of that file to be used as the name.  The Debian default
# is /etc/mailname.
# myorigin = /etc/mailname

smtpd_banner = $myhostname ESMTP $mail_name (Ubuntu)
biff = no

# appending .domain is the MUA's job.
append_dot_mydomain = no

# Uncomment the next line to generate "delayed mail" warnings
# delay_warning_time = 4h

readme_directory = no

# TLS parameters
```

```
smtpd_tls_cert_file=/etc/ssl/certs/ssl-cert-snakeoil.pem
smtpd_tls_key_file=/etc/ssl/private/ssl-cert-snakeoil.key
smtpd_use_tls=yes
smtpd_tls_session_cache_database =
btree:${data_directory}/smtpd_scache
smtp_tls_session_cache_database =
btree:${data_directory}/smtp_scache

# See /usr/share/doc/postfix/TLS_README.gz in the postfix-doc
# package for information on enabling SSL in
# the smtp client.

smtpd_relay_restrictions = permit_mynetworks
permit_sasl_authenticated defer_unauth_destination
myhostname = {{ domain_name }}
alias_maps = hash:/etc/aliases
alias_database = hash:/etc/aliases
mydestination = $myhostname, localhost, localhost.localdomain, ,
 localhost
relayhost =
mynetworks = 127.0.0.0/8 [::ffff:127.0.0.0]/104 [::1]/128
mailbox_size_limit = 0
recipient_delimiter = +
inet_interfaces = all
inet_protocols = all
virtual_alias_domains = {{ domain_name }}
virtual_alias_maps = hash:/etc/postfix/virtual
```

8. Create a template for the email forwarding configuration:

```
{# deployment/ansible_templates/virtual.j2 #}
# /etc/postfix/virtual

hello@{{ domain_name }} admin@example.com
@{{ domain_name }} admin@example.com
```

9. Create a template for the memcached configuration:

```
{# deployment/ansible_templates/memcached.j2 #}
# memcached default config file
# 2003 - Jay Bonci <jaybonci@debian.org>
# This configuration file is read by the start-memcached script
# provided as part of the Debian GNU/Linux
# distribution.

# Run memcached as a daemon. This command is implied, and is not
# needed for the daemon to run. See the README.Debian that
```

```
# comes with this package for more information.
-d

# Log memcached's output to /var/log/memcached
logfile /var/log/memcached.log

# Be verbose
# -v

# Be even more verbose (print client commands as well)
# -vv

# Use 1/16 of server RAM for memcached
-m {{ (ansible_memtotal_mb * 0.0625) | int }}

# Default connection port is 11211
-p 11211

# Run the daemon as root. The start-memcached will default to
# running as root if no -u command is present
# in this config file
-u memcache

# Specify which IP address to listen on. The default is to
# listen on all IP addresses
# This parameter is one of the only security measures that
# memcached has, so make sure it's listening on
# a firewalled interface.
-l 127.0.0.1

# Limit the number of simultaneous incoming connections.
# The daemon default is 1024
# -c 1024

# Lock down all paged memory. Consult with the README and
# homepage before you do this
# -k

# Return error when memory is exhausted (rather than
# removing items)
# -M

# Maximize core file limit
# -r
```

10. Finally, create a Jinja template for the `secrets.json` file:

```
{# deployment/ansible_templates/secrets.json.j2 #}
{
    "DJANGO_SECRET_KEY": "{{ django_secret_key }}",
    "DATABASE_ENGINE": "django.contrib.gis.db.backends.postgis",
    "DATABASE_NAME": "{{ db_name }}",
    "DATABASE_USER": "{{ db_user }}",
    "DATABASE_PASSWORD": "{{ db_password }}",
    "EMAIL_HOST": "{{ email_host }}",
    "EMAIL_PORT": "{{ email_port }}",
    "EMAIL_HOST_USER": "{{ email_host_user }}",
    "EMAIL_HOST_PASSWORD": "{{ email_host_password }}"
}
```

Now, let's work on the Vagrant and Ansible scripts specific to the staging environment:

1. In the `.gitignore` file, add lines to ignore some Vagrant- and Ansible-specific files:

```
# .gitignore
# Secrets
secrets.json
secrets.yml

# Vagrant / Ansible
.vagrant
*.retry
```

2. Create two directories, `deployment/staging` and `deployment/staging/ansible`.

3. Create a `Vagrantfile` file there with the following script to set up a virtual machine with Ubuntu 18 and run the Ansible script in it:

```
# deployment/staging/ansible/Vagrantfile
VAGRANTFILE_API_VERSION = "2"

Vagrant.configure(VAGRANTFILE_API_VERSION) do |config|
  config.vm.box = "bento/ubuntu-18.04"
  config.vm.box_version = "201912.14.0"
  config.vm.box_check_update = false
  config.ssh.insert_key=false
  config.vm.provider "virtualbox" do |v|
    v.memory = 512
    v.cpus = 1
    v.name = "myproject"
  end
```

```
    config.vm.network "private_network", ip: "192.168.50.5"
    config.vm.provision "ansible" do |ansible|
      ansible.limit = "all"
      ansible.playbook = "setup.yml"
      ansible.inventory_path = "./hosts/vagrant"
      ansible.host_key_checking = false
      ansible.verbose = "vv"
      ansible.extra_vars = { ansible_python_interpreter:
      "/usr/bin/python3" }
    end
  end
```

4. Create a `hosts` directory containing a `vagrant` file with the following content:

   # deployment/staging/ansible/hosts/vagrant
   ```
   [servers]
   192.168.50.5
   ```

5. Create a `vars.yml` file there with the variables that will be used in the installation scripts and Jinja templates for configurations:

   # deployment/staging/ansible/vars.yml
   ```
   ---
   # a unix path-friendly name (IE, no spaces or special characters)
   project_name: myproject

   user_username: "{{ project_name }}"

   # the base path to install to. You should not need to change this.
   install_root: /home

   project_root: "{{ install_root }}/{{ project_name }}"

   # the python module path to your project's wsgi file
   wsgi_module: myproject.wsgi

   # any directories that need to be added to the PYTHONPATH.
   python_path: "{{ project_root }}/src/{{ project_name }}"

   # the git repository URL for the project
   project_repo: git@github.com:archatas/django-myproject.git

   # The value of your django project's STATIC_ROOT settings.
   static_root: "{{ python_path }}/static"
   media_root: "{{ python_path }}/media"

   locale: en_US.UTF-8
   timezone: Europe/Berlin
   ```

```
domain_name: myproject.192.168.50.5.xip.io
django_settings: myproject.settings.staging

letsencrypt_email: ""
wsgi_file_name: wsgi_staging.py
```

6. Also, we'll need a `secrets.yml` file with secret values including passwords and authentication keys. First, create a `sample_secrets.yml` file that will have no sensitive information, but only the variable names, and then copy it to `secrets.yml` and fill in the secrets. The former file will be under version control, whereas the latter will be ignored:

   ```
   # deployment/staging/ansible/sample_secrets.yml
   # Django Secret Key
   django_secret_key: "change-this-to-50-characters-
     long-random-string"

   # PostgreSQL database settings
   db_name: "myproject"
   db_user: "myproject"
   db_password: "change-this-to-a-secret-password"
   db_host: "localhost"
   db_port: "5432"

   # Email SMTP settings
   email_host: "localhost"
   email_port: "25"
   email_host_user: ""
   email_host_password: ""

   # a private key that has access to the repository URL
   ssh_github_key: ~/.ssh/id_rsa_github
   ```

7. Now create an Ansible script (a so-called *playbook*) at `deployment/staging/ansible/setup.yml` for installing all the dependencies and configuring services. Copy the content for this file from `https://raw. githubusercontent.com/PacktPublishing/Django-3-Web-Development-Cookbook-Fourth-Edition/master/ch12/myproject_virtualenv/src/django-myproject/deployment-apache/staging/ansible/setup.yml`.

8. Then create another Ansible script at `deployment/staging/ansible/deploy.yml` for dealing with the Django project. Copy the content for this file from `https://raw.githubusercontent.com/PacktPublishing/Django-3-Web-Development-Cookbook-Fourth-Edition/master/ch12/myproject_virtualenv/src/django-myproject/deployment-apache/staging/ansible/deploy.yml`.

9. And create a bash script that you can execute to start the deployment:

```
# deployment/staging/ansible/setup_on_virtualbox.sh
#!/usr/bin/env bash
echo "=== Setting up the local staging server ==="
date

cd "$(dirname "$0")"
vagrant up --provision
```

10. Add execution permissions for the bash script and run it:

```
$ chmod +x setup_on_virtualbox.sh
$ ./setup_on_virtualbox.sh
```

11. If the script fails with errors, it's likely that the virtual machine needs to be rebooted for the changes to take effect. You can do that by connecting to the virtual machine via ssh, changing to the root user, and then rebooting as follows:

```
$ vagrant ssh
Welcome to Ubuntu 18.04.3 LTS (GNU/Linux 4.15.0-72-generic x86_64)

 * Documentation:  https://help.ubuntu.com
 * Management:     https://landscape.canonical.com
 * Support:        https://ubuntu.com/advantage

  System information as of Wed Jan 15 04:44:42 CET 2020

  System load:  0.21              Processes:           126
  Usage of /:   4.0% of 61.80GB   Users logged in:     1
  Memory usage: 35%               IP address for eth0: 10.0.2.15
  Swap usage:   4%                IP address for eth1: 192.168.50.5


0 packages can be updated.
0 updates are security updates.


*** System restart required ***

This system is built by the Bento project by Chef Software
More information can be found at https://github.com/chef/bento
Last login: Wed Jan 15 04:43:32 2020 from 192.168.50.1
vagrant@myproject:~$ sudo su
root@myproject:/home/vagrant#
reboot
Connection to 127.0.0.1 closed by remote host.
Connection to 127.0.0.1 closed.
```

12. To browse the Django project directories, `ssh` to the virtual machine and change the user to `myproject` as follows:

```
$ vagrant ssh
Welcome to Ubuntu 18.04.3 LTS (GNU/Linux 4.15.0-74-generic x86_64)
# ...
vagrant@myproject:~$ sudo su - myproject
(env) myproject@myproject:~$ pwd
/home/myproject
(env) myproject@myproject:~$ ls
commands db_backups logs public_html src env
```

How it works...

VirtualBox allows you to have multiple virtual machines on your computer with different operating systems. Vagrant is a tool allowing you to create those virtual machines and to download and install operating systems on them using a script. Ansible is a Python-based utility that reads instructions from a `.yaml` configuration file and executes them on a remote server.

The deployment scripts we have just written do the following:

- Create a virtual machine in VirtualBox and install Ubuntu 18 there
- Assign the IP of `192.168.50.5` to the virtual machine
- Set a hostname for the virtual machine
- Upgrade the Linux packages
- Set the localization settings for the server
- Install all Linux dependencies, including Python, Apache, PostgreSQL, Postfix, Memcached, and so on
- Create a Linux user and `home` directory for the Django project
- Create a virtual environment for the Django project
- Create the PostgreSQL database user and database
- Configure the Apache web server
- Install a self-signed SSL certificate
- Configure the Memcached caching service
- Configure the Postfix email server
- Clone the Django project repository
- Install Python dependencies
- Create the `secrets.json` file

- Migrate the database
- Collect static files
- Restart Apache

Now the Django website will be accessible
at `https://www.myproject.192.168.50.5.xip.io` and will show you a **Hello,
World!** page. Note that some browsers, such as Chrome, might not want to open a website
with a self-signed SSL certificate and will block it as a security measure.

 xip.io is a wildcard DNS service that points IP-specific subdomains to the
IP and allows you to use that for SSL certificates or other website features
that require a domain.

If you want to experiment with different configurations or additional commands, it is
reasonable to do the changes incrementally in small steps. For some parts, you will need to
test things out directly on the virtual machine before converting the tasks to Ansible
instructions.

 For information how to use Ansible, check the official documentation
at `https://docs.ansible.com/ansible/latest/index.html`. It shows lots
of useful instruction examples for most use cases.

If you get any errors with any service, `ssh` to the virtual machine, switch to the root user,
and inspect the logs of that service. Googling the error messages will get you closer to a
working system.

To rebuild the virtual machine, use the following commands:

```
$ vagrant destroy
$ vagrant up --provision
```

See also

- The *Creating a virtual environment project file structure* recipe in `Chapter 1`, *Getting
  Started with Django 3.0*
- The *Handling project dependencies with pip* recipe in `Chapter 1`, *Getting Started with
  Django 3.0*
- The *Setting up STATIC_URL dynamically for Git users* recipe in `Chapter 1`, *Getting
  Started with Django 3.0*

- The *Deploying on Apache with mod_wsgi for the production environment* recipe
- The *Deploying on Nginx and Gunicorn for the staging environment* recipe
- The *Deploying on Nginx and Gunicorn for the production environment* recipe
- The *Creating and restoring PostgreSQL database backups* recipe in `Chapter 13,` *Maintenance*
- The *Setting up cron jobs for regular tasks* recipe in `Chapter 13`, *Maintenance*

Deploying on Apache with mod_wsgi for the production environment

Apache is one of the most popular web servers. It makes sense to deploy your Django project under Apache if you also have to run some services for server management, monitoring, analytics, blogging, e-commerce, and so on that require Apache on the same server.

In this recipe, we will continue working from the previous recipe and will implement an Ansible script (a *playbook*) to set up a production environment on **Apache** with the **mod_wsgi** module.

Getting ready

Make sure that your project configuration doesn't raise warnings when you run the following:

```
(env)$ python manage.py check --deploy --
settings=myproject.settings.production
```

Make sure you have the latest stable version of Ansible.

Choose a server provider and create a dedicated server there with root access via SSH with private and public key authentication. My provider of choice is DigitalOcean (`https://www.digitalocean.com/`), with which I created a dedicated server (Droplet) with Ubuntu 18. I can connect to the server by its IP, `142.93.167.30`, using a new SSH private and public key-pair, `~/.ssh/id_rsa_django_cookbook` and `~/.ssh/id_rsa_django_cookbook.pub` respectively.

Locally, we need to configure SSH connections by creating or modifying the
`~/.ssh/config` file with the following content:

```
# ~/.ssh/config
Host *
    ServerAliveInterval 240
    AddKeysToAgent yes
    UseKeychain yes

Host github
    Hostname github.com
    IdentityFile ~/.ssh/id_rsa_github

Host myproject-apache
    Hostname 142.93.167.30
    User root
    IdentityFile ~/.ssh/id_rsa_django_cookbook
```

Now, we should be able to connect to the dedicated server as the root user via SSH using
this command:

```
$ ssh myproject-apache
```

In your domain configuration, point the **DNS A record** of your domain to the IP address of
the dedicated server. In our case, we will just be
using `myproject.142.93.167.30.xip.io` to show how to set up the server with an SSL
certificate for the Django website.

> As mentioned before, xip.io is a wildcard DNS service that points IP-
> specific subdomains to the IP and allows you to use that for SSL
> certificates or other website features that require a domain.

How to do it...

To create a deployment script for production, perform these steps:

1. Make sure to have the `deployment/ansible_templates` directory with the
   Jinja templates for service configuration that we created in the previous *Deploying
   on Apache with mod_wsgi for the staging environment* recipe.
2. **Create the** `deployment/production` **and** `deployment/production/ansible`
   directories for the Ansible scripts.

3. There, create a `hosts` directory with a `remote` file containing the following content:

```
# deployment/production/ansible/hosts/remote
[servers]
myproject-apache

[servers:vars]
ansible_python_interpreter=/usr/bin/python3
```

4. Create a `vars.yml` file there with the variables that will be used in the installation scripts and Jinja templates for configurations:

```
# deployment/production/ansible/vars.yml
---
# a unix path-friendly name (IE, no spaces or special characters)
project_name: myproject

user_username: "{{ project_name }}"

# the base path to install to. You should not need to change this.
install_root: /home

project_root: "{{ install_root }}/{{ project_name }}"

# the python module path to your project's wsgi file
wsgi_module: myproject.wsgi

# any directories that need to be added to the PYTHONPATH.
python_path: "{{ project_root }}/src/{{ project_name }}"

# the git repository URL for the project
project_repo: git@github.com:archatas/django-myproject.git

# The value of your django project's STATIC_ROOT settings.
static_root: "{{ python_path }}/static"
media_root: "{{ python_path }}/media"

locale: en_US.UTF-8
timezone: Europe/Berlin

domain_name: myproject.142.93.167.30.xip.io
django_settings: myproject.settings.production

# letsencrypt settings
letsencrypt_email: hello@myproject.com
wsgi_file_name: wsgi_production.py
```

5. Also, we'll need a `secrets.yml` file with secret values including passwords and authentication keys. First, create a `sample_secrets.yml` file that will have no sensitive information, but only the variable names, and then copy it to `secrets.yml` and fill in the secrets. The former file will be under version control whereas the latter will be ignored:

```
# deployment/production/ansible/sample_secrets.yml
# Django Secret Key
django_secret_key: "change-this-to-50-characters-
  long-random-string"

# PostgreSQL database settings
db_name: "myproject"
db_user: "myproject"
db_password: "change-this-to-a-secret-password"
db_host: "localhost"
db_port: "5432"

# Email SMTP settings
email_host: "localhost"
email_port: "25"
email_host_user: ""
email_host_password: ""

# a private key that has access to the repository URL
ssh_github_key: ~/.ssh/id_rsa_github
```

6. Now create an Ansible script (a *playbook*) at `deployment/production/ansible/setup.yml` for installing all the dependencies and configuring services. Copy the content for this file from `https://raw.githubusercontent.com/PacktPublishing/Django-3-Web-Development-Cookbook-Fourth-Edition/master/ch12/myproject_virtualenv/src/django-myproject/deployment-apache/production/ansible/setup.yml`.

7. Then create another Ansible script, `deployment/production/ansible/deploy.yml`, for dealing with the Django project. Copy the content for this file from `https://raw.githubusercontent.com/PacktPublishing/Django-3-Web-Development-Cookbook-Fourth-Edition/master/ch12/myproject_virtualenv/src/django-myproject/deployment-apache/production/ansible/deploy.yml`.

8. Create a bash script that you can execute to start the deployment:

```
# deployment/production/ansible/setup_remotely.sh
#!/usr/bin/env bash
echo "=== Setting up the production server ==="
date

cd "$(dirname "$0")"
ansible-playbook setup.yml -i hosts/remote
```

9. Add execution permissions for the bash script and run it:

```
$ chmod +x setup_remotely.sh
$ ./setup_remotely.sh
```

10. If the script fails with errors, it's likely that the dedicated server needs to be rebooted for the changes to take effect. You can do that by connecting to the server via ssh and rebooting as follows:

```
$ ssh myproject-apache
Welcome to Ubuntu 18.04.3 LTS (GNU/Linux 4.15.0-74-generic x86_64)

 * Documentation: https://help.ubuntu.com
 * Management: https://landscape.canonical.com
 * Support: https://ubuntu.com/advantage

System information as of Wed Jan 15 11:39:51 CET 2020

System load: 0.08 Processes: 104
Usage of /: 8.7% of 24.06GB Users logged in: 0
Memory usage: 35% IP address for eth0: 142.93.167.30
Swap usage: 0%

 * Canonical Livepatch is available for installation.
 - Reduce system reboots and improve kernel security. Activate at:
 https://ubuntu.com/livepatch

0 packages can be updated.
0 updates are security updates.


*** System restart required ***

Last login: Sun Jan 12 12:23:35 2020 from 178.12.115.146
root@myproject:~# reboot
Connection to 142.93.167.30 closed by remote host.
Connection to 142.93.167.30 closed.
```

11. Create another bash script just for updating the Django project:

```
# deployment/production/ansible/deploy_remotely.sh
#!/usr/bin/env bash
echo "=== Deploying project to production server ==="
date

cd "$(dirname "$0")"
ansible-playbook deploy.yml -i hosts/remote
```

12. Add execution permissions for this bash script:

```
$ chmod +x deploy_remotely.sh
```

How it works...

An Ansible script (a *playbook*) is idempotent. It means that you can execute it multiple times and you will always get the same result: an up-to-date dedicated server with a Django website installed and running. If you have any technical hardware issues with the server and have backups of the database and media files, you can relatively quickly install the same configuration on another dedicated server.

The production deployment scripts do these things:

- Set a hostname for the virtual machine
- Upgrade the Linux packages
- Set the localization settings for the server
- Install all Linux dependencies including Python, Apache, PostgreSQL, Postfix, Memcached, and so on
- Create a Linux user and `home` directory for the Django project
- Create a virtual environment for the Django project
- Create the PostgreSQL database user and database
- Configure the Apache web server
- Install the *Let's Encrypt* SSL certificate
- Configure the Memcached caching service
- Configure the Postfix email server
- Clone the Django project repository
- Install Python dependencies
- Create the `secrets.json` file

- Migrate the database
- Collect static files
- Restart Apache

Run the `setup_remotely.sh` script when you need to install the services and dependencies for the first time. Later, you can use `deploy_remotely.sh` if you need to update just the Django project. As you can see, the installation is very similar to the one on the staging server, but, to keep it flexible and more tweakable, we saved it separately in the `deployment/production` directory.

Theoretically, you could skip the staging environment altogether, but it is more practical to try out the deployment procedure in a virtual machine at first rather than experimenting with installing directly on a remote server.

See also

- The *Creating a virtual environment project file structure* recipe in `Chapter 1`, *Getting Started with Django 3.0*
- The *Handling project dependencies with pip* recipe in `Chapter 1`, *Getting Started with Django 3.0*
- The *Setting up STATIC_URL dynamically for Git users* recipe in `Chapter 1`, *Getting Started with Django 3.0*
- The *Deploying on Apache with mod_wsgi for the staging environment* recipe
- The *Deploying on Nginx and Gunicorn for the staging environment* recipe
- The *Deploying on Nginx and Gunicorn for the production environment* recipe
- The *Creating and restoring PostgreSQL database backups* recipe
- The *Setting up cron jobs for regular tasks* recipe

Deploying on Nginx and Gunicorn for the staging environment

Apache with mod_wsgi is a good and stable approach for deployment, but when you need high performance, it is recommended to use **Nginx** with **Gunicorn** to serve your Django website. Gunicorn is a Python server running WSGI scripts. Nginx is a web server that parses domain configurations and passes requests to Gunicorn.

In this recipe, I will show you how to create a script for deploying your project to a staging environment on a virtual machine on your computer. To do this, we are going to use **Ansible**, **Vagrant**, and **VirtualBox**. As mentioned before, there are lots of details to bear in mind and several days are usually necessary to develop an optimal deployment script similar to this.

Getting ready

Go through the deployment checklist and make sure that your configuration passes all security recommendations at `https://docs.djangoproject.com/en/3.0/howto/deployment/checklist/`. At least make sure that your project configuration doesn't raise warnings when you run the following:

```
(env)$ python manage.py check --deploy --
  settings=myproject.settings.staging
```

Install the latest stable versions of Ansible, Vagrant, and VirtualBox. You can get them from the following official websites:

- **Ansible**: `https://docs.ansible.com/ansible/latest/installation_guide/intro_installation.html`
- **VirtualBox**: `https://www.virtualbox.org/wiki/Downloads`
- **Vagrant**: `https://www.vagrantup.com/downloads.html`

On macOS X you can install all of them with **HomeBrew**:

```
$ brew install ansible
$ brew cask install virtualbox
$ brew cask install vagrant
```

How to do it...

First of all, we'll need to create some configuration templates for the different services used on the server. These will be used by both deployment procedures: staging and production.

1. In your Django project, create a `deployment` directory and inside of it create an `ansible_templates` directory.

2. Create a Jinja template file for time zone configuration:

   ```
   {# deployment/ansible_templates/timezone.j2 #}
   {{ timezone }}
   ```

3. Create a Jinja template file for Nginx domain configuration before setting the SSL certificates:

```
{# deployment/ansible_templates/nginx-pre.j2 #}
server{
    listen 80;
    server_name {{ domain_name }};

    location /.well-known/acme-challenge {
        root /var/www/letsencrypt;
        try_files $uri $uri/ =404;
    }
    location / {
        root /var/www/letsencrypt;
    }
}
```

4. Create a Jinja template file at `deployment/ansible_templates/nginx.j2` for our Nginx domain configuration, including the SSL certificates. For this file, copy the content from `https://raw.githubusercontent.com/PacktPublishing/Django-3-Web-Development-Cookbook-Fourth-Edition/master/ch12/myproject_virtualenv/src/django-myproject/deployment-nginx/ansible_templates/nginx.j2`.

5. Create a template for the Gunicorn service configuration:

```
# deployment/ansible_templates/gunicorn.j2
[Unit]
Description=Gunicorn daemon for myproject website
After=network.target

[Service]
PIDFile=/run/gunicorn/pid
Type=simple
User={{ user_username }}
Group=www-data
RuntimeDirectory=gunicorn
WorkingDirectory={{ python_path }}
ExecStart={{ project_root }}/env/bin/gunicorn --pid
/run/gunicorn/pid --log-file={{ project_root }}/logs/gunicorn.log -
-workers {{ ansible_processor_count | int }} --bind 127.0.0.1:8000
{{ project_name }}.wsgi:application --env DJANGO_SETTINGS_MODULE={{
django_settings }} --max-requests 1000
ExecReload=/bin/kill -s HUP $MAINPID
ExecStop=/bin/kill -s TERM $MAINPID
PrivateTmp=true

[Install]
```

```
WantedBy=multi-user.target
```

6. Create a template for the PostgreSQL configuration file
   at `deployment/ansible_templates/postgresql.j2` with content
   from `https://github.com/postgres/postgres/blob/REL_10_STABLE/src/`
   `backend/utils/misc/postgresql.conf.sample`. Later you can tweak the
   configuration in this file.

7. Create a template for the PostgreSQL permissions configuration file (currently, it
   is very permissive, but you can tweak it later according to your needs):

```
{# deployment/ansible_templates/pg_hba.j2 #}
# TYPE    DATABASE          USER              CIDR-ADDRESS        METHOD
local     all               all                                  ident
host      all               all               ::0/0              md5
host      all               all               0.0.0.0/32         md5
host      {{ db_name }}     {{ db_user }}     127.0.0.1/32       md5
```

8. Create a template for the Postfix email server configuration:

```
{# deployment/ansible_templates/postfix.j2 #}
# See /usr/share/postfix/main.cf.dist for a commented, more
# complete version


# Debian specific:  Specifying a file name will cause the first
# line of that file to be used as the name.  The Debian default
# is /etc/mailname.
# myorigin = /etc/mailname

smtpd_banner = $myhostname ESMTP $mail_name (Ubuntu)
biff = no

# appending .domain is the MUA's job.
append_dot_mydomain = no

# Uncomment the next line to generate "delayed mail" warnings
#delay_warning_time = 4h

readme_directory = no

# TLS parameters
smtpd_tls_cert_file=/etc/ssl/certs/ssl-cert-snakeoil.pem
smtpd_tls_key_file=/etc/ssl/private/ssl-cert-snakeoil.key
smtpd_use_tls=yes
smtpd_tls_session_cache_database =
btree:${data_directory}/smtpd_scache
smtp_tls_session_cache_database =
```

```
btree:${data_directory}/smtp_scache

# See /usr/share/doc/postfix/TLS_README.gz in the postfix-doc
# package for information on enabling SSL
# in the smtp client.

smtpd_relay_restrictions = permit_mynetworks
permit_sasl_authenticated defer_unauth_destination
myhostname = {{ domain_name }}
alias_maps = hash:/etc/aliases
alias_database = hash:/etc/aliases
mydestination = $myhostname, localhost, localhost.localdomain, ,
 localhost
relayhost =
mynetworks = 127.0.0.0/8 [::ffff:127.0.0.0]/104 [::1]/128
mailbox_size_limit = 0
recipient_delimiter = +
inet_interfaces = all
inet_protocols = all
virtual_alias_domains = {{ domain_name }}
virtual_alias_maps = hash:/etc/postfix/virtual
```

9. Create a template for the email forwarding configuration:

```
{# deployment/ansible_templates/virtual.j2 #}
# /etc/postfix/virtual

hello@{{ domain_name }} admin@example.com
@{{ domain_name }} admin@example.com
```

10. Create a template for the memcached configuration:

```
{# deployment/ansible_templates/memcached.j2 #}
# memcached default config file
# 2003 - Jay Bonci <jaybonci@debian.org>
# This configuration file is read by the start-memcached script
# provided as part of the Debian GNU/Linux distribution.

# Run memcached as a daemon. This command is implied, and is not
# needed for the daemon to run. See the README.Debian
# that comes with this package for more information.
-d

# Log memcached's output to /var/log/memcached
logfile /var/log/memcached.log

# Be verbose
# -v
```

```
# Be even more verbose (print client commands as well)
# -vv

# Use 1/16 of server RAM for memcached
-m {{ (ansible_memtotal_mb * 0.0625) | int }}

# Default connection port is 11211
-p 11211

# Run the daemon as root. The start-memcached will default to
# running as root if no -u command is present
# in this config file
-u memcache

# Specify which IP address to listen on. The default is to
# listen on all IP addresses
# This parameter is one of the only security measures that
# memcached has, so make sure it's listening
# on a firewalled interface.
-l 127.0.0.1

# Limit the number of simultaneous incoming connections. The
# daemon default is 1024
# -c 1024

# Lock down all paged memory. Consult with the README and homepage
# before you do this
# -k

# Return error when memory is exhausted (rather than
# removing items)
# -M

# Maximize core file limit
# -r
```

11. Finally, create a Jinja template for the secrets.json file:

```
{# deployment/ansible_templates/secrets.json.j2 #}
{
    "DJANGO_SECRET_KEY": "{{ django_secret_key }}",
    "DATABASE_ENGINE": "django.contrib.gis.db.backends.postgis",
    "DATABASE_NAME": "{{ db_name }}",
    "DATABASE_USER": "{{ db_user }}",
    "DATABASE_PASSWORD": "{{ db_password }}",
    "EMAIL_HOST": "{{ email_host }}",
    "EMAIL_PORT": "{{ email_port }}",
    "EMAIL_HOST_USER": "{{ email_host_user }}",
```

```
                    "EMAIL_HOST_PASSWORD": "{{ email_host_password }}"
          }
```

Now let's work on the Vagrant and Ansible scripts specific to the staging environment:

1. In the `.gitignore` file, add the following lines to ignore some Vagrant- and Ansible-specific files:

```
# .gitignore
# Secrets
secrets.json
secrets.yml

# Vagrant / Ansible
.vagrant
*.retry
```

2. Create the `deployment/staging` and `deployment/staging/ansible` directories.

3. In the `deployment/staging/ansible` directory, create a `Vagrantfile` file with the following script to set up a virtual machine with Ubuntu 18 and run the Ansible script in it:

```
# deployment/staging/ansible/Vagrantfile
VAGRANTFILE_API_VERSION = "2"

Vagrant.configure(VAGRANTFILE_API_VERSION) do |config|
  config.vm.box = "bento/ubuntu-18.04"
  config.vm.box_version = "201912.14.0"
  config.vm.box_check_update = false
  config.ssh.insert_key=false
  config.vm.provider "virtualbox" do |v|
    v.memory = 512
    v.cpus = 1
    v.name = "myproject"
  end
  config.vm.network "private_network", ip: "192.168.50.5"
  config.vm.provision "ansible" do |ansible|
    ansible.limit = "all"
    ansible.playbook = "setup.yml"
    ansible.inventory_path = "./hosts/vagrant"
    ansible.host_key_checking = false
    ansible.verbose = "vv"
    ansible.extra_vars = { ansible_python_interpreter:
    "/usr/bin/python3" }
  end
end
```

4. Create a `hosts` directory with a `vagrant` file containing the following content:

```
# deployment/staging/ansible/hosts/vagrant
[servers]
192.168.50.5
```

5. Create a `vars.yml` file there with the variables that will be used in the installation scripts and Jinja templates for configurations:

```
# deployment/staging/ansible/vars.yml
---
# a unix path-friendly name (IE, no spaces or special characters)
project_name: myproject

user_username: "{{ project_name }}"

# the base path to install to. You should not need to change this.
install_root: /home

project_root: "{{ install_root }}/{{ project_name }}"

# the python module path to your project's wsgi file
wsgi_module: myproject.wsgi

# any directories that need to be added to the PYTHONPATH.
python_path: "{{ project_root }}/src/{{ project_name }}"

# the git repository URL for the project
project_repo: git@github.com:archatas/django-myproject.git

# The value of your django project's STATIC_ROOT settings.
static_root: "{{ python_path }}/static"
media_root: "{{ python_path }}/media"

locale: en_US.UTF-8
timezone: Europe/Berlin

domain_name: myproject.192.168.50.5.xip.io
django_settings: myproject.settings.staging

letsencrypt_email: ""
```

6. We'll also need a `secrets.yml` file containing secret values, such as passwords and authentication keys. First, create a `sample_secrets.yml` file that will have no sensitive information, but only the variable names, and then copy it to `secrets.yml` and fill in the secrets. The former file will be under version control whereas the latter will be ignored:

```
# deployment/staging/ansible/sample_secrets.yml
# Django Secret Key
django_secret_key: "change-this-to-50-characters-long-random-
string"

# PostgreSQL database settings
db_name: "myproject"
db_user: "myproject"
db_password: "change-this-to-a-secret-password"
db_host: "localhost"
db_port: "5432"

# Email SMTP settings
email_host: "localhost"
email_port: "25"
email_host_user: ""
email_host_password: ""

# a private key that has access to the repository URL
ssh_github_key: ~/.ssh/id_rsa_github
```

7. Now create an Ansible script (a *playbook*) at `deployment/staging/ansible/setup.yml` for installing all the dependencies and configuring services. Copy the content for this file from https://raw.githubusercontent.com/PacktPublishing/Django-3-Web-Development-Cookbook-Fourth-Edition/master/ch12/myproject_virtualenv/src/django-myproject/deployment-nginx/staging/ansible/setup.yml.

8. Then create another Ansible script at `deployment/staging/ansible/deploy.yml` for dealing with the Django project. Copy the content for this file from https://raw.githubusercontent.com/PacktPublishing/Django-3-Web-Development-Cookbook-Fourth-Edition/master/ch12/myproject_virtualenv/src/django-myproject/deployment-nginx/staging/ansible/deploy.yml.

9. And create a bash script that you can execute to start the deployment:

```
# deployment/staging/ansible/setup_on_virtualbox.sh
#!/usr/bin/env bash
echo "=== Setting up the local staging server ==="
date

cd "$(dirname "$0")"
vagrant up --provision
```

10. Add execution permissions for the bash script and run it:

```
$ chmod +x setup_on_virtualbox.sh
$ ./setup_on_virtualbox.sh
```

11. If the script fails with errors, it's likely that the virtual machine needs to be rebooted for the changes to take effect. You can do that by connecting to the virtual machine via ssh, changing to the root user, and then rebooting as follows:

```
$ vagrant ssh
Welcome to Ubuntu 18.04.3 LTS (GNU/Linux 4.15.0-72-generic x86_64)

 * Documentation:  https://help.ubuntu.com
 * Management:      https://landscape.canonical.com
 * Support:         https://ubuntu.com/advantage

  System information as of Wed Jan 15 04:44:42 CET 2020

  System load:   0.21            Processes:            126
  Usage of /:    4.0% of 61.80GB Users logged in:      1
  Memory usage:  35%             IP address for eth0:  10.0.2.15
  Swap usage:    4%              IP address for eth1:  192.168.50.5


0 packages can be updated.
0 updates are security updates.


*** System restart required ***

This system is built by the Bento project by Chef Software
More information can be found at https://github.com/chef/bento
Last login: Wed Jan 15 04:43:32 2020 from 192.168.50.1
vagrant@myproject:~$ sudo su
root@myproject:/home/vagrant#
reboot
Connection to 127.0.0.1 closed by remote host.
Connection to 127.0.0.1 closed.
```

12. To browse the Django project directories, `ssh` to the virtual machine and change the user to `myproject` as follows:

```
$ vagrant ssh
Welcome to Ubuntu 18.04.3 LTS (GNU/Linux 4.15.0-74-generic x86_64)
# ...
vagrant@myproject:~$ sudo su - myproject
(env) myproject@myproject:~$ pwd
/home/myproject
(env) myproject@myproject:~$ ls
commands db_backups logs public_html src env
```

How it works...

VirtualBox allows you to have multiple virtual machines on your computer with different operating systems. Vagrant is a tool that creates those virtual machines and lets you download and install operating systems on them. Ansible is a Python-based utility that reads instructions from a `.yaml` configuration file and executes them on a remote server.

The deployment scripts we have just written do these things:

- Create a virtual machine in a VirtualBox and installs Ubuntu 18 there
- Assign an IP of `192.168.50.5` to the virtual machine
- Set a hostname for the virtual machine
- Upgrade the Linux packages
- Set localization settings for the server
- Install all Linux dependencies, including Python, Nginx, PostgreSQL, Postfix, Memcached, and so on
- Create a Linux user and `home` directory for the Django project
- Create a virtual environment for the Django project
- Create the PostgreSQL database user and database
- Configure the Nginx web server
- Install the self-signed SSL certificate
- Configure the Memcached caching service
- Configure the Postfix email server
- Clone the Django project repository
- Install Python dependencies
- Set up Gunicorn
- Create the `secrets.json` file

- Migrate the database
- Collect static files
- Restart Nginx

Now the Django website will be accessible
at `https://www.myproject.192.168.50.5.xip.io` and will show you a **Hello, World!** page. Note that some browsers including Chrome might not want to open a website with a self-signed SSL certificate and will block it as a security measure.

 xip.io is a wildcard DNS service that points IP-specific subdomains to the IP and allows you to use that for SSL certificates or other website features that require a domain.

If you want to experiment with different configurations or additional commands, it is reasonable to do the changes incrementally in small steps. For some parts, you will need to test things out directly on the virtual machine before converting the tasks to Ansible instructions.

 For information about how to use Ansible, check the official documentation at `https://docs.ansible.com/ansible/latest/index.html`. It shows lots of useful instruction examples for most use cases.

If you get any errors with any service, `ssh` to the virtual machine, switch to the root user, and inspect the logs of that service. Googling the error messages will get you closer to a working system.

To rebuild the virtual machine, use the following commands:

```
$ vagrant destroy
$ vagrant up --provision
```

See also

- The *Creating a virtual environment project file structure* recipe in `Chapter 1`, *Getting Started with Django 3.0*
- The *Handling project dependencies with pip* recipe in `Chapter 1`, *Getting Started with Django 3.0*
- The *Setting up STATIC_URL dynamically for Git users* recipe in `Chapter 1`, *Getting Started with Django 3.0*

- The *Deploying on Apache with mod_wsgi for the staging environment* recipe
- The *Deploying on Apache with mod_wsgi for the production environment* recipe
- The *Deploying on Nginx and Gunicorn for the production environment* recipe
- The *Creating and restoring PostgreSQL database backups* recipe
- The *Setting up cron jobs for regular tasks* recipe

Deploying on Nginx and Gunicorn for the production environment

In this recipe, we will continue working from the previous recipe and will implement an **Ansible** script (playbook) to set up a production environment with **Nginx** and **Gunicorn**.

Getting ready

Check that your project configuration doesn't raise warnings when you run the following:

```
(env)$ python manage.py check --deploy --
settings=myproject.settings.production
```

Make sure to have the latest stable version of Ansible.

Choose a server provider and create a dedicated server there with root access via `ssh` by private and public key authentication. My provider of choice is DigitalOcean (`https://www.digitalocean.com/`). At DigitalOcean control panel, I created a dedicated server (Droplet) with Ubuntu 18. I can connect to the server by its IP of `46.101.136.102` using a new SSH private and public key pair, `~/.ssh/id_rsa_django_cookbook` and `~/.ssh/id_rsa_django_cookbook.pub` respectively.

Locally, we need to configure SSH connections by creating or modifying a `~/.ssh/config` file with the following content:

```
# ~/.ssh/config
Host *
    ServerAliveInterval 240
    AddKeysToAgent yes
    UseKeychain yes

Host github
    Hostname github.com
```

```
IdentityFile ~/.ssh/id_rsa_github

Host myproject-nginx
    Hostname 46.101.136.102
    User root
    IdentityFile ~/.ssh/id_rsa_django_cookbook
```

Now we should be able to connect to the dedicated server as the root user via `ssh` using this command:

$ ssh myproject-nginx

In your domain configuration, point the **DNS A record** of your domain to the IP address of the dedicated server. In our case, we will just be using `myproject.46.101.136.102.xip.io` to show how to set up the server with an SSL certificate for the Django website.

How to do it...

To create a deployment script for production, perform these steps:

1. Make sure to have a `deployment/ansible_templates` directory with the Jinja templates for service configuration that we created in the previous *Deploying on Nginx with Gunicorn for the staging environment* recipe.

2. Create the `deployment/production` and `deployment/production/ansible` directories for the Ansible scripts.

3. Create a `hosts` directory with a `remote` file containing the following content:

   ```
   # deployment/production/ansible/hosts/remote
   [servers]
   myproject-nginx

   [servers:vars]
   ansible_python_interpreter=/usr/bin/python3
   ```

4. Create a `vars.yml` file there with the variables that will be used in the installation scripts and Jinja templates for configurations:

   ```
   # deployment/production/ansible/vars.yml
   ---
   # a unix path-friendly name (IE, no spaces or special characters)
   project_name: myproject

   user_username: "{{ project_name }}"
   ```

```
# the base path to install to. You should not need to change this.
install_root: /home

project_root: "{{ install_root }}/{{ project_name }}"

# the python module path to your project's wsgi file
wsgi_module: myproject.wsgi

# any directories that need to be added to the PYTHONPATH.
python_path: "{{ project_root }}/src/{{ project_name }}"

# the git repository URL for the project
project_repo: git@github.com:archatas/django-myproject.git

# The value of your django project's STATIC_ROOT settings.
static_root: "{{ python_path }}/static"
media_root: "{{ python_path }}/media"

locale: en_US.UTF-8
timezone: Europe/Berlin

domain_name: myproject.46.101.136.102.xip.io
django_settings: myproject.settings.production

# letsencrypt settings
letsencrypt_email: hello@myproject.com
```

5. We'll also need a `secrets.yml` file with secret values such as passwords and authentication keys. First, create a `sample_secrets.yml` file that will have no sensitive information, but only the variable names, and then copy it to `secrets.yml` and fill in the secrets. The former file will be under version control, whereas the latter will be ignored:

```
# deployment/production/ansible/sample_secrets.yml
# Django Secret Key
django_secret_key: "change-this-to-50-characters-long-random-
string"

# PostgreSQL database settings
db_name: "myproject"
db_user: "myproject"
db_password: "change-this-to-a-secret-password"
db_host: "localhost"
db_port: "5432"

# Email SMTP settings
email_host: "localhost"
```

```
email_port: "25"
email_host_user: ""
email_host_password: ""

# a private key that has access to the repository URL
ssh_github_key: ~/.ssh/id_rsa_github
```

6. Now create an Ansible script (a *playbook*)
   at `deployment/production/ansible/setup.yml` for installing all the
   dependencies and configuring services. Copy the contents for this file
   from `https://raw.githubusercontent.com/PacktPublishing/Django-3-Web-Development-Cookbook-Fourth-Edition/master/ch12/myproject_virtualenv/src/django-myproject/deployment-nginx/production/ansible/setup.yml`.

7. Then create another Ansible script
   at `deployment/production/ansible/deploy.yml` for dealing with the
   Django project. Copy the contents for this file from `https://raw.githubusercontent.com/PacktPublishing/Django-3-Web-Development-Cookbook-Fourth-Edition/master/ch12/myproject_virtualenv/src/django-myproject/deployment-nginx/production/ansible/deploy.yml`.

8. Create a bash script that you can execute to start the deployment:

   ```
   # deployment/production/ansible/setup_remotely.sh
   #!/usr/bin/env bash
   echo "=== Setting up the production server ==="
   date

   cd "$(dirname "$0")"
   ansible-playbook setup.yml -i hosts/remote
   ```

9. Add execution permissions for the bash script and run it:

   ```
   $ chmod +x setup_remotely.sh
   $ ./setup_remotely.sh
   ```

10. If the script fails with errors, it's likely that the dedicated server needs to be
    rebooted for the changes to take effect. You can do that by connecting to the
    server via `ssh` and rebooting as follows:

    ```
    $ ssh myproject-nginx
    Welcome to Ubuntu 18.04.3 LTS (GNU/Linux 4.15.0-74-generic x86_64)

     * Documentation: https://help.ubuntu.com
     * Management:    https://landscape.canonical.com
     * Support:       https://ubuntu.com/advantage

    System information as of Wed Jan 15 11:39:51 CET 2020
    ```

```
System load: 0.08 Processes: 104
Usage of /: 8.7% of 24.06GB Users logged in: 0
Memory usage: 35% IP address for eth0: 142.93.167.30
Swap usage: 0%

* Canonical Livepatch is available for installation.
- Reduce system reboots and improve kernel security. Activate at:
https://ubuntu.com/livepatch

0 packages can be updated.
0 updates are security updates.


*** System restart required ***

Last login: Sun Jan 12 12:23:35 2020 from 178.12.115.146
root@myproject:~# reboot
Connection to 142.93.167.30 closed by remote host.
Connection to 142.93.167.30 closed.
```

11. Create another bash script just for updating the Django project:

```
# deployment/production/ansible/deploy_remotely.sh
#!/usr/bin/env bash
echo "=== Deploying project to production server ==="
date

cd "$(dirname "$0")"
ansible-playbook deploy.yml -i hosts/remote
```

12. Add execution permissions for the bash script:

```
$ chmod +x deploy_remotely.sh
```

How it works...

An Ansible script (a *playbook*) is idempotent. It means that you can execute it multiple times and you will always get the same results, an up-to-date dedicated server with Django website installed and running. If you have any technical hardware issues with the server and have backups of the database and media files, you can relatively quickly install the same configuration on another dedicated server.

The production deployment scripts do these things:

- Set a hostname for the virtual machine
- Upgrade the Linux packages
- Set the localization settings for the server
- Install all Linux dependencies such as Python, Nginx, PostgreSQL, Postfix, Memcached, and so on
- Create a Linux user and `home` directory for the Django projec
- Create a virtual environment for the Django project
- Create the PostgreSQL database user and database
- Configure the Nginx web server
- Install the *Let's Encrypt* SSL certificate
- Configure the Memcached caching service
- Configure the Postfix email server
- Clone the Django project repository
- Install Python dependencies
- Set up Gunicorn
- Create the `secrets.json` file
- Migrate the database
- Collect static files
- Restart Nginx

As you can see, the installation is very similar to the one on the staging server, but, to keep it flexible and more tweakable, we saved it separately in the `deployment/production` directory.

Theoretically, you could skip the staging environment altogether, but it is practical to try out the deployment procedure in a virtual machine rather than experimenting with installing directly on a remote server.

See also

- The *Creating a virtual environment project file structure* recipe in `Chapter 1`, *Getting Started with Django 3.0*
- The *Handling project dependencies with pip* recipe in `Chapter 1`, *Getting Started with Django 3.0*
- The *Setting up STATIC_URL dynamically for Git users* recipe in `Chapter 1`, *Getting Started with Django 3.0*
- The *Deploying on Apache with mod_wsgi for the staging environment* recipe
- The *Deploying on Apache with mod_wsgi for the production environment* recipe
- The *Deploying on Nginx and Gunicorn for the staging environment* recipe
- The *Creating and restoring PostgreSQL database backups* recipe
- The *Setting up cron jobs for regular tasks* recipe

13
Maintenance

In this chapter, we will cover the following topics:

- Creating and restoring MySQL database backups
- Creating and restoring PostgreSQL database backups
- Setting up cron jobs for regular tasks
- Logging events for further introspection
- Getting detailed error reporting via email

Introduction

At this point, you should have one or more Django projects developed and published. For the final steps of the development cycle, we will take a look at how to maintain your projects and monitor them for optimization. Stay tuned for the final bits and pieces!

Technical requirements

To work with the code of this chapter, you will need the latest stable version of Python, MySQL, or PostgreSQL database and a Django project with a virtual environment.

You can find all of the code for this chapter in the `ch13` directory of the GitHub repository: `https://github.com/PacktPublishing/Django-3-Web-Development-Cookbook-Fourth-Edition`.

Creating and restoring MySQL database backups

For website stability, it is very important to be able to recover from hardware failures and hacker attacks. Therefore, you should always make backups and make sure that they work. Your code and static files will usually reside in version control from which it can be recovered, but database and media files should be backed up regularly.

In this recipe, we will show you how to create backups for MySQL databases.

Getting ready

Make sure you have a working Django project running with a MySQL database. Deploy that project to a remote production (or staging) server.

How to do it...

To back up and restore your MySQL database, perform these steps:

1. Under the `commands` directory in your project's home directory, create a bash script: `backup_mysql_db.sh`. Start the script with variable and function definitions, as follows:

   ```
   /home/myproject/commands/backup_mysql_db.sh
   #!/usr/bin/env bash
   SECONDS=0
   export DJANGO_SETTINGS_MODULE=myproject.settings.production
   PROJECT_PATH=/home/myproject
   REPOSITORY_PATH=${PROJECT_PATH}/src/myproject
   LOG_FILE=${PROJECT_PATH}/logs/backup_mysql_db.log
   DAY_OF_THE_WEEK=$(LC_ALL=en_US.UTF-8 date +"%w-%A")
   DAILY_BACKUP_PATH=${PROJECT_PATH}/db_backups/${DAY_OF_THE_WEEK}.sql
   LATEST_BACKUP_PATH=${PROJECT_PATH}/db_backups/latest.sql
   error_counter=0

   echoerr() { echo "$@" 1>&2; }
   ```

```
cd ${PROJECT_PATH}
mkdir -p logs
mkdir -p db_backups

source env/bin/activate
cd ${REPOSITORY_PATH}

DATABASE=$(echo "from django.conf import settings;
print(settings.DATABASES['default']['NAME'])" | python manage.py
shell -i python)
USER=$(echo "from django.conf import settings;
print(settings.DATABASES['default']['USER'])" | python manage.py
shell -i python)
PASSWORD=$(echo "from django.conf import settings;
print(settings.DATABASES['default']['PASSWORD'])" | python
manage.py shell -i python)

EXCLUDED_TABLES=(
django_session
)

IGNORED_TABLES_STRING=''
for TABLE in "${EXCLUDED_TABLES[@]}"; do
    IGNORED_TABLES_STRING+=" --ignore-table=${DATABASE}.${TABLE}"
done
```

2. Then, add commands to create a dump of the database structure and data:

```
echo "=== Creating DB Backup ===" > ${LOG_FILE}
date >> ${LOG_FILE}

echo "- Dump structure" >> ${LOG_FILE}
mysqldump -u "${USER}" -p"${PASSWORD}" --single-transaction --no-
data "${DATABASE}" > "${DAILY_BACKUP_PATH}" 2>> ${LOG_FILE}
function_exit_code=$?
if [[ $function_exit_code -ne 0 ]]; then
    {
        echoerr "Command mysqldump for dumping database structure
          failed with exit code ($function_exit_code)."
        error_counter=$((error_counter + 1))
    } >> "${LOG_FILE}" 2>&1
fi

echo "- Dump content" >> ${LOG_FILE}
# shellcheck disable=SC2086
mysqldump -u "${USER}" -p"${PASSWORD}" "${DATABASE}"
${IGNORED_TABLES_STRING} >> "${DAILY_BACKUP_PATH}" 2>> ${LOG_FILE}
function_exit_code=$?
```

```
      if [[ $function_exit_code -ne 0 ]]; then
          {
              echoerr "Command mysqldump for dumping database content
              failed with exit code ($function_exit_code)."
              error_counter=$((error_counter + 1))
          } >> "${LOG_FILE}" 2>&1
      fi
```

3. Add commands to compress the database dump and to create a symbolic link, `latest.sql.gz`:

```
echo "- Create a *.gz archive" >> ${LOG_FILE}
gzip --force "${DAILY_BACKUP_PATH}"
function_exit_code=$?
if [[ $function_exit_code -ne 0 ]]; then
    {
        echoerr "Command gzip failed with exit code
        ($function_exit_code)."
        error_counter=$((error_counter + 1))
    } >> "${LOG_FILE}" 2>&1
fi

echo "- Create a symlink latest.sql.gz" >> ${LOG_FILE}
if [ -e "${LATEST_BACKUP_PATH}.gz" ]; then
    rm "${LATEST_BACKUP_PATH}.gz"
fi
ln -s "${DAILY_BACKUP_PATH}.gz" "${LATEST_BACKUP_PATH}.gz"
function_exit_code=$?
if [[ $function_exit_code -ne 0 ]]; then
    {
        echoerr "Command ln failed with exit code
        ($function_exit_code)."
        error_counter=$((error_counter + 1))
    } >> "${LOG_FILE}" 2>&1
fi
```

4. Finalize the script by logging the time taken to execute the previous commands:

```
duration=$SECONDS
echo "-------------------------------------------------" >> ${LOG_FILE}
echo "The operation took $((duration / 60)) minutes and $((duration
% 60)) seconds." >> ${LOG_FILE}
exit $error_counter
```

5. In the same directory, create a bash script, `restore_mysql_db.sh`, with the following content:

```
# home/myproject/commands/restore_mysql_db.sh
#!/usr/bin/env bash
SECONDS=0
PROJECT_PATH=/home/myproject
REPOSITORY_PATH=${PROJECT_PATH}/src/myproject
LATEST_BACKUP_PATH=${PROJECT_PATH}/db_backups/latest.sql
export DJANGO_SETTINGS_MODULE=myproject.settings.production

cd "${PROJECT_PATH}"
source env/bin/activate

echo "=== Restoring DB from a Backup ==="

echo "- Fill the database with schema and data"
cd "${REPOSITORY_PATH}"
zcat "${LATEST_BACKUP_PATH}.gz" | python manage.py dbshell

duration=$SECONDS
echo "----------------------------------------"
echo "The operation took $((duration / 60)) minutes and $((duration
% 60)) seconds."
```

6. Make both scripts executable:

```
$ chmod +x *.sh
```

7. Run the database backup script:

```
$ ./backup_mysql_db.sh
```

8. Run the database restoration script (with caution if in production):

```
$ ./restore_mysql_db.sh
```

How it works...

The backup script will create backup files under `/home/myproject/db_backups/` and will save the log at `/home/myproject/logs/backup_mysql_db.log`, similar to this:

```
=== Creating DB Backup ===
Fri Jan 17 02:12:14 CET 2020
- Dump structure
mysqldump: [Warning] Using a password on the command line interface can be
```

```
insecure.
- Dump content
mysqldump: [Warning] Using a password on the command line interface can be
insecure.
- Create a *.gz archive
- Create a symlink latest.sql.gz
------------------------------------------
The operation took 0 minutes and 2 seconds.
```

If the operation is successful, the script will return exit code 0; otherwise, the exit code will be the number of errors while executing the script. And the log file will show the error messages.

In the db_backups directory, there will be one compressed SQL backup with the day of the week, such as 0-Sunday.sql.gz, 1-Monday.sql.gz, and so on, and another file, a symbolic link actually, called latest.sql.gz. The weekday-based backup allows you to have recent backups of the last 7 days when set properly under cron jobs, and the symbolic link allows you to quickly or automatically transfer the latest backup to another computer via SSH.

Note that we take the database credentials from the Django settings and then use them in the bash script.

We are dumping all data except the sessions table because the sessions are temporary anyway and very memory-consuming.

When we run the restore_mysql_db.sh script, we get output like this:

```
=== Restoring DB from a Backup ===
- Fill the database with schema and data
mysql: [Warning] Using a password on the command line interface can be
insecure.
------------------------------------------
The operation took 0 minutes and 2 seconds.
```

See also

- The *Deploying on Apache with mod_wsgi for the production environment* recipe in Chapter 12, *Deployment*
- The *Deploying on Nginx and Gunicorn for the production environment* recipe in Chapter 12, *Deployment*

- The *Creating and restoring PostgreSQL database backups* recipe
- The *Setting up cron jobs for regular tasks* recipe

Creating and restoring PostgreSQL database backups

In this recipe, you will learn how to back up PostgreSQL databases and recover them in the event of hardware failure or hacker attacks.

Getting ready

Make sure to have a working Django project running with a PostgreSQL database. Deploy that project to a remote staging or production server.

How to do it...

To back up and restore your MySQL database, perform these steps:

1. Under the `commands` directory in your project's home directory, create a bash script, `backup_postgresql_db.sh`. Start the script with variable and function definitions, as follows:

   /home/myproject/commands/backup_postgresql_db.sh
   ```
   #!/usr/bin/env bash
   SECONDS=0
   PROJECT_PATH=/home/myproject
   REPOSITORY_PATH=${PROJECT_PATH}/src/myproject
   LOG_FILE=${PROJECT_PATH}/logs/backup_postgres_db.log
   DAY_OF_THE_WEEK=$(LC_ALL=en_US.UTF-8 date +"%w-%A")
   DAILY_BACKUP_PATH=${PROJECT_PATH}/db_backups/${DAY_OF_THE_WEEK}.bac
   kup
   LATEST_BACKUP_PATH=${PROJECT_PATH}/db_backups/latest.backup
   error_counter=0

   echoerr() { echo "$@" 1>&2; }

   cd ${PROJECT_PATH}
   mkdir -p logs
   mkdir -p db_backups
   ```

```
source env/bin/activate
cd ${REPOSITORY_PATH}

DATABASE=$(echo "from django.conf import settings;
print(settings.DATABASES['default']['NAME'])" | python manage.py
shell -i python)
```

2. Then, add a command to create a database dump:

```
echo "=== Creating DB Backup ===" > ${LOG_FILE}
date >> ${LOG_FILE}

echo "- Dump database" >> ${LOG_FILE}
pg_dump --format=p --file="${DAILY_BACKUP_PATH}" ${DATABASE}
function_exit_code=$?
if [[ $function_exit_code -ne 0 ]]; then
    {
        echoerr "Command pg_dump failed with exit code
        ($function_exit_code)."
        error_counter=$((error_counter + 1))
    } >> "${LOG_FILE}" 2>&1
fi
```

3. Add commands to compress the database dump and create a symbolic link, latest.backup.gz, to it:

```
echo "- Create a *.gz archive" >> ${LOG_FILE}
gzip --force "${DAILY_BACKUP_PATH}"
function_exit_code=$?
if [[ $function_exit_code -ne 0 ]]; then
    {
        echoerr "Command gzip failed with exit code
        ($function_exit_code)."
        error_counter=$((error_counter + 1))
    } >> "${LOG_FILE}" 2>&1
fi

echo "- Create a symlink latest.backup.gz" >> ${LOG_FILE}
if [ -e "${LATEST_BACKUP_PATH}.gz" ]; then
    rm "${LATEST_BACKUP_PATH}.gz"
fi
ln -s "${DAILY_BACKUP_PATH}.gz" "${LATEST_BACKUP_PATH}.gz"
function_exit_code=$?
if [[ $function_exit_code -ne 0 ]]; then
    {
        echoerr "Command ln failed with exit code
        ($function_exit_code)."
```

```
          error_counter=$((error_counter + 1))
      } >> "${LOG_FILE}" 2>&1
fi
```

4. Finalize the script by logging the time taken to execute the previous commands:

```
duration=$SECONDS
echo "------------------------------------------" >> ${LOG_FILE}
echo "The operation took $((duration / 60)) minutes and $((duration
% 60)) seconds." >> ${LOG_FILE}
exit $error_counter
```

5. In the same directory, create a bash script, `restore_postgresql_db.sh`, with the following content:

```
# /home/myproject/commands/restore_postgresql_db.sh
#!/usr/bin/env bash
SECONDS=0
PROJECT_PATH=/home/myproject
REPOSITORY_PATH=${PROJECT_PATH}/src/myproject
LATEST_BACKUP_PATH=${PROJECT_PATH}/db_backups/latest.backup
export DJANGO_SETTINGS_MODULE=myproject.settings.production

cd "${PROJECT_PATH}"
source env/bin/activate

cd "${REPOSITORY_PATH}"

DATABASE=$(echo "from django.conf import settings;
print(settings.DATABASES['default']['NAME'])" | python manage.py
shell -i python)
USER=$(echo "from django.conf import settings;
print(settings.DATABASES['default']['USER'])" | python manage.py
shell -i python)
PASSWORD=$(echo "from django.conf import settings;
print(settings.DATABASES['default']['PASSWORD'])" | python
manage.py shell -i python)

echo "=== Restoring DB from a Backup ==="

echo "- Recreate the database"
psql --dbname=$DATABASE --command='SELECT
pg_terminate_backend(pg_stat_activity.pid) FROM pg_stat_activity
WHERE datname = current_database() AND pid <> pg_backend_pid();'

dropdb $DATABASE

createdb --username=$USER $DATABASE
```

```
echo "- Fill the database with schema and data"
zcat "${LATEST_BACKUP_PATH}.gz" | python manage.py dbshell

duration=$SECONDS
echo "----------------------------------------"
echo "The operation took $((duration / 60)) minutes and $((duration
% 60)) seconds."
```

6. Make both scripts executable:

   ```
   $ chmod +x *.sh
   ```

7. Run the database backup script:

   ```
   $ ./backup_postgresql_db.sh
   ```

8. Run the database restoration script (with caution if in production):

   ```
   $ ./restore_postgresql_db.sh
   ```

How it works...

The backup script will create backup files under /home/myproject/db_backups/ and will save the log at /home/myproject/logs/backup_postgresql_db.log, similar to this:

```
=== Creating DB Backup ===
Fri Jan 17 02:40:55 CET 2020
- Dump database
- Create a *.gz archive
- Create a symlink latest.backup.gz
----------------------------------------
The operation took 0 minutes and 1 seconds.
```

If the operation is successful, the script will return exit code 0; otherwise, the exit code will be the number of errors while executing the script. And the log file will show the error messages.

In the db_backups directory, there will be one compressed SQL backup file with the day of the week, such as 0-Sunday.backup.gz, 1-Monday.backup.gz, and so on, and another file, a symbolic link actually, called latest.backup.gz. The weekday-based backup allows you to have recent backups of the last 7 days when set properly under cron jobs, and the symbolic link allows you to quickly or automatically transfer the latest backup to another computer via SSH.

Note that we take the database credentials from the Django settings and then use them in the bash script.

When we run the `restore_postgresql_db.sh` script, we get output like this:

```
=== Restoring DB from a Backup ===
- Recreate the database
 pg_terminate_backend
---------------------
(0 rows)

- Fill the database with schema and data
SET
SET
SET
SET
SET
 set_config
-----------

(1 row)

SET

...

ALTER TABLE
ALTER TABLE
ALTER TABLE
---------------------------------------
The operation took 0 minutes and 2 seconds.
```

See also

- The *Deploying on Apache with mod_wsgi for the production environment* recipe in `Chapter 12`, *Deployment*
- The *Deploying on Nginx and Gunicorn for the production environment* recipe in `Chapter 12`, *Deployment*
- The *Creating and restoring PostgreSQL database backups* recipe
- The *Setting up cron jobs for regular tasks* recipe

Setting up cron jobs for regular tasks

Usually, websites have some management tasks to perform in the background on a regular interval, such as once a week, once a day, or every hour. This can be achieved by using scheduled tasks, commonly known as cron jobs. These are scripts that run on the server after the specified period of time. In this recipe, we will create two cron jobs: one to clear sessions from the database and another to back up the database data. Both will be run every night.

Getting ready

To start, deploy your Django project to a remote server. Then, connect to the server by SSH. These steps are written with the assumption that you are using a virtual environment, but a similar cron job can be created for a Docker project, and it can even run directly within the app container. Code files are provided with the alternate syntax, and the steps are otherwise largely the same.

How to do it...

Let's create the two scripts and make them run regularly, via the following steps:

1. On the production or staging server, navigate to the project user's home directory where your env and src directories are located.
2. If these don't exist yet, create the commands, db_backups, and logs folders alongside the env directory, as follows:

   ```
   (env)$ mkdir commands db_backups logs
   ```

3. In the commands directory, create a clear_sessions.sh file. You can edit it with a terminal editor, such as vim or nano, adding the following content:

   ```
   # /home/myproject/commands/clear_sessions.sh
   #!/usr/bin/env bash
   SECONDS=0
   export DJANGO_SETTINGS_MODULE=myproject.settings.production
   PROJECT_PATH=/home/myproject
   REPOSITORY_PATH=${PROJECT_PATH}/src/myproject
   LOG_FILE=${PROJECT_PATH}/logs/clear_sessions.log
   error_counter=0

   echoerr() { echo "$@" 1>&2; }
   ```

```
cd ${PROJECT_PATH}
mkdir -p logs

echo "=== Clearing up Outdated User Sessions ===" > ${LOG_FILE}
date >> ${LOG_FILE}

source env/bin/activate
cd ${REPOSITORY_PATH}
python manage.py clearsessions >> "${LOG_FILE}" 2>&1
function_exit_code=$?
if [[ $function_exit_code -ne 0 ]]; then
    {
        echoerr "Clearing sessions failed with exit code
        ($function_exit_code)."
        error_counter=$((error_counter + 1))
    } >> "${LOG_FILE}" 2>&1
fi

duration=$SECONDS
echo "--------------------------------------------------" >> ${LOG_FILE}
echo "The operation took $((duration / 60)) minutes and $((duration
% 60)) seconds." >> ${LOG_FILE}
exit $err
or_counter
```

4. Make the `clear_sessions.sh` file executable, as follows:

    $ chmod +x *.sh

5. Let's assume that you are using PostgreSQL as the database for your project. Then, in the same directory, create a backup script following the instructions from the previous recipe, *Creating and restoring PostgreSQL database backups*.

6. Test the scripts to see whether they are executed correctly, by running them and then checking the `*.log` files in the logs directory, as follows:

    $ ./clear_sessions.sh
    $ ./backup_postgresql_db.sh

7. In your project's home directory on the remote server, create a `crontab.txt` file, with the following content:

    # /home/myproject/crontab.txt
    ```
    MAILTO=""
    HOME=/home/myproject
    PATH=/home/myproject/env/bin:/usr/local/sbin:/usr/local/bin:/usr/sb
    in:/usr/bin:/sbin:/bin:/usr/games:/usr/local/games:/snap/bin
    SHELL=/bin/bash
    ```

```
00 01 * * * /home/myproject/commands/clear_sessions.sh
00 02 * * * /home/myproject/commands/backup_postgresql_db.sh
```

8. Install the `crontab` tasks as the `myproject` user, as follows:

(env)$ crontab crontab.txt

How it works...

With the current setup, every night, `clear_sessions.sh` will be executed at 1:00 A.M., and `backup_postgresql_db.sh` will be executed at 2:00 A.M. The execution logs will be saved in `~/logs/clear_sessions.sh` and `~/logs/backup_postgresql_db.log`. If you get any errors, you should check these files for the traceback.

Every day, `clear_sessions.sh` will execute the `clearsessions` management command, which, as its name alludes to, clears expired sessions from the database, using the default database settings.

The database backup script is a little more complex. Every day of the week, it creates a backup file for that day, using a naming scheme of `0-Sunday.backup.gz`, `1-Monday.backup.gz`, and so on. Therefore, you will be able to restore data that was backed up 7 days ago or later.

The crontab file follows a specific syntax. Each line contains a specific time of day, indicated by a series of numbers, and then a task to run at that given moment. The time is defined in five parts, separated by spaces, as shown in the following list:

- Minutes, from 0 to 59
- Hours, from 0 to 23
- Days of the month, from 1 to 31
- Months, from 1 to 12
- Days of the week, from 0 to 7, where 0 is Sunday, 1 is Monday, and so on—7 is Sunday again

An asterisk (*) means that every time frame will be used. Therefore, the following task defines that `clear_sessions.sh` is to be executed at 1:00 A.M. every day of each month, every month, and every day of the week:

```
00 01 * * * /home/myproject/commands/clear_sessions.sh
```

You can learn more about the specifics of the crontab at `https://en.wikipedia.org/wiki/Cron`.

There's more...

We defined commands that will be executed at regular intervals, and the logging of results is also activated, but we can't yet tell whether a cron job was executed successfully or whether it failed unless we log into the server and check the logs every day manually. To solve the problem of monotonic manual labor, you can monitor the cron jobs automatically using the **Healthchecks** service (`https://healthchecks.io/`).

With Healthchecks, you would modify the crontab so that it pings a specific URL after each successful job is executed. If the script fails and exits with a non-zero code, Healthchecks will know that it was not executed successfully. Every day, you will get an overview of cron jobs and their execution statuses by email.

See also

- The *Deploying on Apache with mod_wsgi for the production environment* recipe in `Chapter 12`, *Deployment*
- The *Deploying on Nginx and Gunicorn for the production environment* recipe in `Chapter 12`, *Deployment*
- The *Creating and restoring MySQL database backups* recipe
- The *Creating and restoring PostgreSQL database backups* recipe

Logging events for further introspection

In the previous recipes, you could see how logging works for bash scripts. But you can also log events happening on your Django website, such as user registration, adding a product to a cart, buying tickets, bank transactions, sending SMS messages, server errors, and similar.

You should never log sensitive information such as user passwords or credit card details.

Also, use an analytics tool instead of Python logging for tracking overall website usage.

In this recipe, we will guide you through how to log structured information about your website into log files.

Getting ready

Let's start with the `likes` apps from the *Implementing the Like widget* recipe in `Chapter 4`, *Templates and JavaScript*.

In the virtual environment of a Django project, install `django-structlog`, as follows:

```
(env)$ pip install django-structlog==1.3.5
```

How to do it...

To set up structured logging in your Django website, follow these steps:

1. Add `RequestMiddleware` in your project's settings:

```python
# myproject/settings/_base.py
MIDDLEWARE = [
    "django.middleware.security.SecurityMiddleware",
    "django.contrib.sessions.middleware.SessionMiddleware",
    "django.middleware.common.CommonMiddleware",
    "django.middleware.csrf.CsrfViewMiddleware",
    "django.contrib.auth.middleware.AuthenticationMiddleware",
    "django.contrib.messages.middleware.MessageMiddleware",
    "django.middleware.clickjacking.XFrameOptionsMiddleware",
    "django.middleware.locale.LocaleMiddleware",
    "django_structlog.middlewares.RequestMiddleware",
]
```

2. Also in the same file, add Django logging configuration:

```python
# myproject/settings/_base.py
LOGGING = {
    "version": 1,
    "disable_existing_loggers": False,
    "formatters": {
        "json_formatter": {
            "()": structlog.stdlib.ProcessorFormatter,
            "processor": structlog.processors.JSONRenderer(),
        },
        "plain_console": {
            "()": structlog.stdlib.ProcessorFormatter,
```

```
                "processor": structlog.dev.ConsoleRenderer(),
            },
            "key_value": {
                "()": structlog.stdlib.ProcessorFormatter,
                "processor":
                structlog.processors.KeyValueRenderer(key_order=
                ['timestamp', 'level', 'event', 'logger']),
            },
        },
        "handlers": {
            "console": {
                "class": "logging.StreamHandler",
                "formatter": "plain_console",
            },
            "json_file": {
                "class": "logging.handlers.WatchedFileHandler",
                "filename": os.path.join(BASE_DIR, "tmp", "json.log"),
                "formatter": "json_formatter",
            },
            "flat_line_file": {
                "class": "logging.handlers.WatchedFileHandler",
                "filename": os.path.join(BASE_DIR, "tmp",
                "flat_line.log"),
                "formatter": "key_value",
            },
        },
        "loggers": {
            "django_structlog": {
                "handlers": ["console", "flat_line_file", "json_file"],
                "level": "INFO",
            },
        }
    }
}
```

3. Also, set `structlog` configuration there:

```
# myproject/settings/_base.py
structlog.configure(
    processors=[
        structlog.stdlib.filter_by_level,
        structlog.processors.TimeStamper(fmt="iso"),
        structlog.stdlib.add_logger_name,
        structlog.stdlib.add_log_level,
        structlog.stdlib.PositionalArgumentsFormatter(),
        structlog.processors.StackInfoRenderer(),
        structlog.processors.format_exc_info,
        structlog.processors.UnicodeDecoder(),
        structlog.processors.ExceptionPrettyPrinter(),
```

```
                    structlog.stdlib.ProcessorFormatter.wrap_for_formatter,
        ],
        context_class=structlog.threadlocal.wrap_dict(dict),
        logger_factory=structlog.stdlib.LoggerFactory(),
        wrapper_class=structlog.stdlib.BoundLogger,
        cache_logger_on_first_use=True,
    )
```

4. In `views.py` of the `likes` app, let's log the object that will be liked or unliked:

```python
# myproject/apps/likes/views.py
import structlog

from django.contrib.contenttypes.models import ContentType
from django.http import JsonResponse
from django.views.decorators.cache import never_cache
from django.views.decorators.csrf import csrf_exempt

from .models import Like
from .templatetags.likes_tags import liked_count

logger = structlog.get_logger("django_structlog")


@never_cache
@csrf_exempt
def json_set_like(request, content_type_id, object_id):
    """
    Sets the object as a favorite for the current user
    """
    result = {
        "success": False,
    }
    if request.user.is_authenticated and request.method == "POST":
        content_type = ContentType.objects.get(id=content_type_id)
        obj = content_type.get_object_for_this_type(pk=object_id)

        like, is_created = Like.objects.get_or_create(
            content_type=ContentType.objects.get_for_model(obj),
            object_id=obj.pk,
            user=request.user)
        if is_created:
            logger.info("like_created",
            content_type_id=content_type.pk,
            object_id=obj.pk)
        else:
            like.delete()
            logger.info("like_deleted",
```

```
            content_type_id=content_type.pk,
            object_id=obj.pk)

    result = {
        "success": True,
        "action": "add" if is_created else "remove",
        "count": liked_count(obj),
    }

    return JsonResponse(result)
```

How it works...

When visitors browse your website, the specific events will be logged in the `tmp/json.log` and `tmp/flat_line.log` files. `django_structlog.middlewares.RequestMiddleware` logs the start and end of the HTTP request processing. In addition, we are logging when a `Like` instance is created or deleted.

The `json.log` file contains logs in JSON format. That means that you can programmatically parse, inspect, and analyze them:

```
{"request_id": "ad0ef355-77ef-4474-a91a-2d9549a0e15d", "user_id": 1, "ip":
"127.0.0.1", "request": "<WSGIRequest: POST
'/en/likes/7/1712dfe4-2e77-405c-aa9b-bfa64a1abe98/'>", "user_agent":
"Mozilla/5.0 (Macintosh; Intel Mac OS X 10_15_2) AppleWebKit/537.36 (KHTML,
like Gecko) Chrome/79.0.3945.130 Safari/537.36", "event":
"request_started", "timestamp": "2020-01-18T04:27:00.556135Z", "logger":
"django_structlog.middlewares.request", "level": "info"}
{"request_id": "ad0ef355-77ef-4474-a91a-2d9549a0e15d", "user_id": 1, "ip":
"127.0.0.1", "content_type_id": 7, "object_id": "UUID('1712dfe4-2e77-405c-
aa9b-bfa64a1abe98')", "event": "like_created", "timestamp":
"2020-01-18T04:27:00.602640Z", "logger": "django_structlog", "level":
"info"}
{"request_id": "ad0ef355-77ef-4474-a91a-2d9549a0e15d", "user_id": 1, "ip":
"127.0.0.1", "code": 200, "request": "<WSGIRequest: POST
'/en/likes/7/1712dfe4-2e77-405c-aa9b-bfa64a1abe98/'>", "event":
"request_finished", "timestamp": "2020-01-18T04:27:00.604577Z", "logger":
"django_structlog.middlewares.request", "level": "info"}
```

The `flat_line.log` file contains the logs in a shorter format, which might be easier to read manually:

```
(env)$ tail -3 tmp/flat_line.log
timestamp='2020-01-18T04:27:03.437759Z' level='info'
event='request_started' logger='django_structlog.middlewares.request'
request_id='a74808ff-c682-4336-aeb9-f043f11a7316' user_id=1 ip='127.0.0.1'
request=<WSGIRequest: POST '/en/likes/7/1712dfe4-2e77-405c-aa9b-
bfa64a1abe98/'> user_agent='Mozilla/5.0 (Macintosh; Intel Mac OS X 10_15_2)
AppleWebKit/537.36 (KHTML, like Gecko) Chrome/79.0.3945.130 Safari/537.36'
timestamp='2020-01-18T04:27:03.489198Z' level='info' event='like_deleted'
logger='django_structlog' request_id='a74808ff-c682-4336-aeb9-f043f11a7316'
user_id=1 ip='127.0.0.1' content_type_id=7
object_id=UUID('1712dfe4-2e77-405c-aa9b-bfa64a1abe98')
timestamp='2020-01-18T04:27:03.491927Z' level='info'
event='request_finished' logger='django_structlog.middlewares.request'
request_id='a74808ff-c682-4336-aeb9-f043f11a7316' user_id=1 ip='127.0.0.1'
code=200 request=<WSGIRequest: POST '/en/likes/7/1712dfe4-2e77-405c-aa9b-
bfa64a1abe98/'>
```

See also

- The *Creating and restoring MySQL database backups* recipe
- The *Creating and restoring PostgreSQL database backups* recipe
- The *Setting up cron jobs for regular tasks* recipe

Getting detailed error reporting via email

To perform system logging, Django uses Python's built-in logging module or the `structlog` module mentioned in the previous recipe. The default Django configuration seems to be quite complex. In this recipe, you will learn how to tweak it to send error emails with complete HTML, similar to what is provided by Django in the DEBUG mode when an error happens.

Getting ready

Locate the Django project in your virtual environment.

How to do it...

The following procedure will send detailed emails about errors to you:

1. If you do not already have `LOGGING` settings set up for your project, set those up first. Find the Django logging utilities file, available at `env/lib/python3.7/site-packages/django/utils/log.py`. Copy the `DEFAULT_LOGGING` dictionary to your project's settings as the `LOGGING` dictionary.

2. Add the `include_html` setting to the `mail_admins` handler. The result of the first two steps should be something like the following:

```python
# myproject/settings/production.py
LOGGING = {
    'version': 1,
    'disable_existing_loggers': False,
    'filters': {
        'require_debug_false': {
            '()': 'django.utils.log.RequireDebugFalse',
        },
        'require_debug_true': {
            '()': 'django.utils.log.RequireDebugTrue',
        },
    },
    'formatters': {
        'django.server': {
            '()': 'django.utils.log.ServerFormatter',
            'format': '[{server_time}] {message}',
            'style': '{',
        }
    },
    'handlers': {
        'console': {
            'level': 'INFO',
            'filters': ['require_debug_true'],
            'class': 'logging.StreamHandler',
        },
        'django.server': {
            'level': 'INFO',
            'class': 'logging.StreamHandler',
            'formatter': 'django.server',
        },
        'mail_admins': {
            'level': 'ERROR',
            'filters': ['require_debug_false'],
            'class': 'django.utils.log.AdminEmailHandler',
```

```
                    'include_html': True,
            }
    },
    'loggers': {
        'django': {
            'handlers': ['console', 'mail_admins'],
            'level': 'INFO',
        },
        'django.server': {
            'handlers': ['django.server'],
            'level': 'INFO',
            'propagate': False,
        },
    }
}
```

How it works...

The logging configuration consists of four parts: loggers, handlers, filters, and formatters. The following list describes them:

- **Loggers** are entry points into the logging system. Each logger can have a log level: DEBUG, INFO, WARNING, ERROR, or CRITICAL. When a message is written to the logger, the log level of the message is compared with the logger's level. If it meets or exceeds the log level of the logger, it will be further processed by a handler. Otherwise, the message will be ignored.

- **Handlers** are engines that define what happens to each message in the logger. They can be written to a console, sent by email to the administrator, saved to a log file, sent to the Sentry error-logging service, and so on. In our case, we set the include_html parameter for the mail_admins handler, as we want the full HTML with traceback and local variables for the error messages that happen in our Django project.

- **Filters** provide additional control over the messages that are passed from the loggers to handlers. For example, in our case, the emails will only be sent when the DEBUG mode is set to false.

- **Formatters** are used to define how to render a log message as a string. They are not used in this example; however, for more information about logging, you can refer to the official documentation at https://docs.djangoproject.com/en/3.0/topics/logging/.

There's more...

The configuration we have just defined will send emails about each server error that happens on your website. If you have high traffic and, let's say, the database crashes, you will get tons of emails that will flood your inbox or even hang your email server.

To avoid such problems, you can use Sentry (`https://sentry.io/for/python/`). It tracks all server errors at their server and sends only one notification email to you for each error type.

See also

- The *Deploying on Apache with mod_wsgi for the production environment* recipe in `Chapter 12`, *Deployment*
- The *Deploying on Nginx and Gunicorn for the production environment* recipe in `Chapter 12`, *Deployment*
- The *Logging events for further introspection* recipe

Other Books You May Enjoy

If you enjoyed this book, you may be interested in these other books by Packt:

Django Design Patterns and Best Practices - Second Edition
Arun Ravindran

ISBN: 978-1-78883-134-5

- Make use of common design patterns to help you write better code
- Implement best practices and idioms in this rapidly evolving framework
- Deal with legacy code and debugging
- Use asynchronous tools such as Celery, Channels, and asyncio
- Use patterns while designing API interfaces with the Django REST Framework
- Reduce the maintenance burden with well-tested, cleaner code
- Host, deploy, and secure your Django projects

Hands-On RESTful Python Web Services - Second Edition
Gaston C. Hillar

ISBN: 978-1-78953-222-7

- Select the most appropriate framework based on requirements
- Develop complex RESTful APIs from scratch using Python
- Use requests handlers, URL patterns, serialization, and validations
- Add authentication, authorization, and interaction with ORMs and databases
- Debug, test, and improve RESTful APIs with four frameworks
- Design RESTful APIs with frameworks and create automated tests

Leave a review - let other readers know what you think

Please share your thoughts on this book with others by leaving a review on the site that you bought it from. If you purchased the book from Amazon, please leave us an honest review on this book's Amazon page. This is vital so that other potential readers can see and use your unbiased opinion to make purchasing decisions, we can understand what our customers think about our products, and our authors can see your feedback on the title that they have worked with Packt to create. It will only take a few minutes of your time, but is valuable to other potential customers, our authors, and Packt. Thank you!

Index

Made in the USA
Coppell, TX
29 December 2021

70330636R00334